THIS

IS YOUR CHANCE TO SAVE BIG!

If you act now you may be able to save yourself

IS IT TIME?

DON'T WAIT!

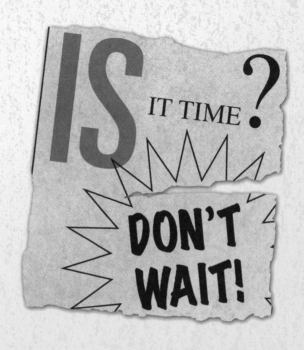

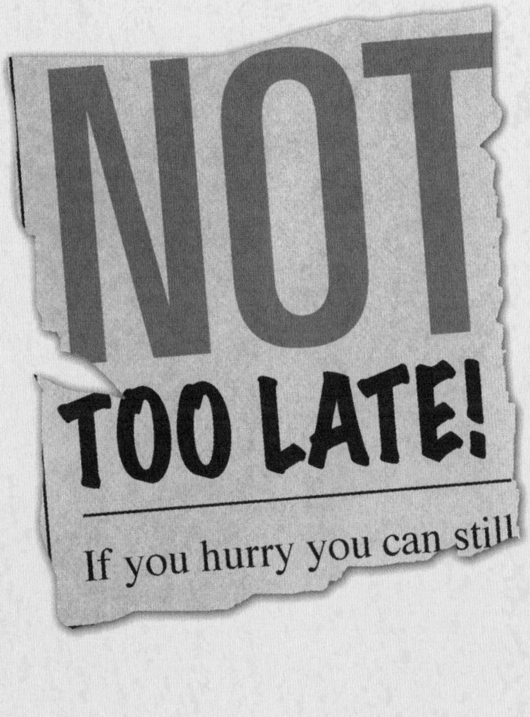
NOT
TOO LATE!
If you hurry you can still

MIND
MGMT

MIND MGMT

VOLUME ONE: THE MANAGER

CREATED, WRITTEN,
AND ILLUSTRATED BY

MATT KINDT

FOREWORD BY
DAMON LINDELOF

DARK HORSE BOOKS

PRESIDENT AND PUBLISHER
MIKE RICHARDSON

DIGITAL PRODUCTION
CLAY JANES

DESIGN
ADAM GRANO
with MATT KINDT

ASSISTANT EDITOR
SHANTEL LaROCQUE

EDITOR
BRENDAN WRIGHT

Special thanks to DIANA SCHUTZ and CHARLIE OLSEN.

MIND MGMT VOLUME 1: THE MANAGER

This volume collects issues #0–#6 of the Dark Horse comic-book series *MIND MGMT.*

Published by Dark Horse Books
A division of Dark Horse Comics, Inc.
10956 SE Main Street
Milwaukie, OR 97222

DarkHorse.com

International Licensing: (503) 905-2377
To find a comics shop in your area, call the Comic Shop Locator Service toll-free at (888) 266-4226.

First edition: April 2013

Library of Congress Cataloging-in-Publication Data

Kindt, Matt.
  Mind MGMT. Volume one, The manager / created, written, and illustrated by Matt Kindt ; foreword by
                    Damon Lindelof. — 1st ed.
      p. cm.
  ISBN 978-1-59582-797-5
  1. Women journalists—Comic books, strips, etc. 2. Graphic novels. I. Title. II. Title: Manager.
  PN6727.K54M56 2013
  741.5'973—dc23
                            2012041667

10 9 8 7 6 5 4 3 2
Printed in China

Neil Hankerson, Executive Vice President I Tom Weddle, Chief Financial Officer I Randy Stradley, Vice President of Publishing I Michael Martens, Vice President of Book Trade Sales I Anita Nelson, Vice President of Business Affairs I Scott Allie, Editor in Chief I Matt Parkinson, Vice President of Marketing I David Scroggy, Vice President of Product Development I Dale LaFountain, Vice President of Information Technology I Darlene Vogel, Senior Director of Print, Design, and Production I Ken Lizzi, General Counsel I Davey Estrada, Editorial Director I Chris Warner, Senior Books Editor I Diana Schutz, Executive Editor I Cary Grazzini, Director of Print and Development I Lia Ribacchi, Art Director I Cara Niece, Director of Scheduling I Tim Wiesch, Director of International Licensing I Mark Bernardi, Director of Digital Publishing

FOREWORD

Before we get too deep, allow me to skip to the end of the lesson:

Flight 815s are bad news.

They also happen to make fairly cool jumping-off points for stories, and I consider myself to be in rather excellent company to share that distinction with one Mr. Matt Kindt, author and artist of the rather fantastic book you are about to read.

Or have you read it *already*?

Is it possible that those vague tugs of *déjà vu* as you flip the pages are, in fact, actual memories . . . memories that were blocked, or even worse, *stolen* from your brain?

But who would do such a thing? And why? Not to mention, last I checked, manipulating or erasing one's very thoughts was impossible . . . at least outside of popular fiction and alien abduction tales.

But what if it *was* possible? What if there was a society right under our noses—an organization with its own secret history and a roster of agents who were gifted in areas that far transcended brainwashing . . . agents who were so powerful they could manipulate reality itself?

That would be pretty effing cool, would it not?

Welcome to *MIND MGMT*.

You are about to depart on a journey you can never fully trust . . . but every step of it is as thrilling as it is original. You will be surprised. Shocked. Entertained. And if you're like me, you will be desperate for *more*.

This is a world so much like our own, it's hard to not feel Mr. Kindt knows a little *too* much about it. But I'm not brave enough to accuse him of such here . . .

After all, I don't want to end up on Flight 815.

That being said, I'm jealous that you get to read this for the very first time. I guarantee, amnesia aside, you're not gonna forget it.

So put on your helmets, kiddies . . .

You're about to get mindfucked.

Damon Lindelof
November 2012

Damon Lindelof is a writer of comics, television, and film. He is the cocreator, with J. J. Abrams, of Lost *and the cowriter of Ridley Scott's* Prometheus.

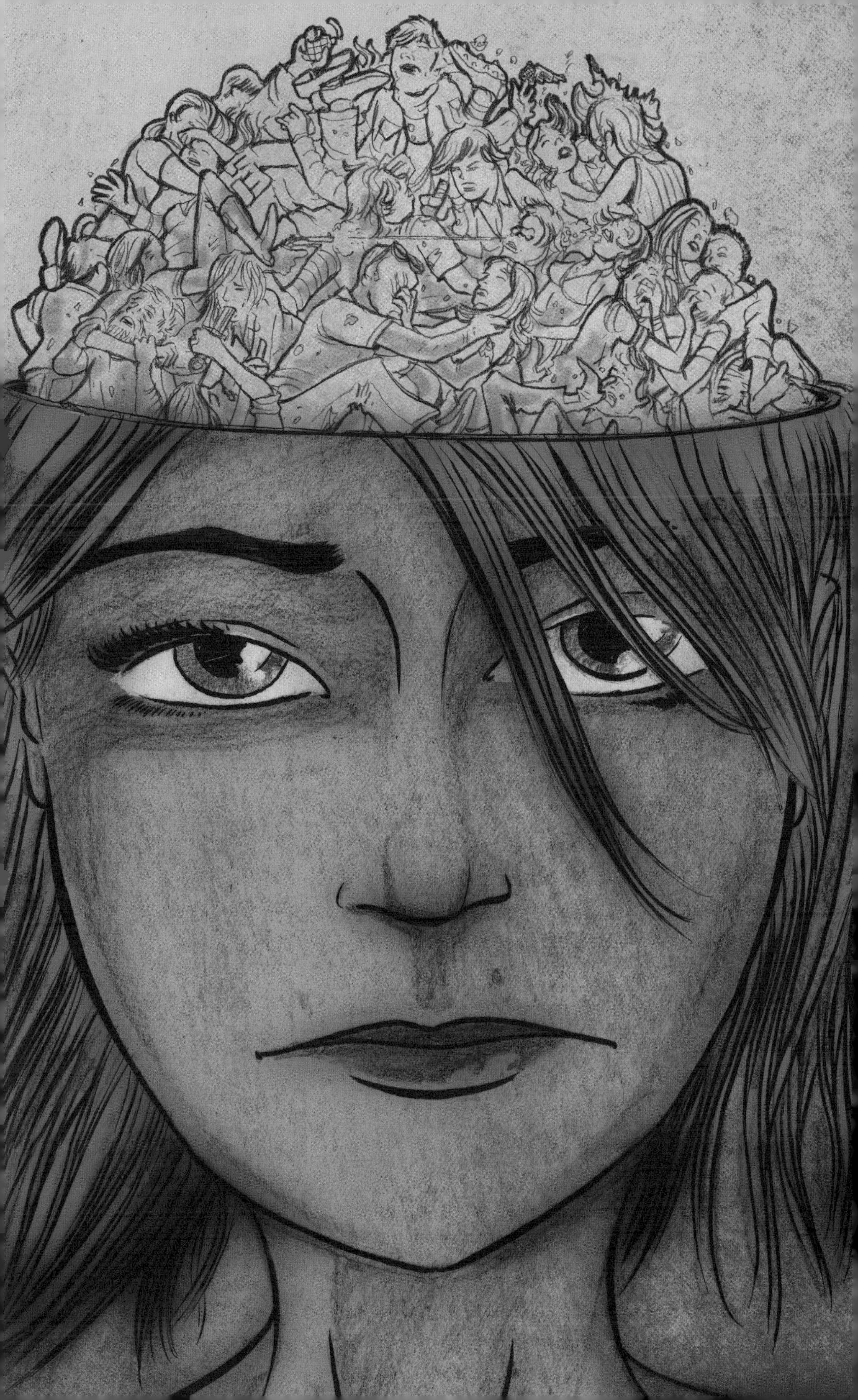

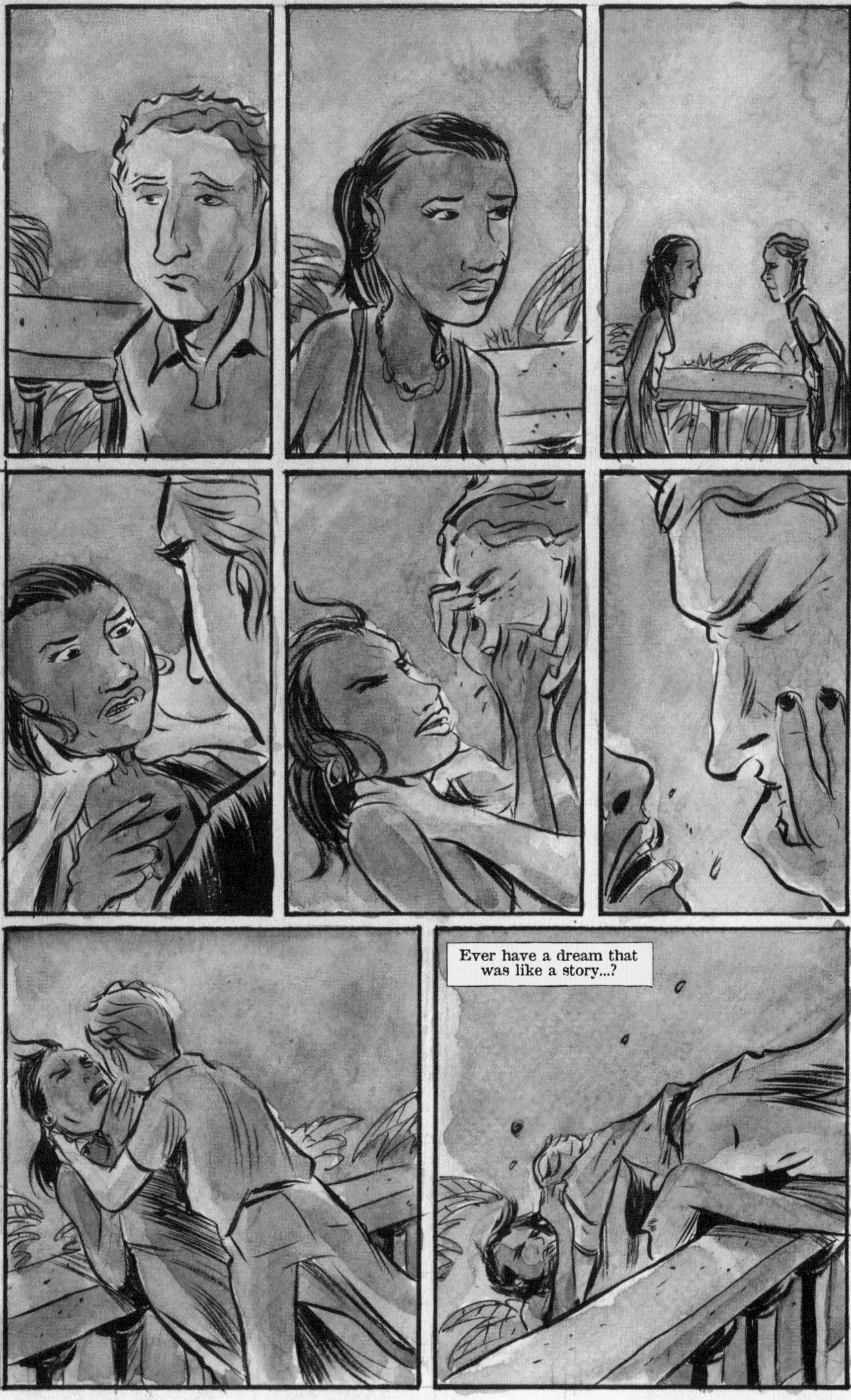
Ever have a dream that
was like a story...?

WHEN FILING REPORT ALL ESSENTIAL DETAILS MUST FALL WITHIN THIS SOLID "LIVE AREA" BOX. THIS IS THE BORDER FOR A STANDARD, NON-BLEED FIELD REPORT

MIND MGMT FIELD GUIDE. 1.2. When confronted with violence, reference the protocol flow chart and if all else fails, follow the "3 E's": Evince, Evade, and as a last resort, Exterminate.

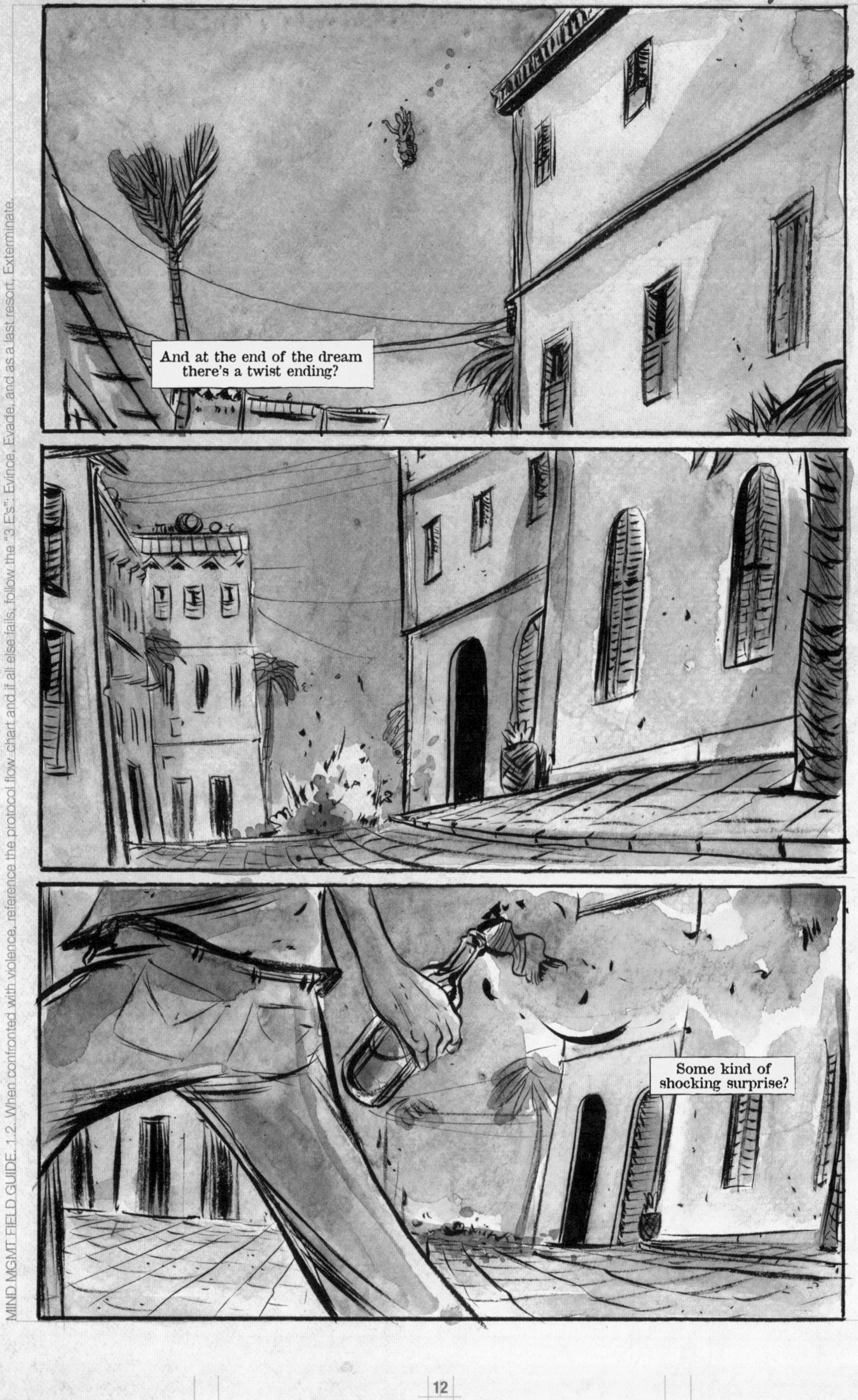
And at the end of the dream there's a twist ending?
Some kind of shocking surprise?

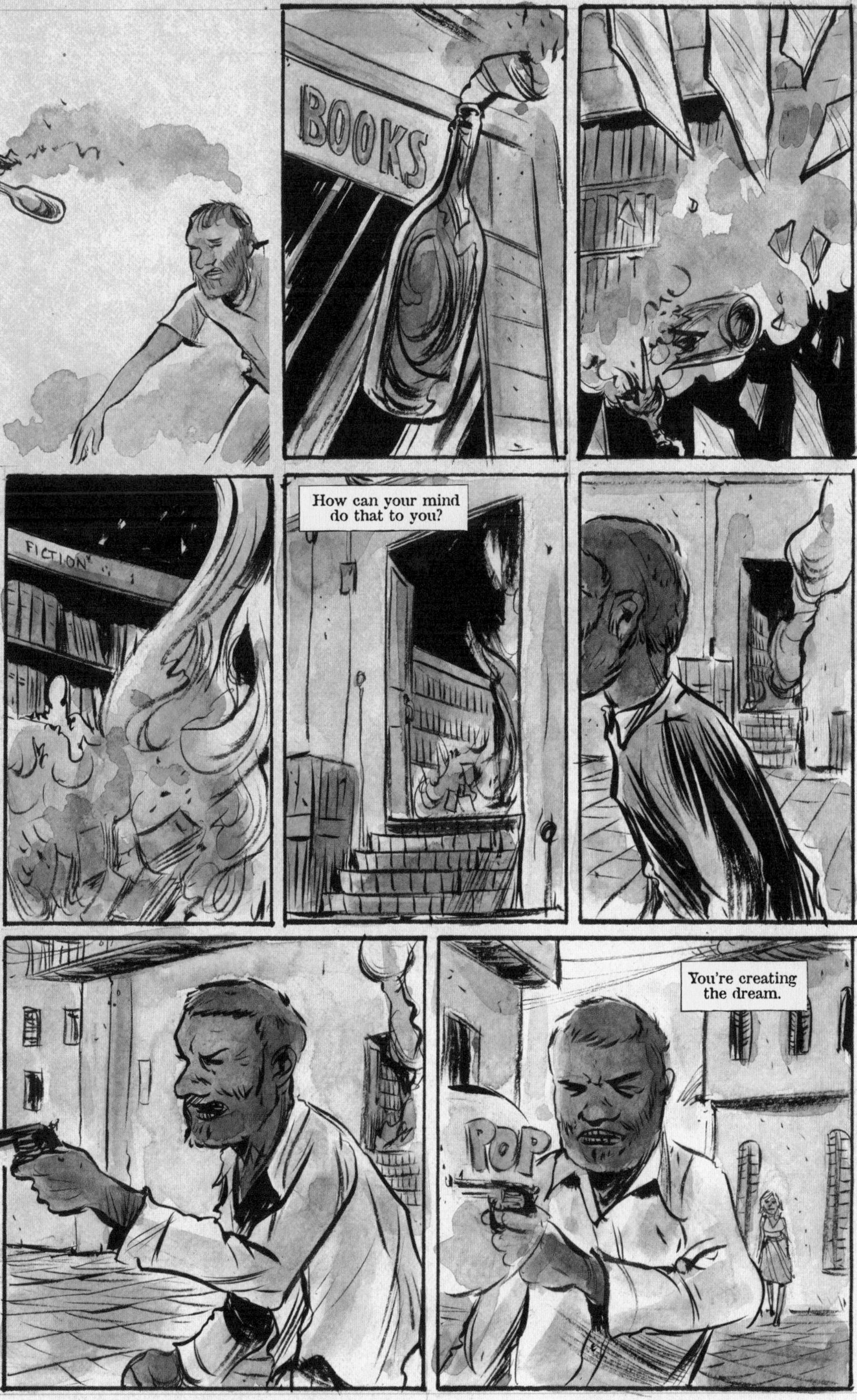
BOOKS
FICTION
How can your mind do that to you?
You're creating the dream.
POP

MIND MGMT FIELD GUIDE. 1.4. Corpse removal is a team effort. After body disposal, Cadaver Disposal requisitions must be filled out within 24 hours.

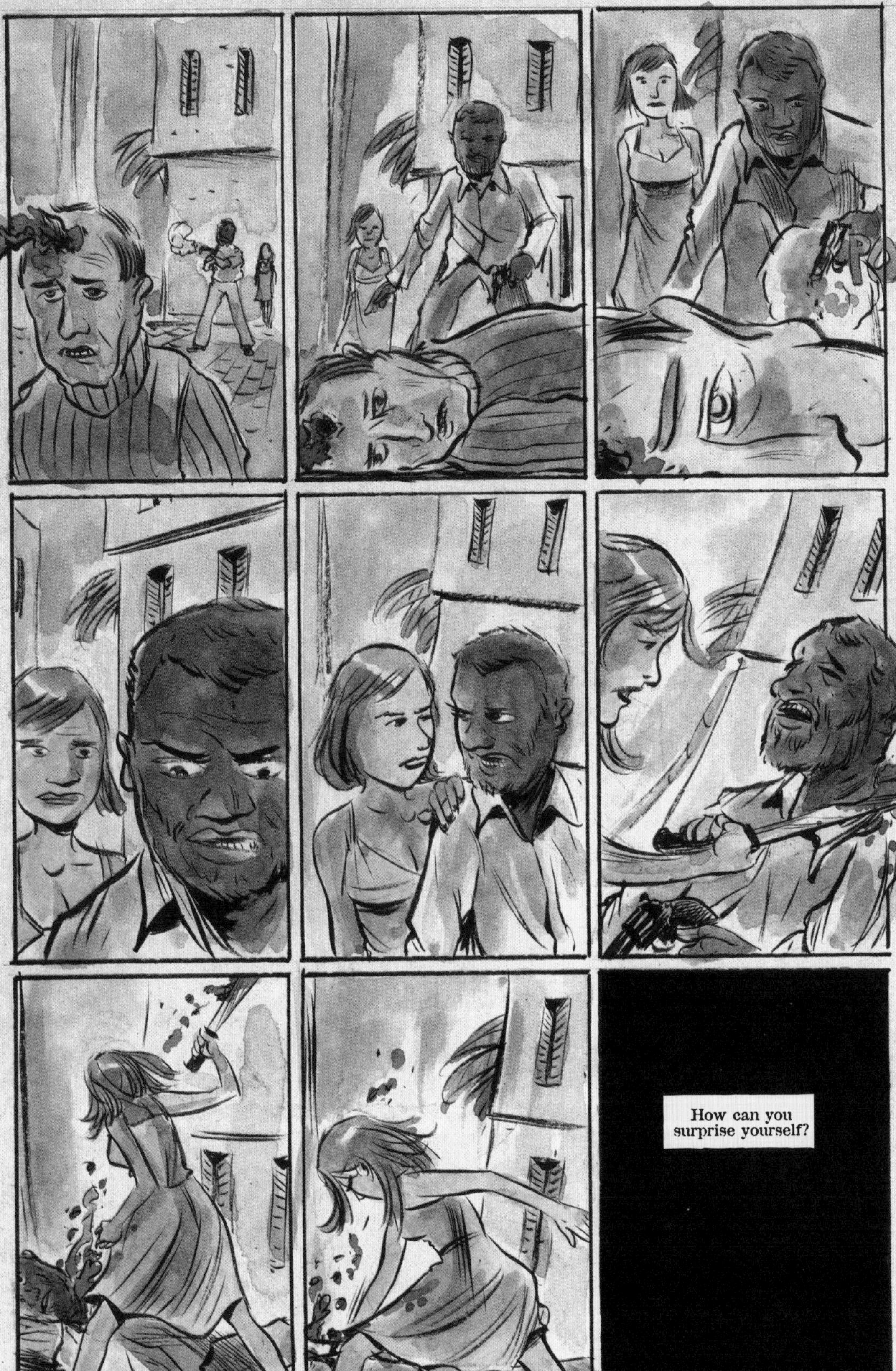
POP
How can you surprise yourself?

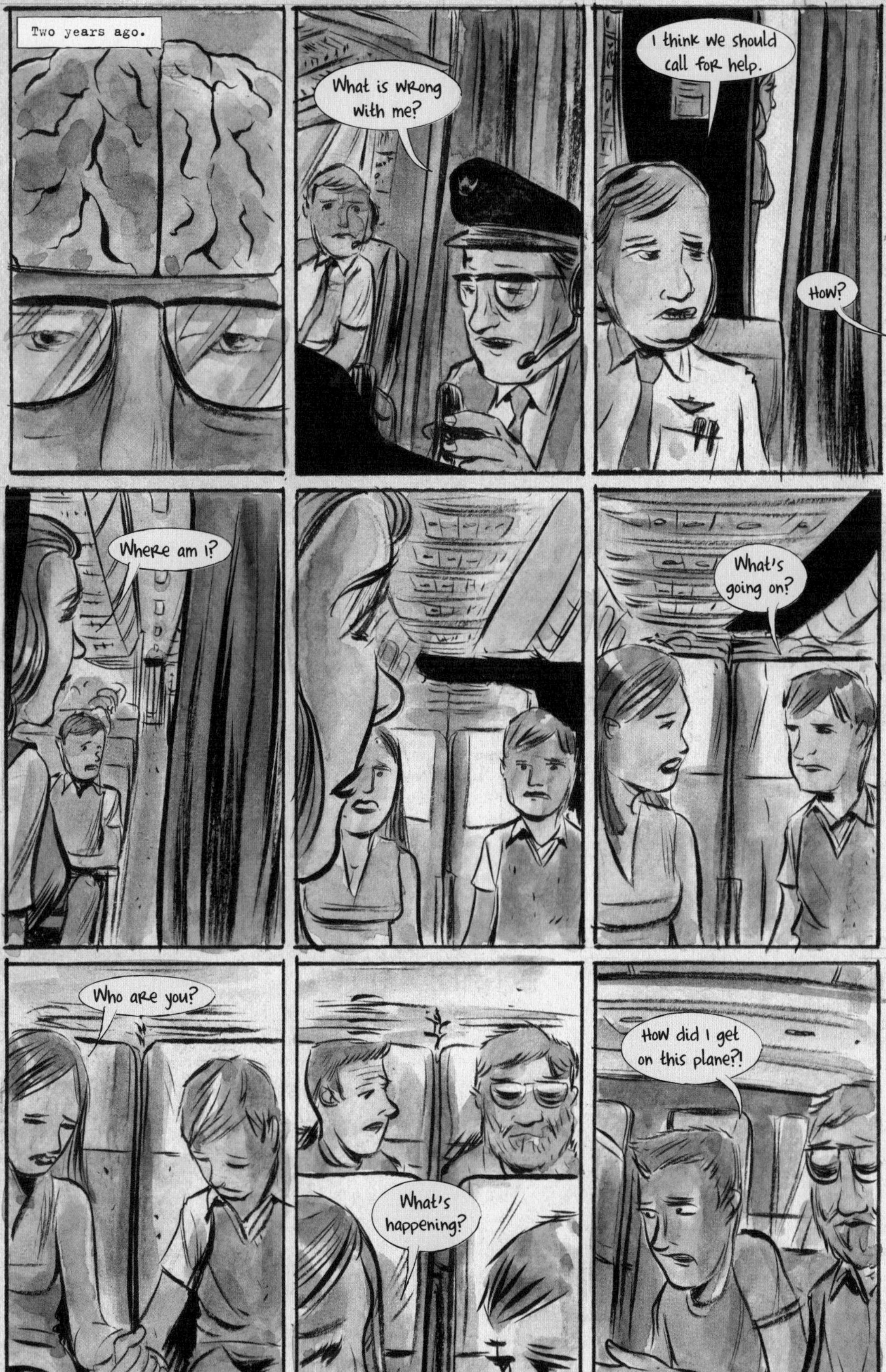
Two years ago.
What is wrong with me?
I think we should call for help.
How?
Where am I?
What's going on?
Who are you?
What's happening?
How did I get on this plane?!

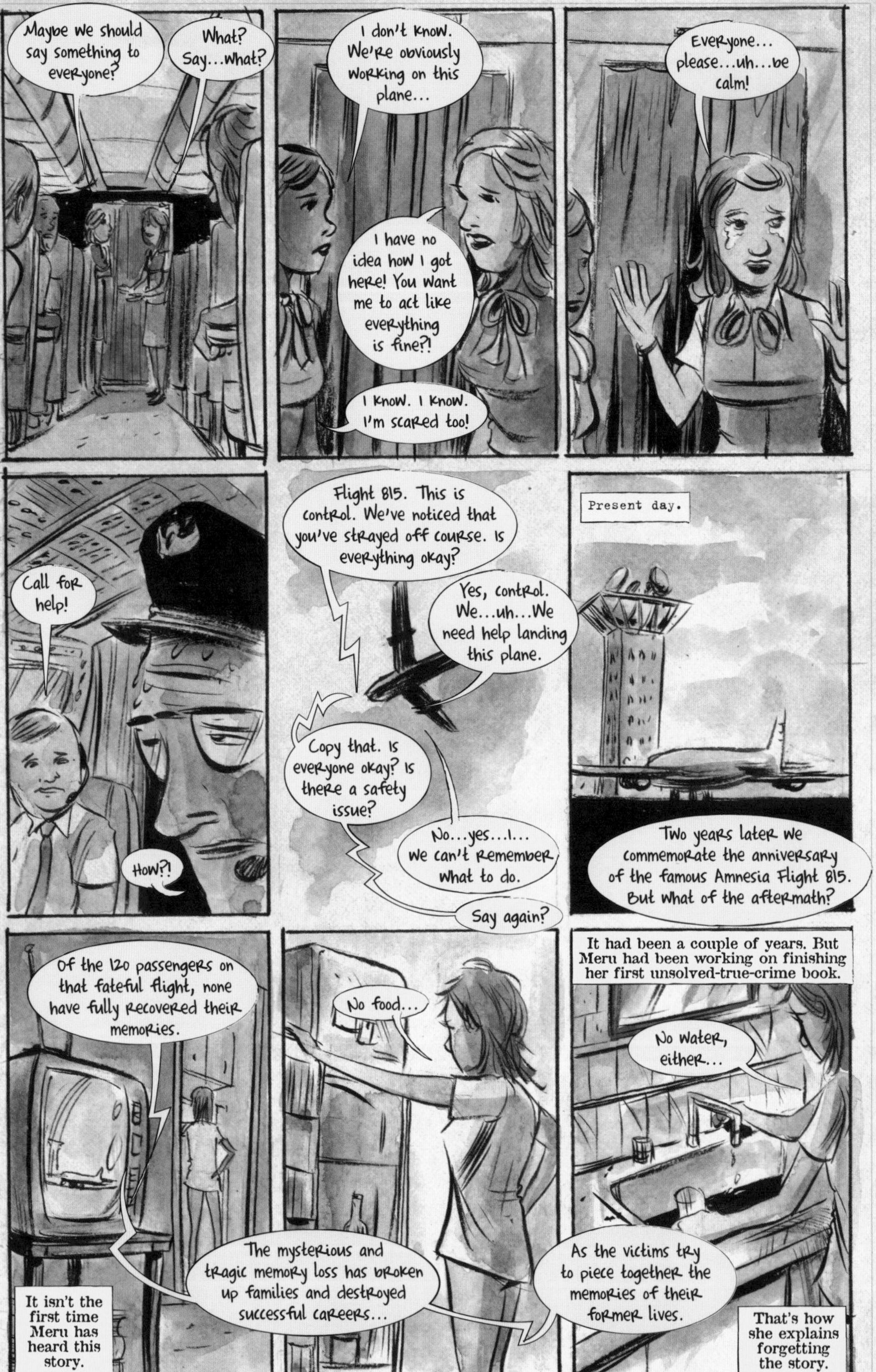
Maybe we should say something to everyone?
What? Say...what?
I don't know. We're obviously working on this plane...
I have no idea how I got here! You want me to act like everything is fine?!
I know. I know. I'm scared too!
Everyone... please...uh...be calm!
Call for help!
How?!
Flight 815. This is control. We've noticed that you've strayed off course. Is everything okay?
Yes, control. We...uh...We need help landing this plane.
Copy that. Is everyone okay? Is there a safety issue?
No...yes...I... we can't remember what to do.
Say again?
Present day.
Two years later we commemorate the anniversary of the famous Amnesia Flight 815. But what of the aftermath?
Of the 120 passengers on that fateful flight, none have fully recovered their memories.
It isn't the first time Meru has heard this story.
No food...
The mysterious and tragic memory loss has broken up families and destroyed successful careers...
It had been a couple of years. But Meru had been working on finishing her first unsolved-true-crime book.
No water, either...
As the victims try to piece together the memories of their former lives.
That's how she explains forgetting the story.

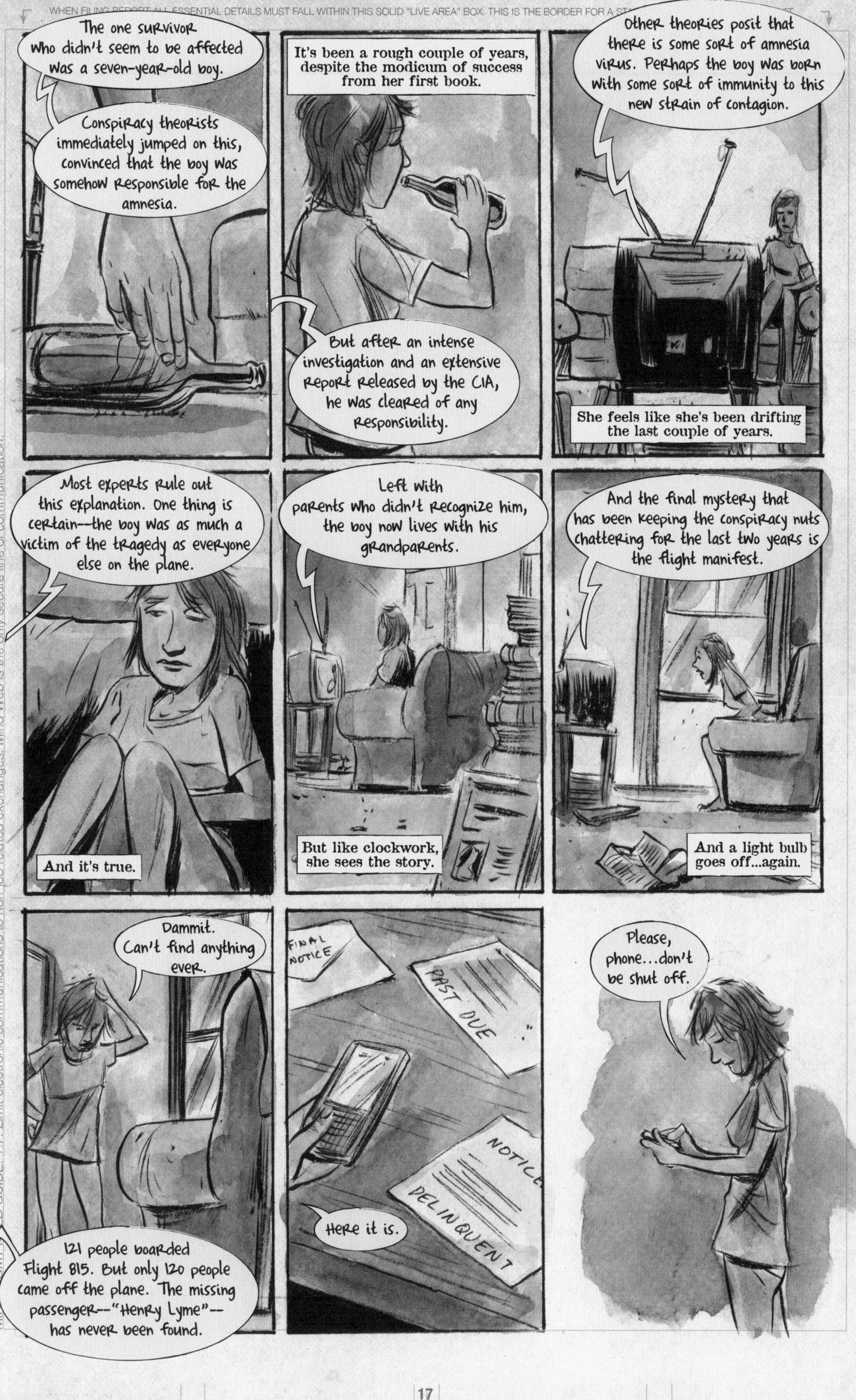
The one survivor who didn't seem to be affected was a seven-year-old boy.
Conspiracy theorists immediately jumped on this, convinced that the boy was somehow responsible for the amnesia.
It's been a rough couple of years, despite the modicum of success from her first book.
But after an intense investigation and an extensive report released by the CIA, he was cleared of any responsibility.
Other theories posit that there is some sort of amnesia virus. Perhaps the boy was born with some sort of immunity to this new strain of contagion.
She feels like she's been drifting the last couple of years.
Most experts rule out this explanation. One thing is certain--the boy was as much a victim of the tragedy as everyone else on the plane.
And it's true.
Left with parents who didn't recognize him, the boy now lives with his grandparents.
But like clockwork, she sees the story.
And the final mystery that has been keeping the conspiracy nuts chattering for the last two years is the flight manifest.
And a light bulb goes off...again.
Dammit. Can't find anything ever.
121 people boarded Flight 815. But only 120 people came off the plane. The missing passenger--"Henry Lyme"--has never been found.
FINAL NOTICE
PAST DUE
NOTICE
DELINQUENT
Here it is.
Please, phone...don't be shut off.
Limit electronic communications to non-job-related exchanges. Mind Web is the only secure line of communication.

Charlie?

Meru? What's up?

She makes the call to her literary agent, like she always does.

I've got a new book idea. It's good.

Excitement over the prospect of a new idea. A new lead...

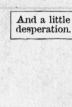

And a little desperation.

...

Don't you want to hear it?

Sure.

She hears the doubt in Charlie's voice.

What's wrong?

And isn't quite sure why it's there.

I've heard all of this before. It's been over two years since your last book.

Best-selling book.

Two years is a long time. You've been chasing this new idea for too long. You need to just start typing. Anything.

You **had** a bestseller.

PREM PREM PREM PREM PREM

A TRUE STORY

PREMEDITATED

MERU

Stop chasing ghosts. True crime is what sells. Finding truth in crime. That's what you're good at.

You didn't even hear my idea...

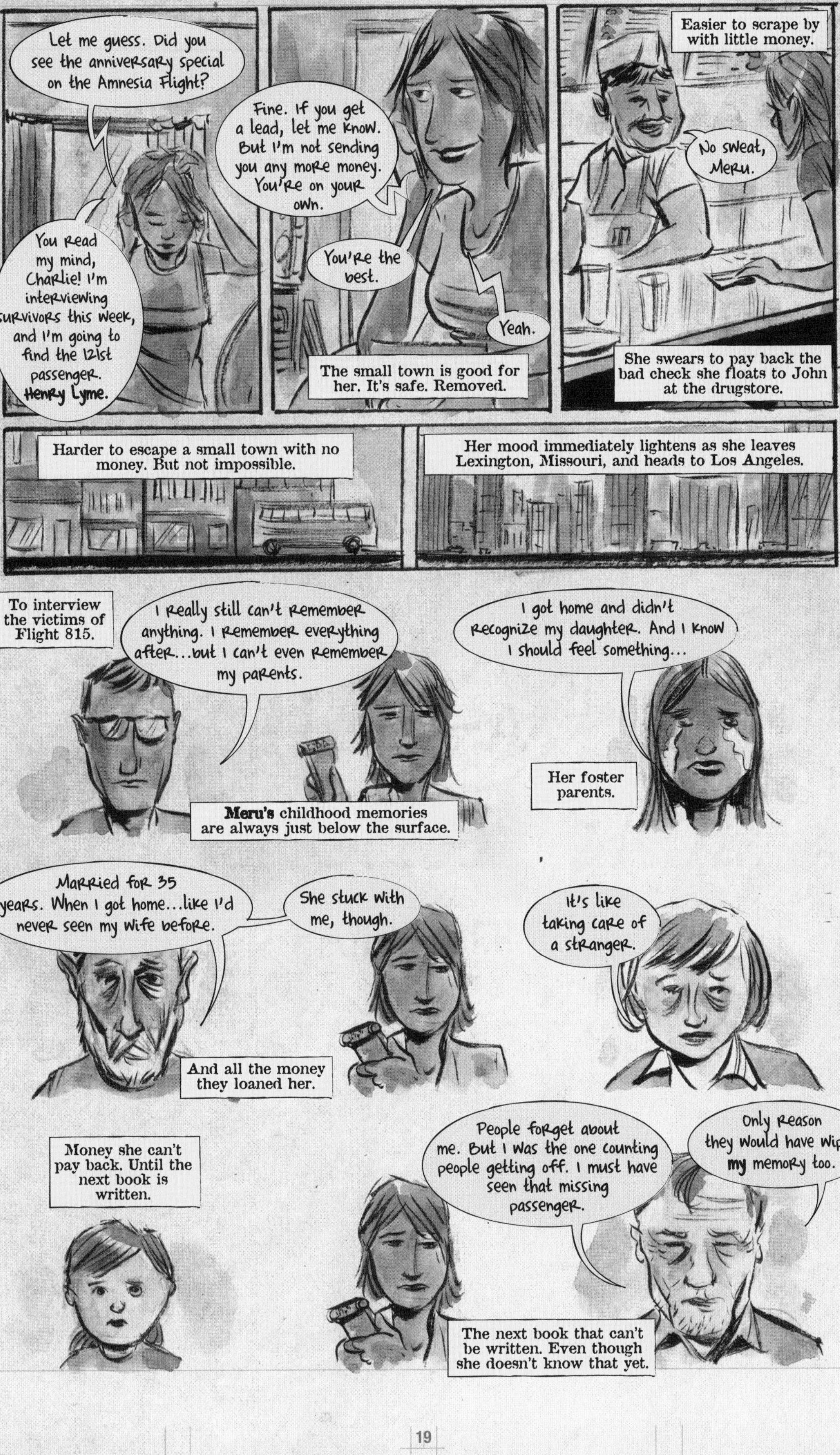
Let me guess. Did you see the anniversary special on the Amnesia Flight?
You read my mind, Charlie! I'm interviewing survivors this week, and I'm going to find the 121st passenger. Henry Lyme.
Fine. If you get a lead, let me know. But I'm not sending you any more money. You're on your own.
You're the best.
Yeah.
The small town is good for her. It's safe. Removed.
Easier to scrape by with little money.
No sweat, Meru.
She swears to pay back the bad check she floats to John at the drugstore.
Harder to escape a small town with no money. But not impossible.
Her mood immediately lightens as she leaves Lexington, Missouri, and heads to Los Angeles.
To interview the victims of Flight 815.
I really still can't remember anything. I remember everything after...but I can't even remember my parents.
Meru's childhood memories are always just below the surface.
I got home and didn't recognize my daughter. And I know I should feel something...
Her foster parents.
Married for 35 years. When I got home...like I'd never seen my wife before.
She stuck with me, though.
And all the money they loaned her.
It's like taking care of a stranger.
Money she can't pay back. Until the next book is written.
People forget about me. But I was the one counting people getting off. I must have seen that missing passenger.
Only reason they would have wiped my memory too.
The next book that can't be written. Even though she doesn't know that yet.

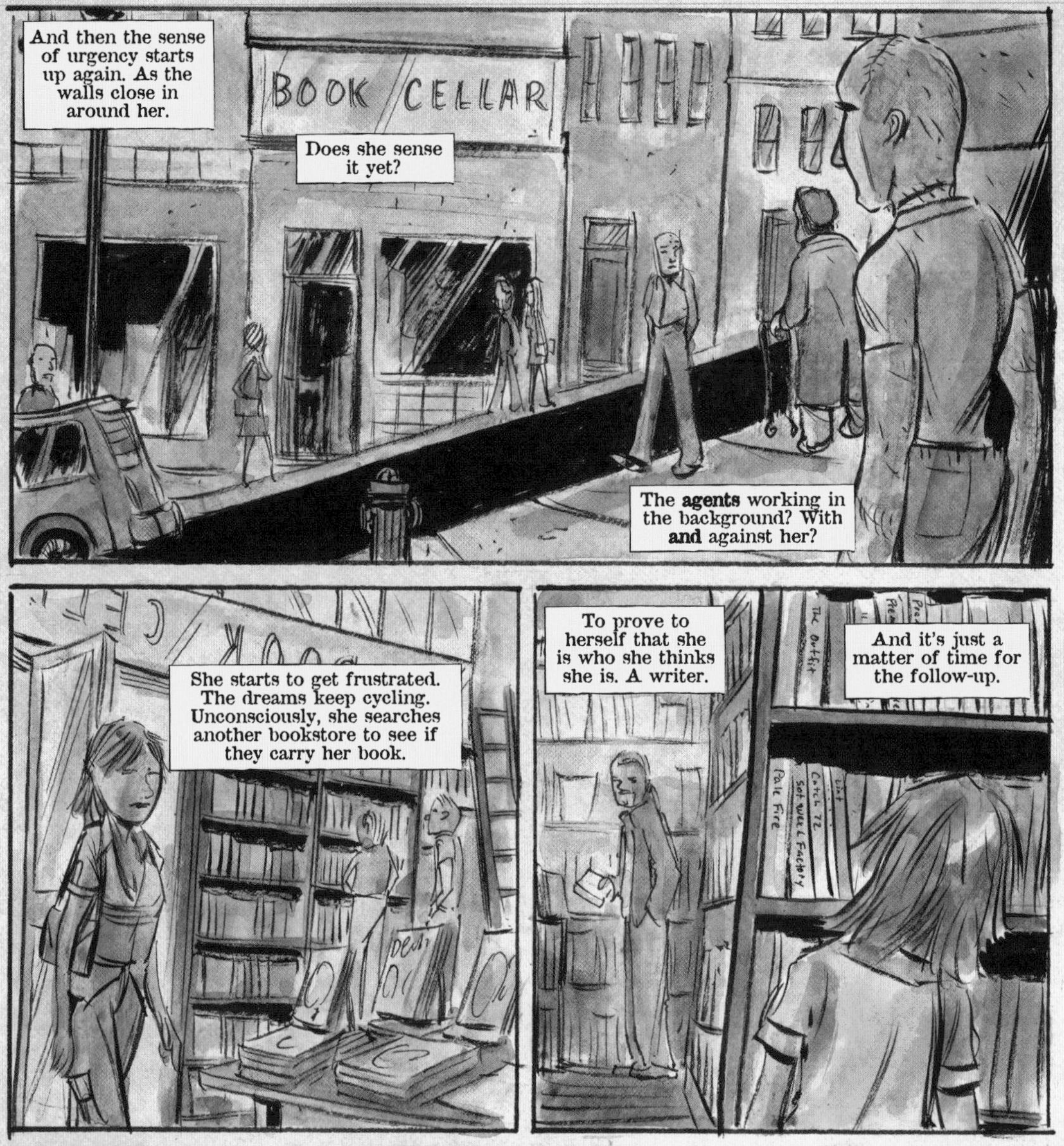
And then the sense of urgency starts up again. As the walls close in around her.
BOOK CELLAR
Does she sense it yet?
The **agents** working in the background? With **and** against her?
She starts to get frustrated. The dreams keep cycling. Unconsciously, she searches another bookstore to see if they carry her book.
To prove to herself that she is who she thinks she is. A writer.
And it's just a matter of time for the follow-up.
And she tries to forget that she's once again at the end of her rope.
No money.
No leads.

MIND MGMT FIELD GUIDE. 1.10. Maintained concentration and continued use of Psychic Psonar will prevent enemy agents from gaining the element of surprise.

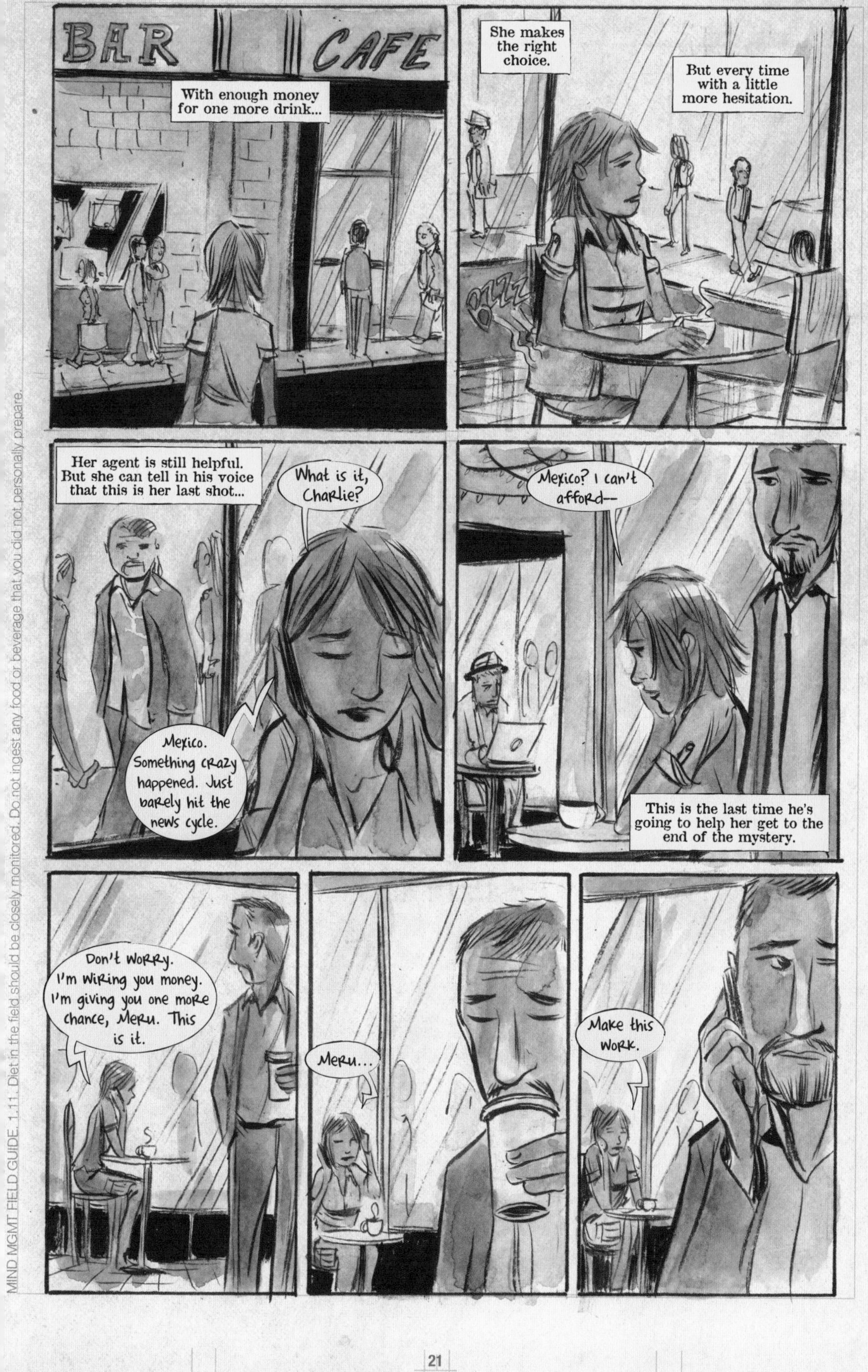
BAR
CAFE
With enough money for one more drink...
She makes the right choice.
But every time with a little more hesitation.
Her agent is still helpful. But she can tell in his voice that this is her last shot...
What is it, Charlie?
Mexico. Something crazy happened. Just barely hit the news cycle.
Mexico? I can't afford--
This is the last time he's going to help her get to the end of the mystery.
Don't worry. I'm wiring you money. I'm giving you one more chance, Meru. This is it.
Meru...
Make this work.

The plane ticket Charlie buys for her could have paid her rent for two months.
She tries to forget about it.
CERVEZA
To focus.
She spins the facts around in her head. Trying to ignore the sense of dread.
As if she knows what's coming.
CANTINA
And she does. Getting closer to **Henry Lyme** with every breadcrumb she tracks down.
As the shadow players revolve around her.
Filling their roles.
Looks like she's in for the night.
I gotta piss.
BAÑO
BAÑO
Different names. But always the same.

MIND MGMT FIELD GUIDE. 1.12. When establishing a base of operations the recommendation is to scan a perimeter of 400 yards for enemy agents. Twice-daily scans are optimal.

WHEN FILING REPORT ALL ESSENTIAL DETAILS MUST FALL WITHIN THIS SOLID "LIVE AREA" BOX. THIS IS THE BORDER FOR A STANDARD, NON-BLEED FIELD REPORT

MIND MGMT FIELD GUIDE 1.13. Public confrontations should be avoided at all costs. If a public alteration does occur, be sure to use Mental Masking to protect your identity.

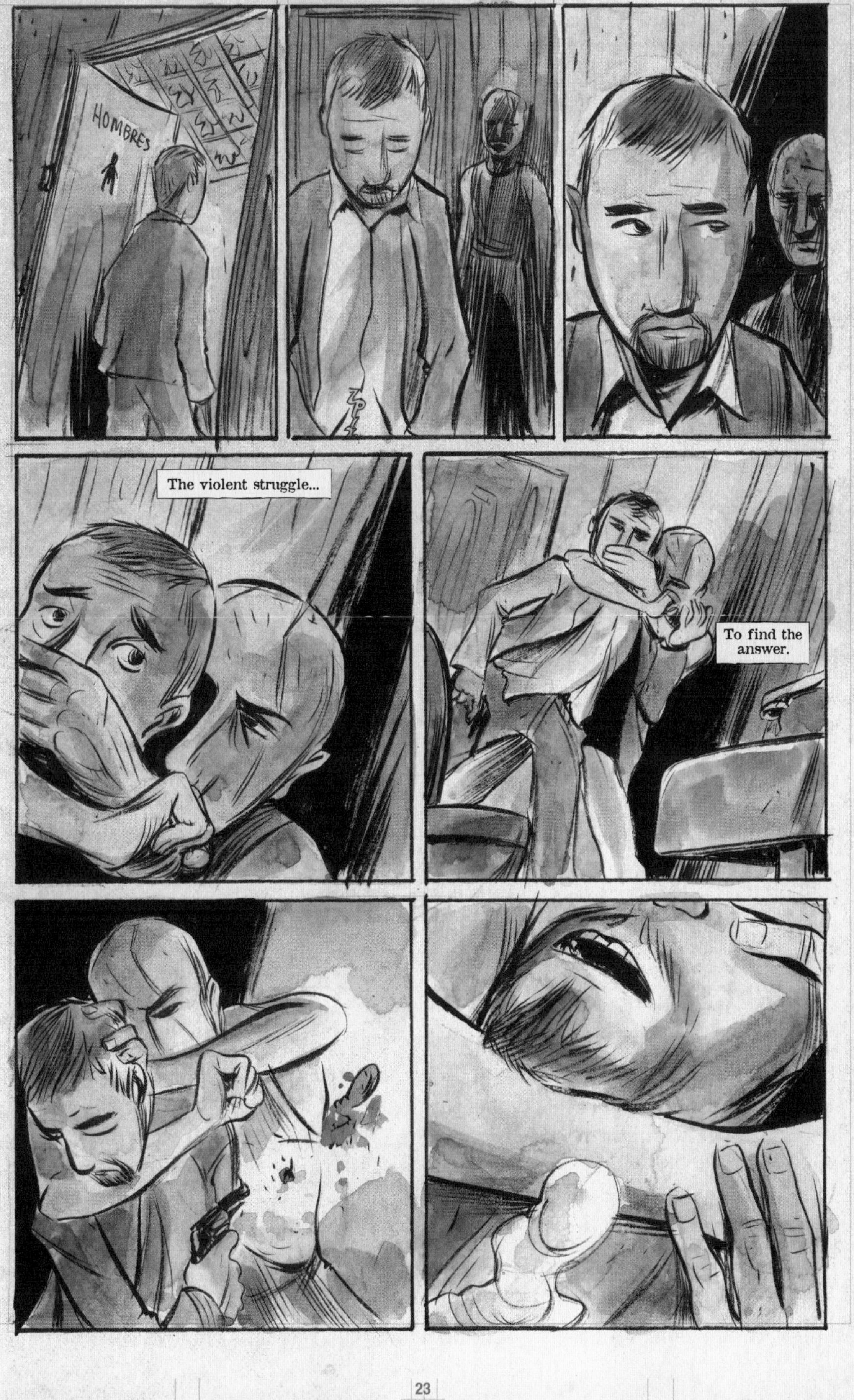
HOMBRES
The violent struggle...
To find the answer.

WHEN FILING REPORT ALL ESSENTIAL DETAILS MUST FALL WITHIN THIS SOLID "LIVE AREA" BOX. THIS IS THE BORDER FOR A STANDARD, NON-BLEED FIELD REPORT

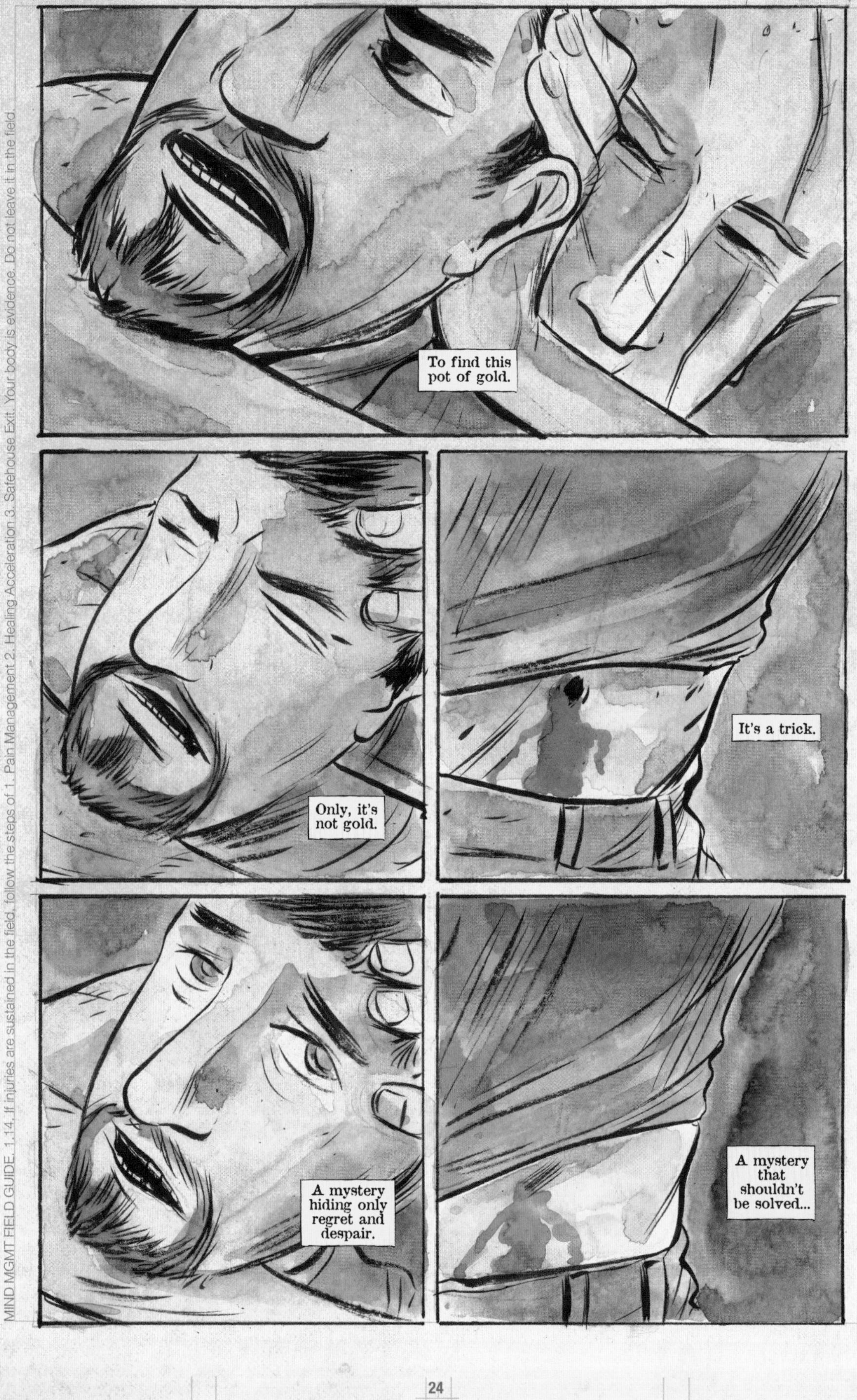

To find this pot of gold.
Only, it's not gold.
It's a trick.
A mystery hiding only regret and despair.
A mystery that shouldn't be solved...

MIND MGMT FIELD GUIDE. 1.14. If injuries are sustained in the field, follow the steps of 1. Pain Management 2. Healing Acceleration 3. Safehouse Exit. Your body is evidence. Do not leave it in the field.

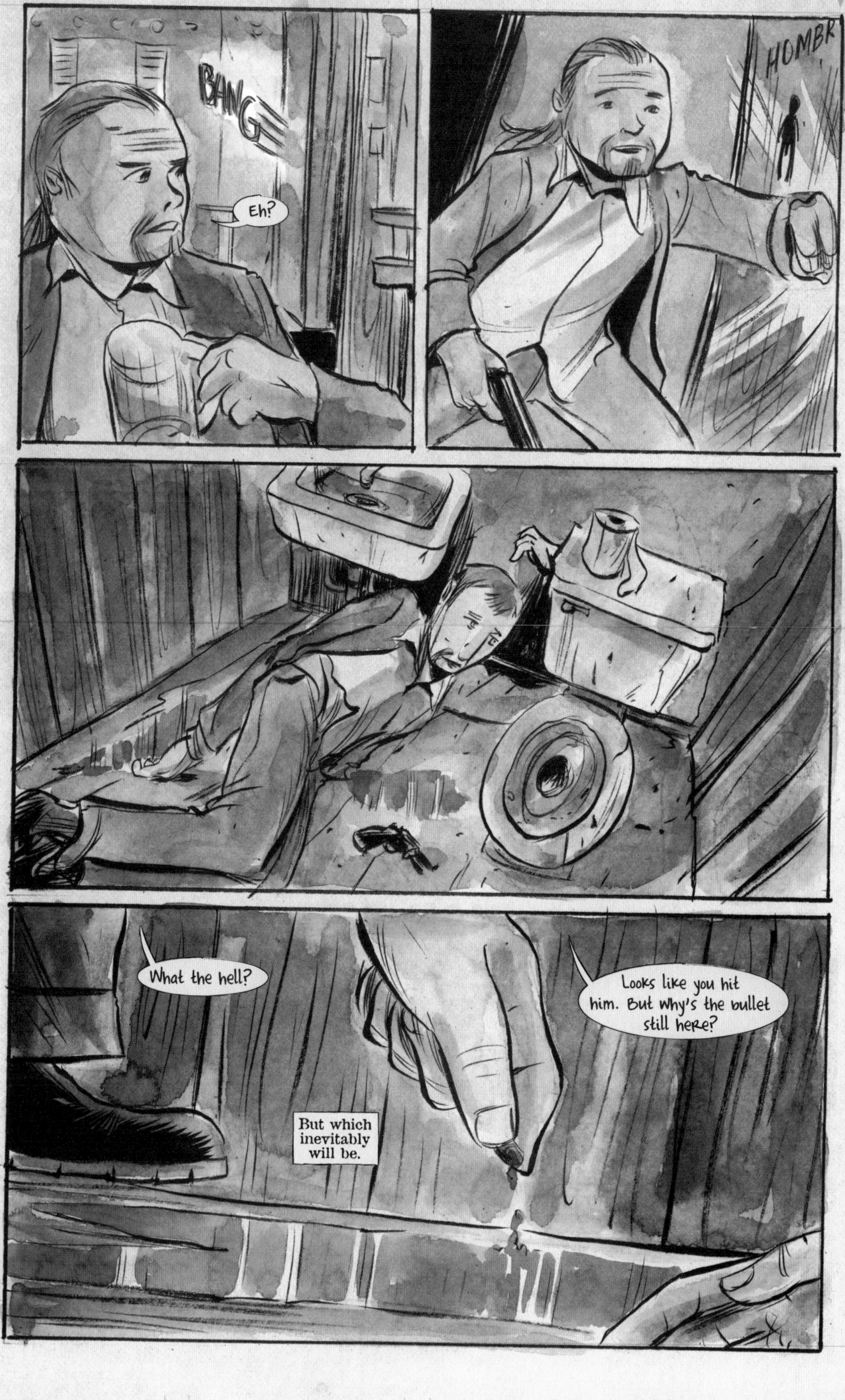
BANG
Eh?
HOMBR
What the hell?
Looks like you hit him. But why's the bullet still here?
But which inevitably will be.

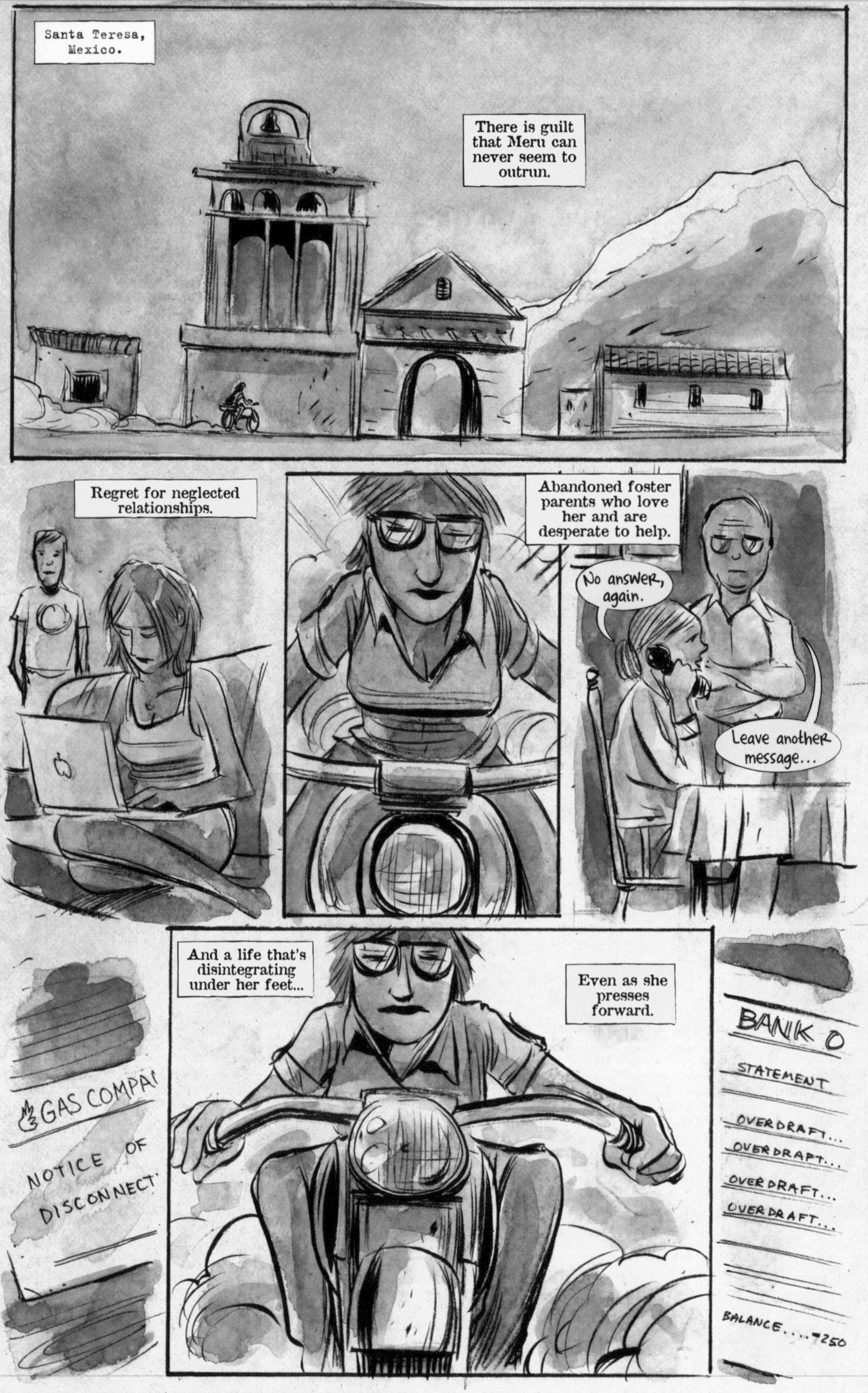
Santa Teresa, Mexico.
There is guilt that Meru can never seem to outrun.
Regret for neglected relationships.
Abandoned foster parents who love her and are desperate to help.
No answer, again.
Leave another message...
And a life that's disintegrating under her feet...
Even as she presses forward.
GAS COMPA
NOTICE OF DISCONNECT
BANK O
STATEMENT
OVERDRAFT...
OVERDRAFT...
OVERDRAFT...
OVERDRAFT...
BALANCE.....-250

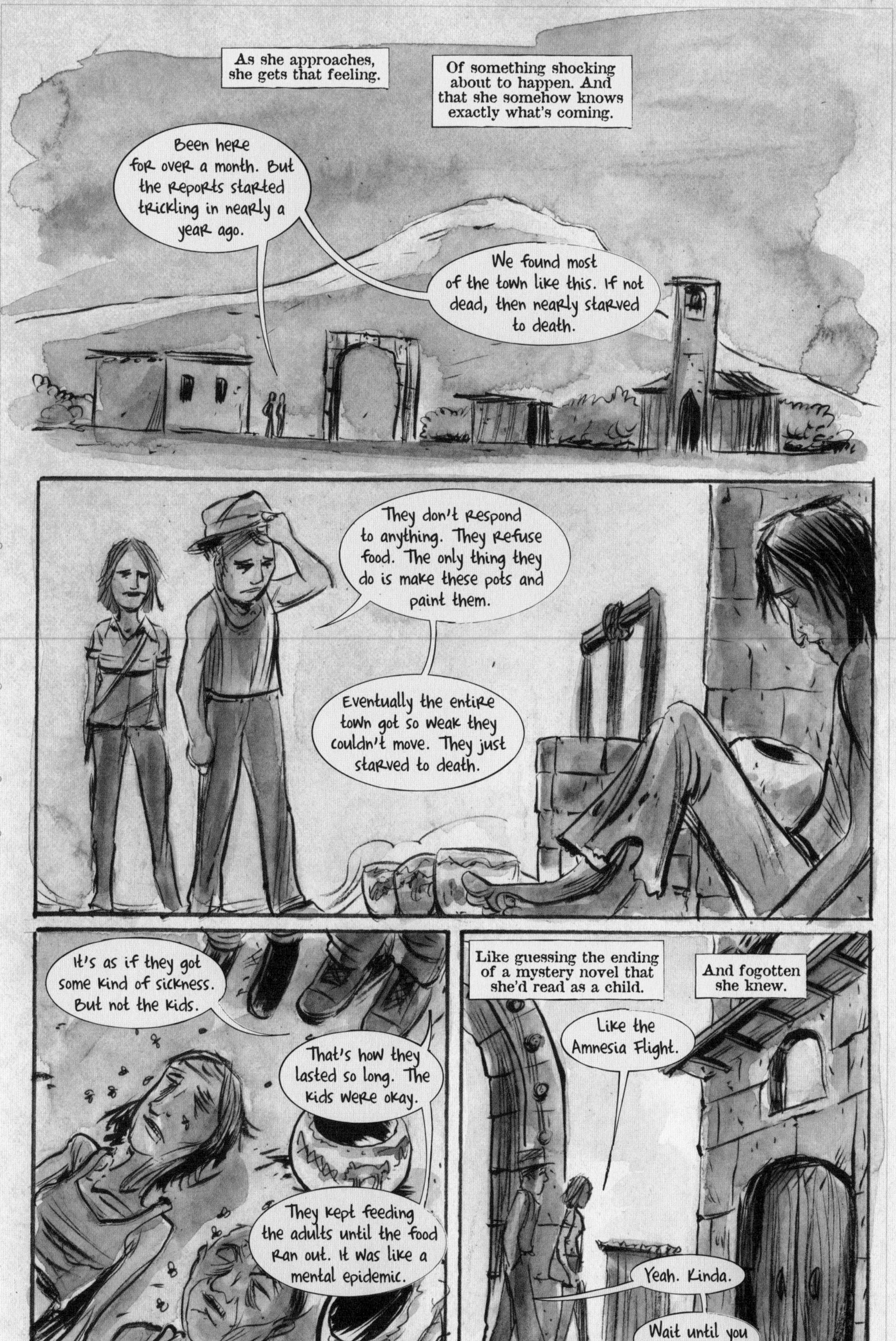
As she approaches, she gets that feeling.
Of something shocking about to happen. And that she somehow knows exactly what's coming.
Been here for over a month. But the reports started trickling in nearly a year ago.
We found most of the town like this. If not dead, then nearly starved to death.
They don't respond to anything. They refuse food. The only thing they do is make these pots and paint them.
Eventually the entire town got so weak they couldn't move. They just starved to death.
It's as if they got some kind of sickness. But not the kids.
That's how they lasted so long. The kids were okay.
They kept feeding the adults until the food ran out. It was like a mental epidemic.
Like guessing the ending of a mystery novel that she'd read as a child.
And fogotten she knew.
Like the Amnesia Flight.
Yeah. Kinda.
Wait until you see this.

MIND MGMT FIELD GUIDE. 1.17. Use of art and found objects is ideal for embedding messages and leaving breadcrumbs if an agent is unable to surface.

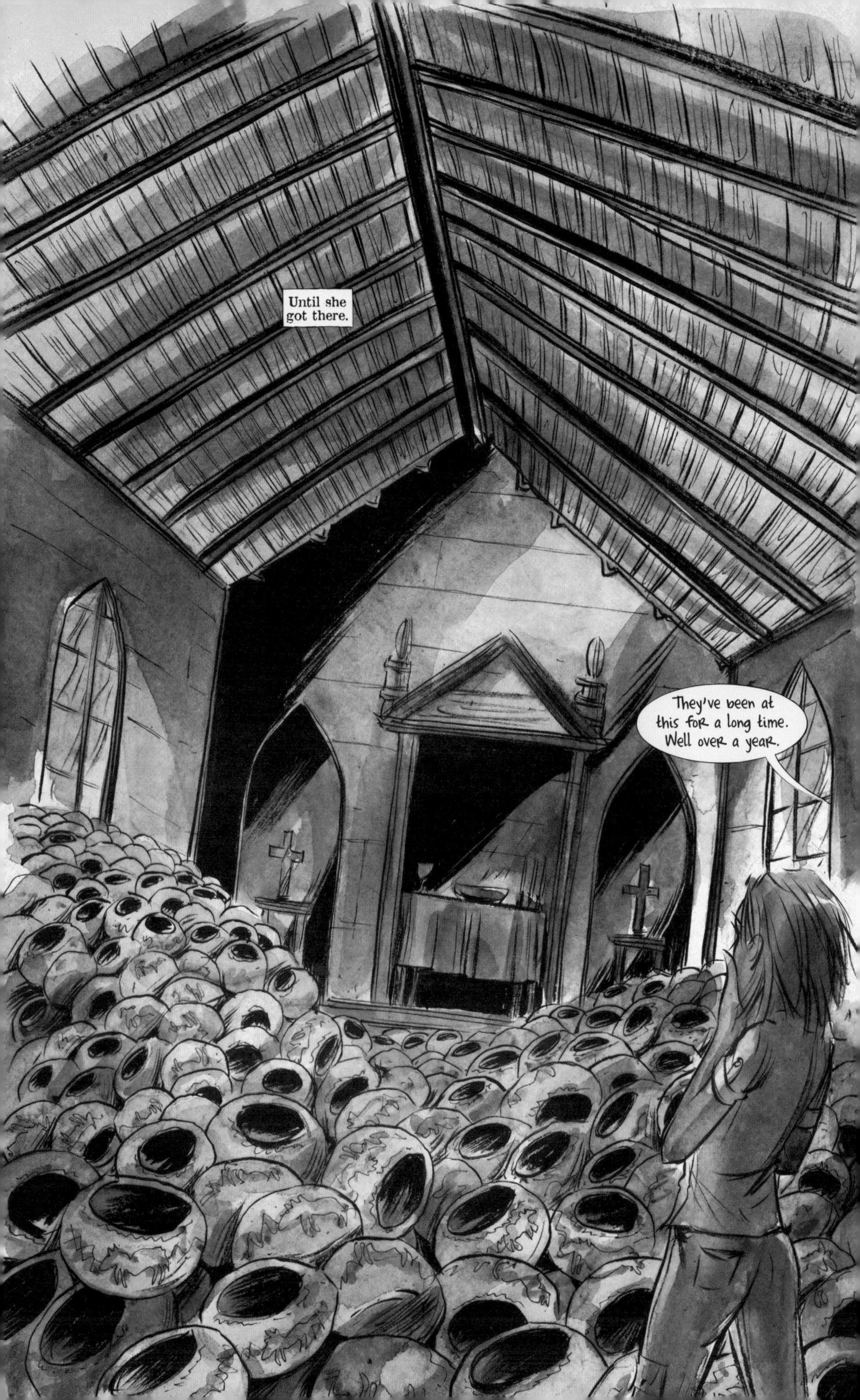
Until she got there.
They've been at this for a long time. Well over a year.

MIND MGMT FIELD GUIDE. 1.19. Use electronic devices to leave false breadcrumbs only. Rely on the Mind Web® for all research, background checks, and personnel histories.

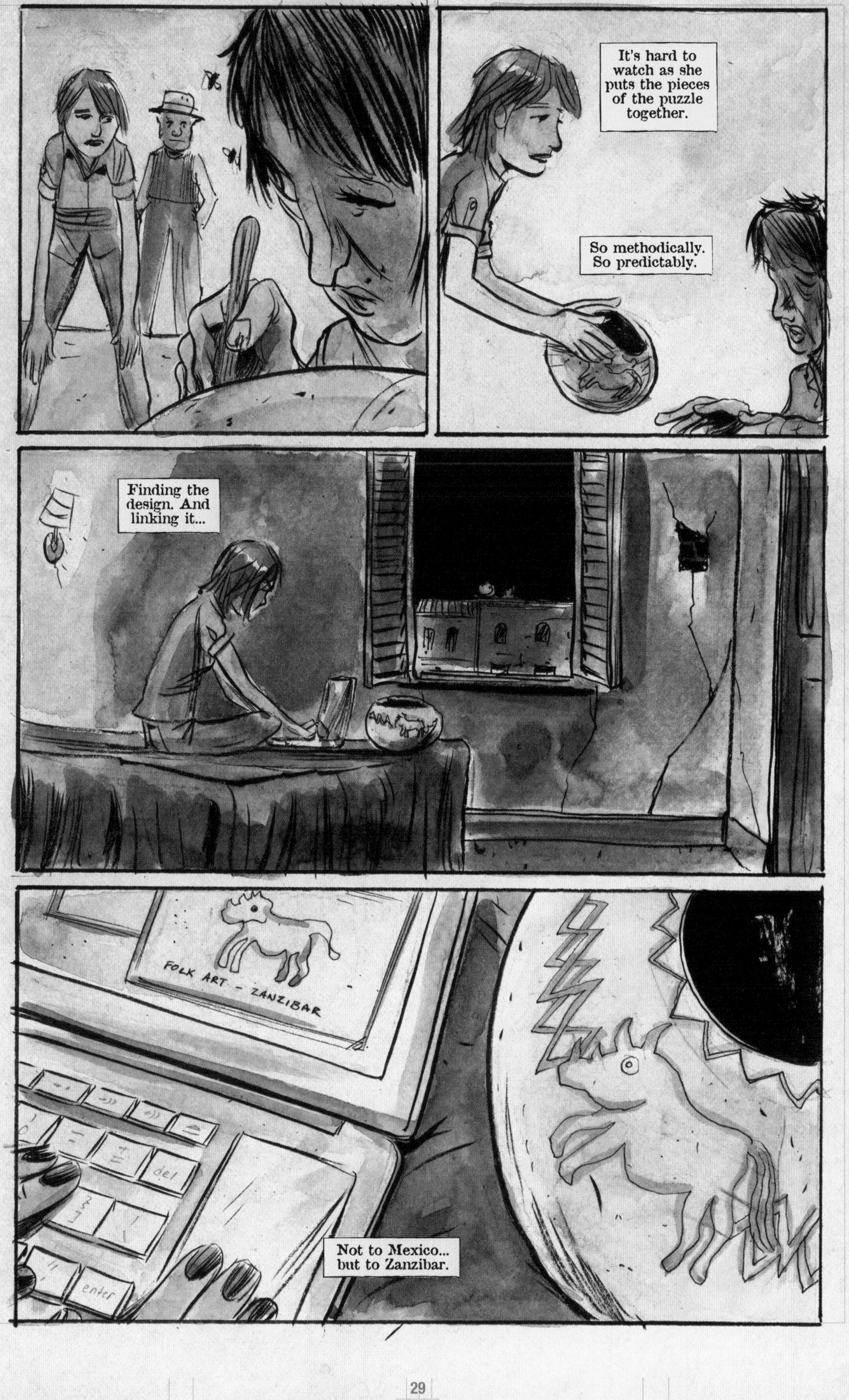
It's hard to watch as she puts the pieces of the puzzle together.
So methodically. So predictably.
Finding the design. And linking it...
FOLK ART - ZANZIBAR
del
enter
Not to Mexico... but to Zanzibar.

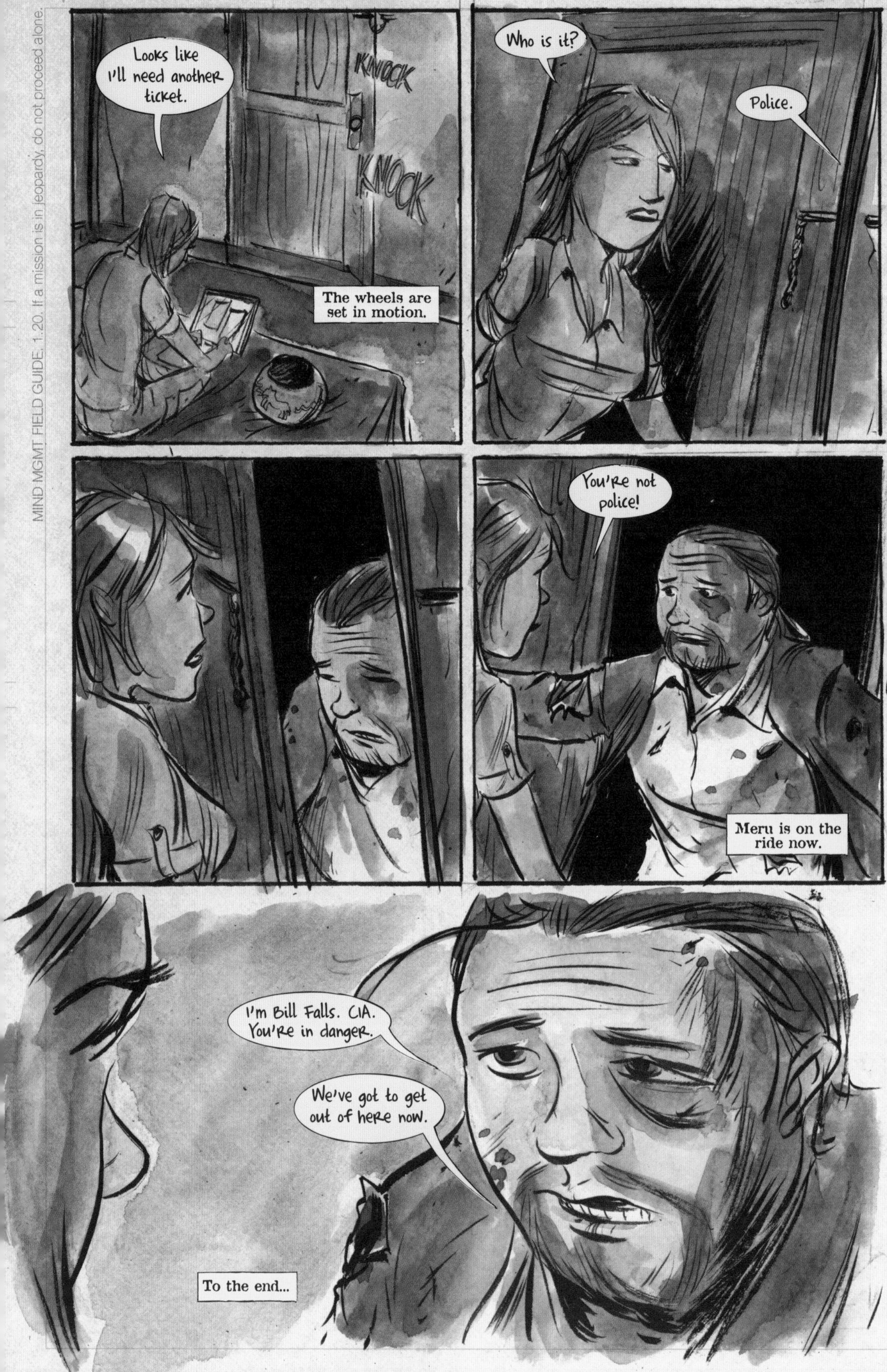
Looks like I'll need another ticket.
KNOCK
KNOCK
The wheels are set in motion.
Who is it?
Police.
You're not police!
Meru is on the ride now.
I'm Bill Falls. CIA. You're in danger.
We've got to get out of here now.
To the end...

MIND MGMT FIELD GUIDE. 1.21. When establishing a base of operations, agents should have a minimum of two escape routes planned as well as a Mind-Wipe Capsule ready to ingest in case of capture.

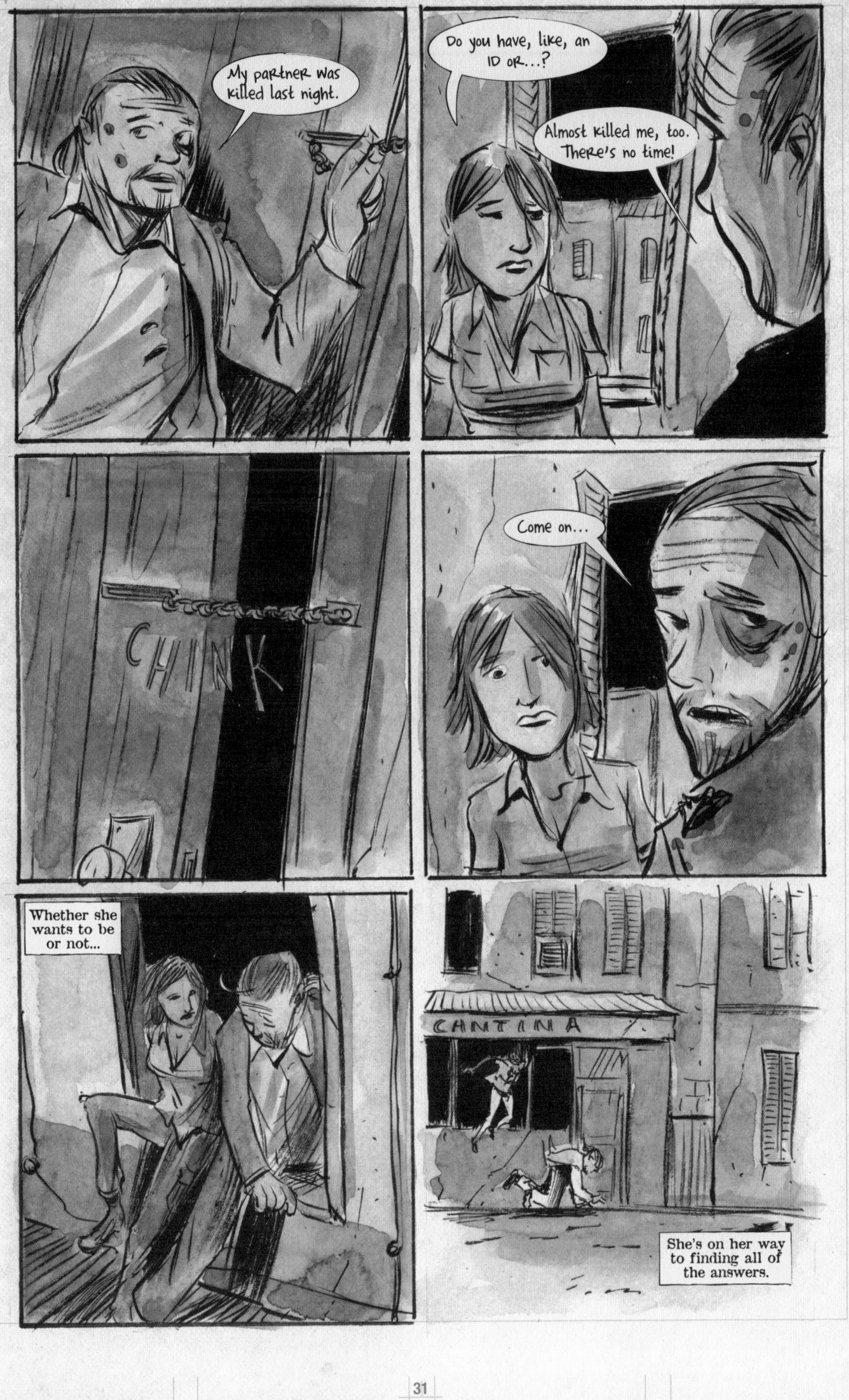
My partner was killed last night.
Do you have, like, an ID or...?
Almost killed me, too. There's no time!
CHINK
Come on...
Whether she wants to be or not...
CANTINA
She's on her way to finding all of the answers.

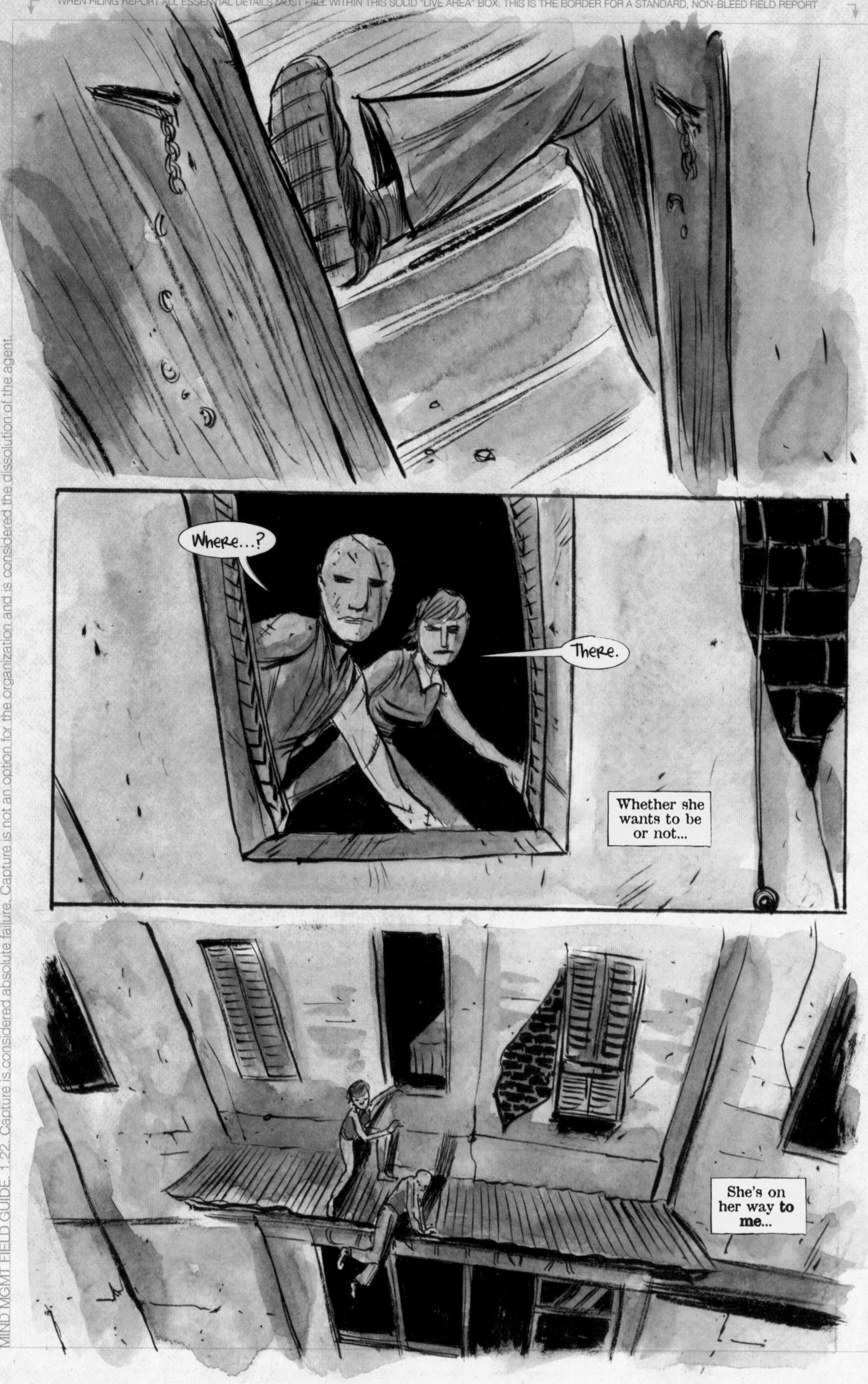
Where...?
There.
Whether she wants to be or not...
She's on her way **to me**...

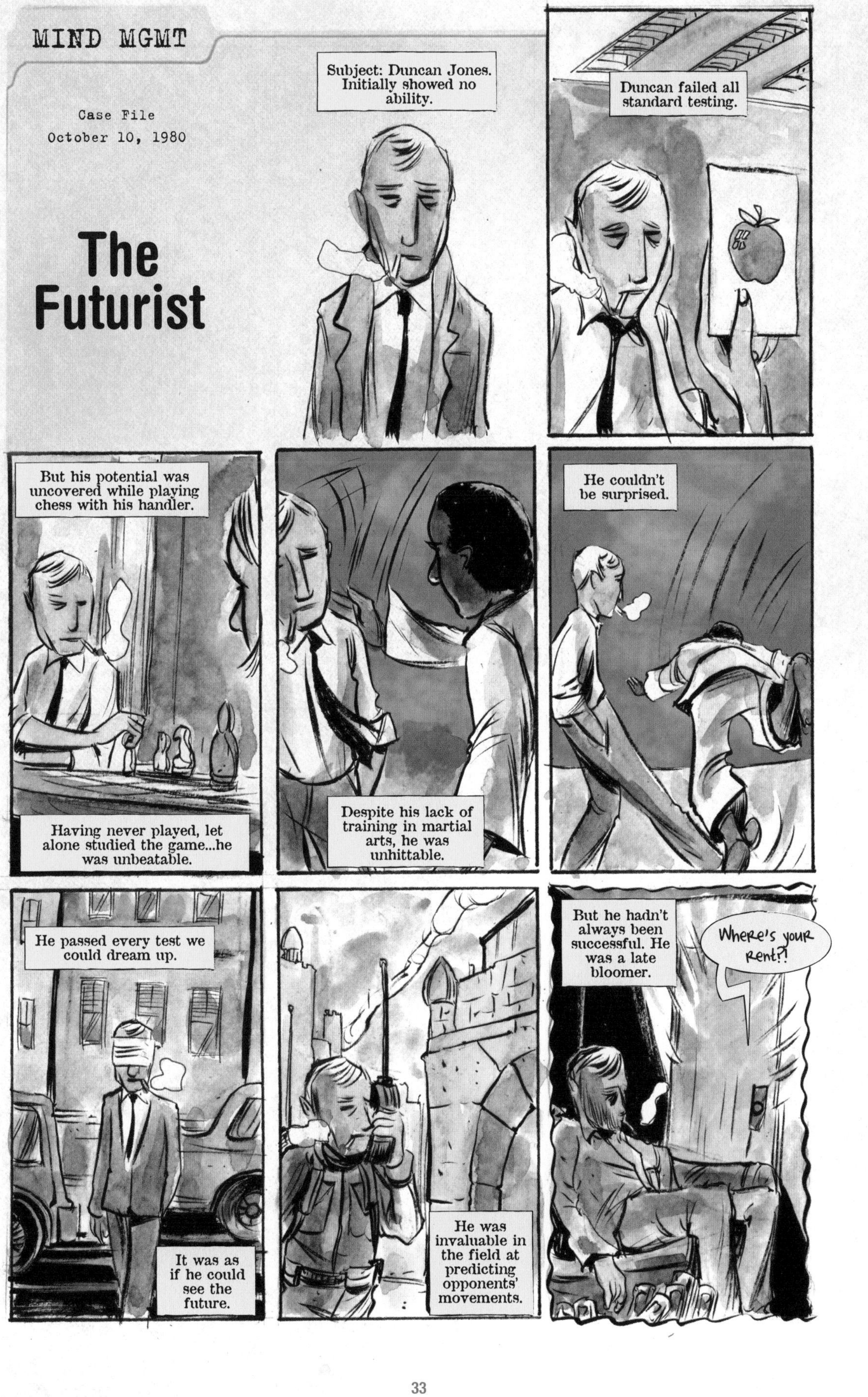
MIND MGMT
Case File
October 10, 1980
The Futurist
Subject: Duncan Jones. Initially showed no ability.
Duncan failed all standard testing.
But his potential was uncovered while playing chess with his handler.
Having never played, let alone studied the game...he was unbeatable.
Despite his lack of training in martial arts, he was unhittable.
He couldn't be surprised.
He passed every test we could dream up.
It was as if he could see the future.
He was invaluable in the field at predicting opponents' movements.
But he hadn't always been successful. He was a late bloomer.
Where's your Rent?!

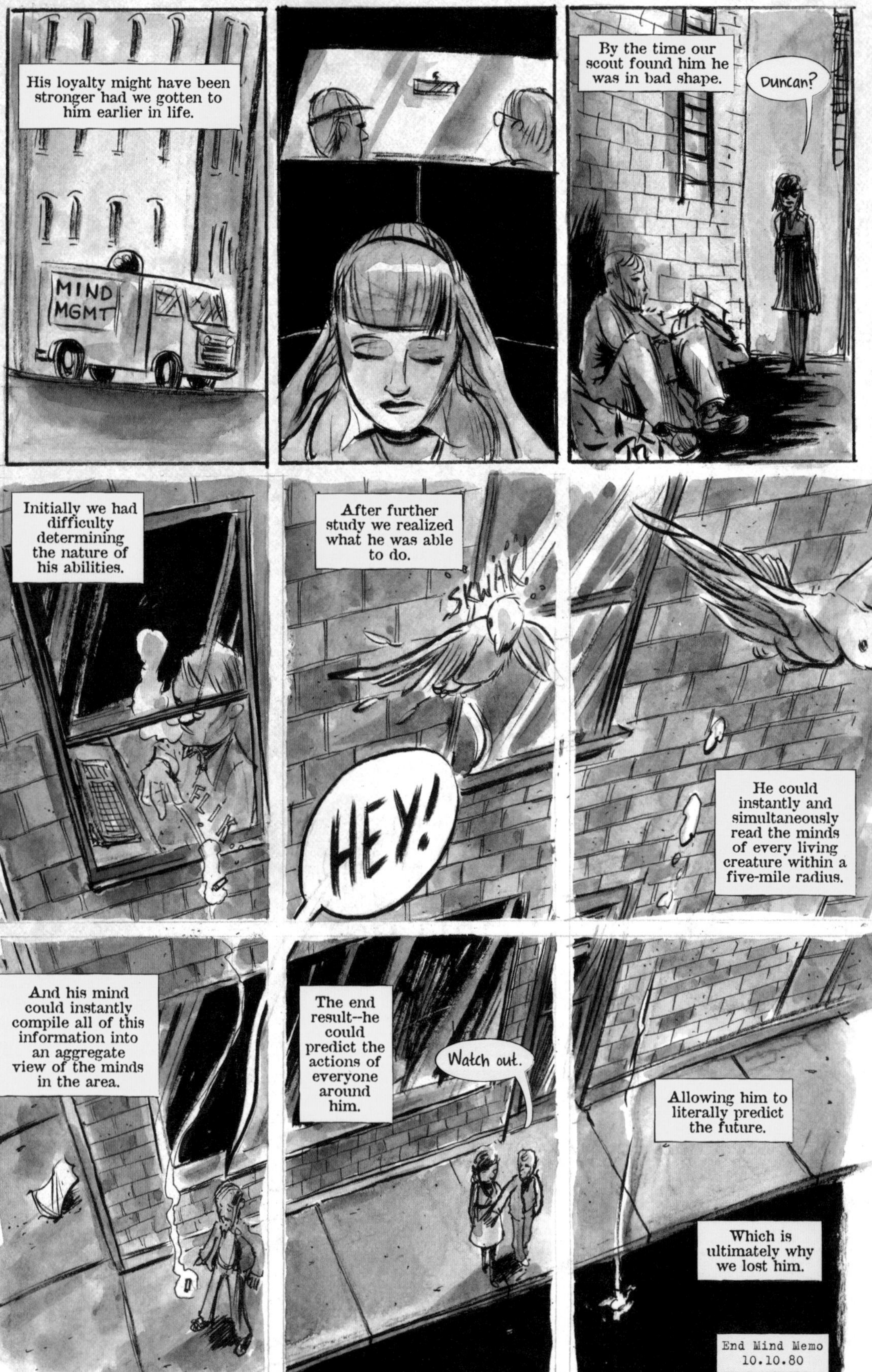
His loyalty might have been stronger had we gotten to him earlier in life.
MIND MGMT
By the time our scout found him he was in bad shape.
Duncan?
Initially we had difficulty determining the nature of his abilities.
FLIK
After further study we realized what he was able to do.
SKWAK!
HEY!
He could instantly and simultaneously read the minds of every living creature within a five-mile radius.
And his mind could instantly compile all of this information into an aggregate view of the minds in the area.
The end result--he could predict the actions of everyone around him.
Watch out.
Allowing him to literally predict the future.
Which is ultimately why we lost him.
End Mind Memo
10.10.80

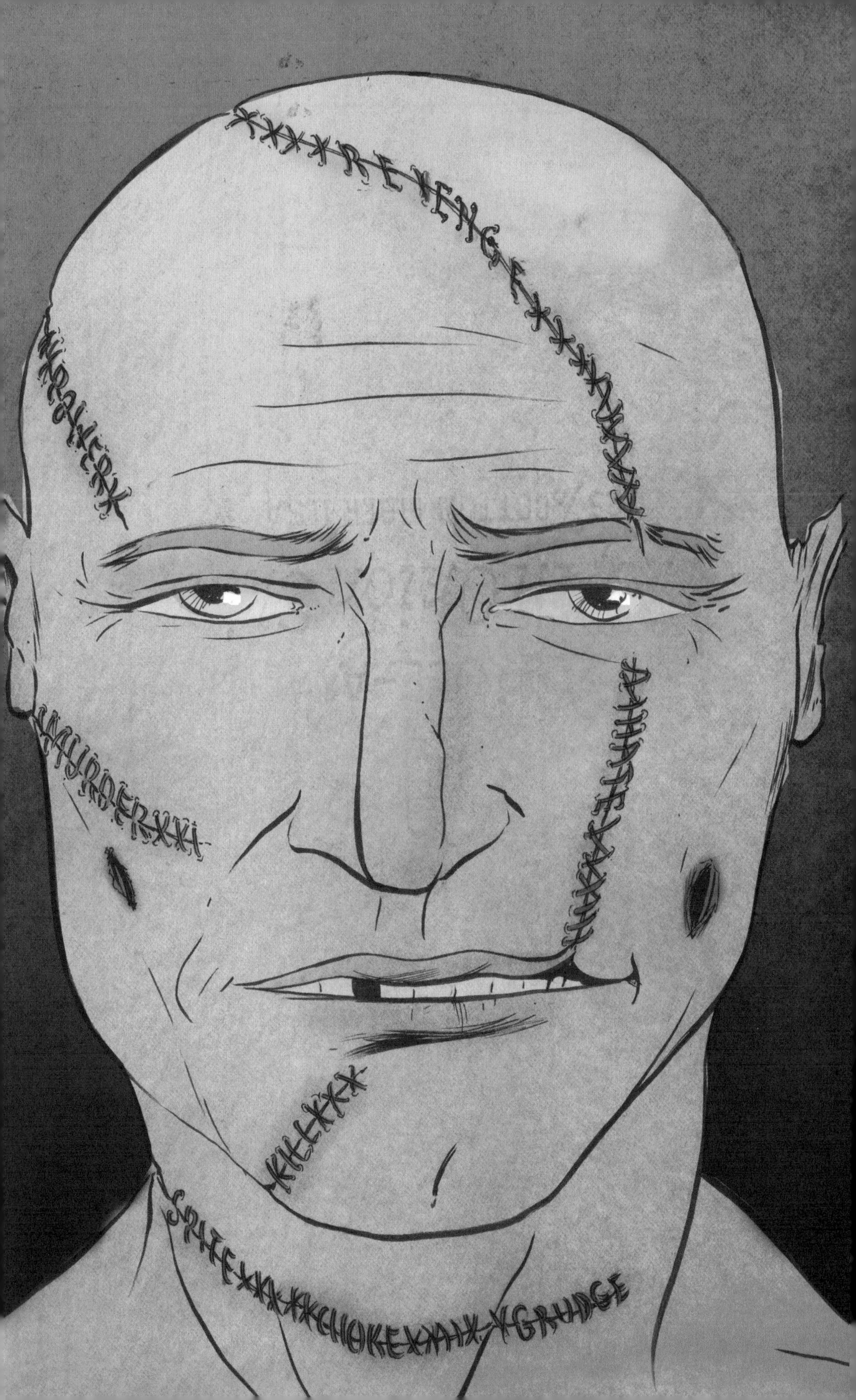
REVENGE
MURDER
KILL
SPITE
CHOKE
GRUDGE

WHEN FILING REPORT ALL ESSENTIAL DETAILS MUST FALL WITHIN THIS SOLID "LIVE AREA" BOX. THIS IS THE BORDER FOR A STANDARD, NON-BLEED FIELD REPORT

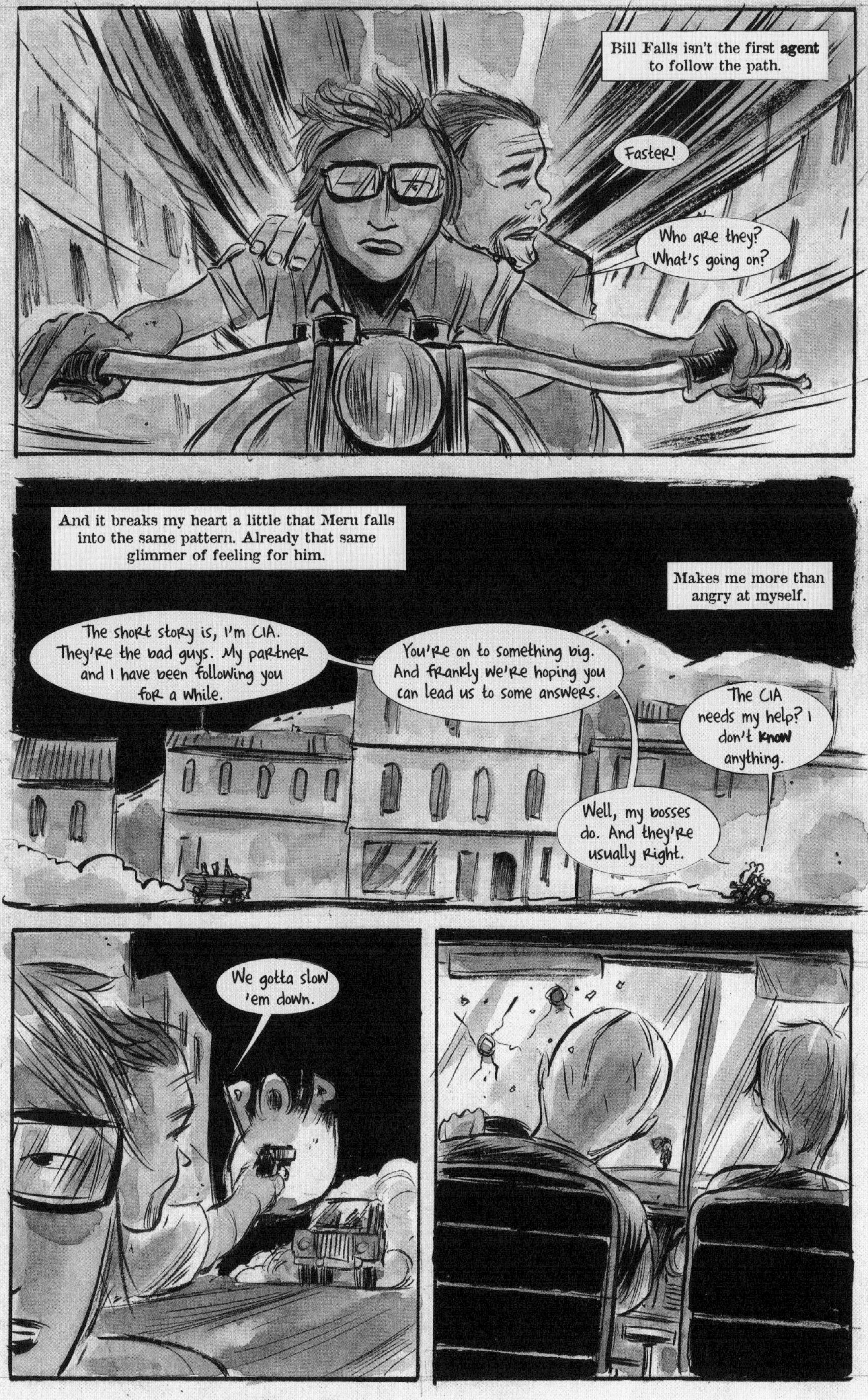

Bill Falls isn't the first **agent** to follow the path.
Faster!
Who are they? What's going on?
And it breaks my heart a little that Meru falls into the same pattern. Already that same glimmer of feeling for him.
Makes me more than angry at myself.
The short story is, I'm CIA. They're the bad guys. My partner and I have been following you for a while.
You're on to something big. And frankly we're hoping you can lead us to some answers.
The CIA needs my help? I don't **know** anything.
Well, my bosses do. And they're usually right.
We gotta slow 'em down.

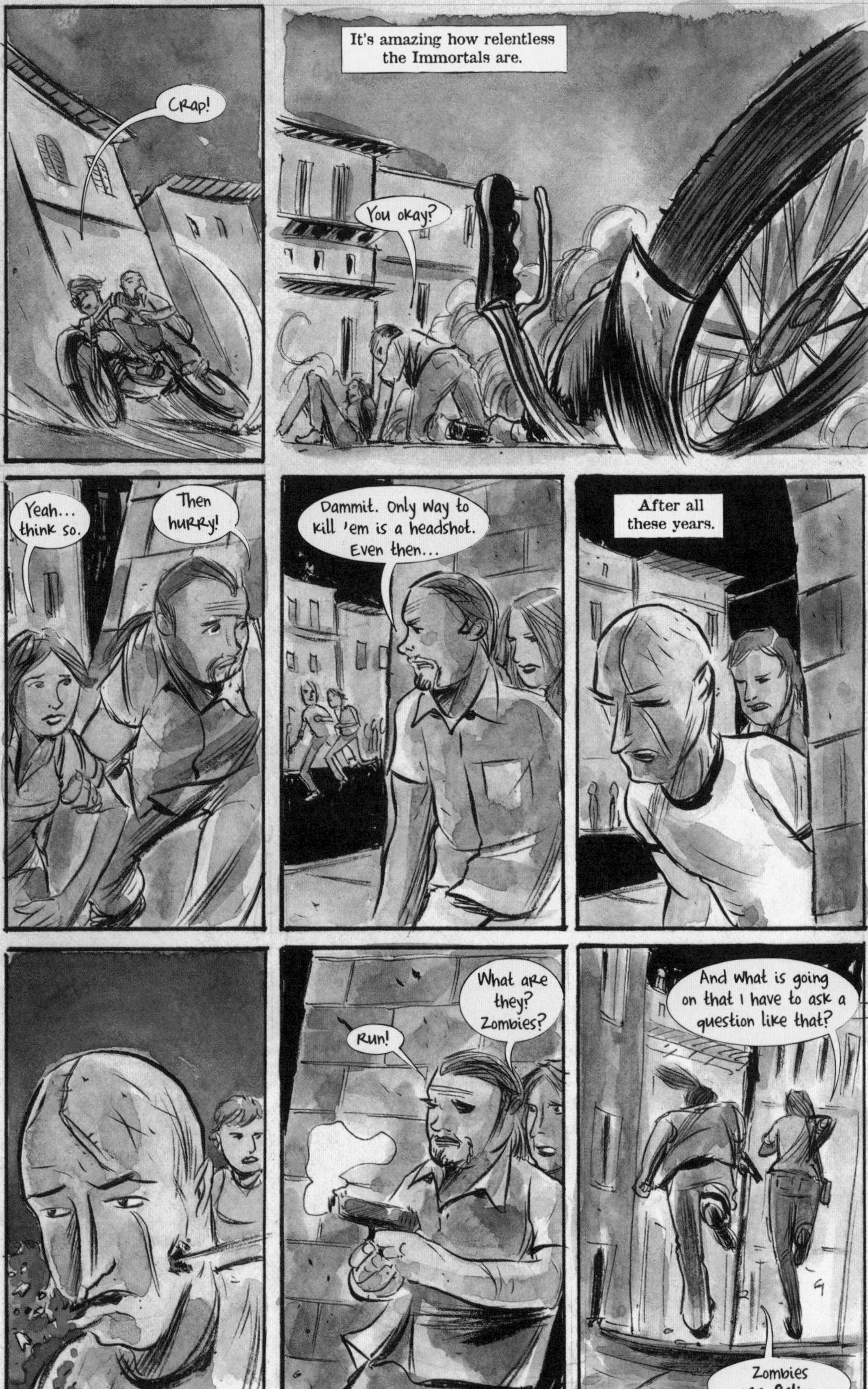
Crap!
It's amazing how relentless the Immortals are.
You okay?
Yeah... think so.
Then hurry!
Dammit. Only way to kill 'em is a headshot. Even then...
After all these years.
Run!
What are they? Zombies?
And what is going on that I have to ask a question like that?
Zombies are fiction.

MIND MGMT FIELD GUIDE. 2.2. Always aim for the trunk of an enemy unless using Mind Mirror ammunition in which case head shots are suggested.

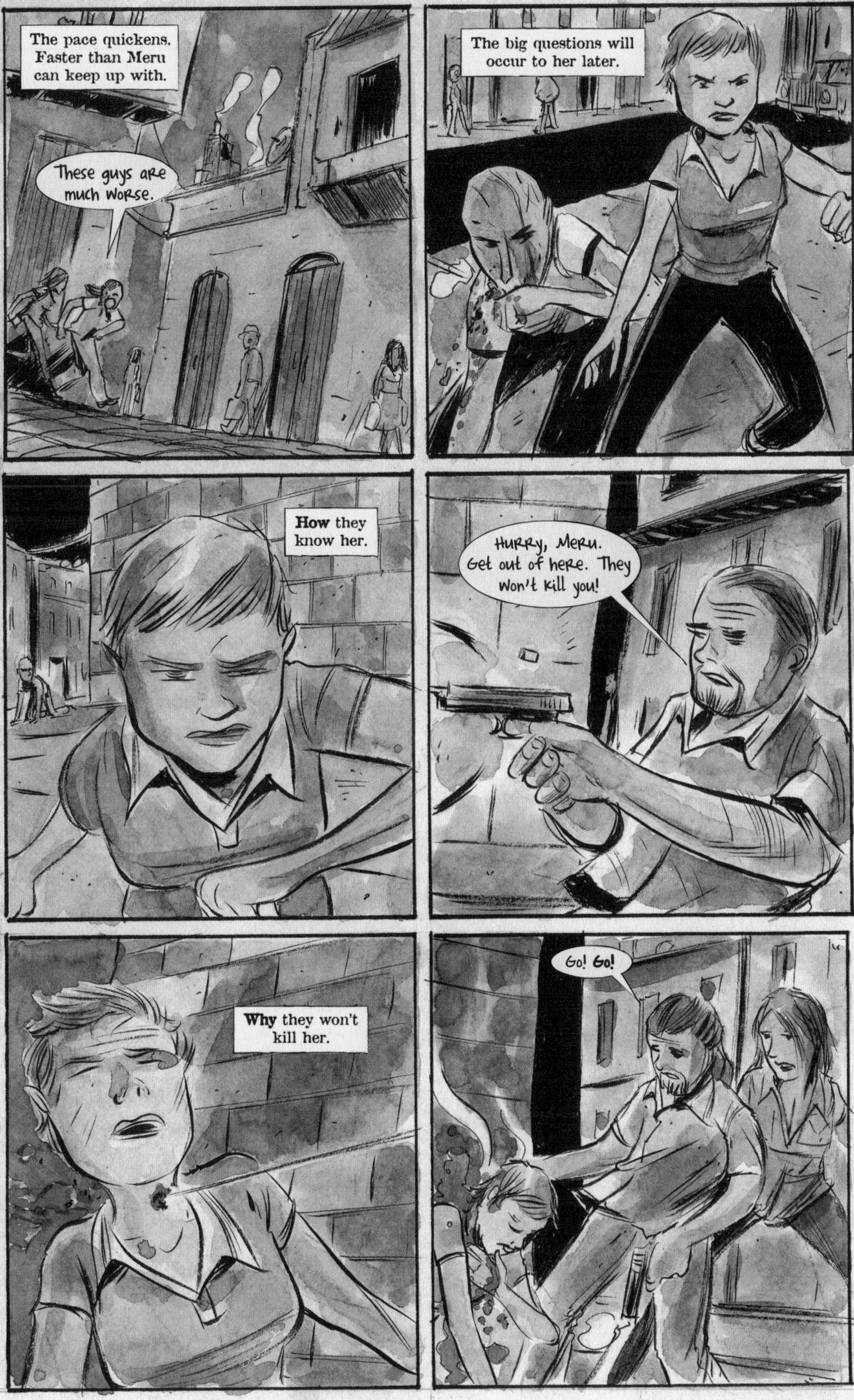
The pace quickens. Faster than Meru can keep up with.
These guys are much worse.
The big questions will occur to her later.
How they know her.
Hurry, Meru. Get out of here. They won't kill you!
Why they won't kill her.
Go! Go!

MIND MGMT FIELD GUIDE. 2.3. When encountering threats of violence in the field, always call for back up Immortal agents to act as spearheads.

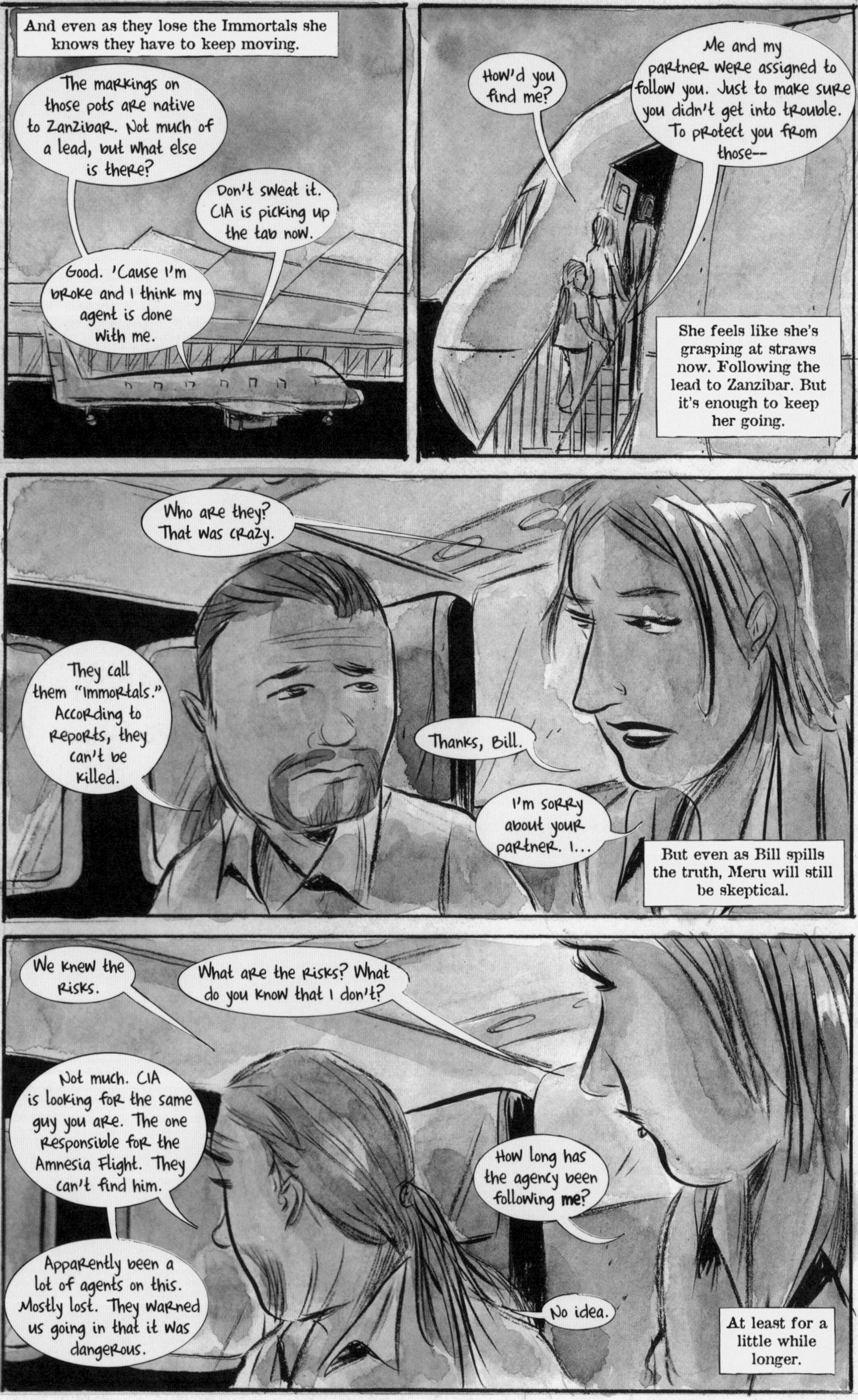
And even as they lose the Immortals she knows they have to keep moving.
The markings on those pots are native to Zanzibar. Not much of a lead, but what else is there?
Don't sweat it. CIA is picking up the tab now.
Good. 'Cause I'm broke and I think my agent is done with me.
How'd you find me?
Me and my partner were assigned to follow you. Just to make sure you didn't get into trouble. To protect you from those--
She feels like she's grasping at straws now. Following the lead to Zanzibar. But it's enough to keep her going.
Who are they? That was crazy.
They call them "Immortals." According to reports, they can't be killed.
Thanks, Bill.
I'm sorry about your partner. I...
But even as Bill spills the truth, Meru will still be skeptical.
We knew the risks.
What are the risks? What do you know that I don't?
Not much. CIA is looking for the same guy you are. The one responsible for the Amnesia Flight. They can't find him.
Apparently been a lot of agents on this. Mostly lost. They warned us going in that it was dangerous.
How long has the agency been following **me**?
No idea.
At least for a little while longer.

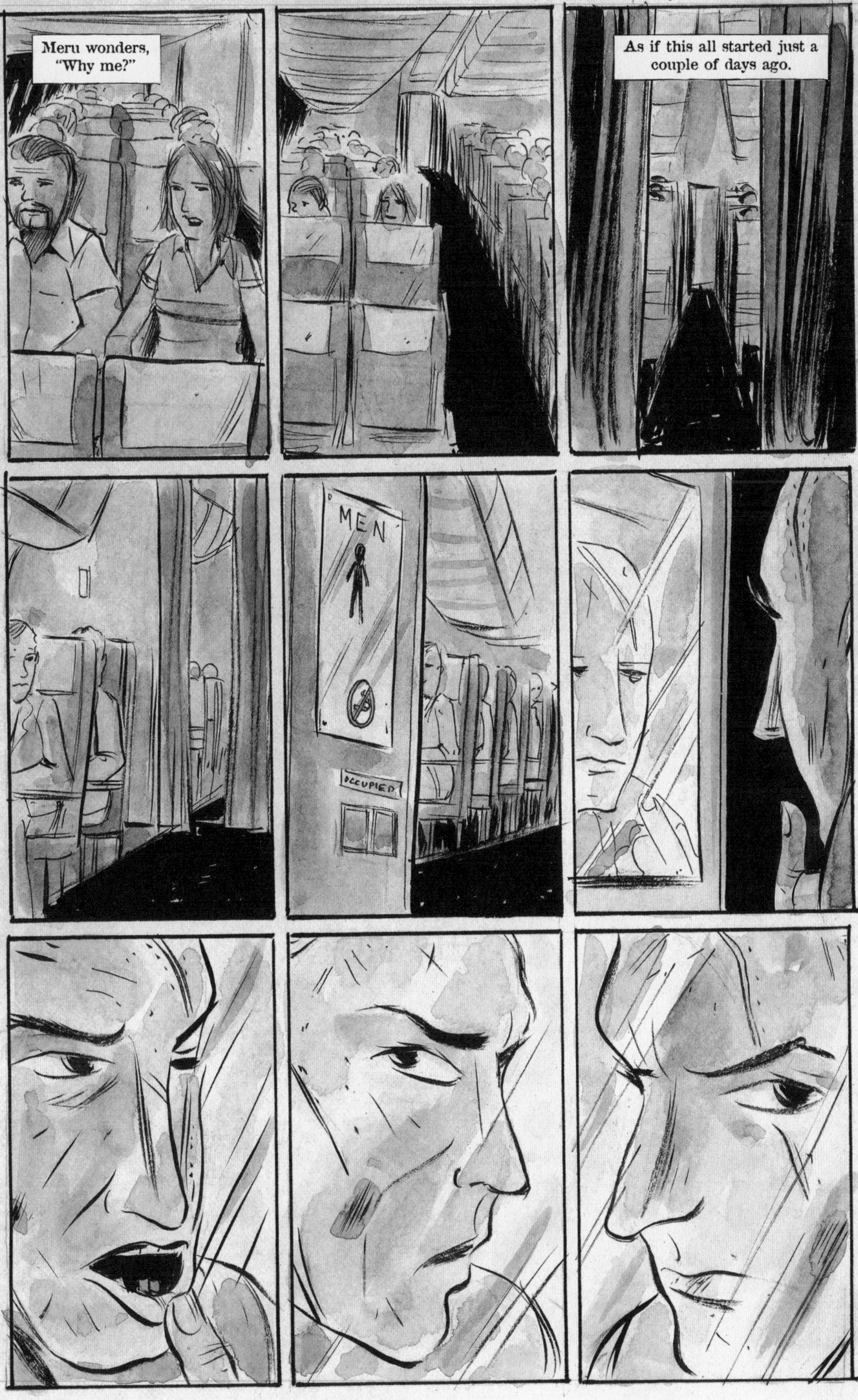
Meru wonders, "Why me?"
As if this all started just a couple of days ago.
MEN
OCCUPIED

MIND MGMT FIELD GUIDE: 2.5. When traveling in pairs, never sit together. Use a staggered seating pattern to watch the front and rear flanks.

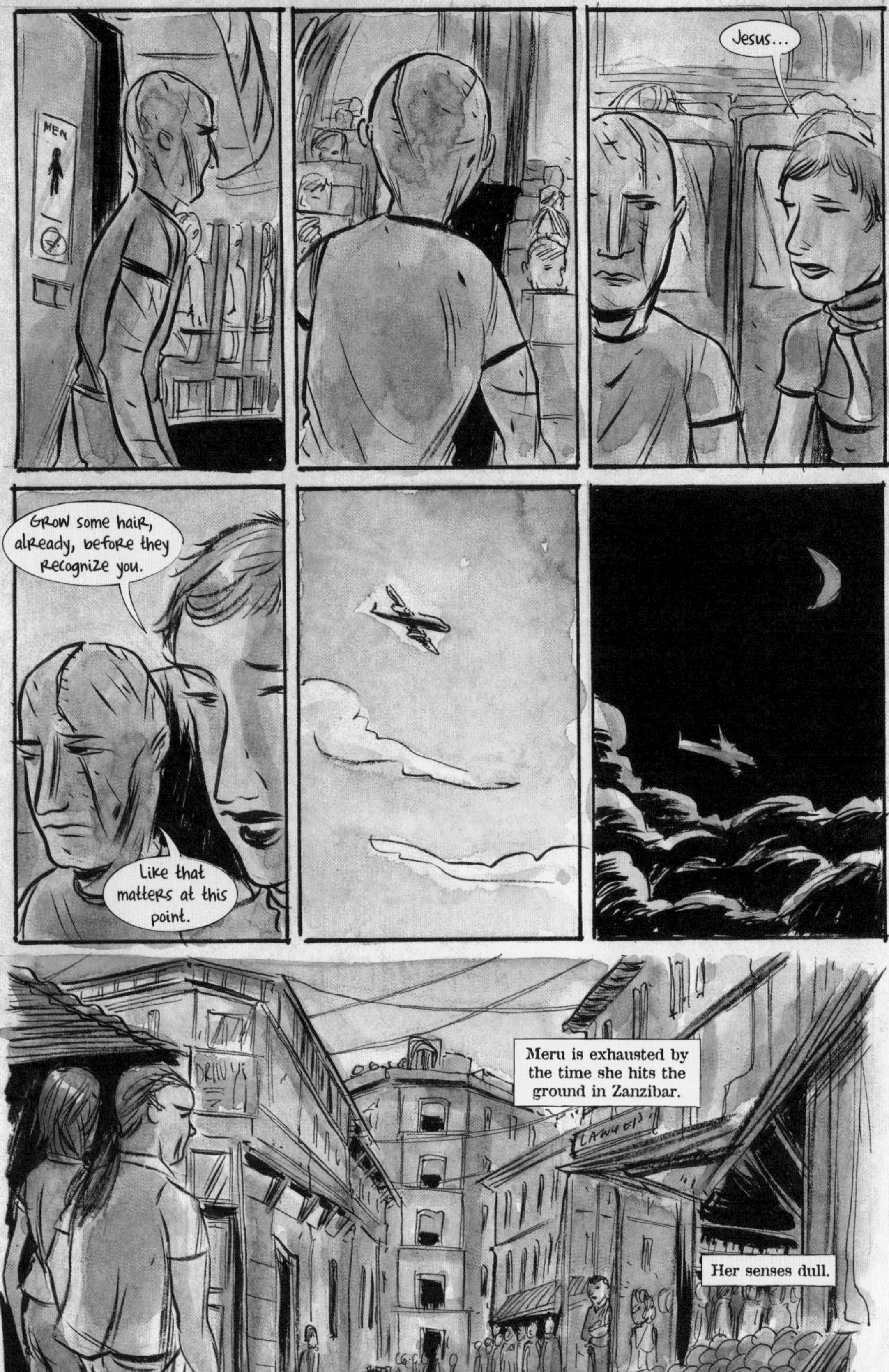
MEN
Jesus...
GROW some hair, already, before they recognize you.
Like that matters at this point.
Meru is exhausted by the time she hits the ground in Zanzibar.
Her senses dull.

MIND MGMT FIELD GUIDE. 2.6. When traveling abroad, make sure Remote Imaging periphery agents are in place at least 24 hours in advance of arrival.

WHEN FILING REPORT ALL ESSENTIAL DETAILS MUST FALL WITHIN THIS SOLID "LIVE AREA" BOX. THIS IS THE BORDER FOR A STANDARD, NON-BLEED FIELD REPORT

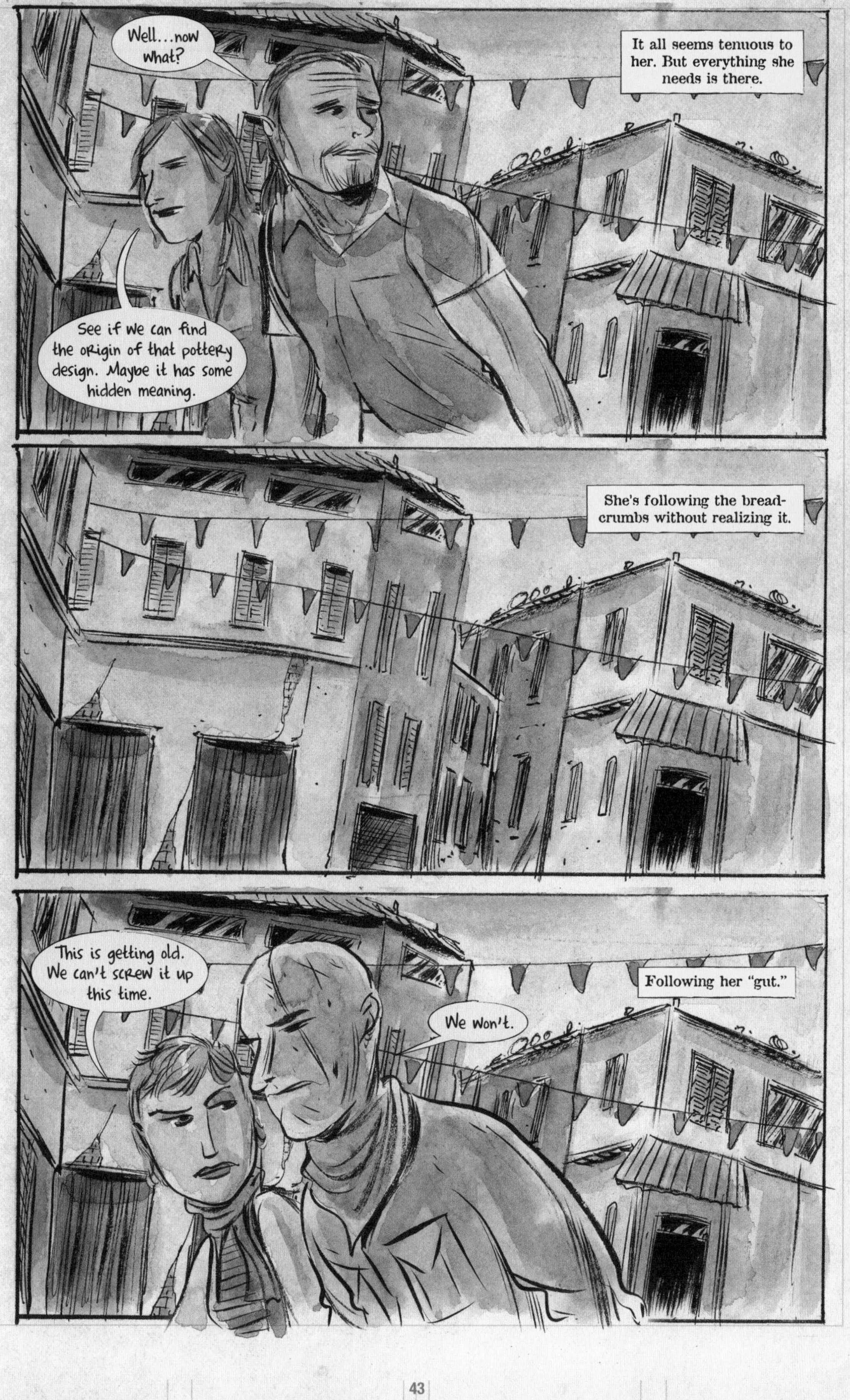
Well...now what?
It all seems tenuous to her. But everything she needs is there.
See if we can find the origin of that pottery design. Maybe it has some hidden meaning.
She's following the bread-crumbs without realizing it.
This is getting old. We can't screw it up this time.
Following her "gut."
We won't.

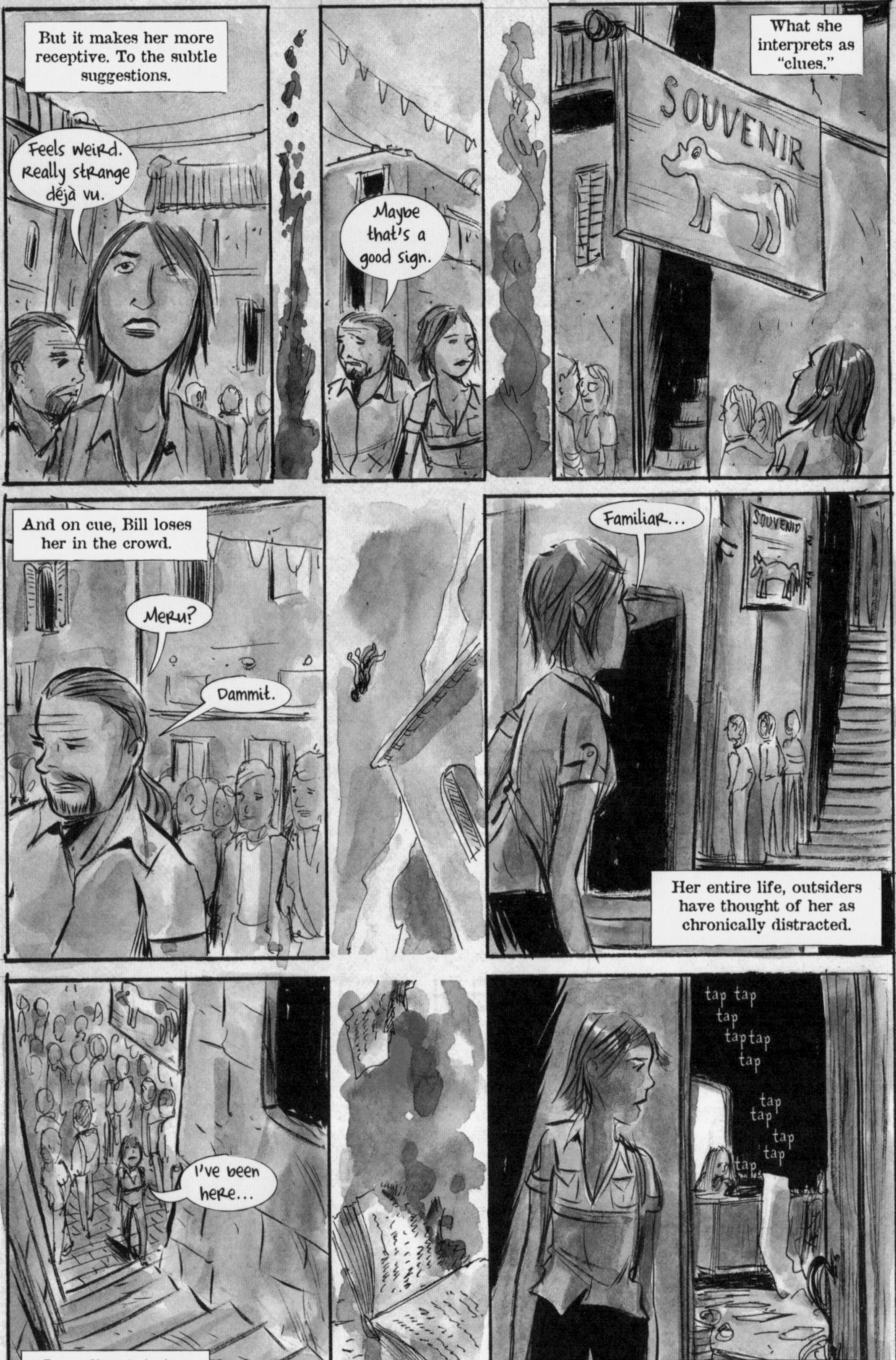
But it makes her more receptive. To the subtle suggestions.
Feels weird. Really strange déjà vu.
Maybe that's a good sign.
What she interprets as "clues."
SOUVENIR
And on cue, Bill loses her in the crowd.
Meru?
Dammit.
Familiar...
SOUVENIR
Her entire life, outsiders have thought of her as chronically distracted.
I've been here...
In reality she's just focused. Pushing everything else to the background.
tap tap tap taptap tap tap tap tap tap tap
Following the script, she reaches the next piece of wreckage.

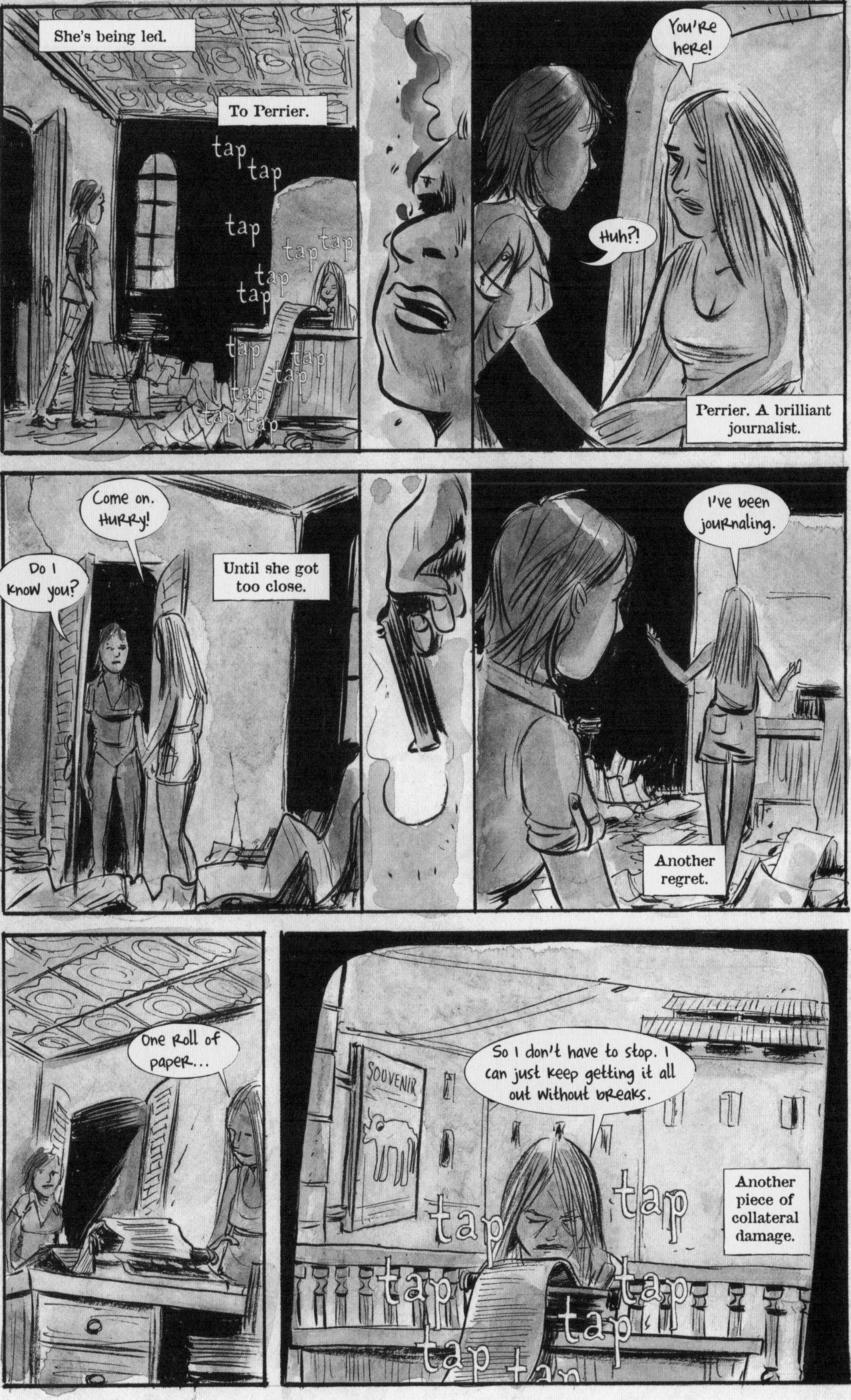
She's being led.
To Perrier.
tap tap tap tap tap tap tap tap tap tap tap tap tap
You're here!
Huh?!
Perrier. A brilliant journalist.
Come on. Hurry!
Do I know you?
Until she got too close.
I've been journaling.
Another regret.
One roll of paper...
So I don't have to stop. I can just keep getting it all out without breaks.
Another piece of collateral damage.
tap tap tap tap tap tap

MIND MGMT FIELD GUIDE 2.9: When in liaison with other field agents, always pick a neutral crash site and use traditional greeting protocols.

You think I'm crazy?

Don't you? I'm not. I don't think.

I just...he won't let me.

I...maybe I'm seeing the future. Like **Duncan** does.

Another casualty.

No. Only **he** does that.

Another breadcrumb.

Yes—somewhere around there.

Serving her purpose.

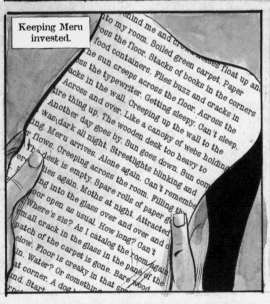

Keeping Meru invested.

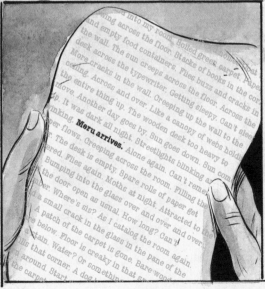

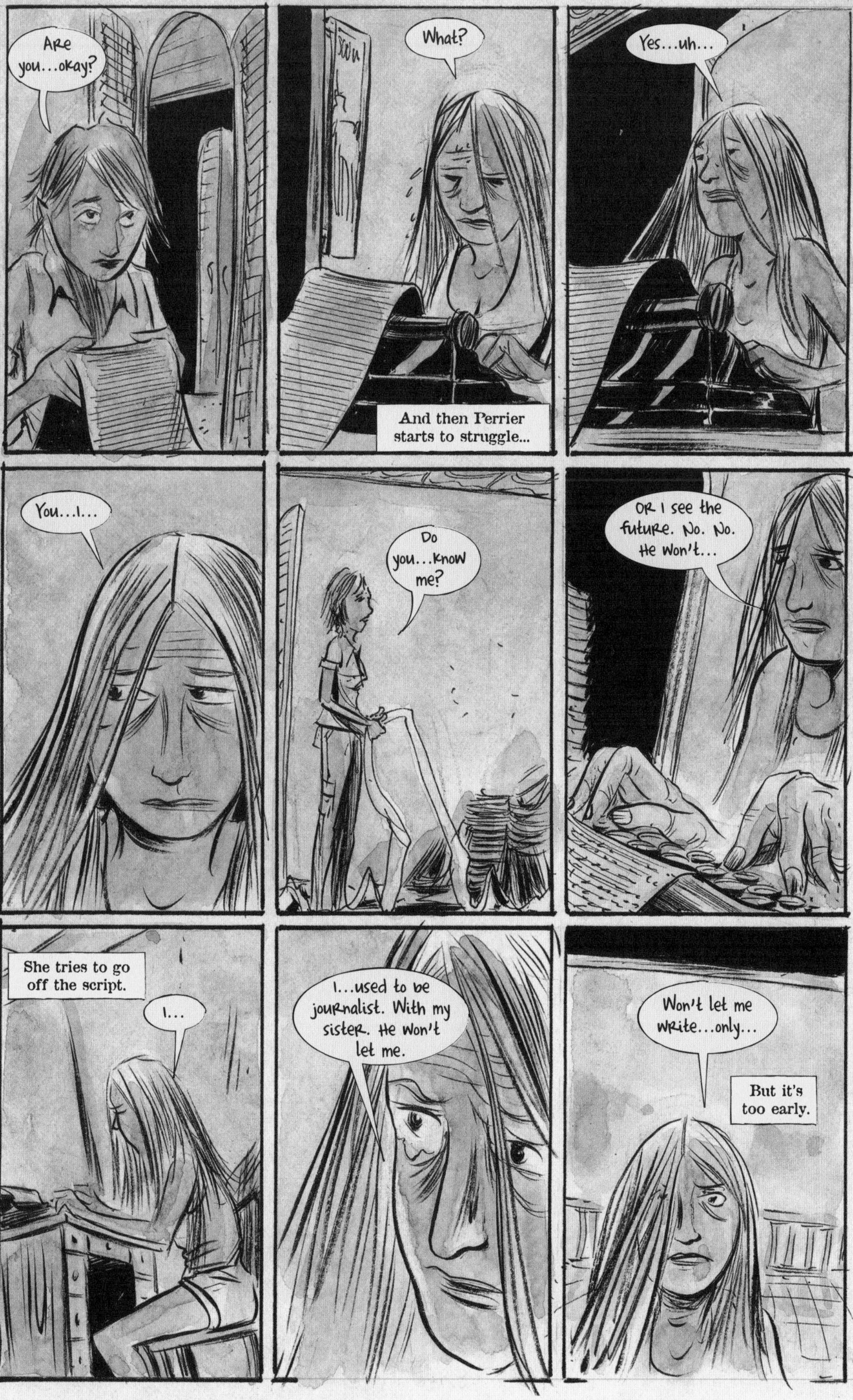
Are you...okay?
What?
And then Perrier starts to struggle...
Yes...uh...
You...I...
Do you...know me?
Or I see the future. No. No. He won't...
She tries to go off the script.
I...
I...used to be journalist. With my sister. He won't let me.
Won't let me write...only...
But it's too early.

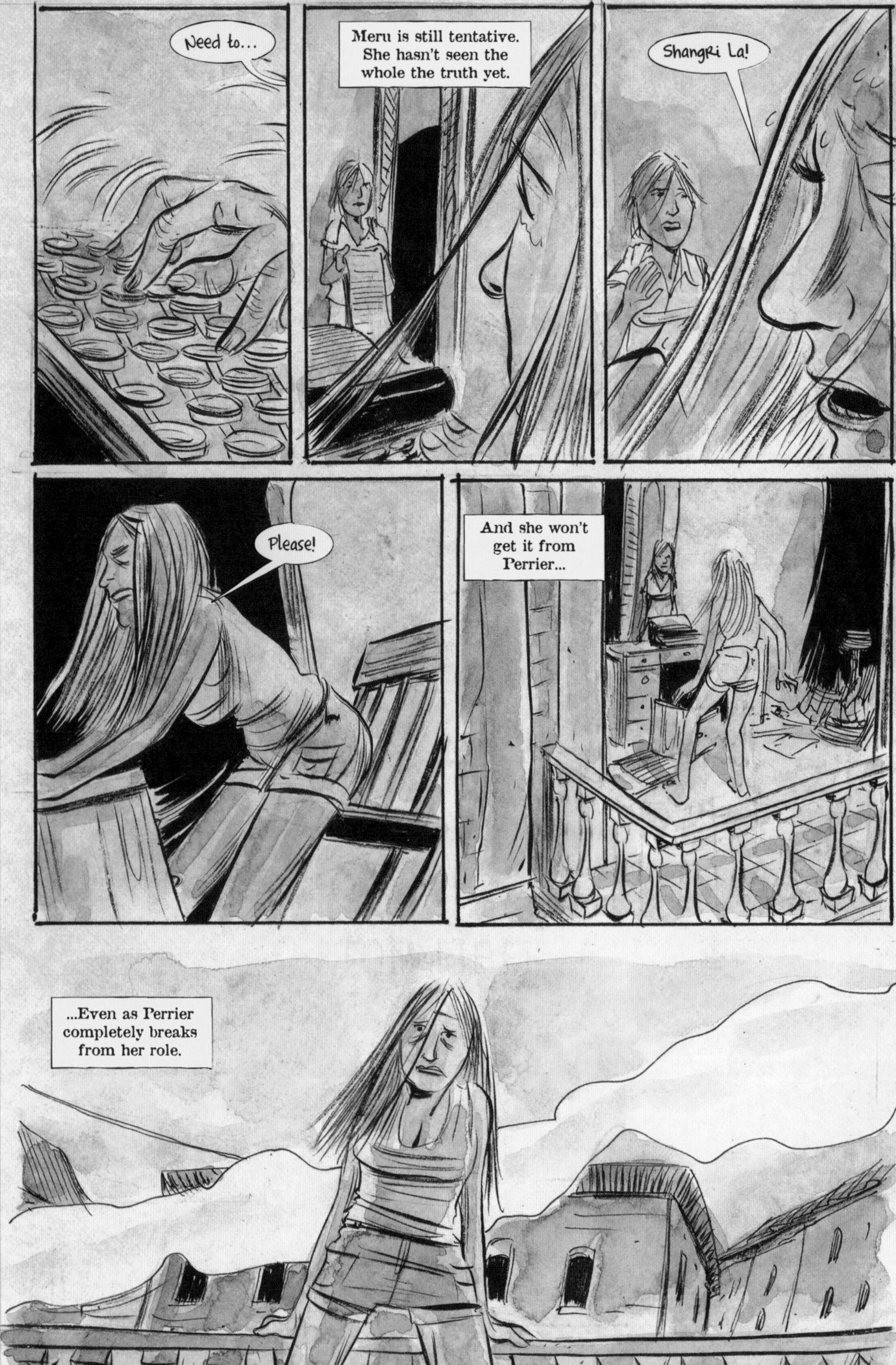
Need to...
Meru is still tentative. She hasn't seen the whole the truth yet.
Shangri La!
Please!
And she won't get it from Perrier...
...Even as Perrier completely breaks from her role.

MIND MGMT FIELD GUIDE. 2.12. When Brain-Embedded Words start to break down, any physical meeting should immediately be concluded until a new safe zone can be found.

WHEN FILING REPORT ALL ESSENTIAL DETAILS MUST FALL WITHIN THIS SOLID "LIVE AREA" BOX. THIS IS THE BORDER FOR A STANDARD, NON-BLEED FIELD REPORT

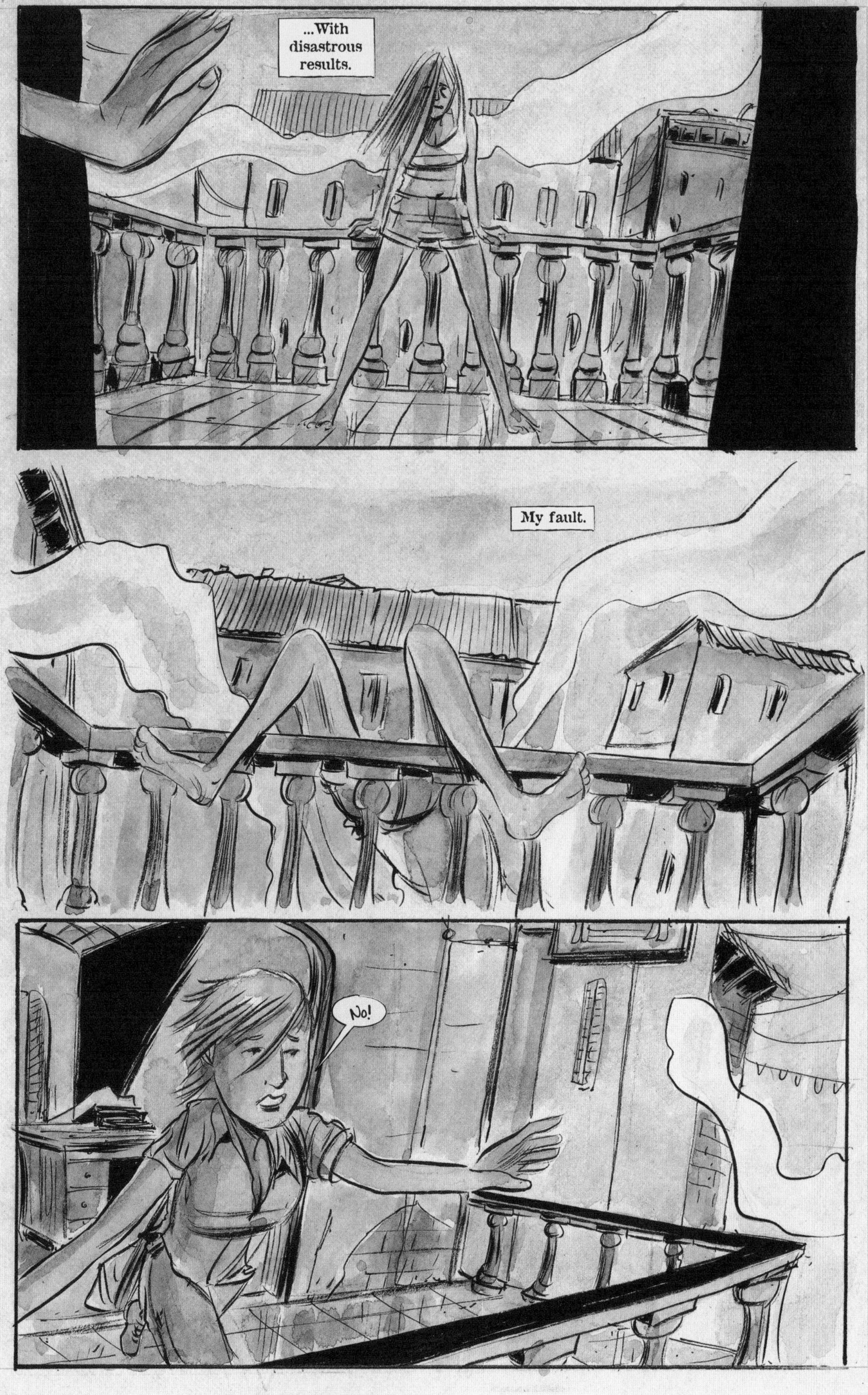

...With disastrous results.
My fault.
No!

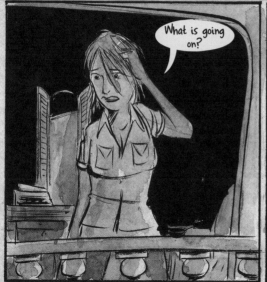

What is going on?
Beyond crazy...
The sad truth is that Perrier isn't irreplaceable...
...and Meru will still be on her way.
Talk to the dolphins.
Despite Perrier's best efforts to change her course.
CLIK
Meru?

MIND MGMT FIELD GUIDE. 2.14. Gray-Matter Paper, when left behind and unprimed can be difficult to read. Don't force the paper--allow the paper to speak to you.

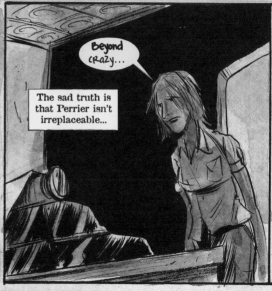

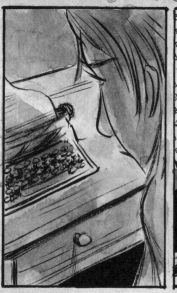

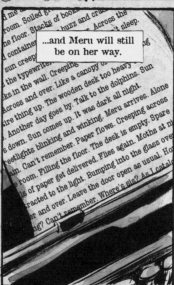

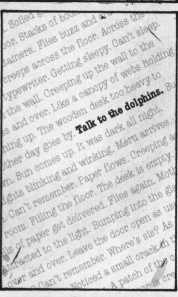

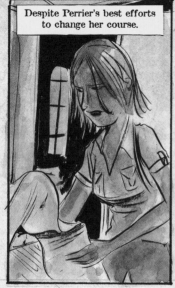

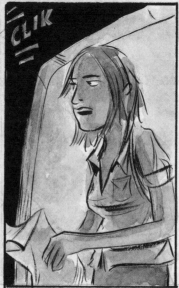

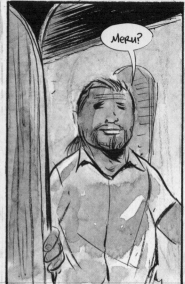

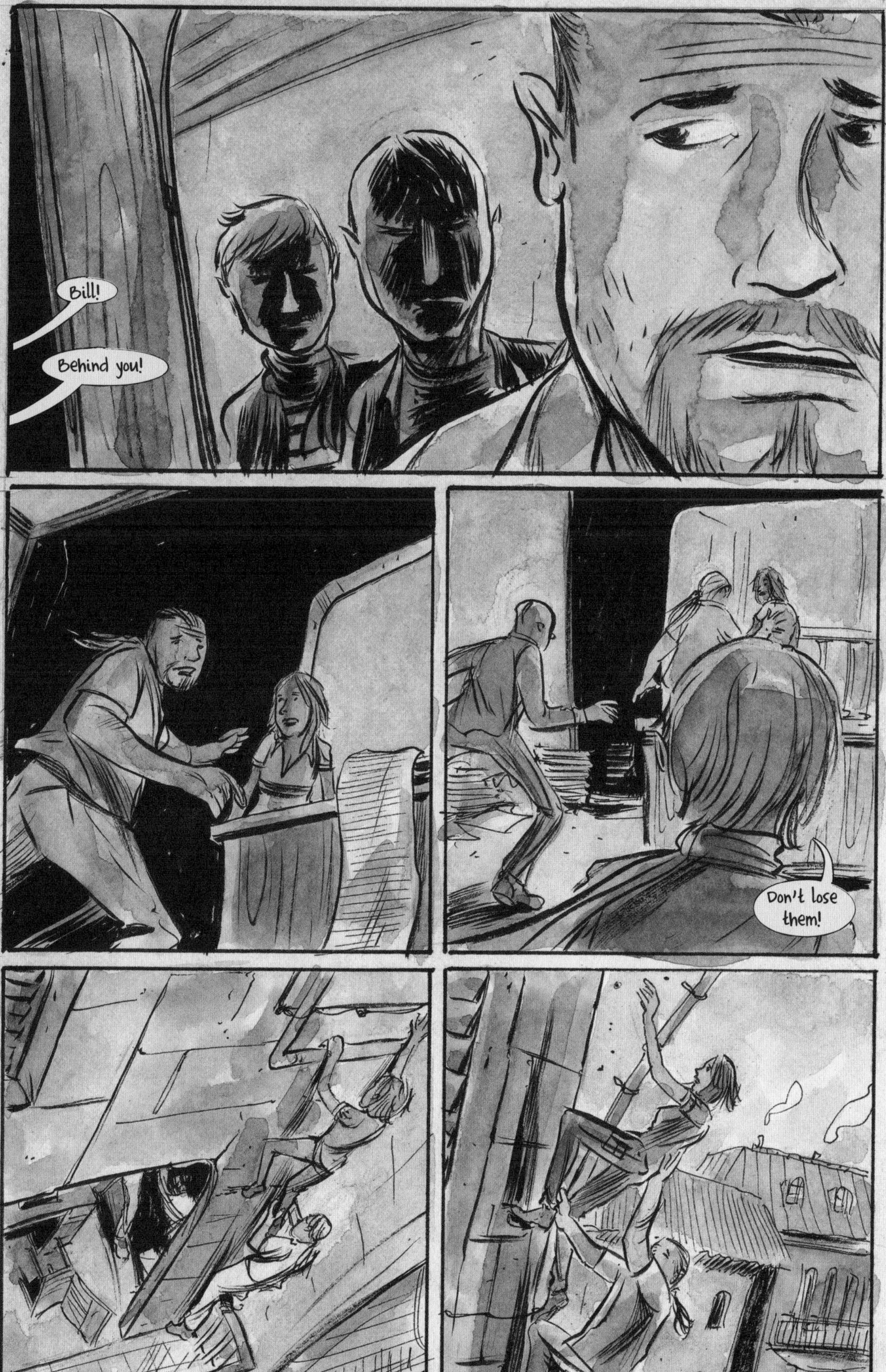
Bill!
Behind you!
Don't lose them!

MIND MGMT FIELD GUIDE 2.15: If all perimeter defenses fail and retreat is unavoidable, use all of your Clean House mind-wipe techniques to clean your safe house.

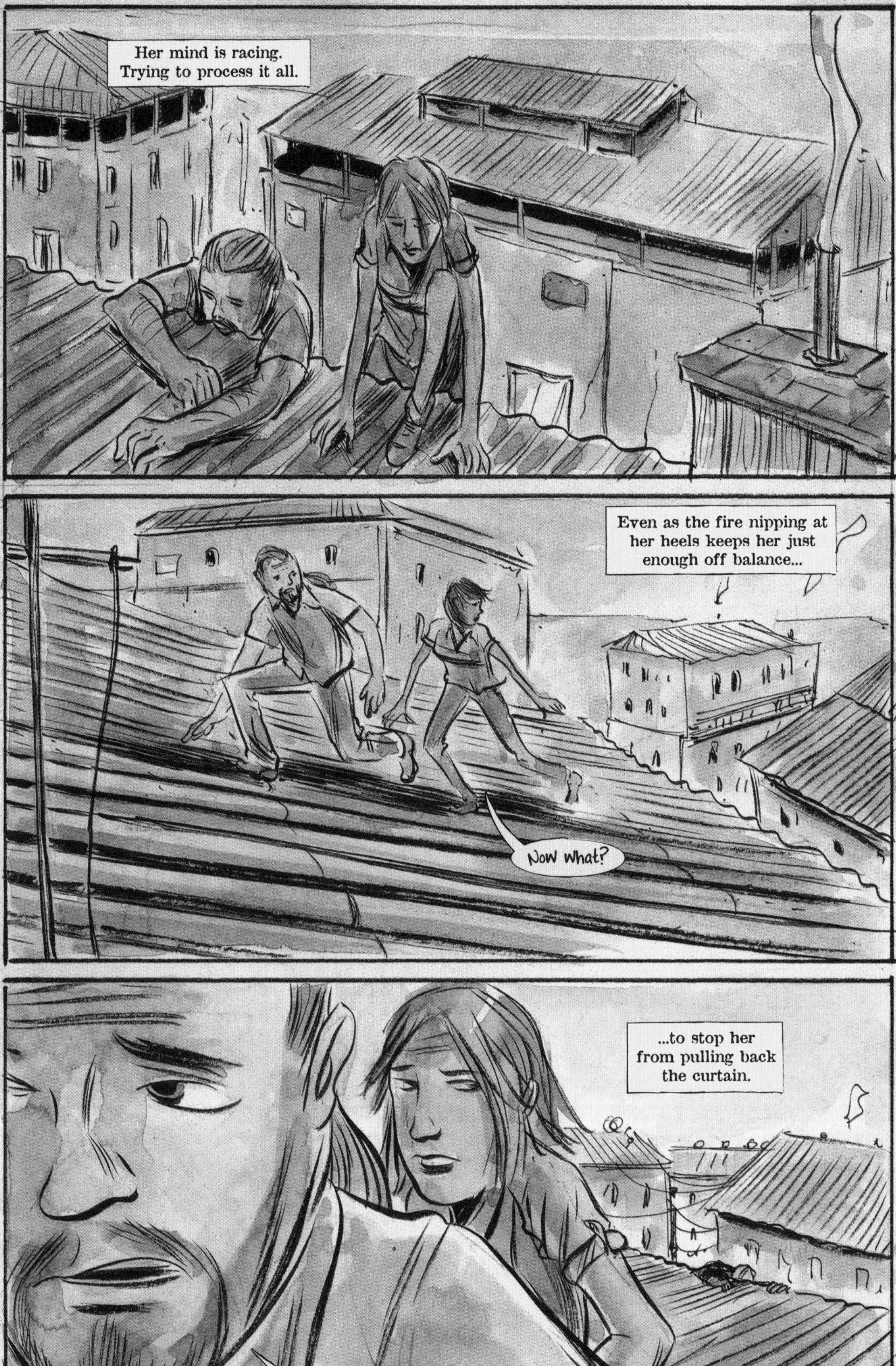
Her mind is racing. Trying to process it all.
Even as the fire nipping at her heels keeps her just enough off balance...
Now what?
...to stop her from pulling back the curtain.
Keep moving.
Not yet...

MIND MGMT FIELD GUIDE. 2.16. When in danger, remember to use all of your traditional evasion techniques in combination with Mind Ventriloquism techniques to throw pursuers off of your trail.

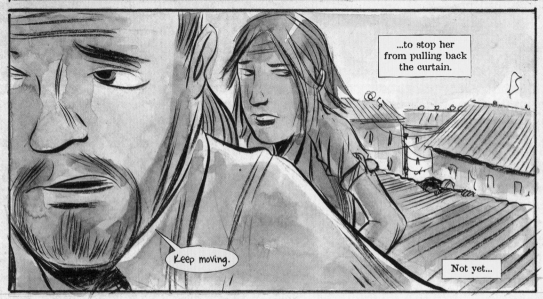

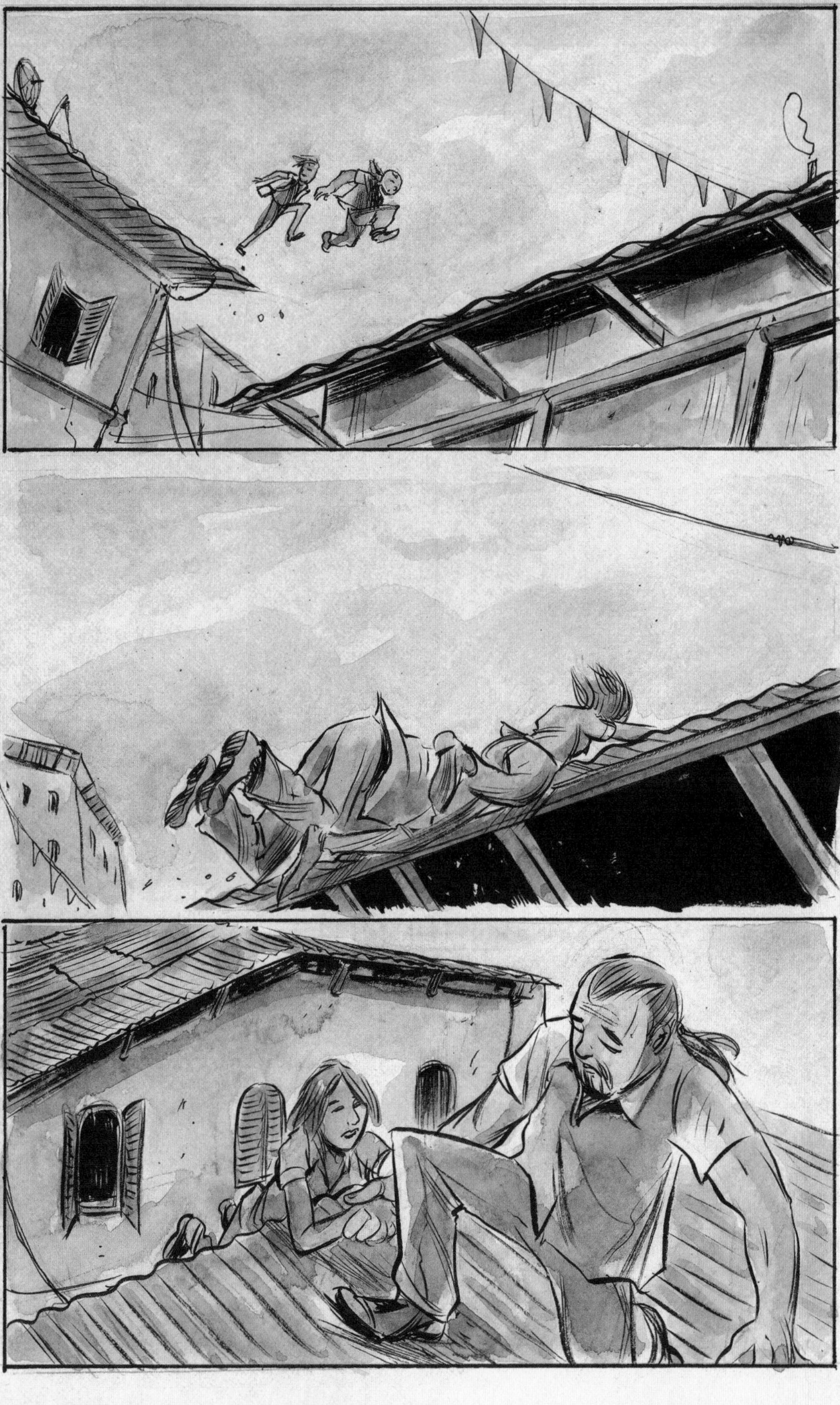

MIND MGMT FIELD GUIDE. 2.17. When in pursuit or being pursued with a partner, always rely on Mental Blasts to coordinate movements rather than verbal communication.

WHEN FILING REPORT ALL ESSENTIAL DETAILS MUST FALL WITHIN THIS SOLID "LIVE AREA" BOX. THIS IS THE BORDER FOR A STANDARD, NON-BLEED FIELD REPORT

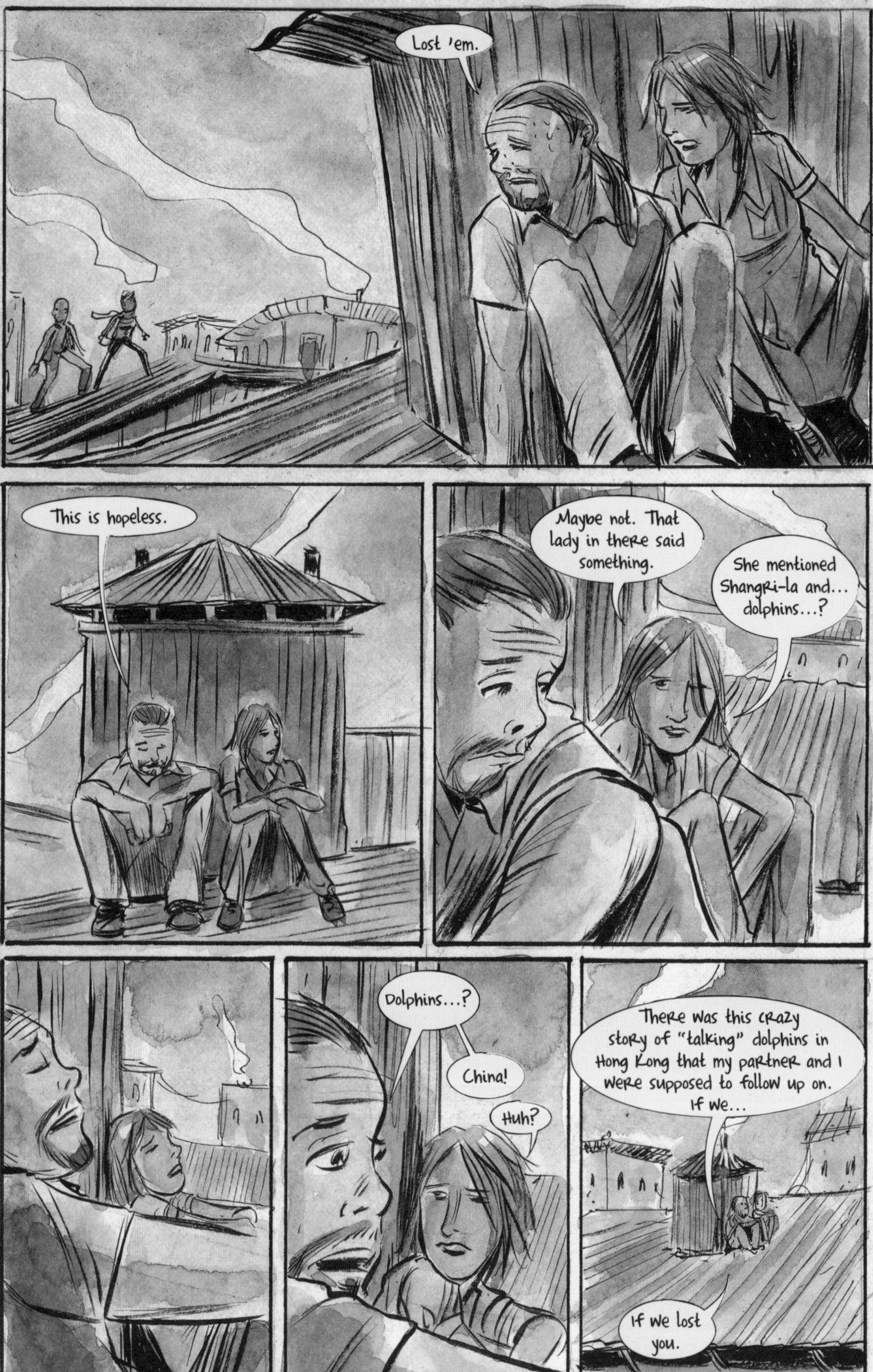
Lost 'em.
This is hopeless.
Maybe not. That lady in there said something.
She mentioned Shangri-la and... dolphins...?
Dolphins...?
China!
Huh?
There was this crazy story of "talking" dolphins in Hong Kong that my partner and I were supposed to follow up on. If we...
If we lost you.

MIND MGMT FIELD GUIDE. 2.18. After escaping pursuers, always take time to use your Mind Underground techniques to disappear off of the Mental Map.

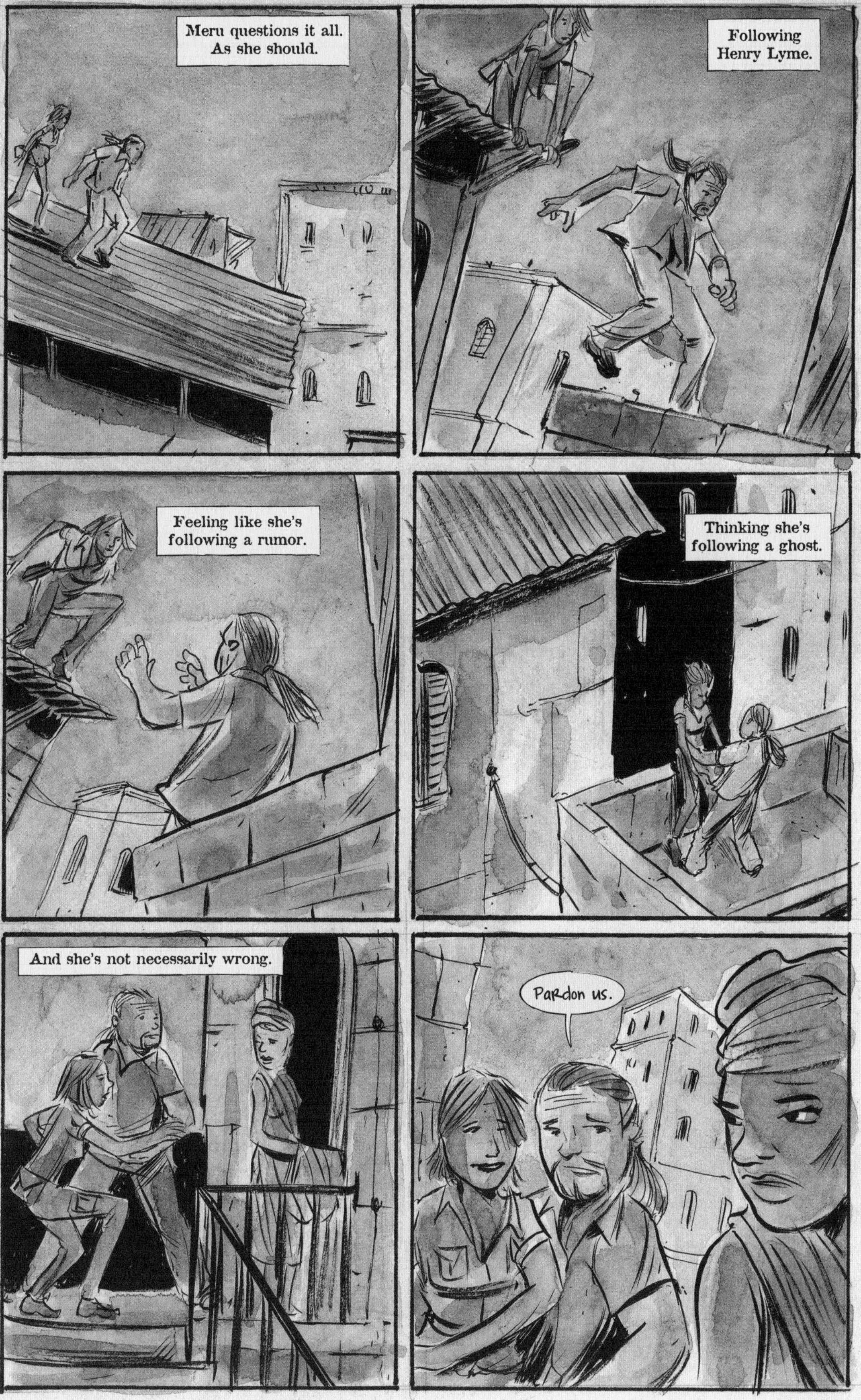
Meru questions it all. As she should.
Following Henry Lyme.
Feeling like she's following a rumor.
Thinking she's following a ghost.
And she's not necessarily wrong.
Pardon us.

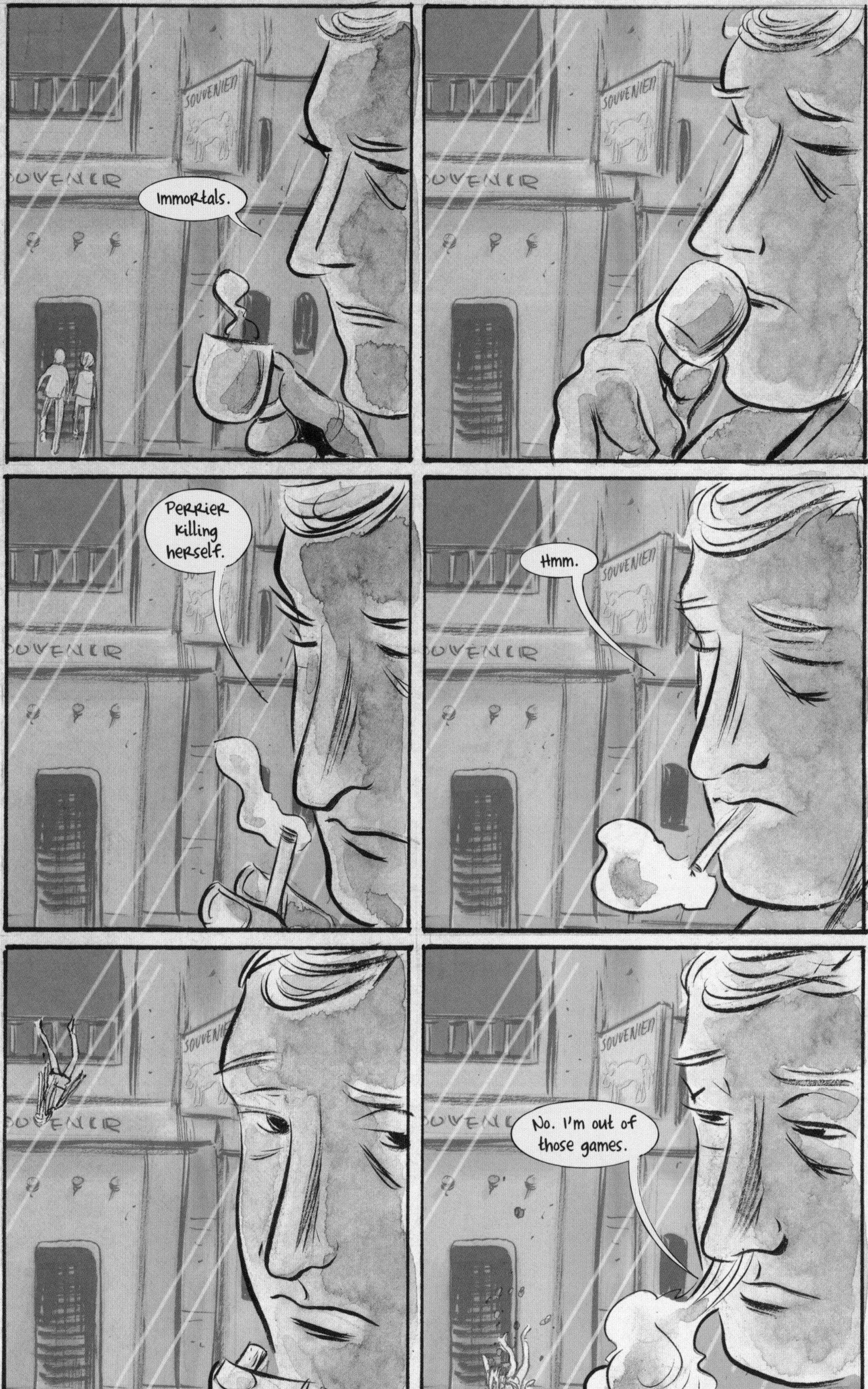
SOUVENIER
SOUVENIER
Immortals.
Perrier killing herself.
Hmm.
No. I'm out of those games.

MIND MGMT FIELD GUIDE. 2.20. Always be aware of your surroundings and of ex-or retired agents that may be lurking in the shadows, waiting to come into play.

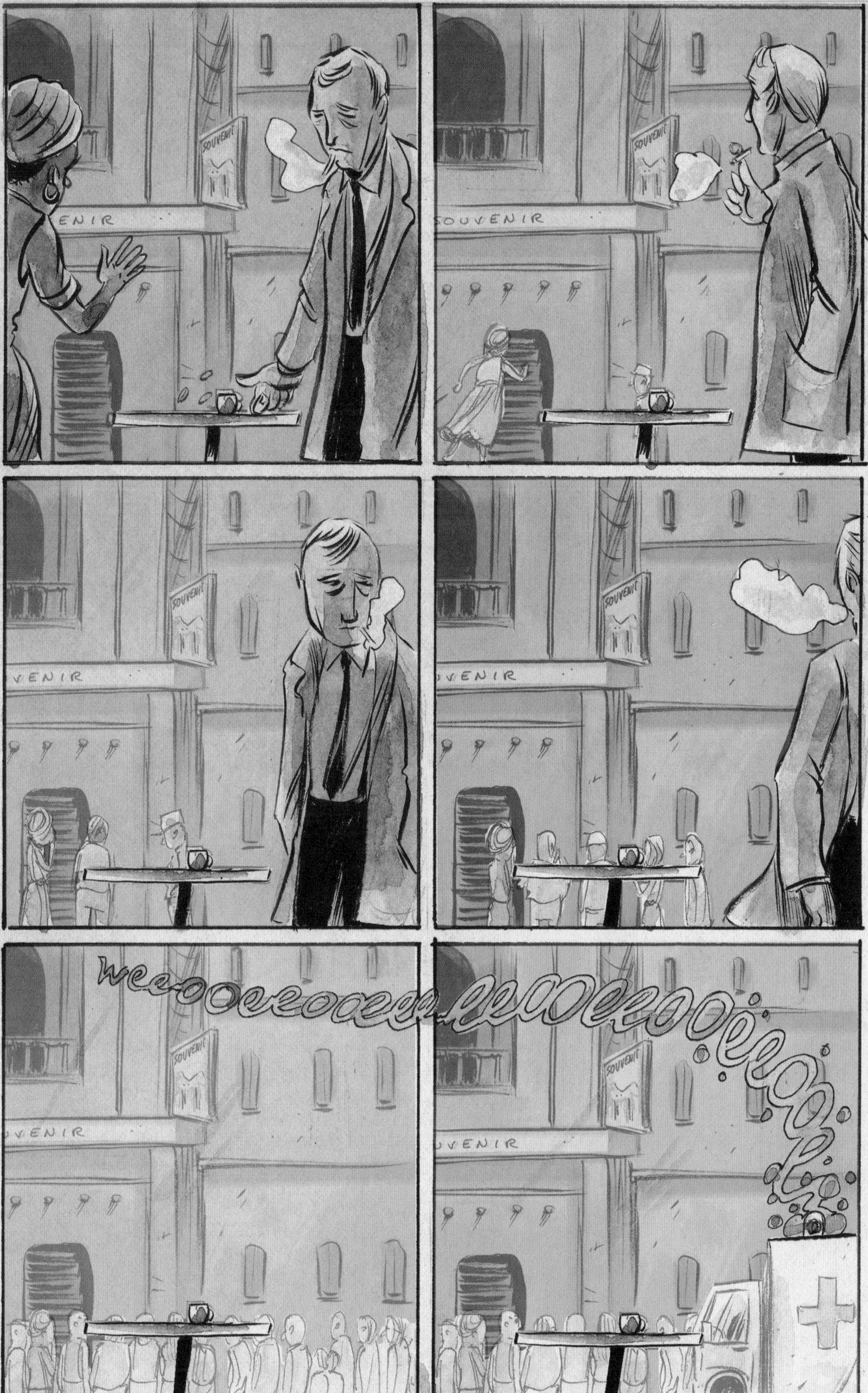
SOUVENIR
SOUVENIR

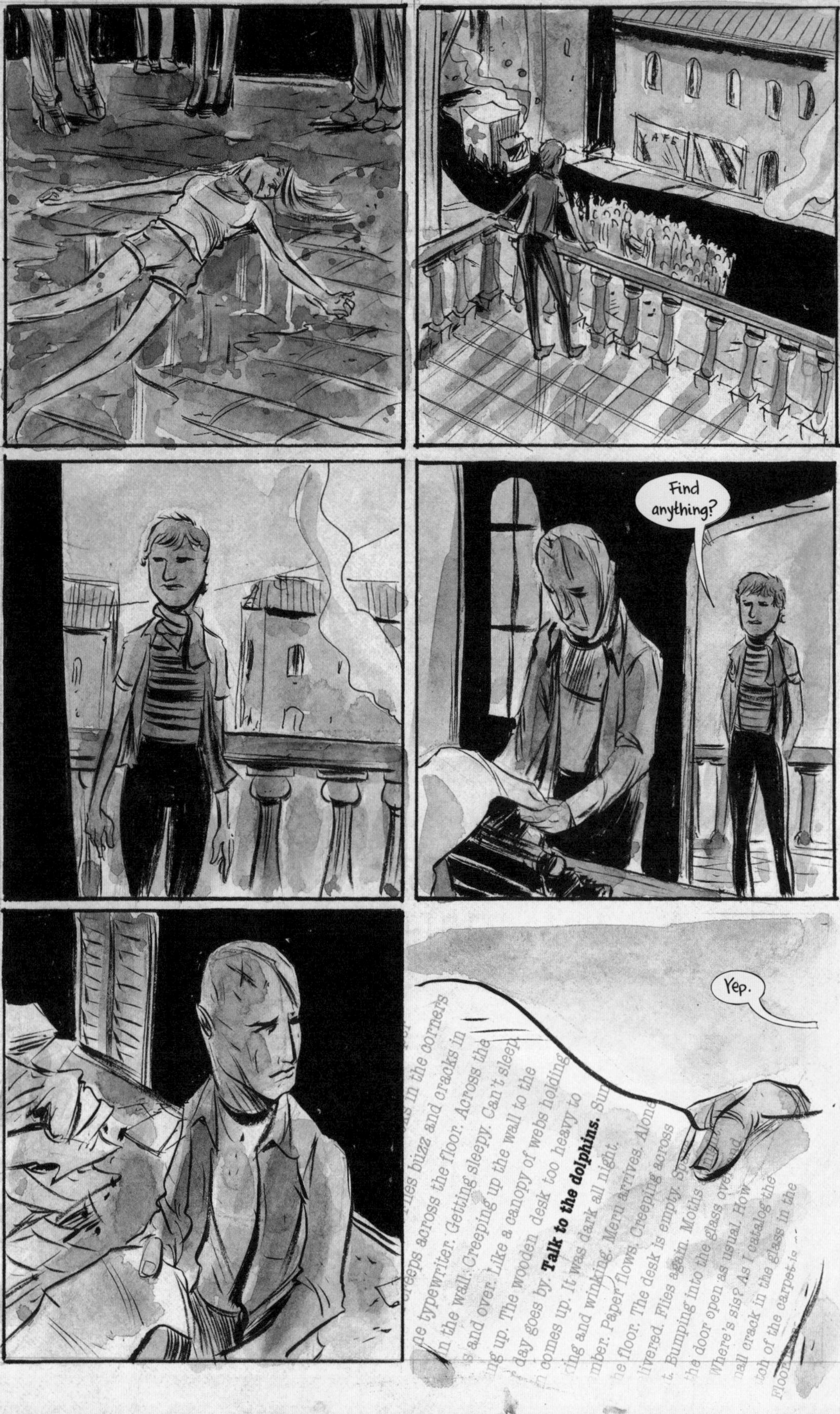
CAFE
Find anything?
Yep.
Talk to the dolphins.

MIND MGMT FIELD GUIDE. 2.22. Again, it can't be stressed enough. Use Gray-Matter Paper at all times when leaving written message to avoid interception by enemy agents.

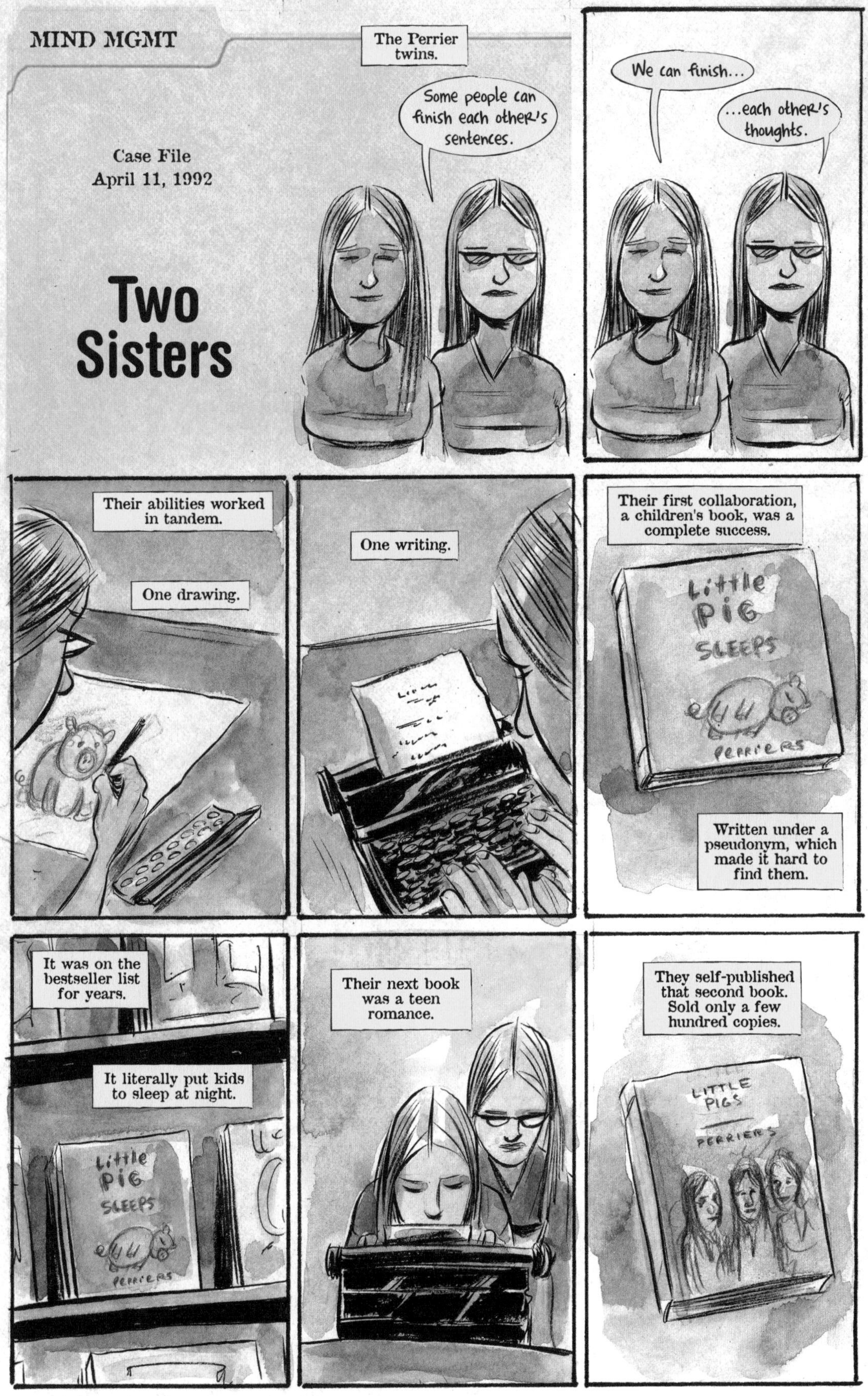
MIND MGMT
Case File
April 11, 1992
Two Sisters
The Perrier twins.
Some people can finish each other's sentences.
We can finish...
...each other's thoughts.
Their abilities worked in tandem.
One drawing.
One writing.
Their first collaboration, a children's book, was a complete success.
Little Pig Sleeps
Written under a pseudonym, which made it hard to find them.
It was on the bestseller list for years.
It literally put kids to sleep at night.
Little Pig Sleeps
Their next book was a teen romance.
They self-published that second book. Sold only a few hundred copies.
Little Pigs

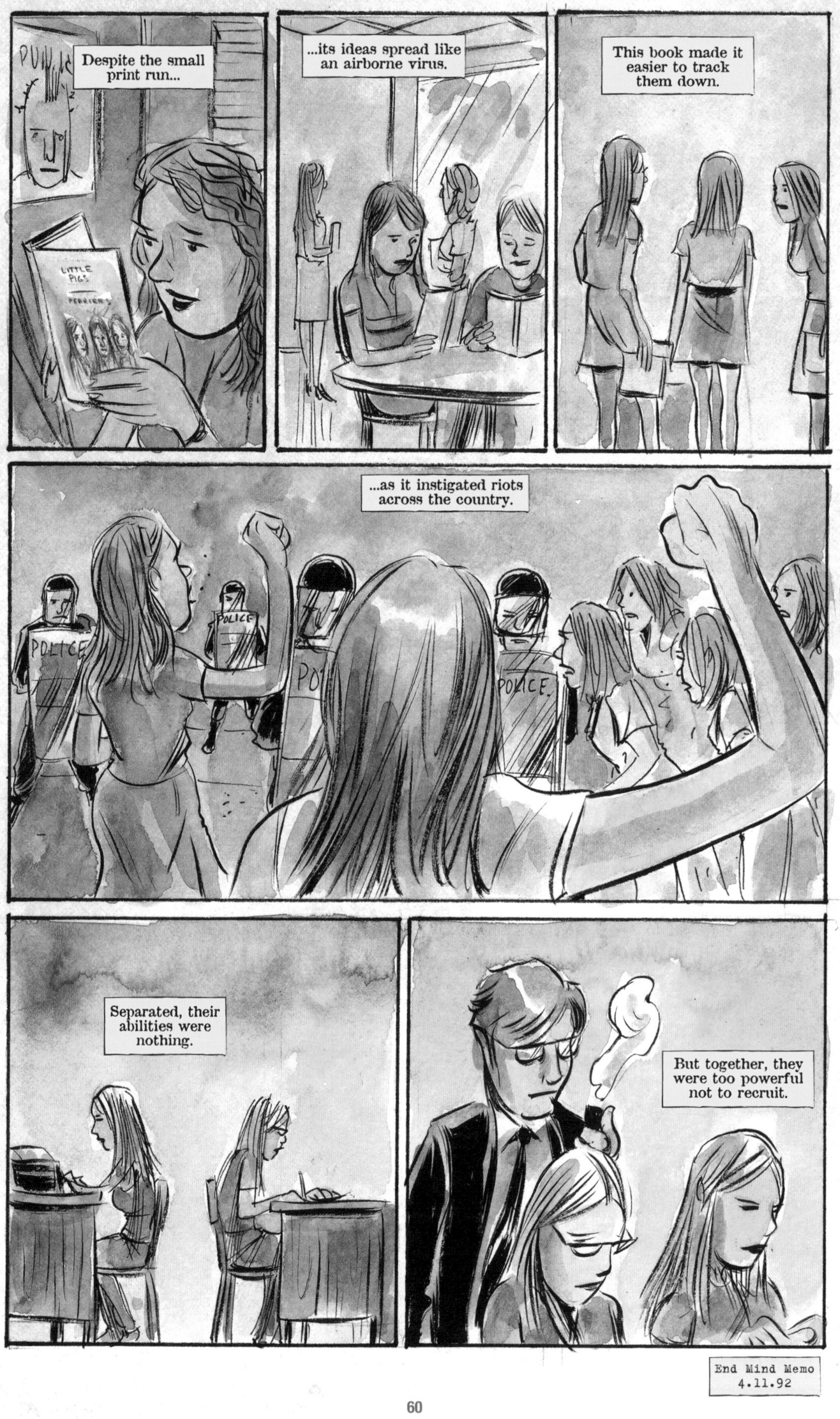
Despite the small print run...
LITTLE PIGS
...its ideas spread like an airborne virus.
This book made it easier to track them down.
...as it instigated riots across the country.
POLICE
POLICE
POLICE
Separated, their abilities were nothing.
But together, they were too powerful not to recruit.

End Mind Memo
4.11.92

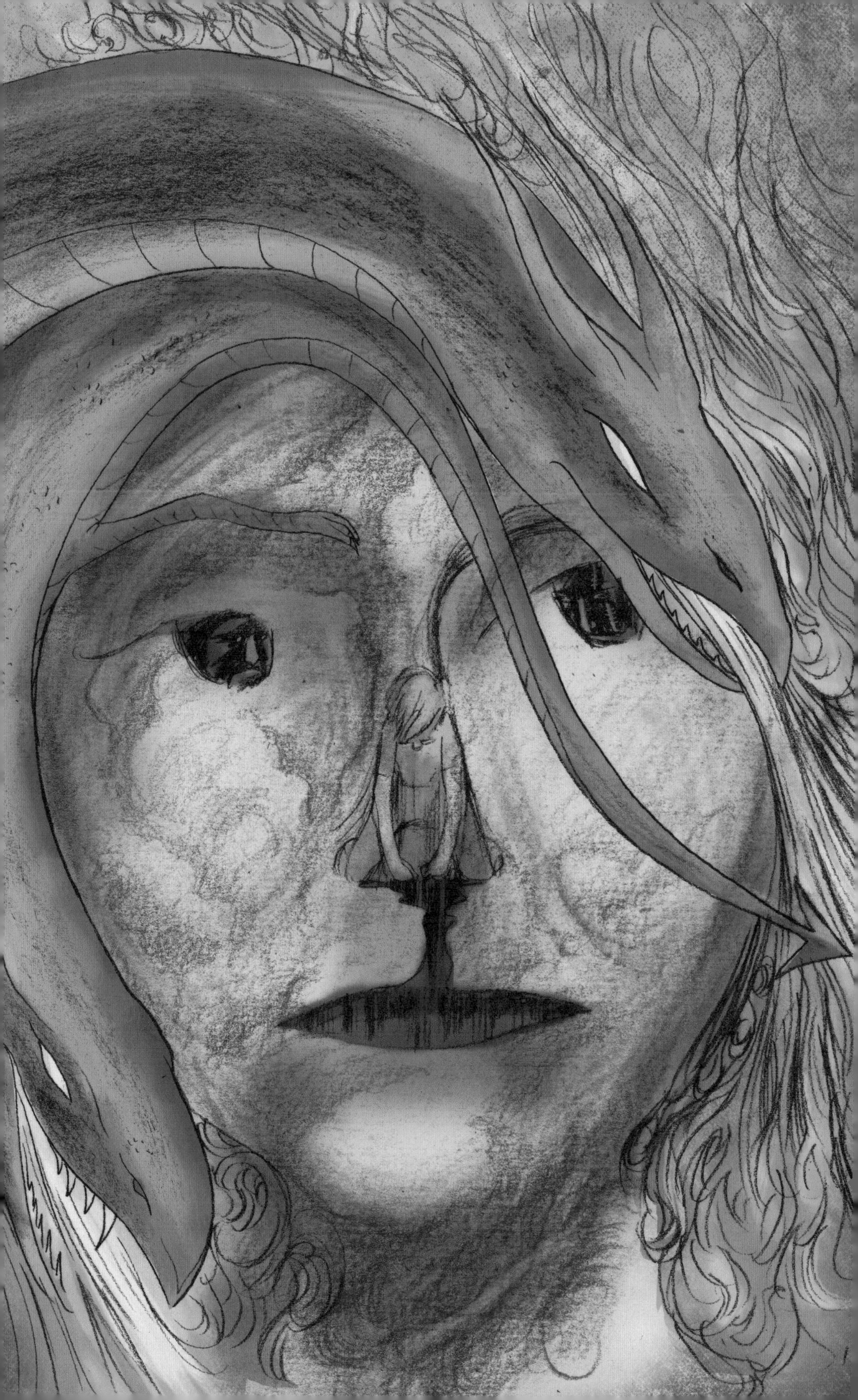

3

WHEN FILING REPORT ALL ESSENTIAL DETAILS MUST FALL WITHIN THIS SOLID "LIVE AREA" BOX. THIS IS THE BORDER FOR A STANDARD, NON-BLEED FIELD REPORT

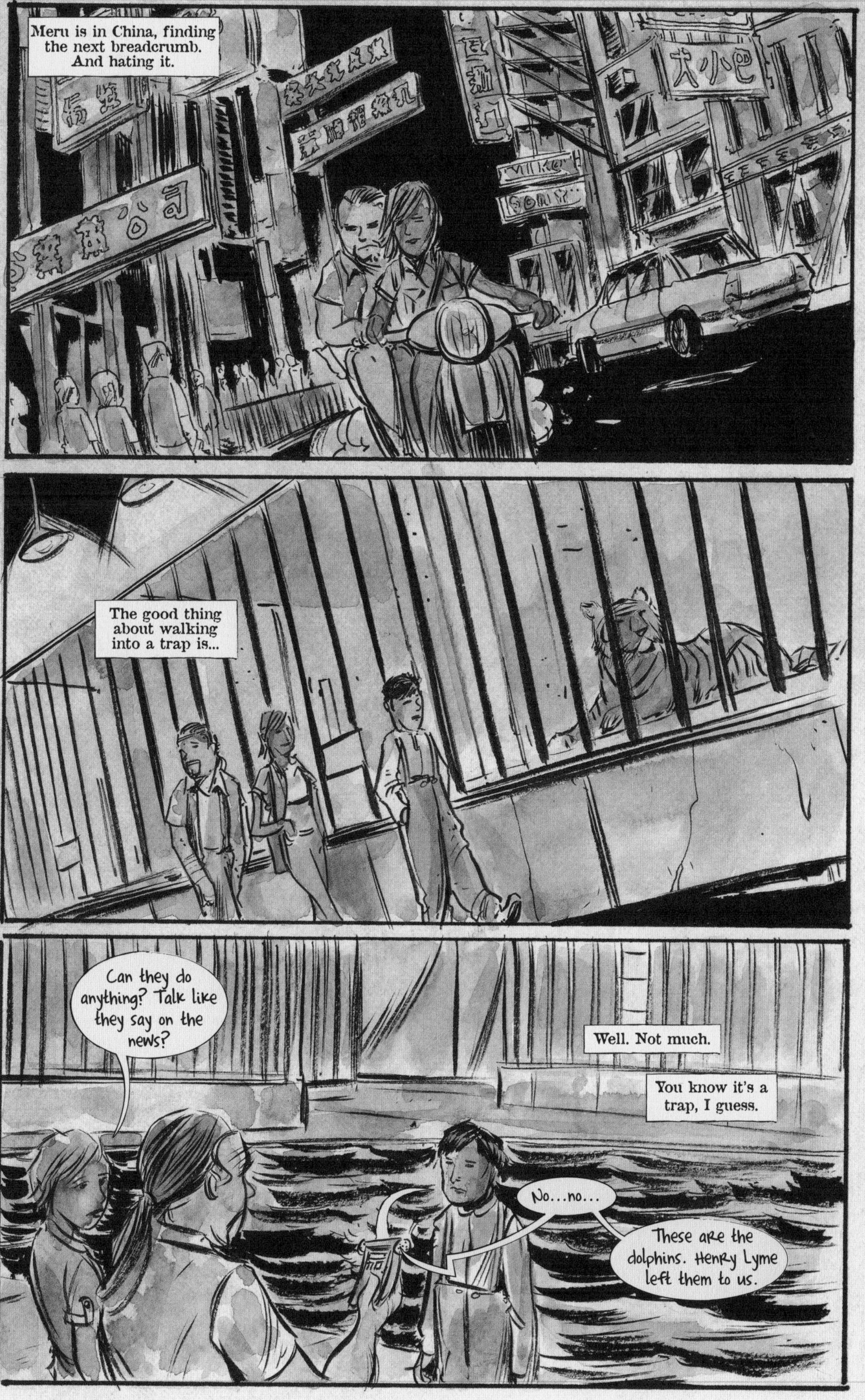

Meru is in China, finding the next breadcrumb. And hating it.
SONY
The good thing about walking into a trap is...
Can they do anything? Talk like they say on the news?
Well. Not much.
You know it's a trap, I guess.
No...no...
These are the dolphins. Henry Lyme left them to us.

MIND MGMT FIELD GUIDE. 3.1. Agents should be paired with translator agents in the field at all times. If your translator becomes injured or killed refer to 3.3 guideline.

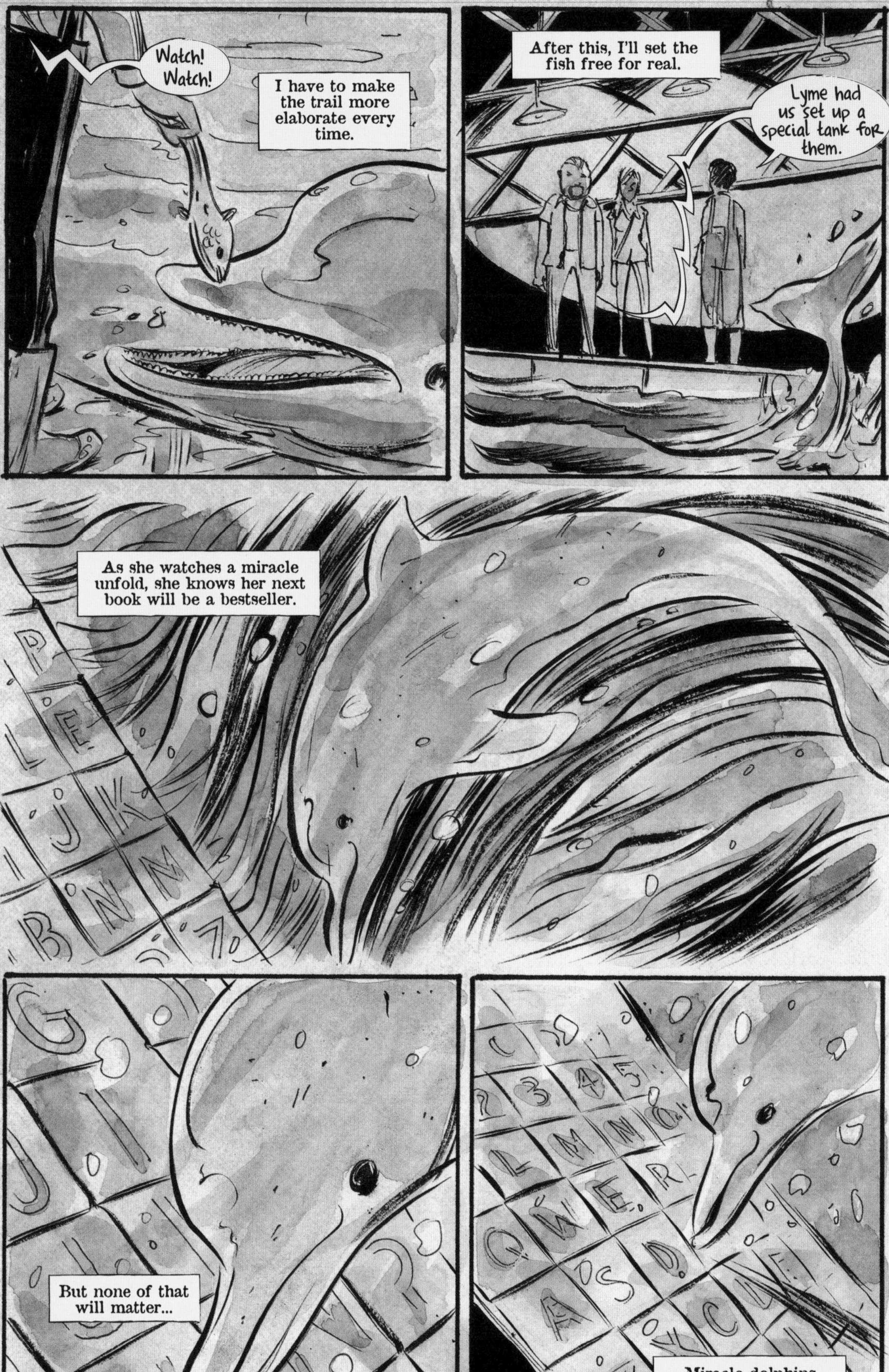
Watch! Watch!
I have to make the trail more elaborate every time.
After this, I'll set the fish free for real.
Lyme had us set up a special tank for them.
As she watches a miracle unfold, she knows her next book will be a bestseller.
But none of that will matter...
Miracle dolphins won't matter. It all hinges on finding "Henry Lyme."

MIND MGMT FIELD GUIDE. 3.2. There are two stages to encounters with animal agents. One: Scan the agent for explosives. Two: Scan the surrounding area for a control agent.

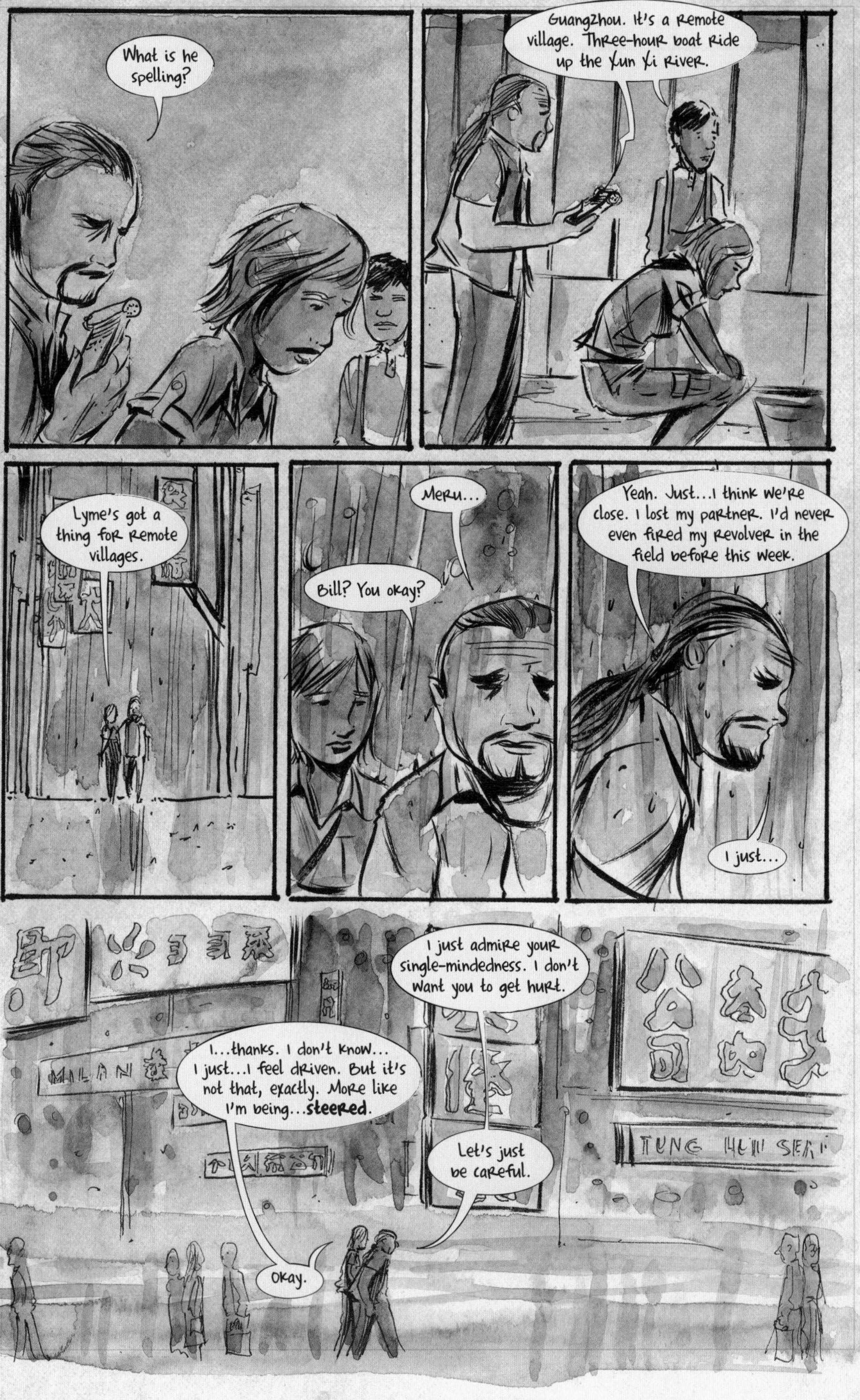
What is he spelling?
Guangzhou. It's a remote village. Three-hour boat ride up the Xun Xi River.
Lyme's got a thing for remote villages.
Meru...
Bill? You okay?
Yeah. Just...I think we're close. I lost my partner. I'd never even fired my revolver in the field before this week.
I just...
I just admire your single-mindedness. I don't want you to get hurt.
I...thanks. I don't know... I just...I feel driven. But it's not that, exactly. More like I'm being...**steered**.
Let's just be careful.
Okay.

MIND MGMT FIELD GUIDE 3.3: In the event of a translator agent injury or death, rely on your general brain-vapor visualization to determine the intent of the speaker.

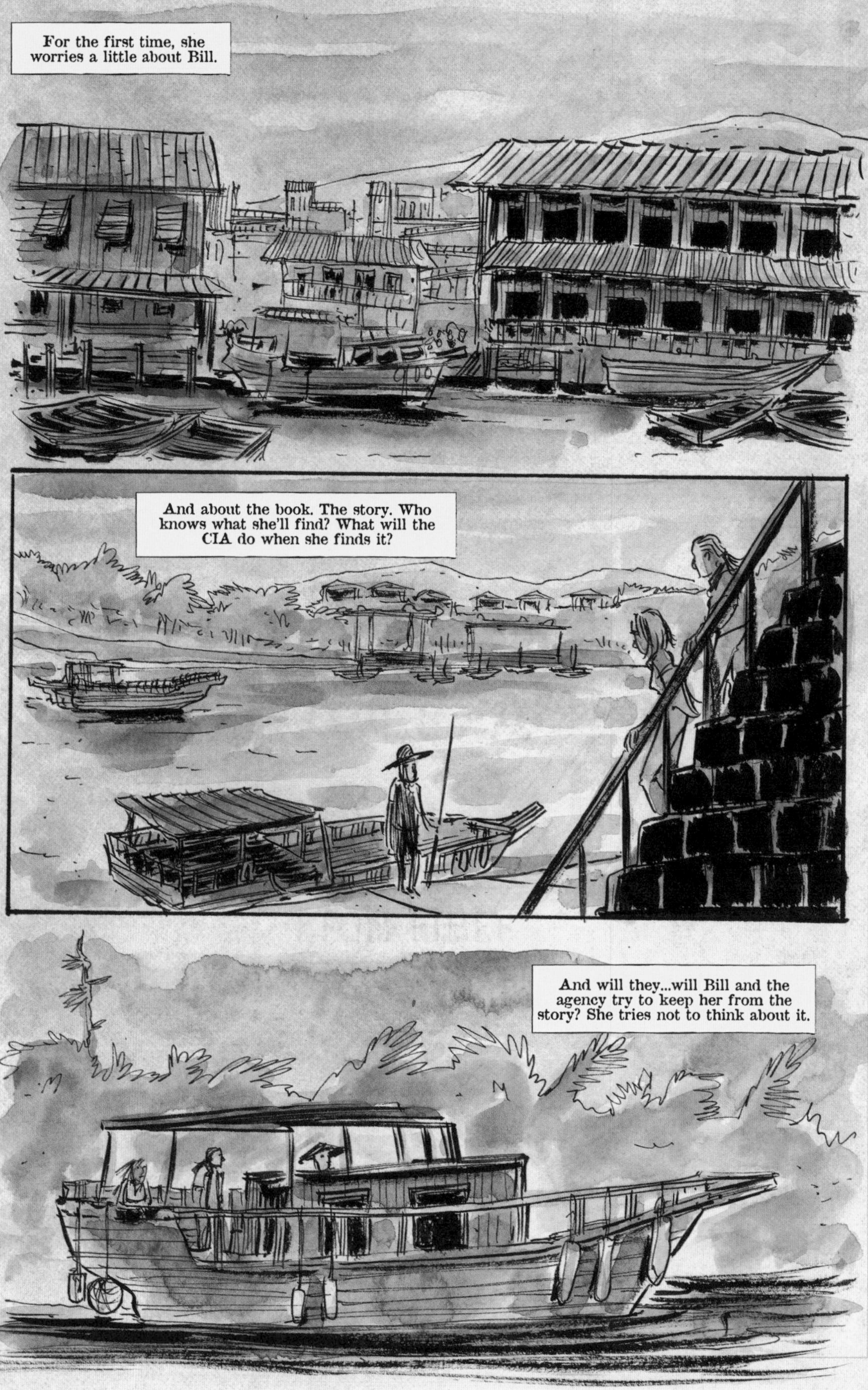
For the first time, she worries a little about Bill.
And about the book. The story. Who knows what she'll find? What will the CIA do when she finds it?
And will they...will Bill and the agency try to keep her from the story? She tries not to think about it.

MIND MGMT FIELD GUIDE. 3.4. If you find that you are short of funds in the field, remember that any paper can be mind augmented to perform in the place of real money.

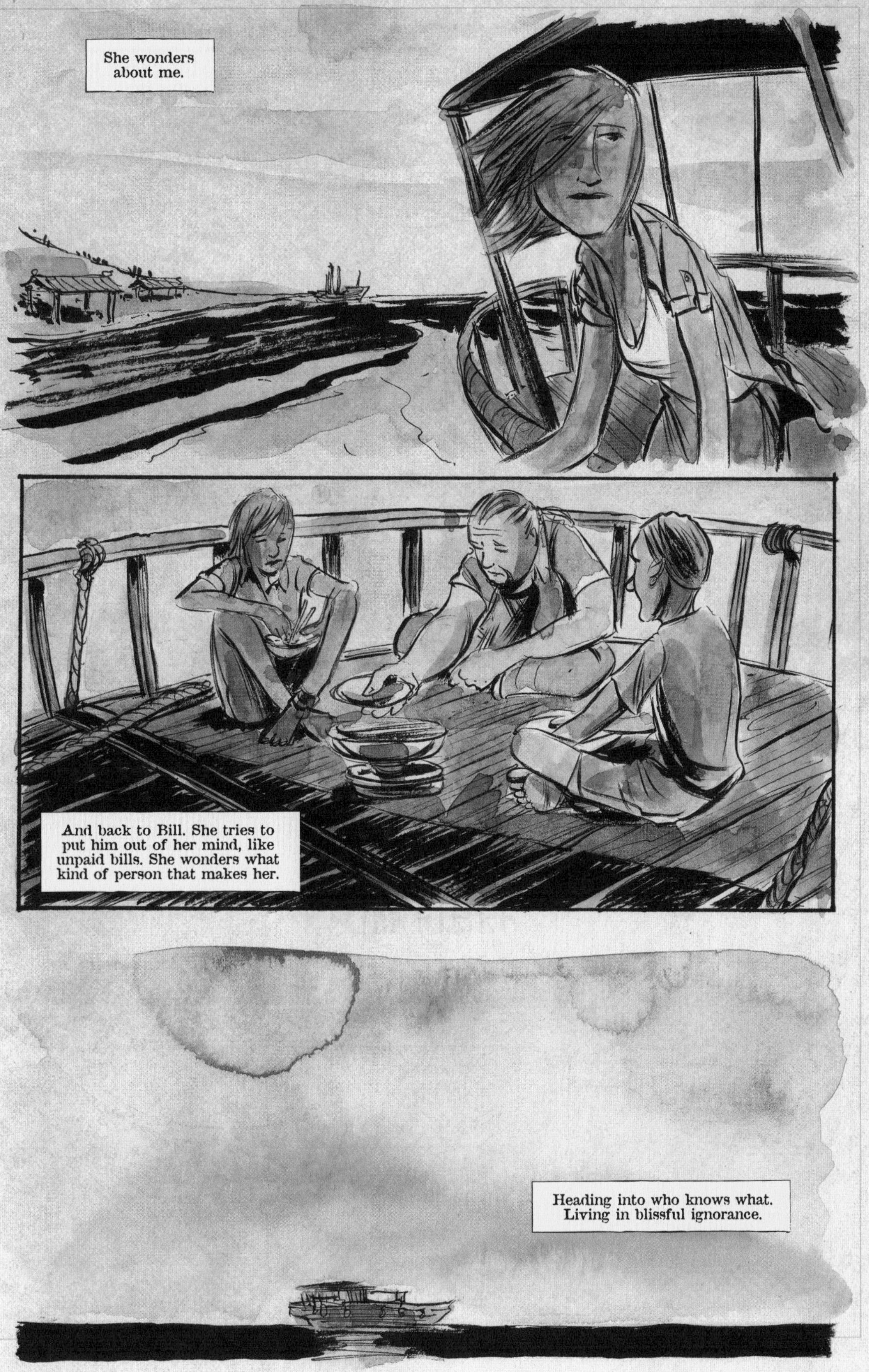
She wonders about me.
And back to Bill. She tries to put him out of her mind, like unpaid bills. She wonders what kind of person that makes her.
Heading into who knows what. Living in blissful ignorance.

MIND MGMT FIELD GUIDE 3.6: Open spaces and sparsely populated areas should be avoided, as maintenance of Activity Camouflage is much harder to maintain.

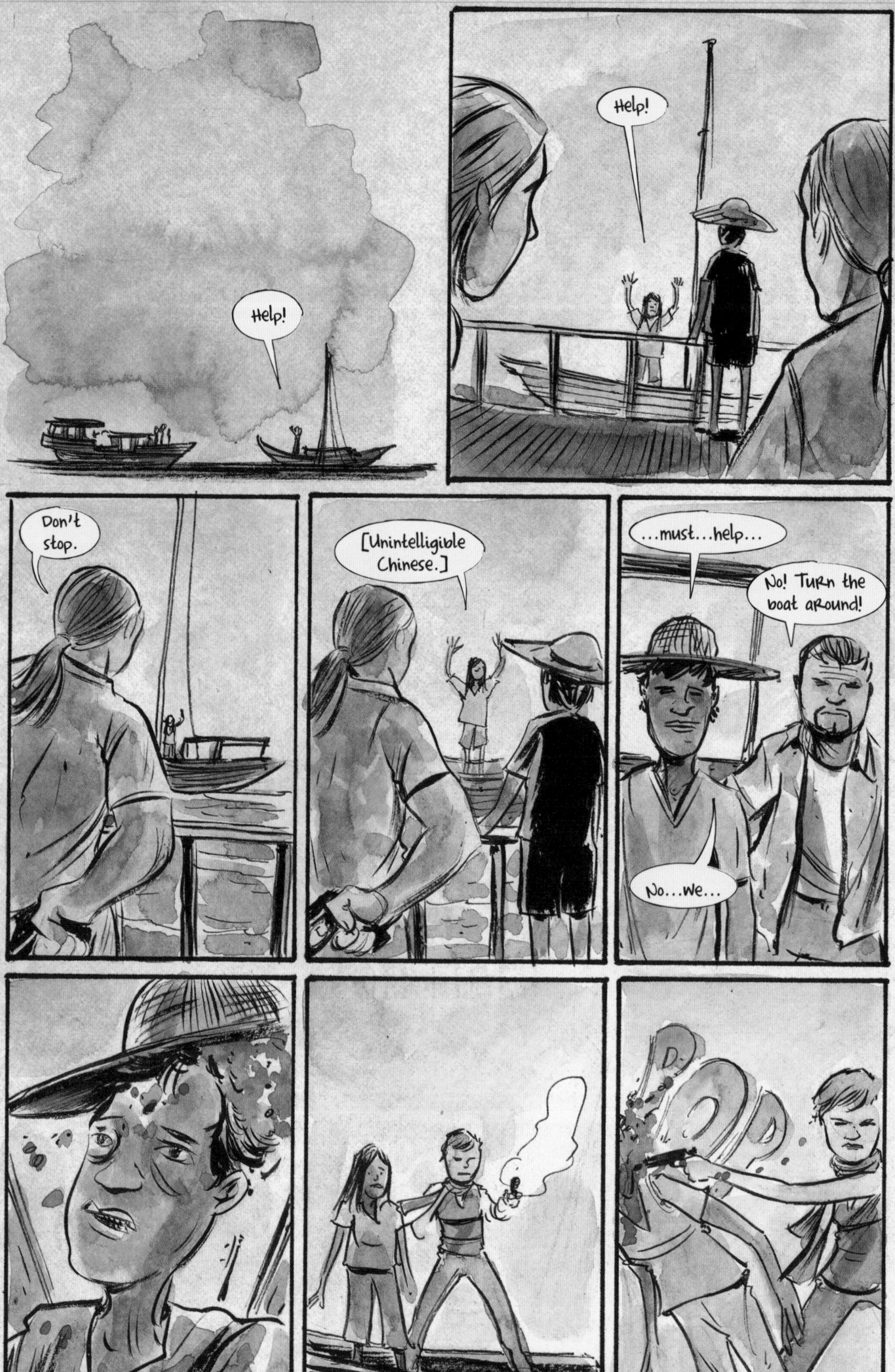
Help!
Help!
Don't stop.
[Unintelligible Chinese.]
...must...help...
No! Turn the boat around!
No...we...

MIND MGMT FIELD GUIDE. 3.6. Using your Anticipation Lobe exercises on a regular basis will ensure that you are never surprised.

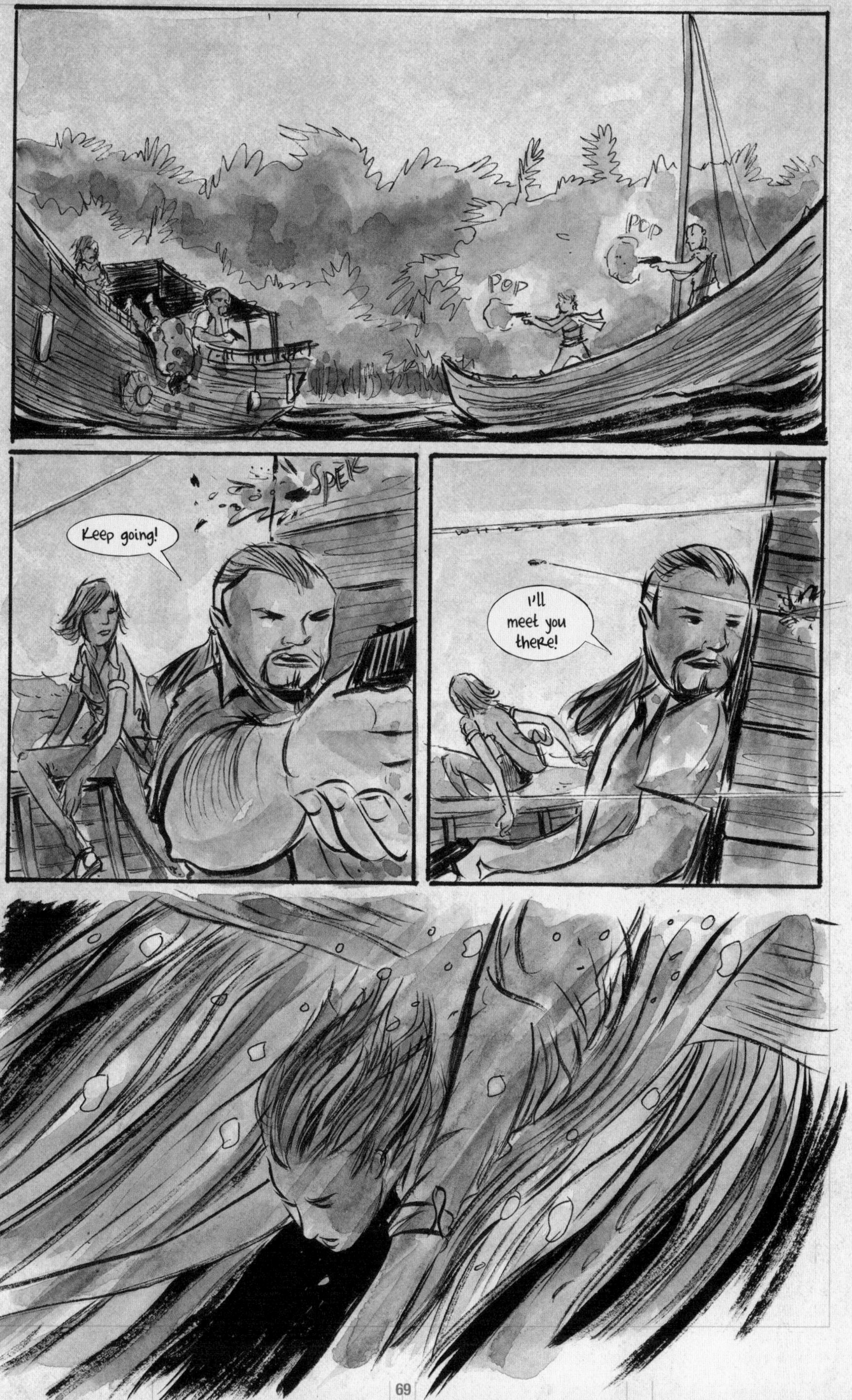
POP
POP
SPEK
Keep going!
I'll meet you there!

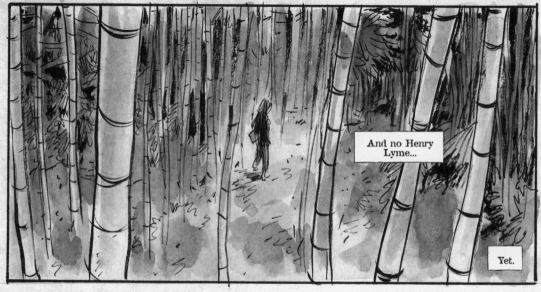

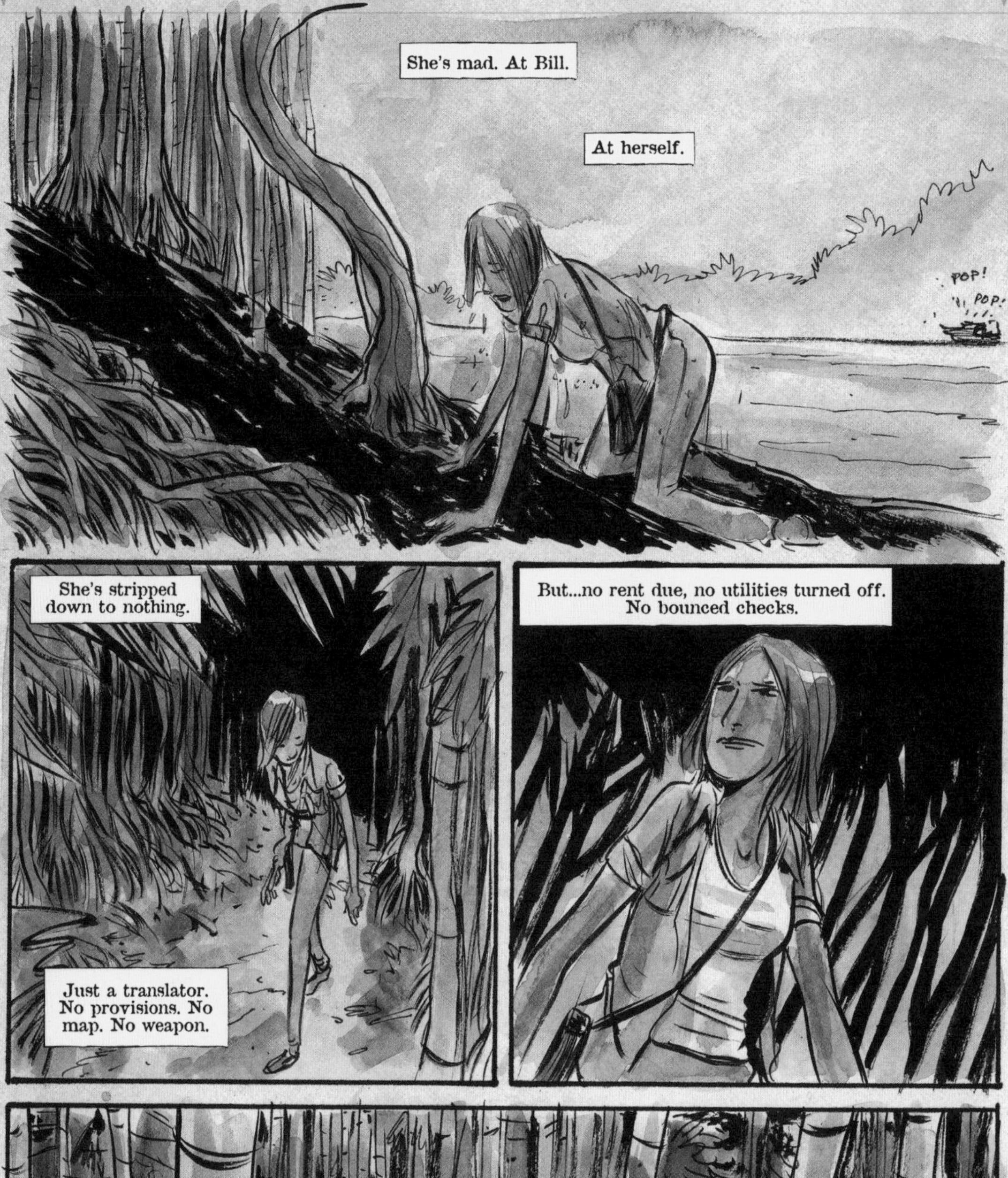
She's mad. At Bill.
At herself.
POP!
POP!
She's stripped down to nothing.
Just a translator. No provisions. No map. No weapon.
But...no rent due, no utilities turned off. No bounced checks.
And no Henry Lyme...
Yet.

MIND MGMT FIELD GUIDE. 3.8. When lost, use of standard navigational techniques as well as dipping into small surrounding animal psyches can provide a nearly comprehensive Mind Map.

WHEN FILING REPORT ALL ESSENTIAL DETAILS MUST FALL WITHIN THIS SOLID "LIVE AREA" BOX. THIS IS THE BORDER FOR A STANDARD, NON-BLEED FIELD REPORT

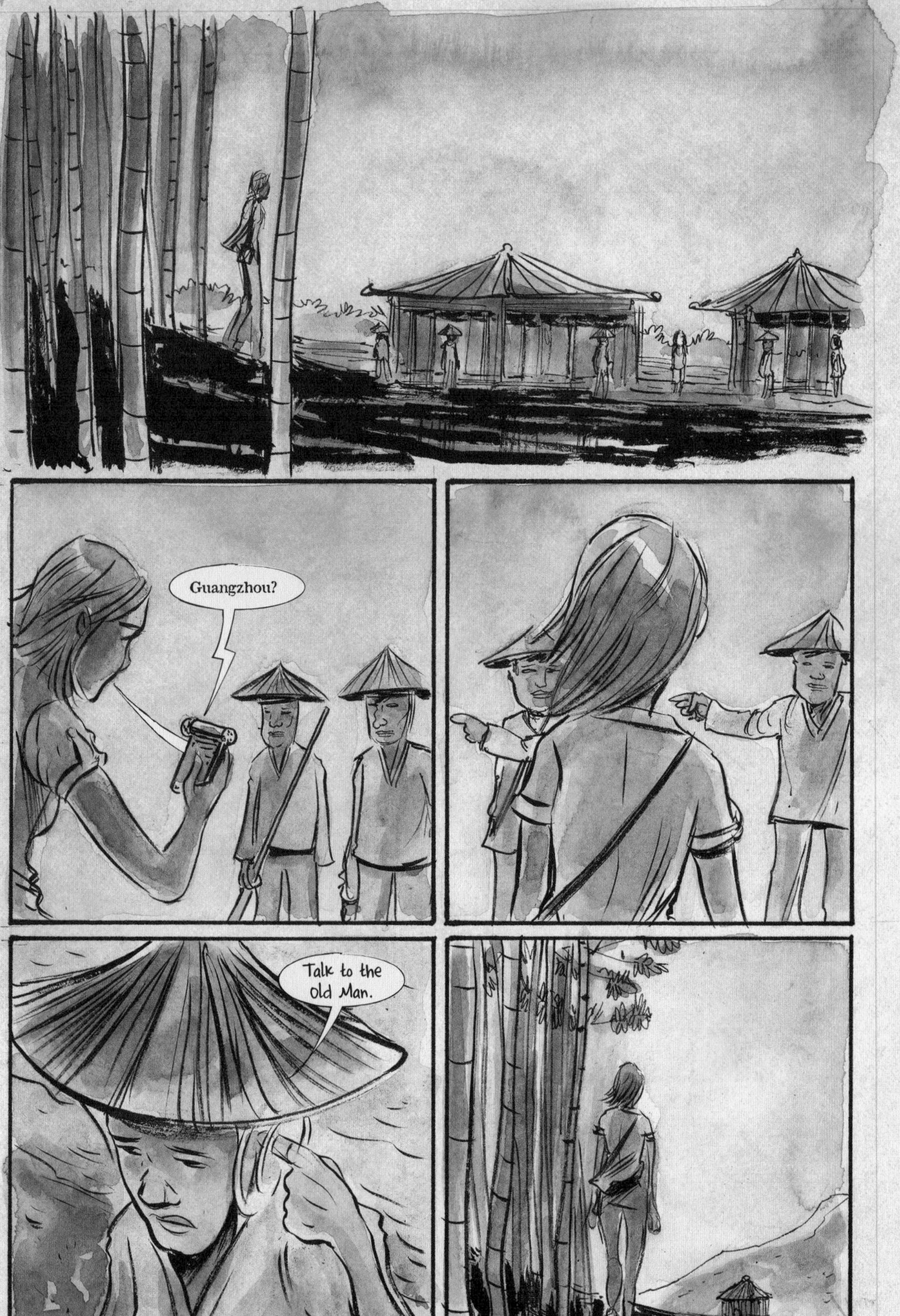
Guangzhou?
Talk to the old Man.

MIND MGMT FIELD GUIDE. 3.10. When questioning subjects, always compare available evidence with the live "brain patter" of the subject and the subjects in close proximity.

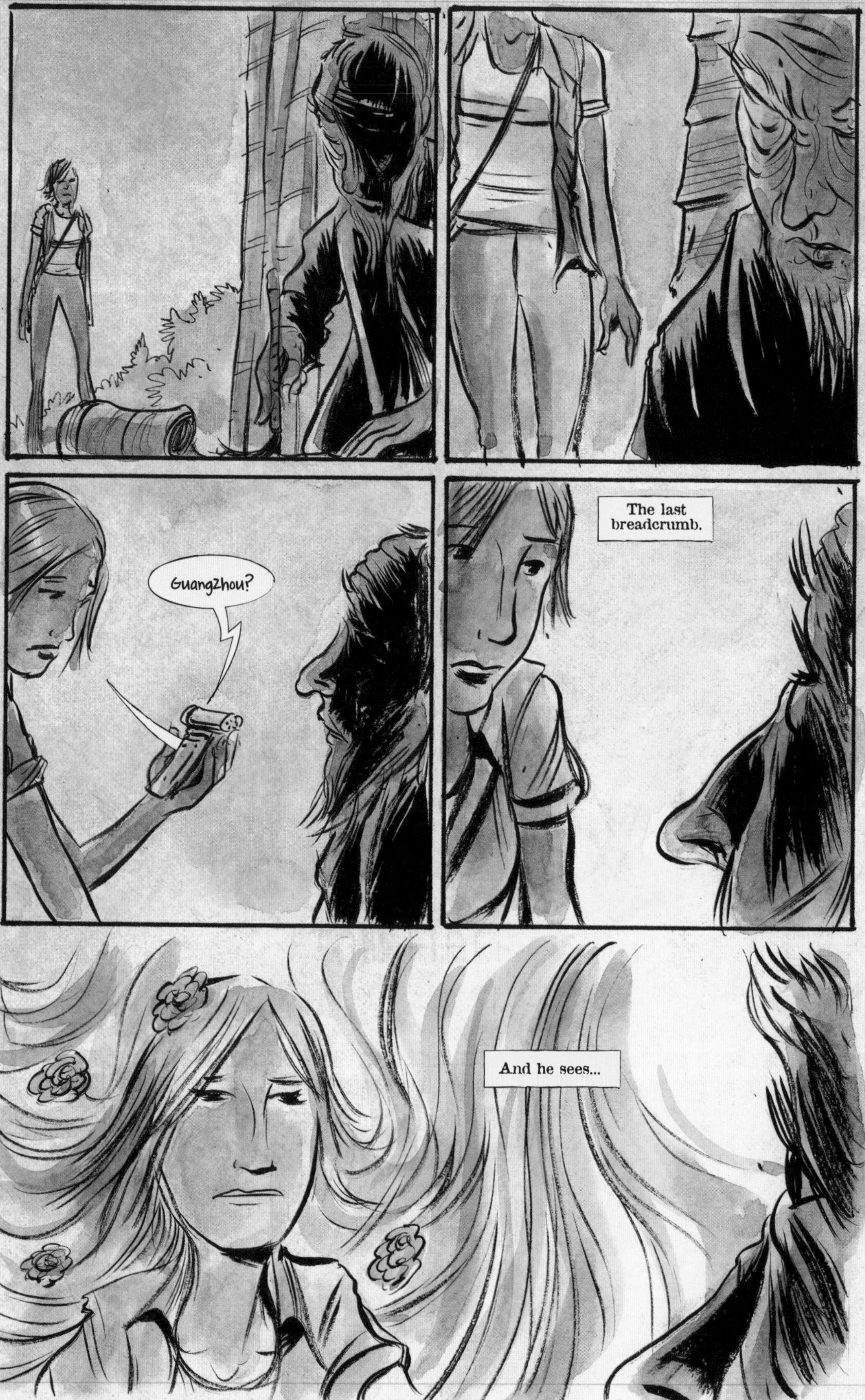
Guangzhou?
The last breadcrumb.
And he sees...

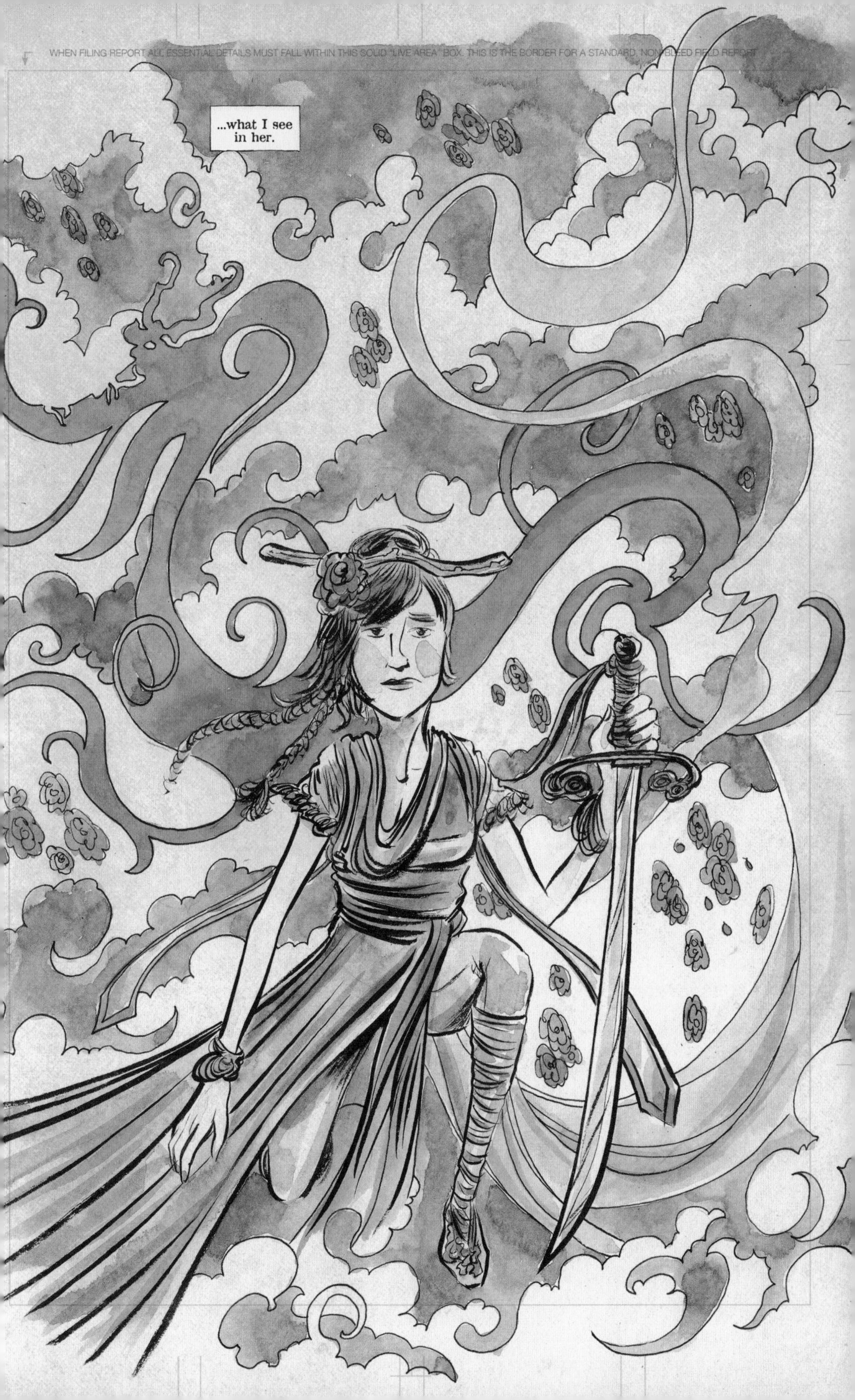
WHEN FILING REPORT ALL ESSENTIAL DETAILS MUST FALL WITHIN THIS SOLID "LIVE AREA" BOX. THIS IS THE BORDER FOR A STANDARD, NON-BLEED FIELD REPORT
...what I see in her.

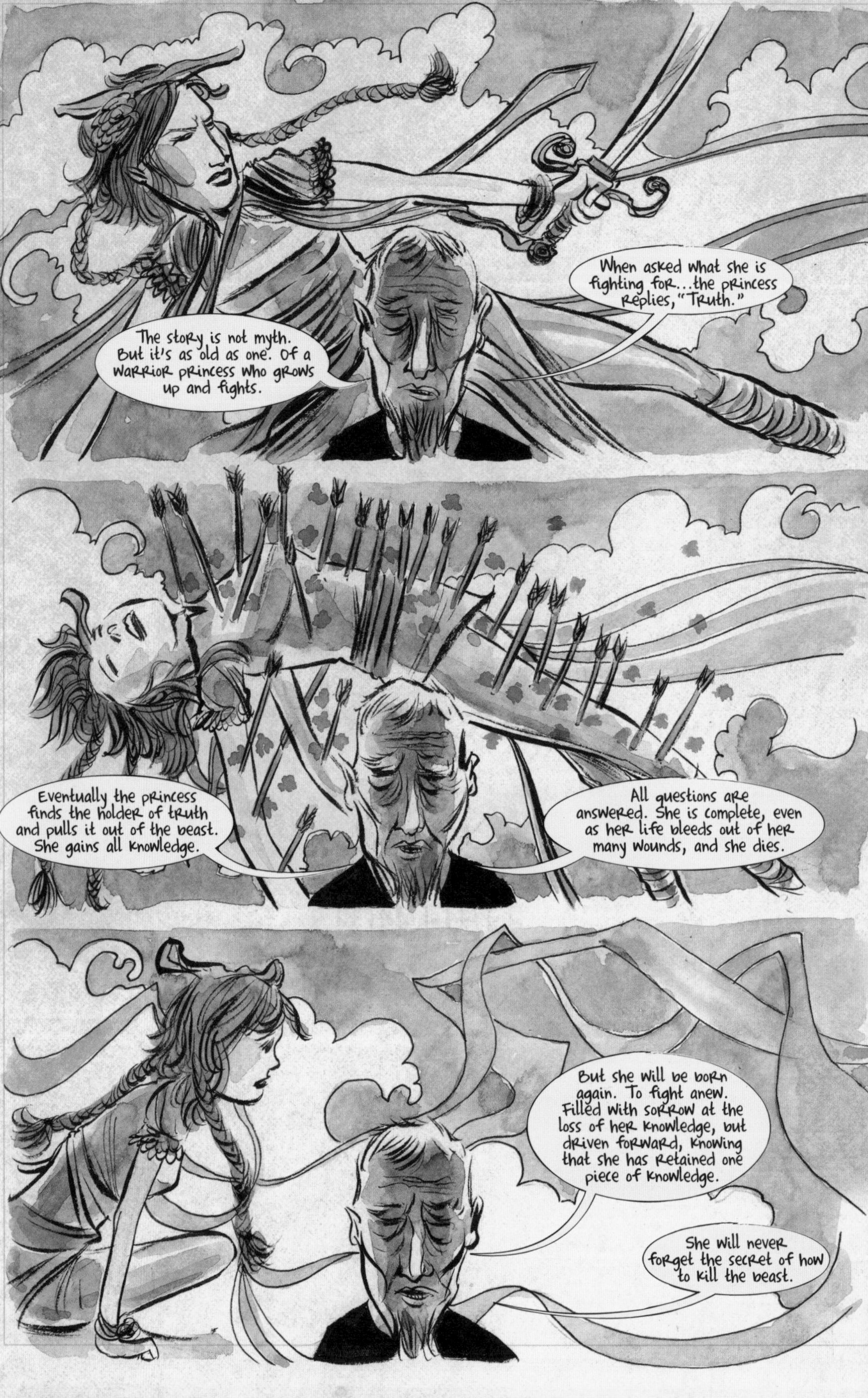
The story is not myth. But it's as old as one. Of a warrior princess who grows up and fights.
When asked what she is fighting for...the princess replies, "Truth."
Eventually the princess finds the holder of truth and pulls it out of the beast. She gains all knowledge.
All questions are answered. She is complete, even as her life bleeds out of her many wounds, and she dies.
But she will be born again. To fight anew. Filled with sorrow at the loss of her knowledge, but driven forward, knowing that she has retained one piece of knowledge.
She will never forget the secret of how to kill the beast.

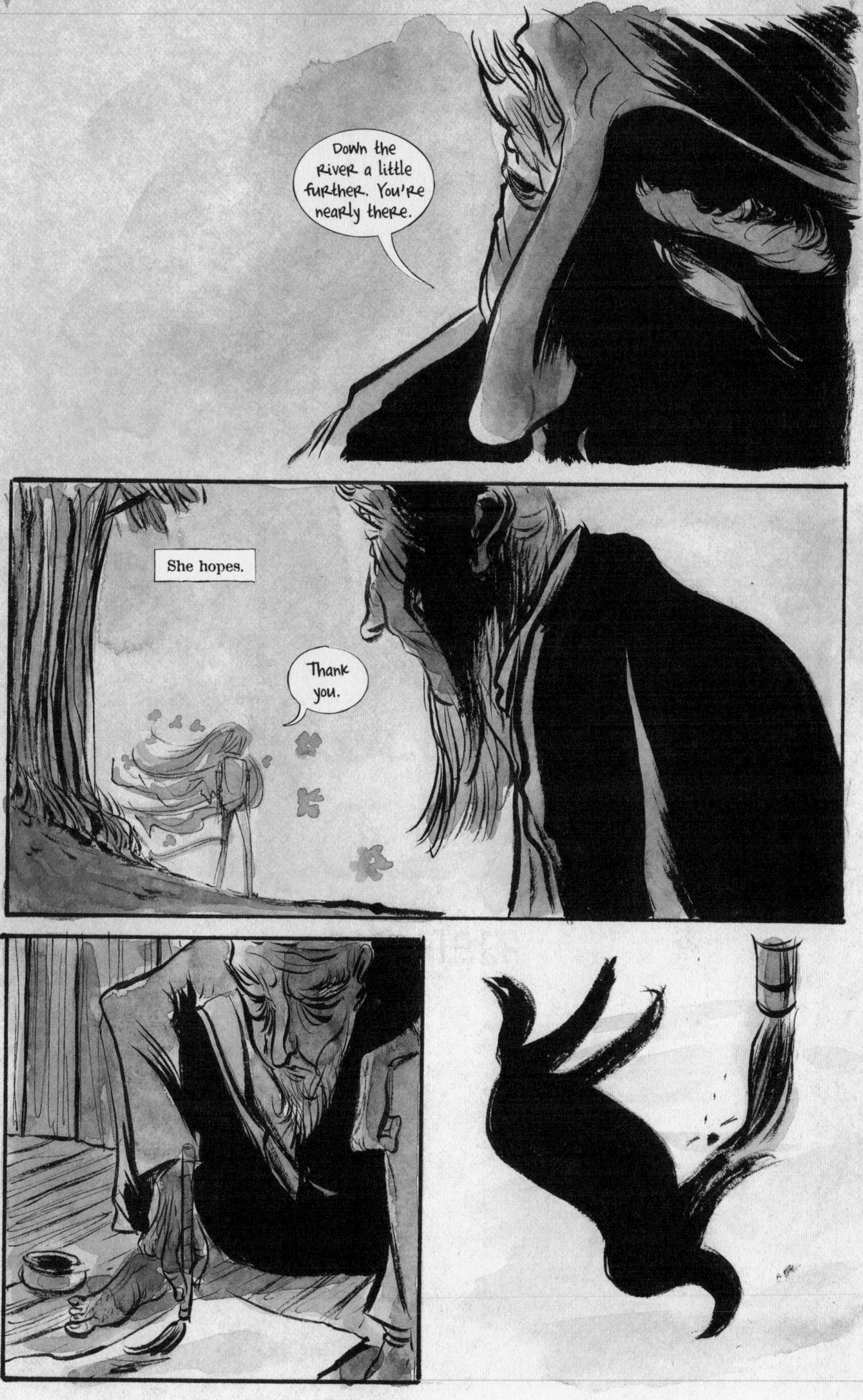
Down the river a little further. You're nearly there.
She hopes.
Thank you.

MIND MGMT FIELD GUIDE. 3.13. After tri-scanning a subject with visual, psychic, and residual questioning, always test the subject afterwards for side effects that could lead to psychosis.

WHEN FILING REPORT ALL ESSENTIAL DETAILS MUST FALL WITHIN THIS SOLID "LIVE AREA" BOX. THIS IS THE BORDER FOR A STANDARD, NON-BLEED FIELD REPORT

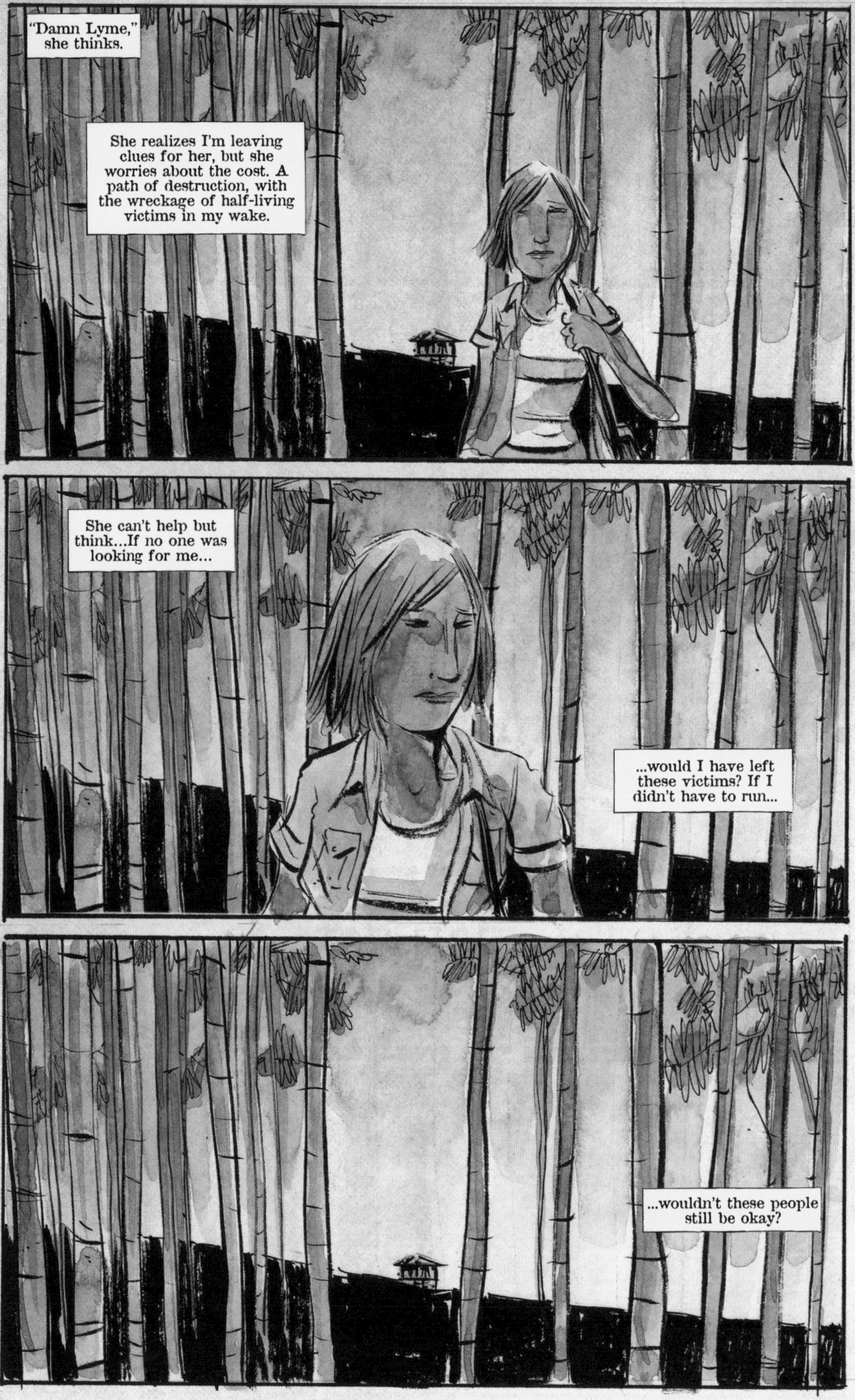
"Damn Lyme," she thinks.
She realizes I'm leaving clues for her, but she worries about the cost. A path of destruction, with the wreckage of half-living victims in my wake.
She can't help but think...If no one was looking for me...
...would I have left these victims? If I didn't have to run...
...wouldn't these people still be okay?

MIND MGMT FIELD GUIDE. 3.14. Remember that when you are "alone with your thoughts"--you are NEVER alone with your thoughts.

MIND MGMT FIELD GUIDE. 3.15. Always perform the Six-Second Sanitizer on the subject to clear your whereabouts from said subject, in case you are being followed.

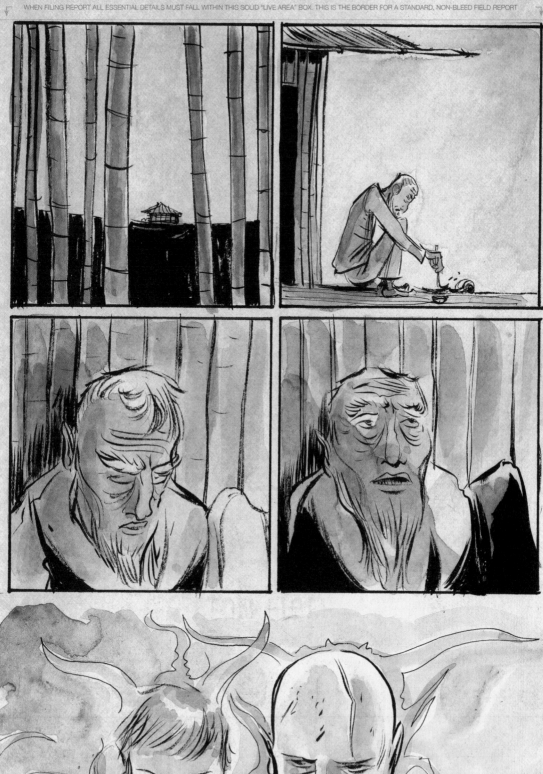

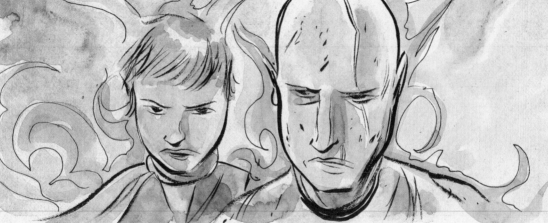

MIND MGMT FIELD GUIDE. 3.16. A common technique in anticipation of conflict is to dampen your body's dopamine levels.

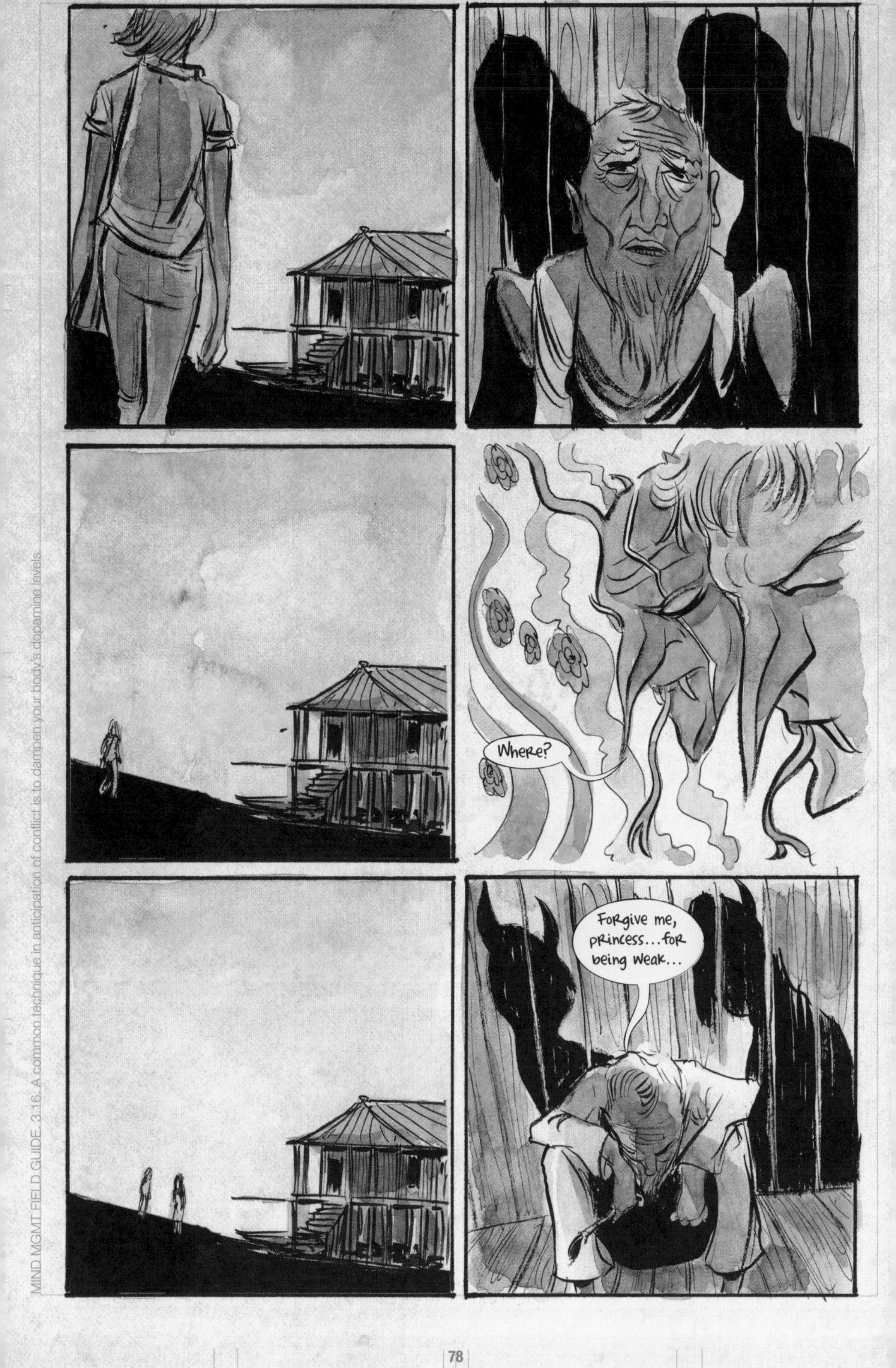
Where?
Forgive me, princess...for being weak...

WHEN FILING REPORT ALL ESSENTIAL DETAILS MUST FALL WITHIN THIS SOLID "LIVE AREA" BOX. THIS IS THE BORDER FOR A STANDARD, NON-BLEED FIELD REPORT

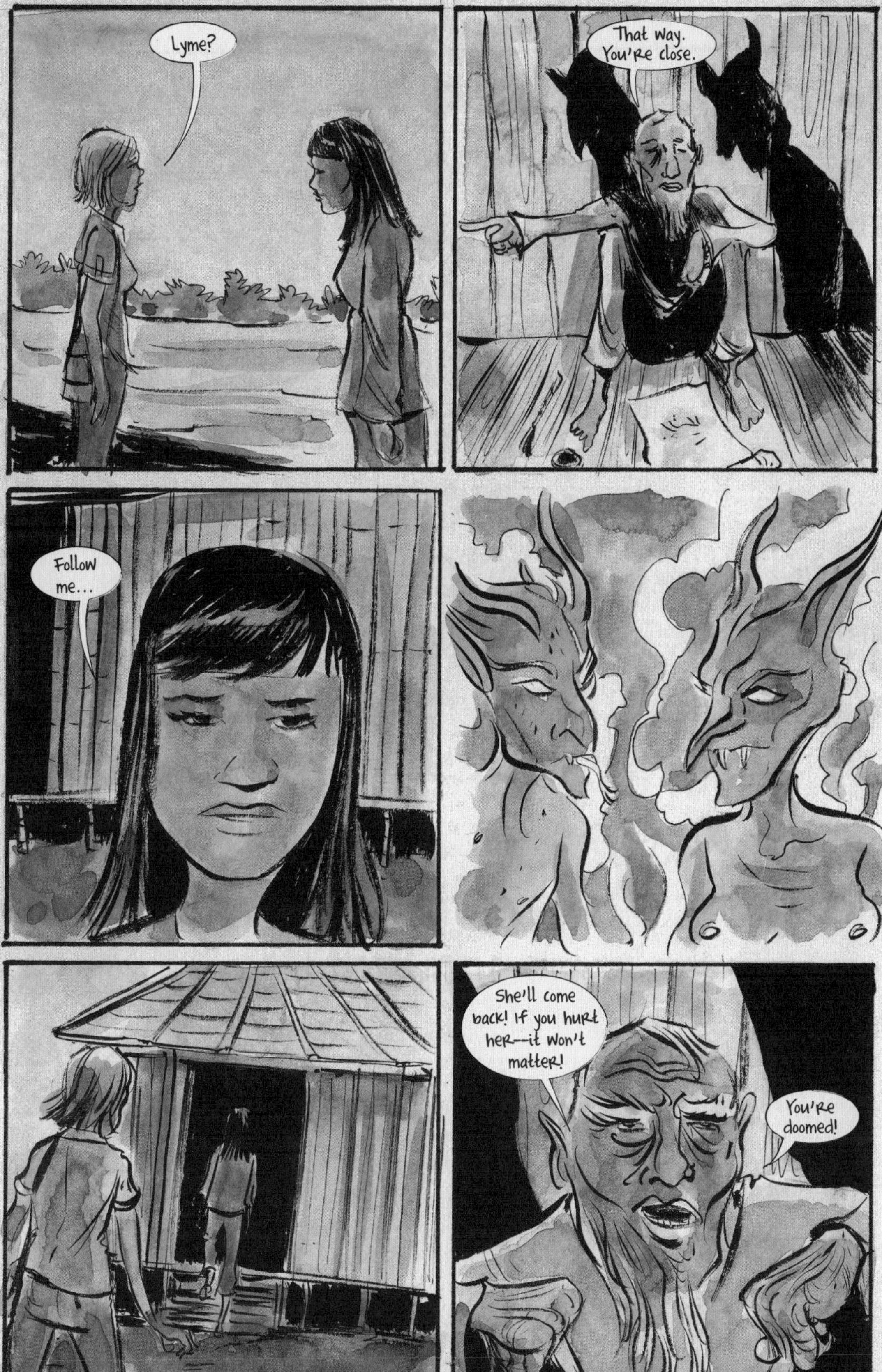

Lyme?
That way. You're close.
Follow me...
She'll come back! If you hurt her--it won't matter!
You're doomed!

MIND MGMT FIELD GUIDE, 3.17: However, a common mistake when dampening adrenaline levels is to dampen it in excess, which will slow your reaction time and fighting ability.

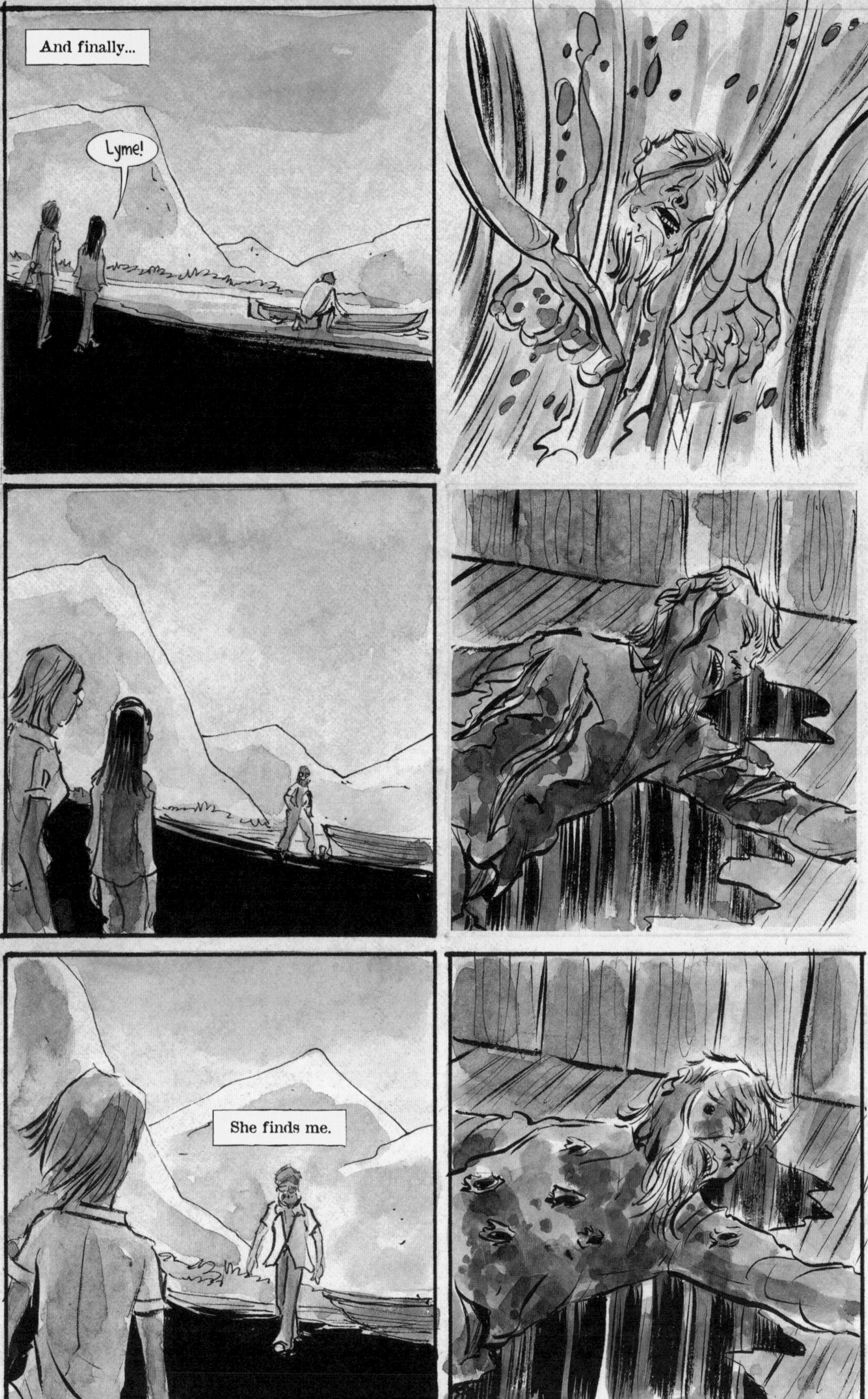
And finally...
Lyme!
She finds me.

MIND MGMT FIELD GUIDE. 3.18. It is ideal to use an Expiration Tag on subjects, so you will know immediately if said subject has been terminated.

MIND MGMT FIELD GUIDE 3.19: When acquiring a target for the first time, always do so in as populated and busy an area as possible to allow for a maximum of neurotransmitter static.

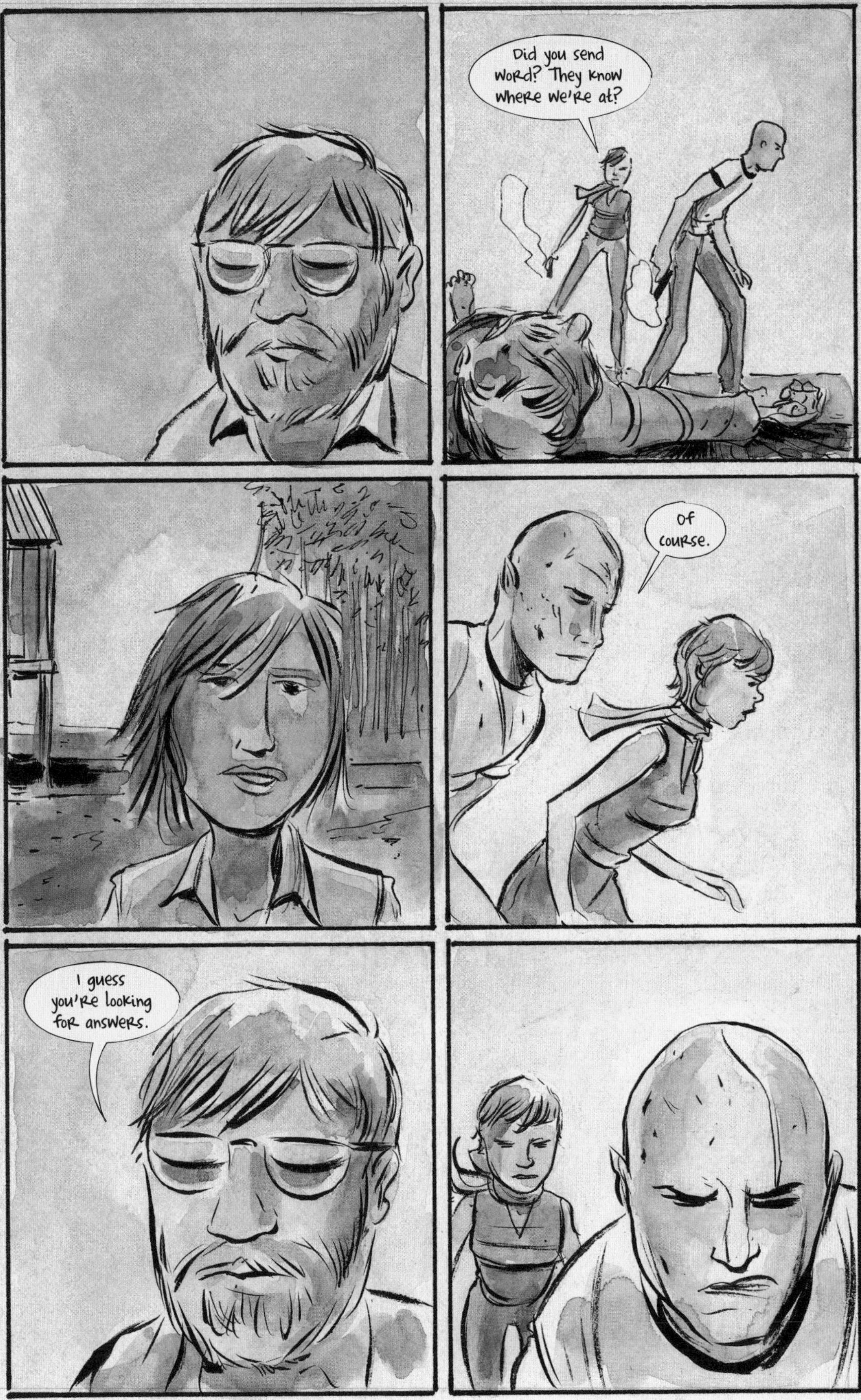
Did you send word? They know where we're at?
Of course.
I guess you're looking for answers.

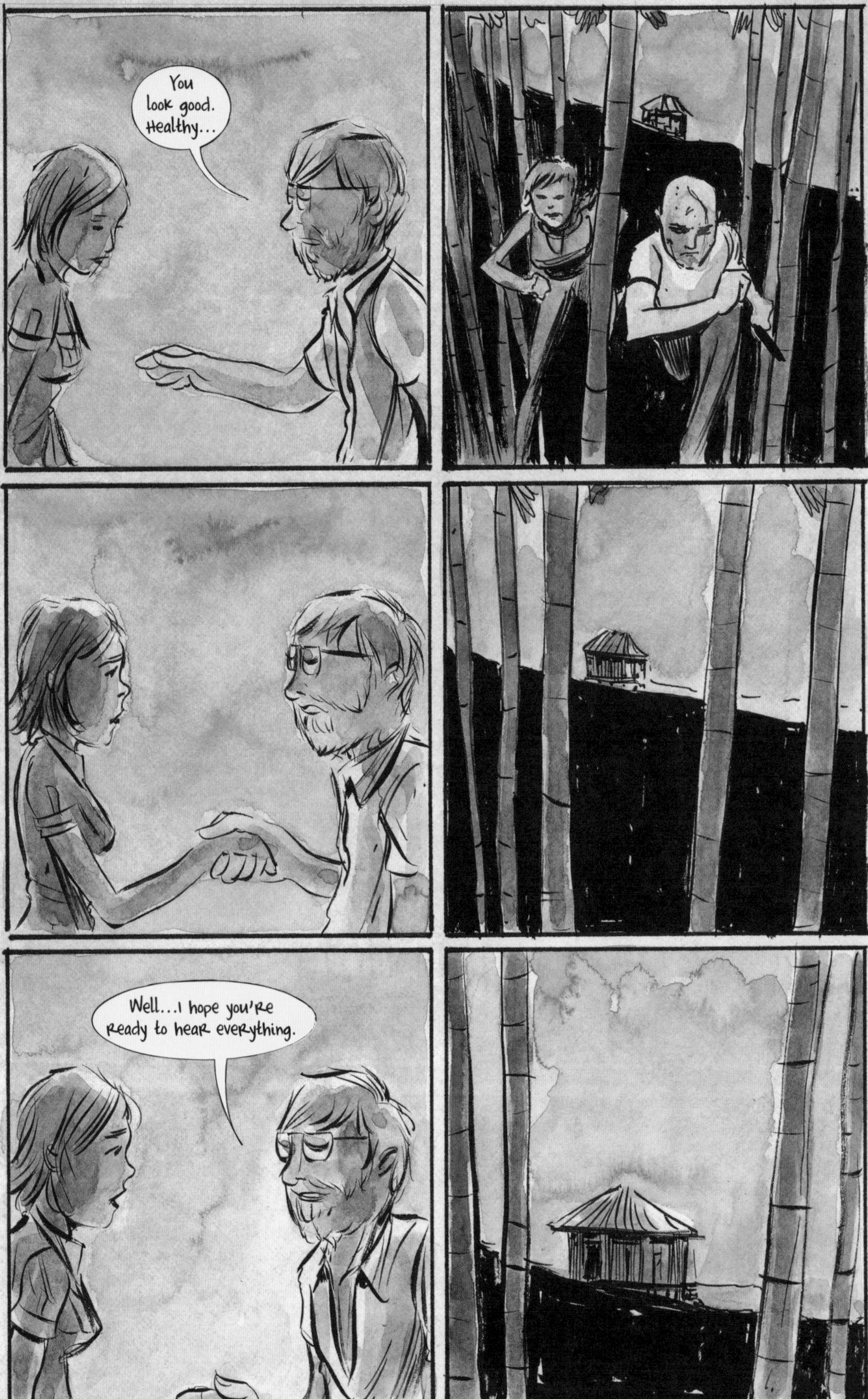
You look good. Healthy...
Well...I hope you're ready to hear everything.

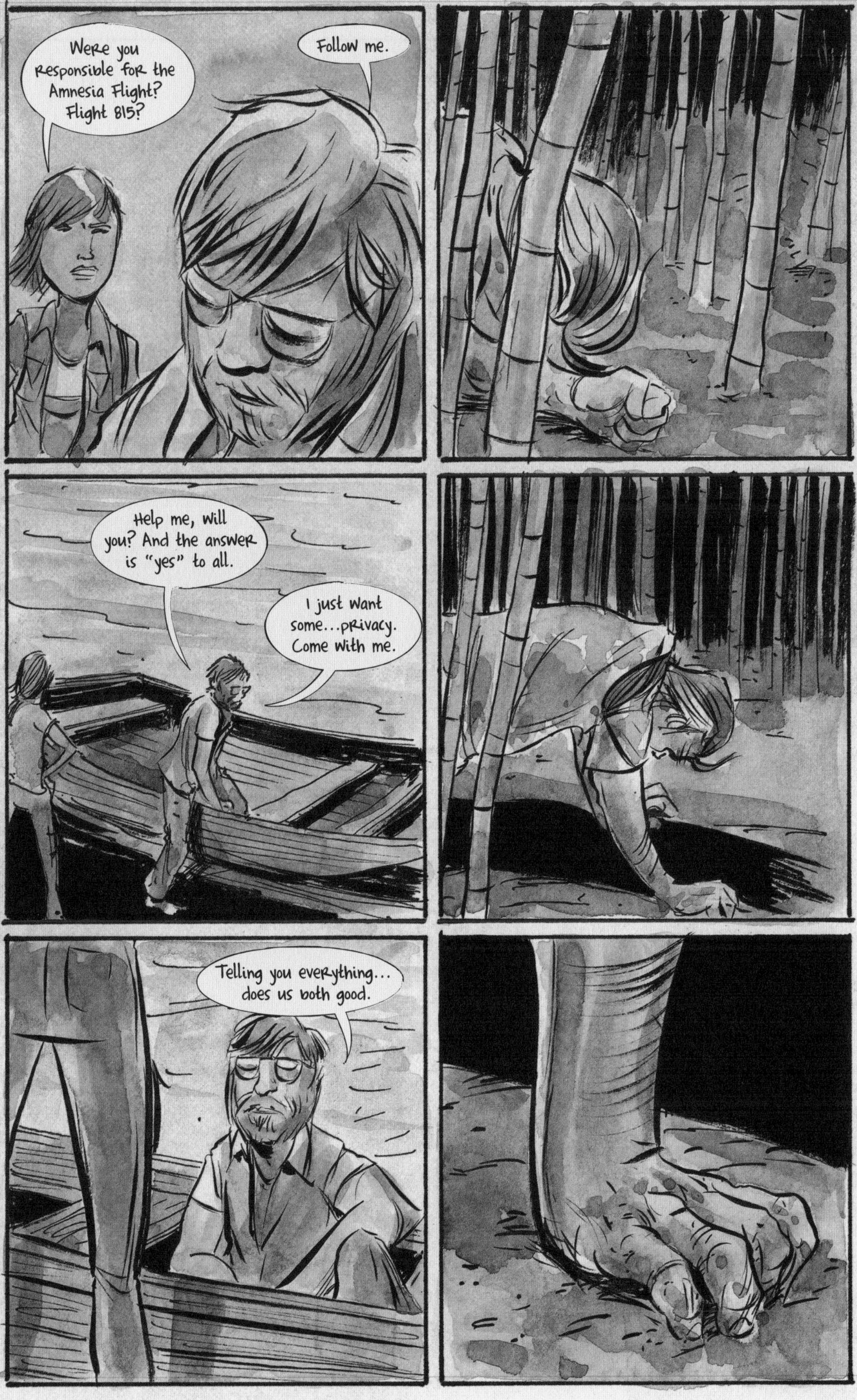
Were you responsible for the Amnesia Flight? Flight 815?
Follow me.
Help me, will you? And the answer is "yes" to all.
I just want some...privacy. Come with me.
Telling you everything... does us both good.

WHEN FILING REPORT ALL ESSENTIAL DETAILS MUST FALL WITHIN THIS SOLID "LIVE AREA" BOX. THIS IS THE BORDER FOR A STANDARD, NON-BLEED FIELD REPORT

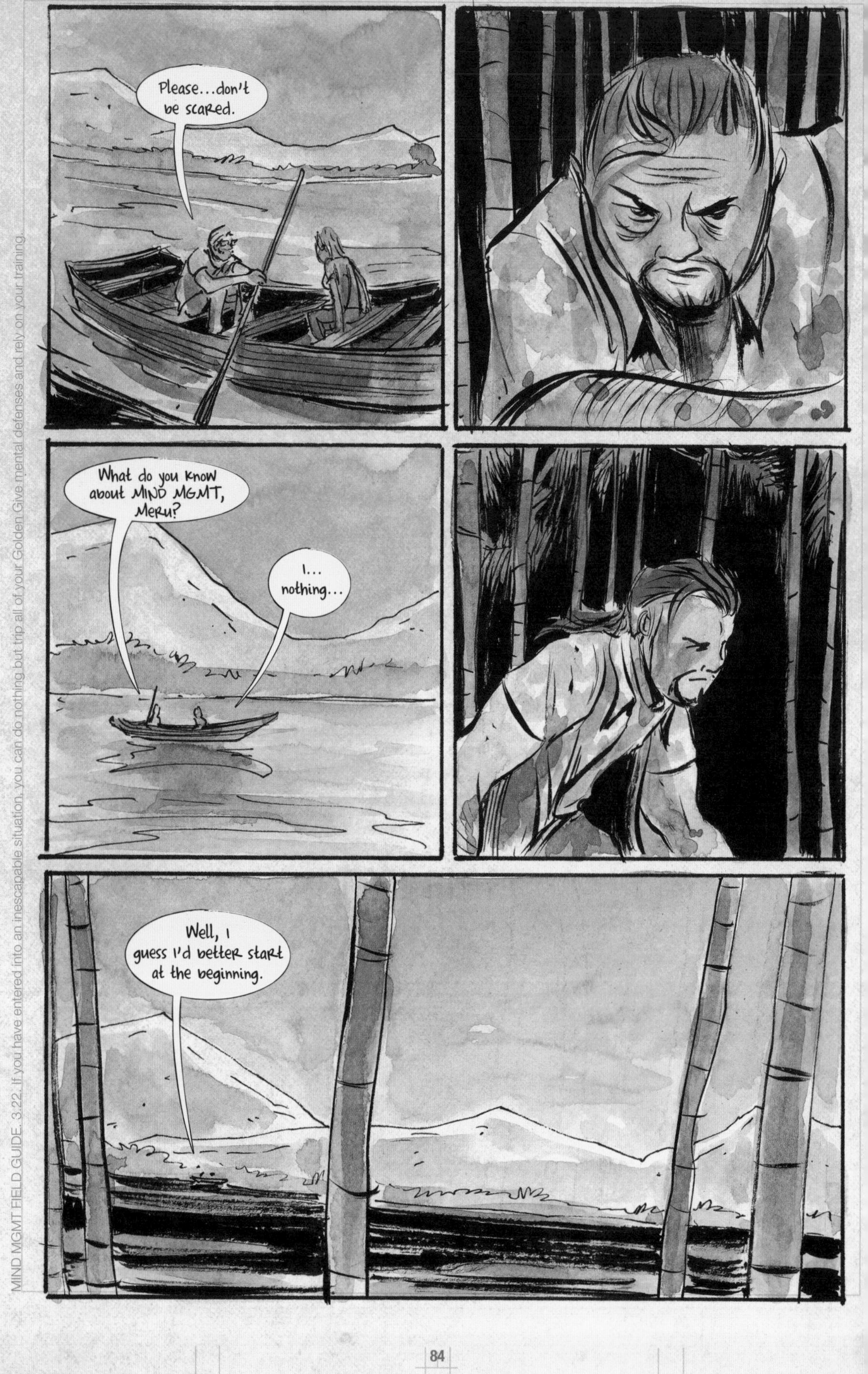
Please...don't be scared.
What do you know about MIND MGMT, Meru?
I... nothing...
Well, I guess I'd better start at the beginning.

MIND MGMT FIELD GUIDE. 3.22. If you have entered into an inescapable situation, you can do nothing but trip all of your Golden Give mental defenses and rely on your training.

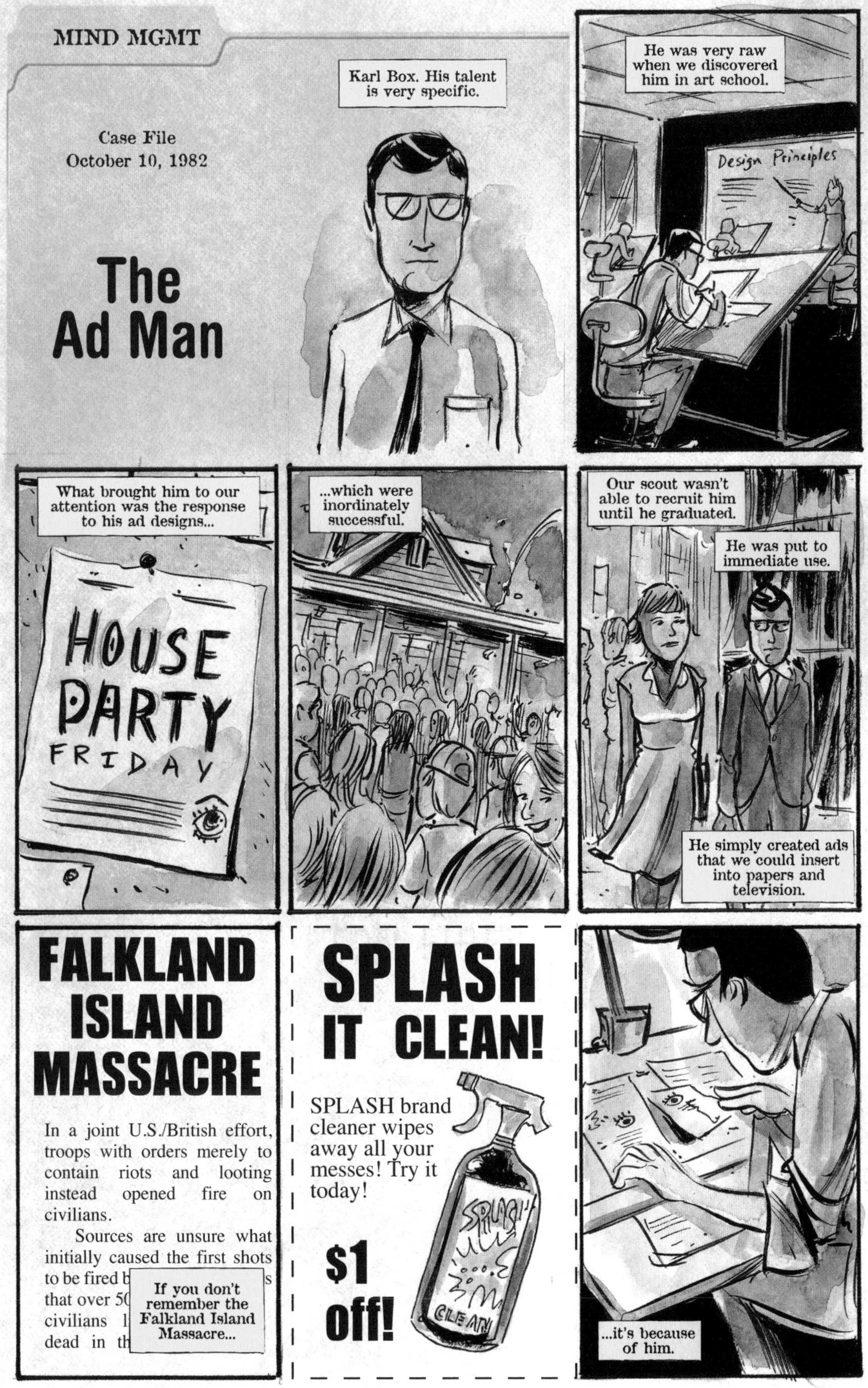

MIND MGMT
Case File
October 10, 1982
The Ad Man
Karl Box. His talent is very specific.
He was very raw when we discovered him in art school.
Design Principles
What brought him to our attention was the response to his ad designs...
HOUSE PARTY
FRIDAY
...which were inordinately successful.
Our scout wasn't able to recruit him until he graduated.
He was put to immediate use.
He simply created ads that we could insert into papers and television.
FALKLAND ISLAND MASSACRE
In a joint U.S./British effort, troops with orders merely to contain riots and looting instead opened fire on civilians.
Sources are unsure what initially caused the first shots to be fired b
that over 5
civilians l
dead in th
If you don't remember the Falkland Island Massacre...
SPLASH IT CLEAN!
SPLASH brand cleaner wipes away all your messes! Try it today!
$1 off!
SPLASH
CLEAN
...it's because of him.

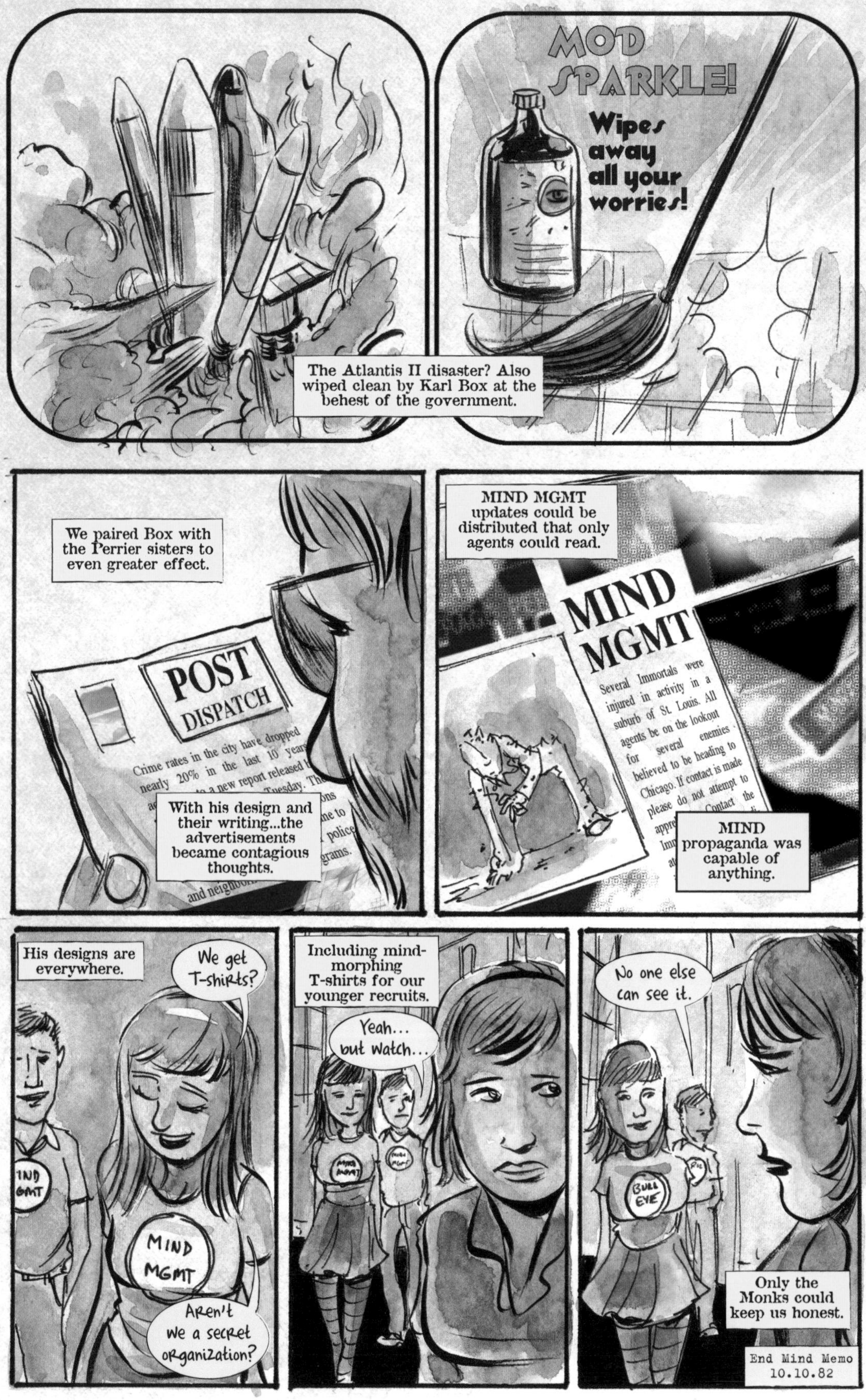
MOD SPARKLE!
Wipes away all your worries!
The Atlantis II disaster? Also wiped clean by Karl Box at the behest of the government.
We paired Box with the Perrier sisters to even greater effect.
POST DISPATCH
Crime rates in the city have dropped
With his design and their writing...the advertisements became contagious thoughts.
MIND MGMT updates could be distributed that only agents could read.
MIND MGMT
Several Immortals were injured in activity in a suburb of St. Louis. All agents be on the lookout for several enemies believed to be heading to Chicago. If contact is made please do not attempt to
MIND propaganda was capable of anything.
His designs are everywhere.
We get T-shirts?
MIND MGMT
Aren't we a secret organization?
Including mind-morphing T-shirts for our younger recruits.
Yeah... but watch...
No one else can see it.
BULL EYE
Only the Monks could keep us honest.
End Mind Memo
10.10.82

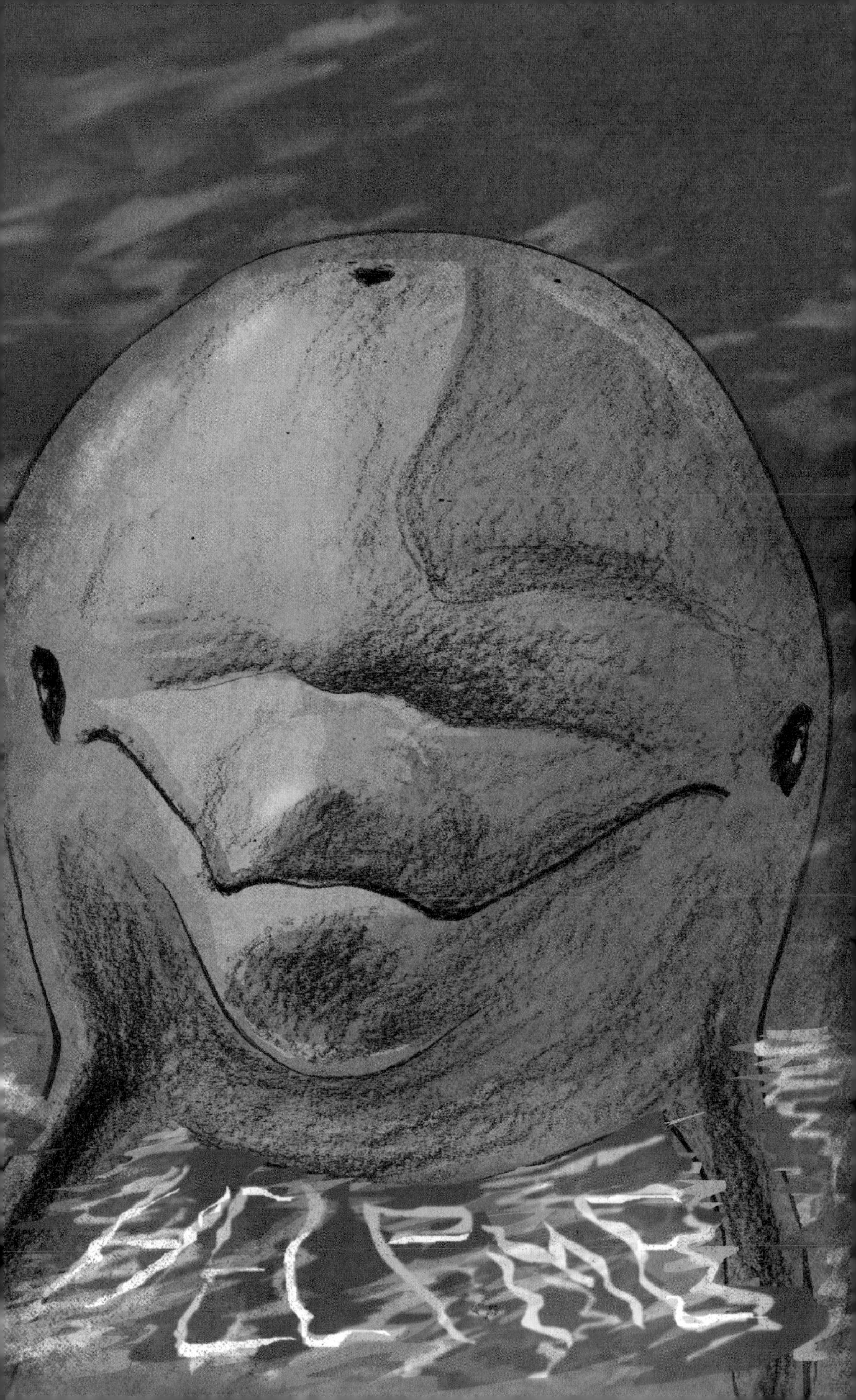

4

WHEN FILING REPORT ALL ESSENTIAL DETAILS MUST FALL WITHIN THIS SOLID "LIVE AREA" BOX. THIS IS THE BORDER FOR A STANDARD, NON-BLEED FIELD REPORT

MIND MGMT FIELD GUIDE 4.1: If Reflection interrogation devices are not available, don't forget that any reflective surface can be used for Hypno-Memory retrieval and disposal.

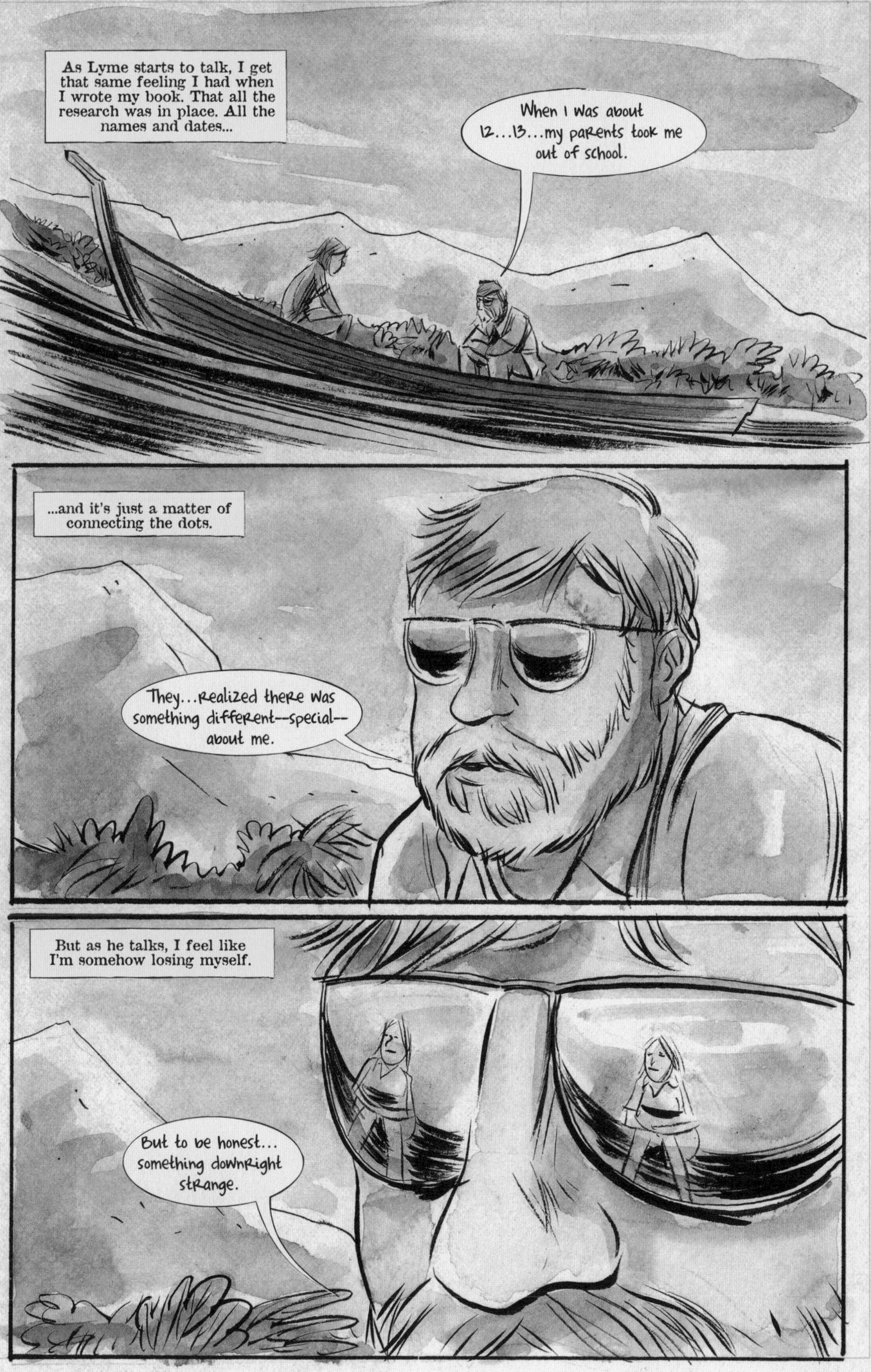

As Lyme starts to talk, I get that same feeling I had when I wrote my book. That all the research was in place. All the names and dates...
When I was about 12...13...my parents took me out of school.
...and it's just a matter of connecting the dots.
They...realized there was something different--special--about me.
But as he talks, I feel like I'm somehow losing myself.
But to be honest... something downright strange.

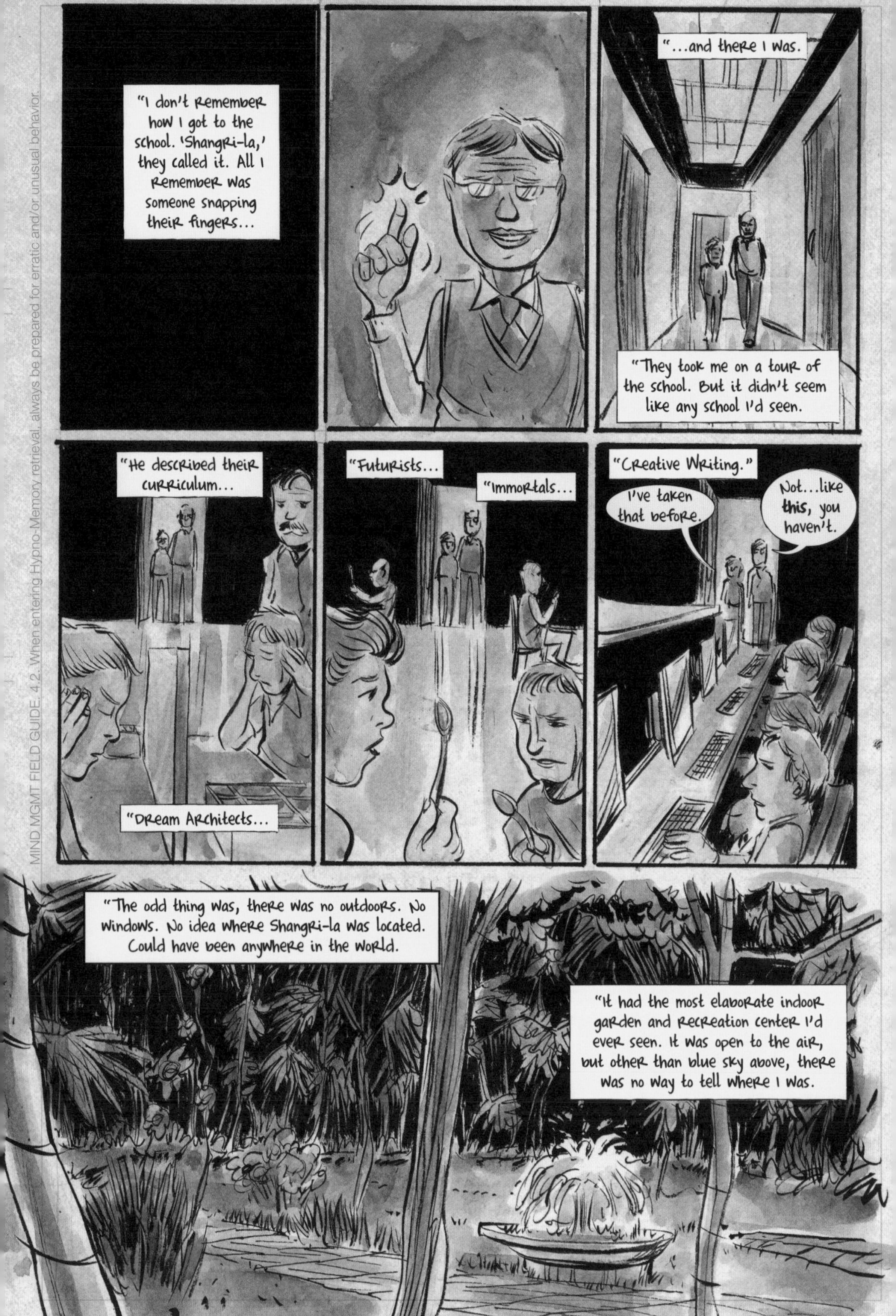
"I don't remember how I got to the school. 'Shangri-la,' they called it. All I remember was someone snapping their fingers...
"...and there I was.
"They took me on a tour of the school. But it didn't seem like any school I'd seen.
"He described their curriculum...
"Dream Architects...
"Futurists...
"Immortals...
"Creative Writing."
I've taken that before.
Not...like this, you haven't.
"The odd thing was, there was no outdoors. No windows. No idea where Shangri-la was located. Could have been anywhere in the world.
"It had the most elaborate indoor garden and recreation center I'd ever seen. It was open to the air, but other than blue sky above, there was no way to tell where I was.

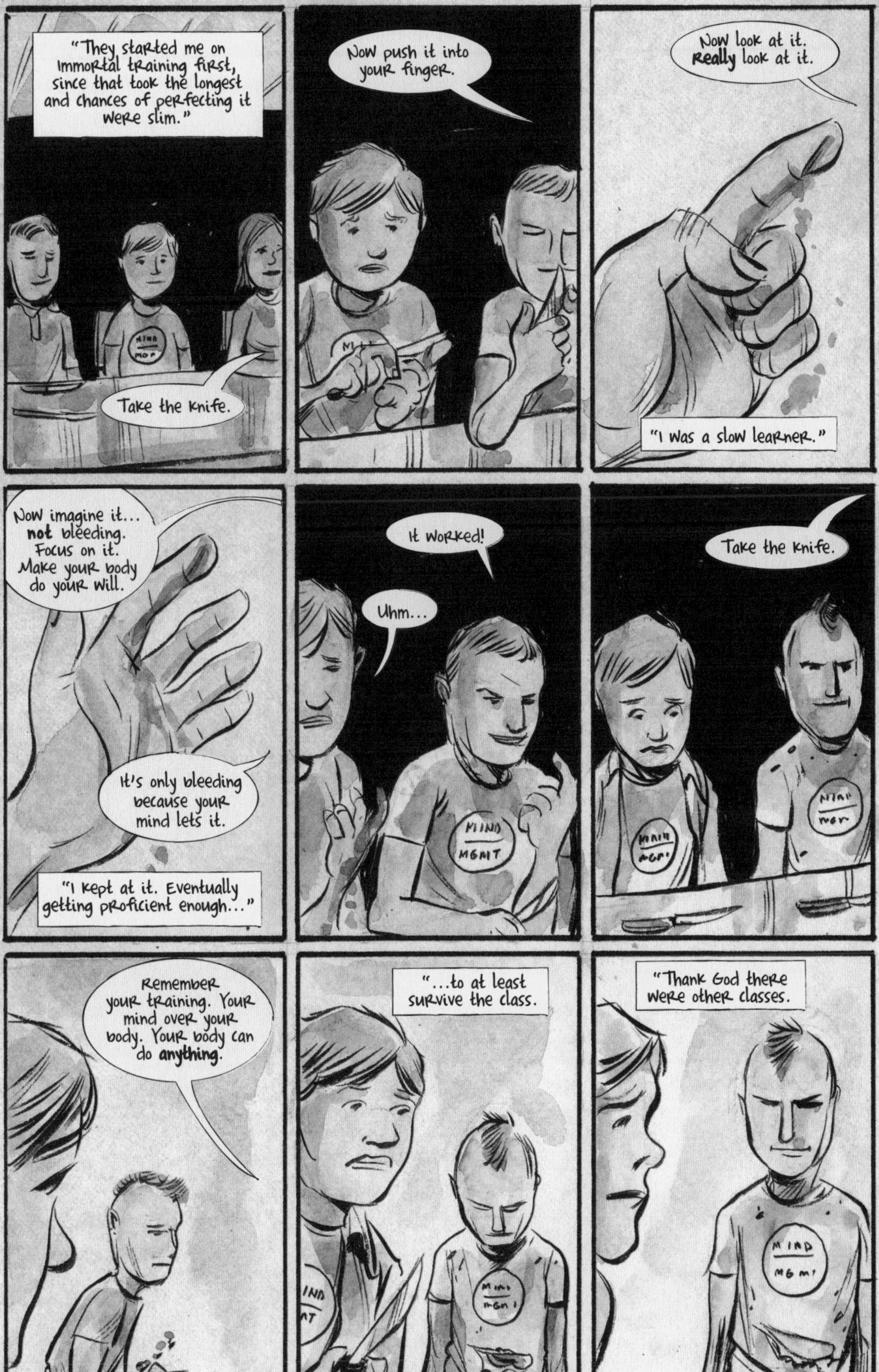
"They started me on Immortal training first, since that took the longest and chances of perfecting it were slim."
Take the knife.
Now push it into your finger.
Now look at it. **Really** look at it.
"I was a slow learner."
Now imagine it... **not** bleeding. Focus on it. Make your body do your will.
It's only bleeding because your mind lets it.
"I kept at it. Eventually getting proficient enough..."
It worked!
Uhm...
Take the knife.
Remember your training. Your mind over your body. Your body can do **anything**.
"...to at least survive the class.
"Thank God there were other classes.

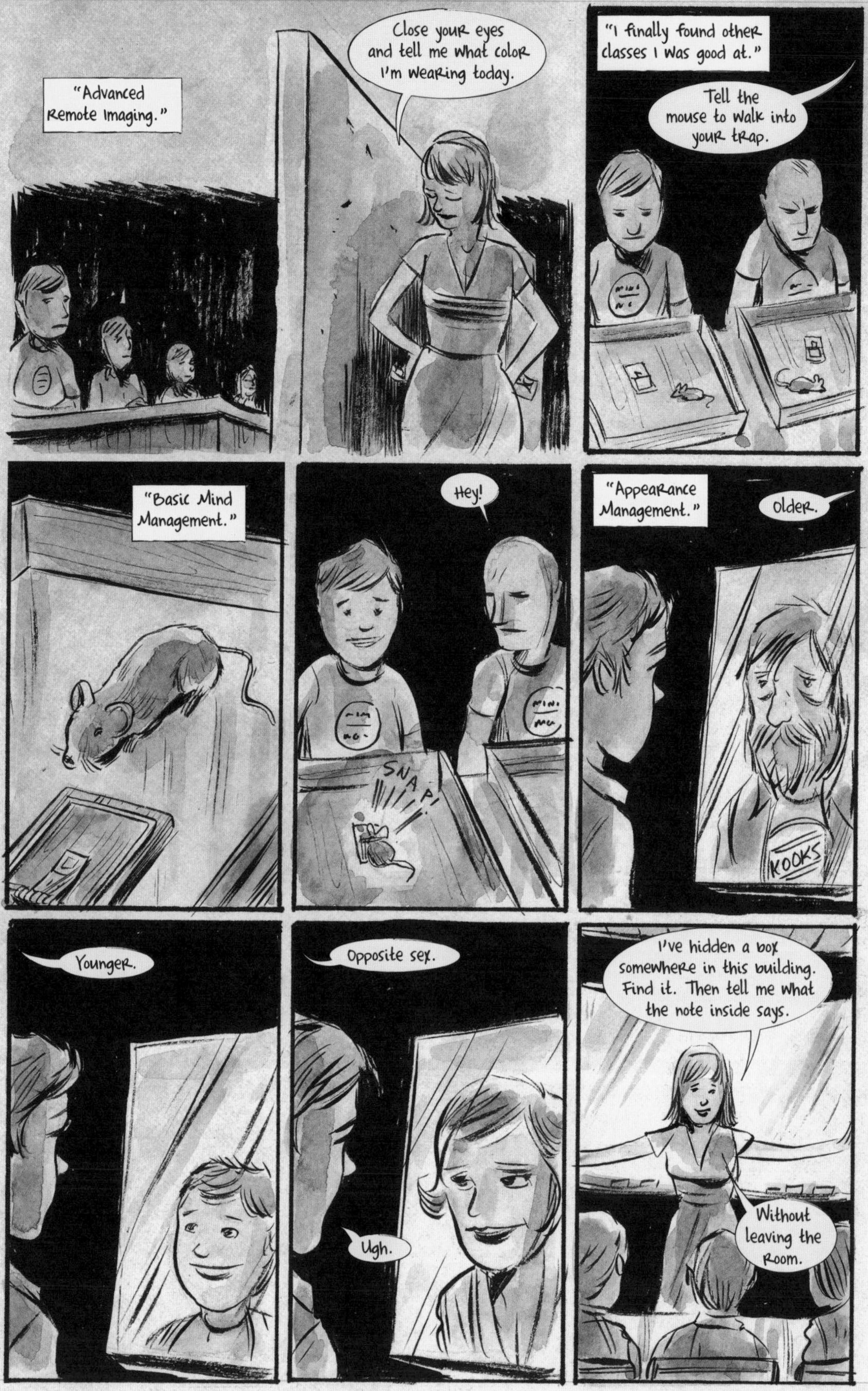
"Advanced Remote Imaging."
Close your eyes and tell me what color I'm wearing today.
"I finally found other classes I was good at."
Tell the mouse to walk into your trap.
"Basic Mind Management."
Hey!
SNAP!
"Appearance Management."
Older.
KOOKS
Younger.
Opposite sex.
Ugh.
I've hidden a box somewhere in this building. Find it. Then tell me what the note inside says.
Without leaving the room.

MIND MGMT FIELD GUIDE. 4.4. Memories of love are usually buried deeper and are harder to retrieve reliably.

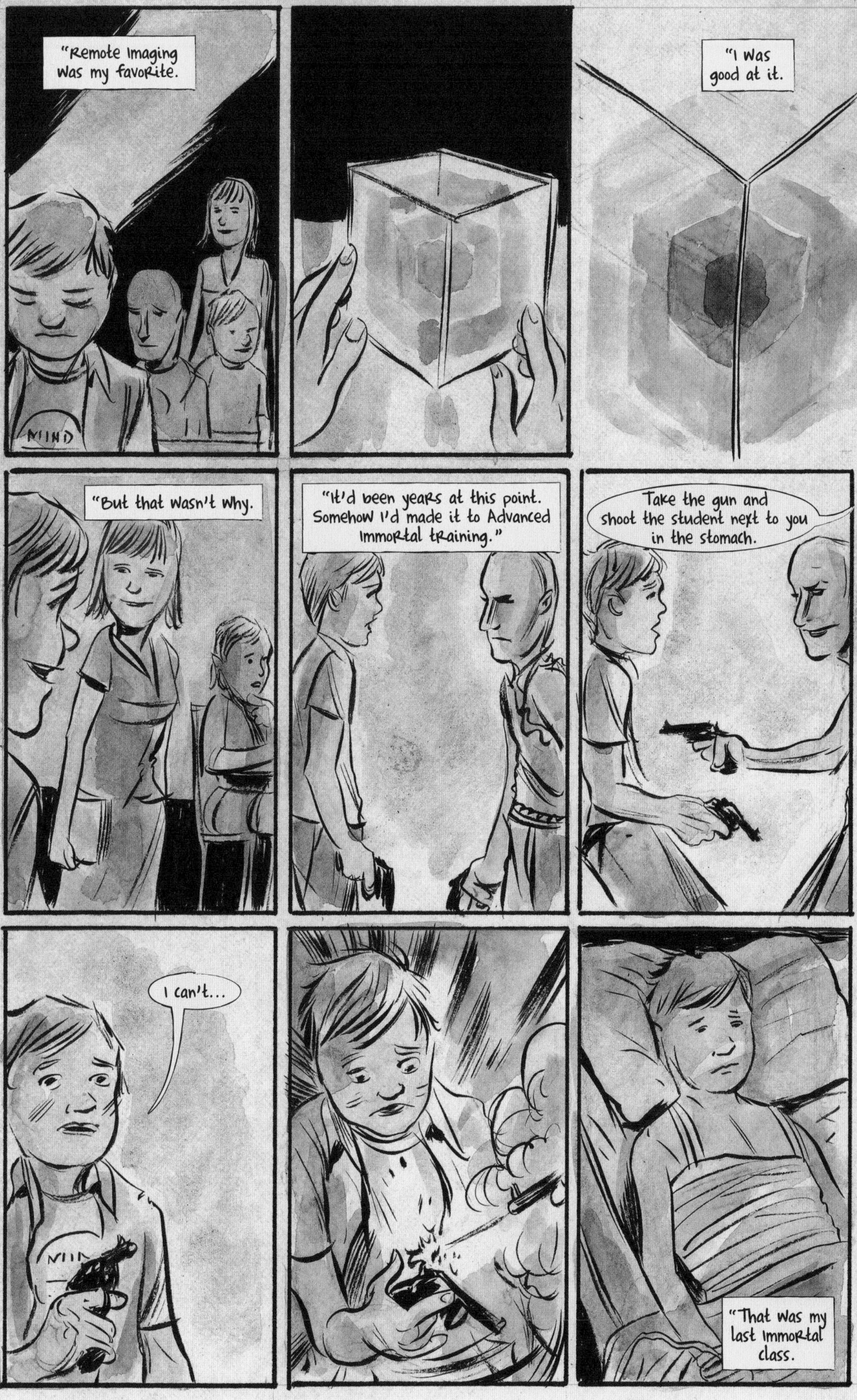
"Remote Imaging was my favorite.
MIND
"I was good at it.
"But that wasn't why.
"It'd been years at this point. Somehow I'd made it to Advanced Immortal training."
Take the gun and shoot the student next to you in the stomach.
I can't...
"That was my last Immortal class.

WHEN FILING REPORT ALL ESSENTIAL DETAILS MUST FALL WITHIN THIS SOLID "LIVE AREA" BOX. THIS IS THE BORDER FOR A STANDARD, NON-BLEED FIELD REPORT

MIND MGMT FIELD GUIDE. 4.6. Remote Imaging techniques can be used to uncover hidden weapons, or to reveal something as simple as a hidden message.

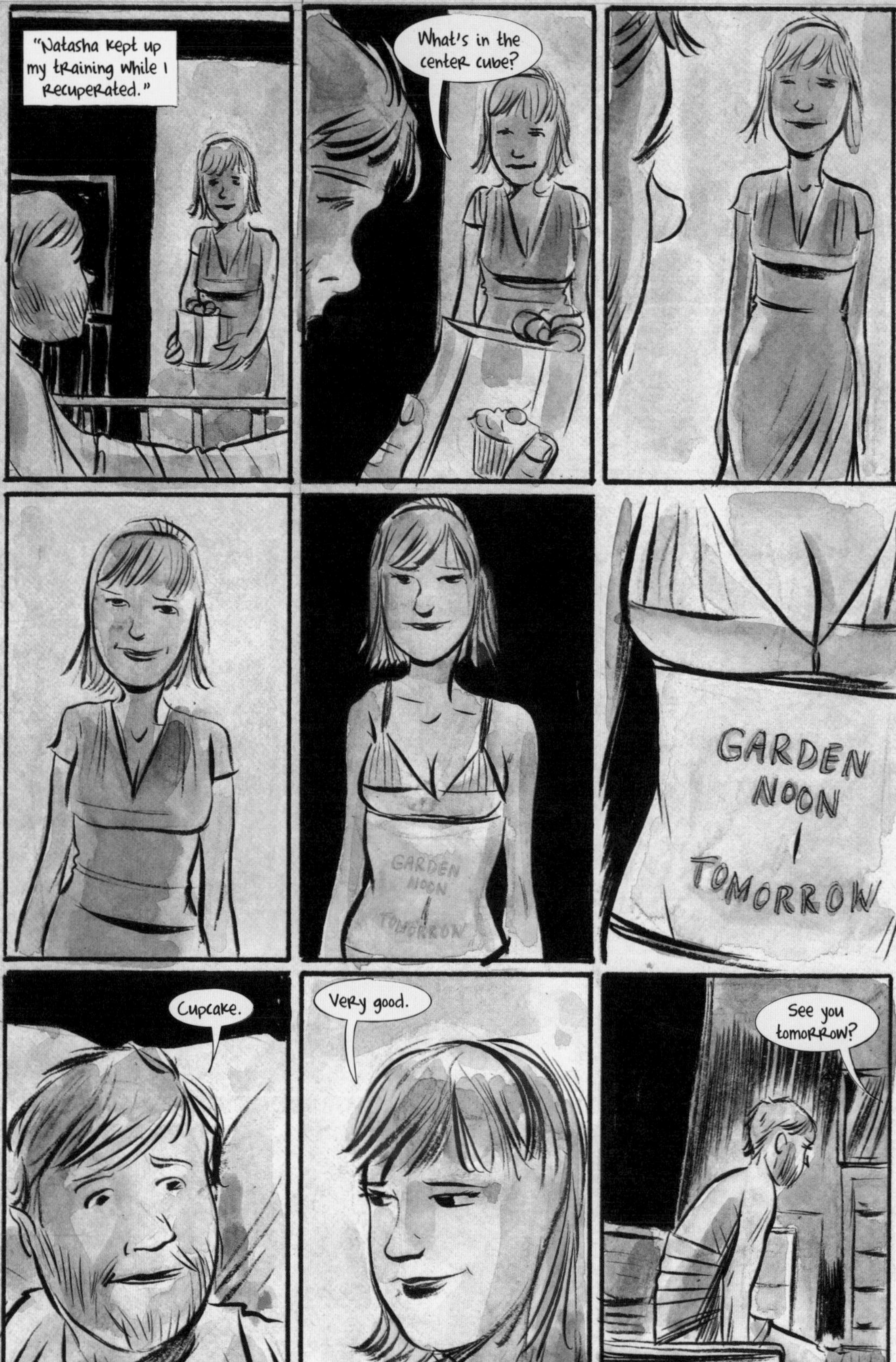
"Natasha kept up my training while I recuperated."
What's in the center cube?
GARDEN NOON 1 TOMORROW
GARDEN NOON 1 TOMORROW
Cupcake.
Very good.
See you tomorrow?

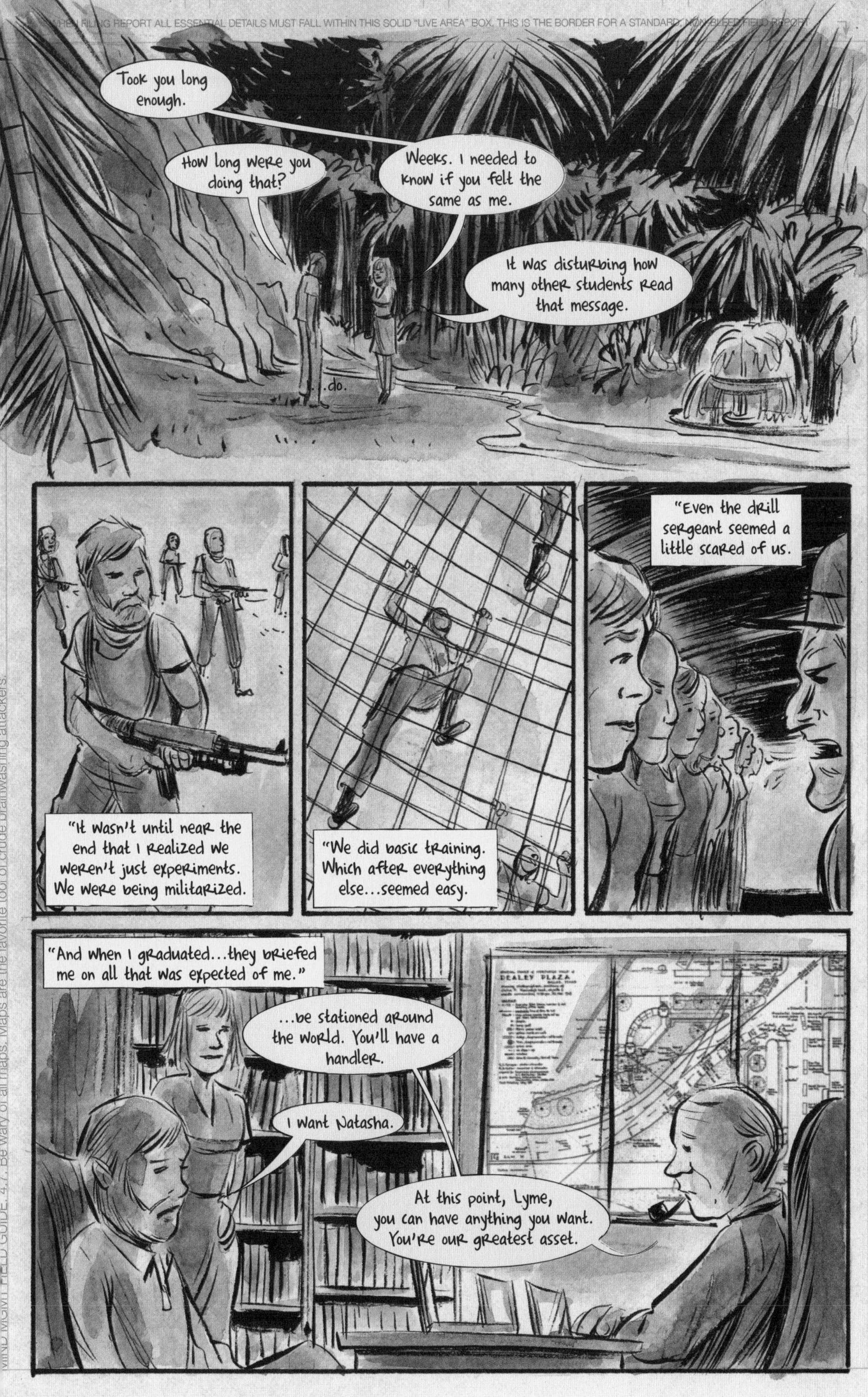
WHEN FILING REPORT ALL ESSENTIAL DETAILS MUST FALL WITHIN THIS SOLID "LIVE AREA" BOX. THIS IS THE BORDER FOR A STANDARD, NON-BLEED FIELD REPORT
Took you long enough.
How long were you doing that?
Weeks. I needed to know if you felt the same as me.
It was disturbing how many other students read that message.
...do.
"It wasn't until near the end that I realized we weren't just experiments. We were being militarized.
"We did basic training. Which after everything else...seemed easy.
"Even the drill sergeant seemed a little scared of us.
"And when I graduated...they briefed me on all that was expected of me."
...be stationed around the world. You'll have a handler.
I want Natasha.
At this point, Lyme, you can have anything you want. You're our greatest asset.
MIND MGMT FIELD GUIDE 4.7: Be wary of all maps. Maps are the favorite tool of crude brainwashing attackers.

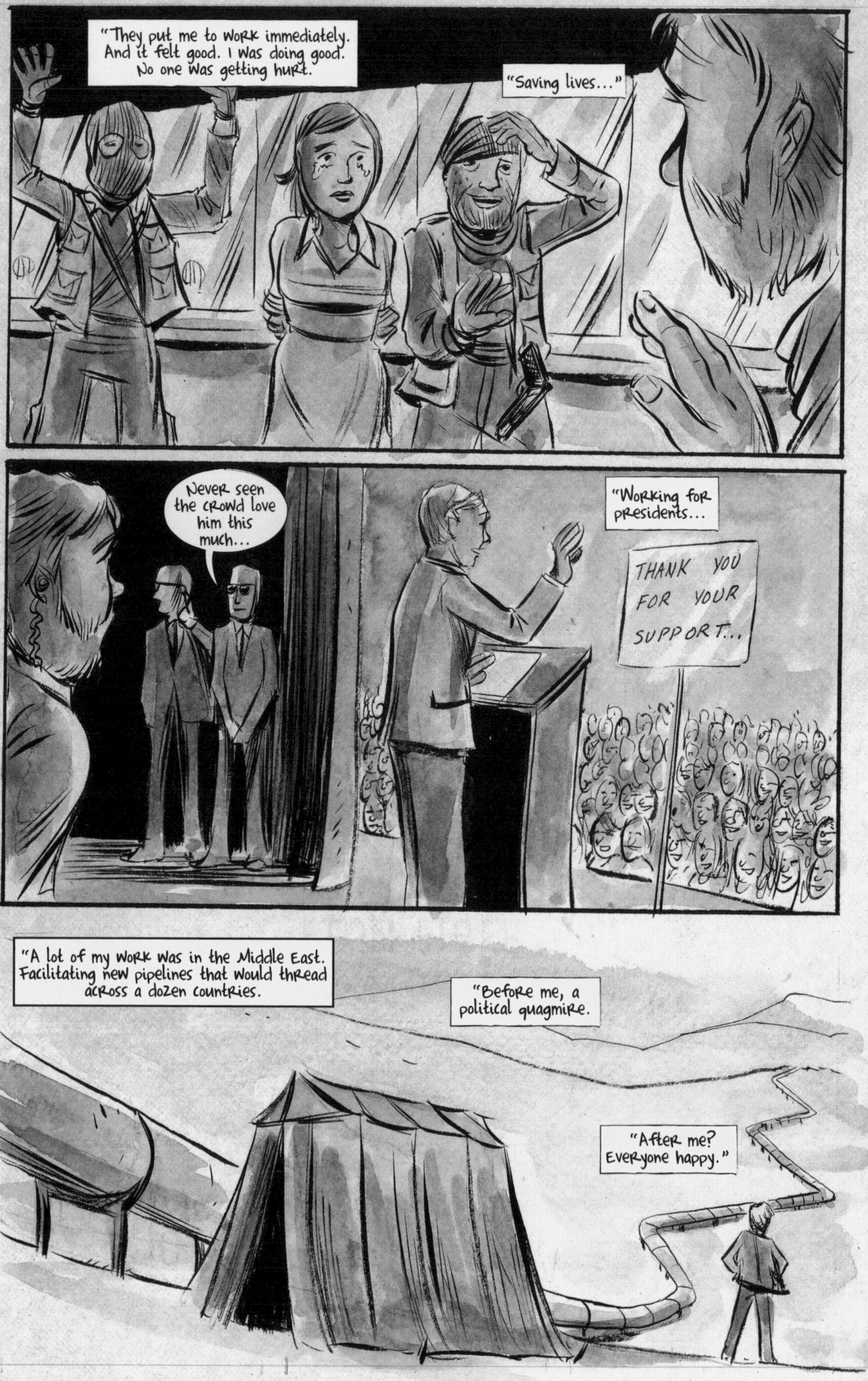
"They put me to work immediately. And it felt good. I was doing good. No one was getting hurt.
"Saving lives..."
Never seen the crowd love him this much...
"Working for presidents...
THANK YOU FOR YOUR SUPPORT...
"A lot of my work was in the Middle East. Facilitating new pipelines that would thread across a dozen countries.
"Before me, a political quagmire.
"After me? Everyone happy."

MIND MGMT FIELD GUIDE. 4.8. Cover stories are your best defense when confronted by an enemy. The more colorful and unbelievable, the better.

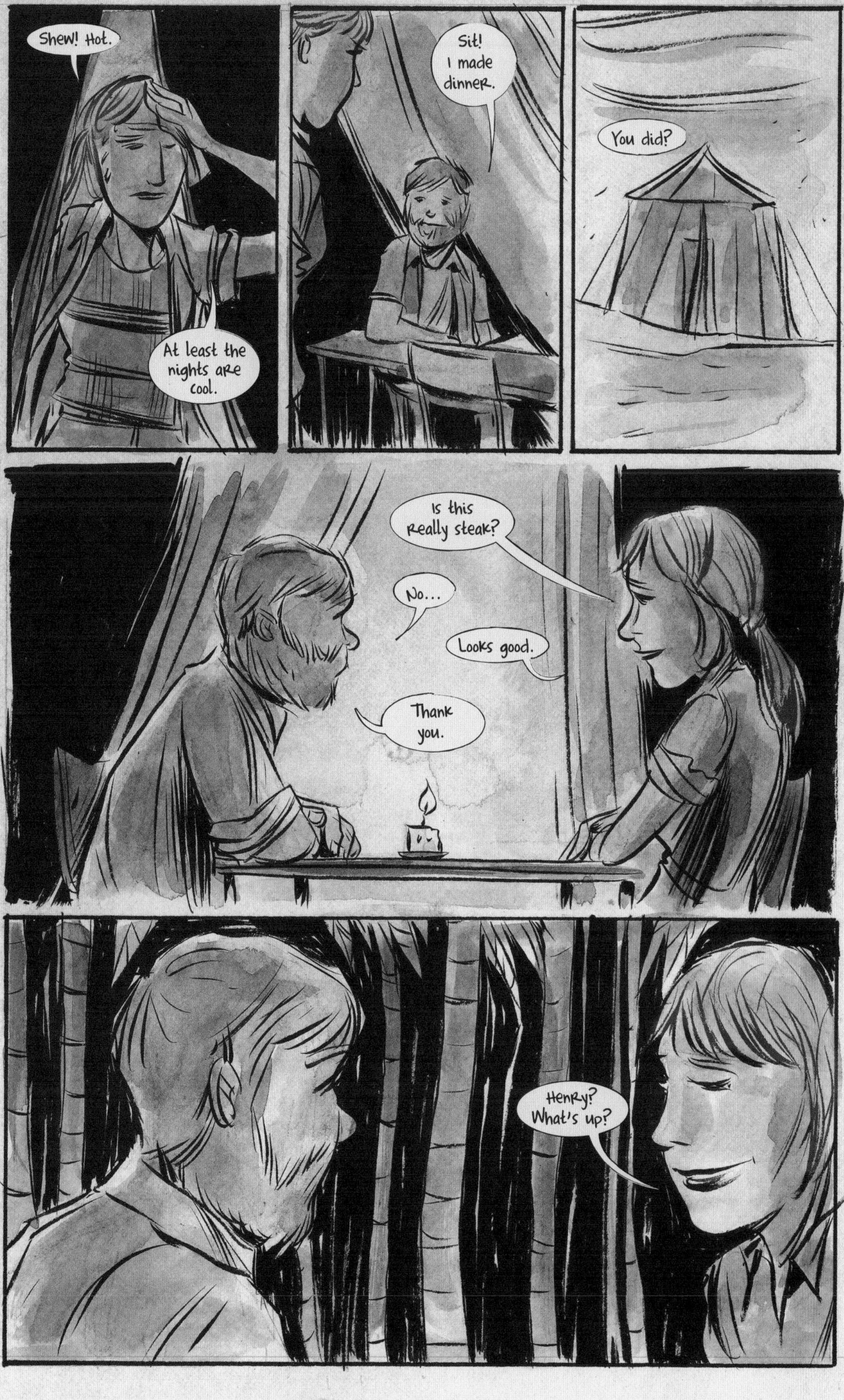
Shew! Hot.
At least the nights are cool.
Sit! I made dinner.
You did?
Is this really steak?
No...
Looks good.
Thank you.
Henry? What's up?

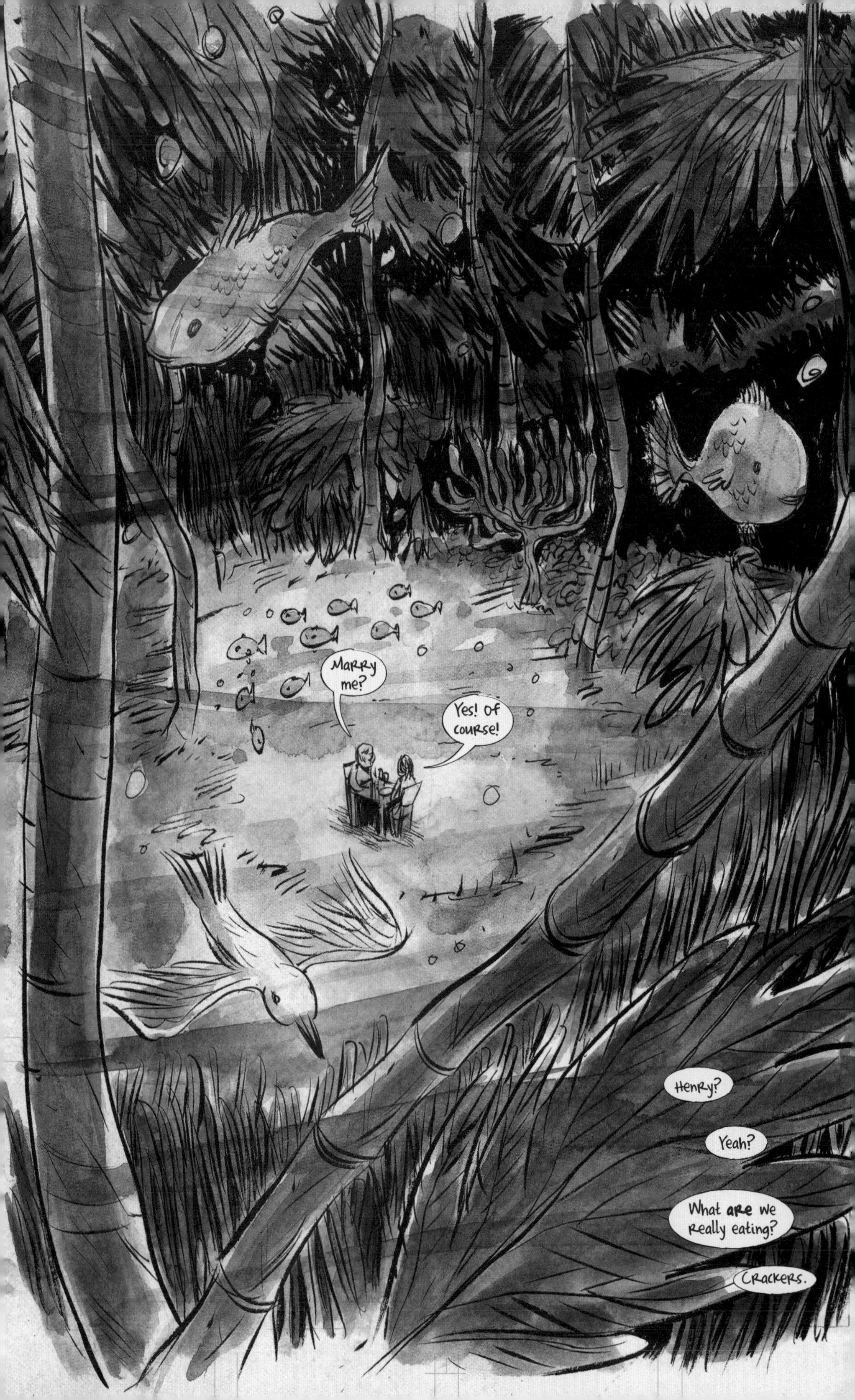
Marry me?
Yes! Of course!
Henry?
Yeah?
What are we really eating?
Crackers.

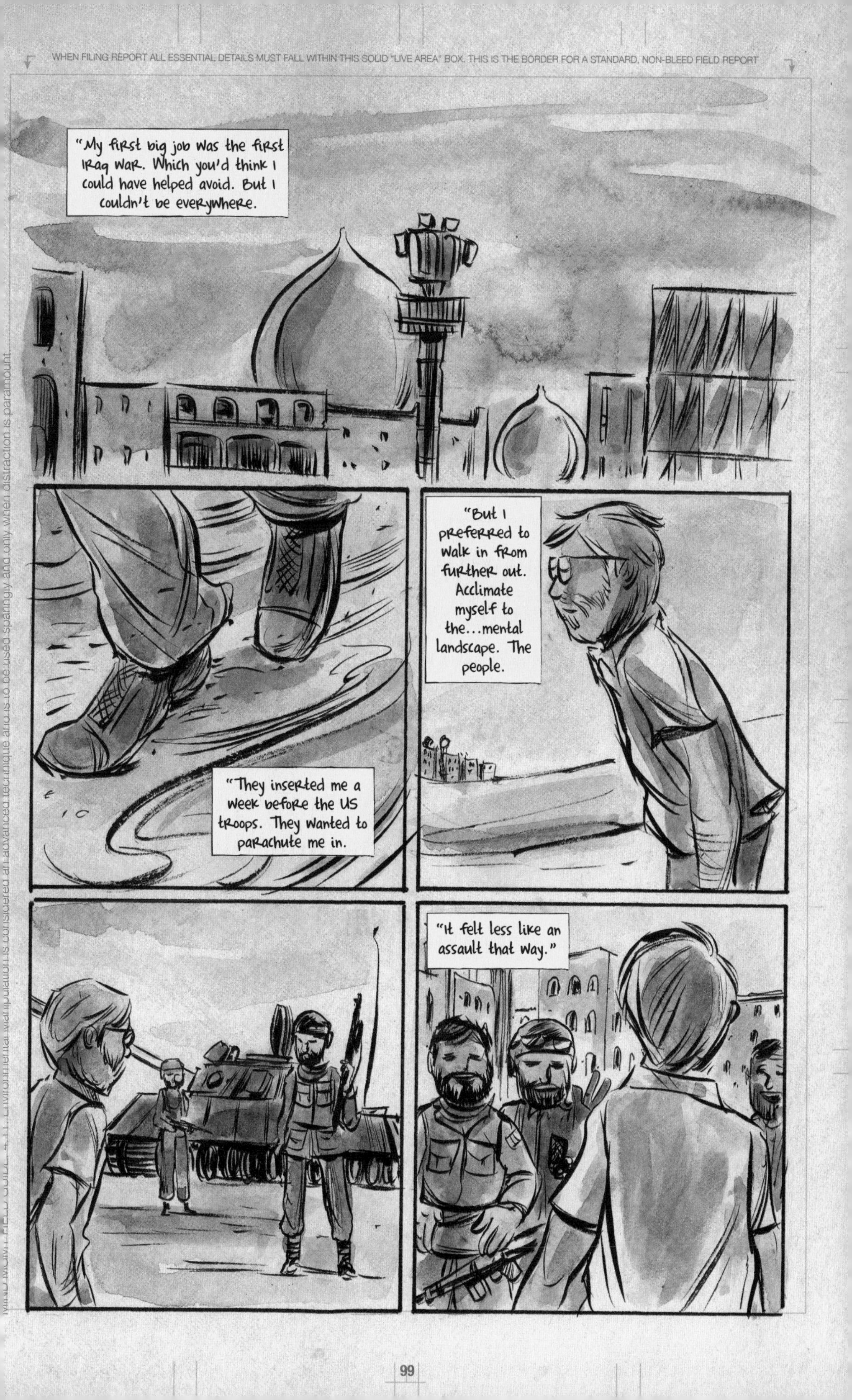
"My first big job was the first Iraq war. Which you'd think I could have helped avoid. But I couldn't be everywhere.
"They inserted me a week before the US troops. They wanted to parachute me in.
"But I preferred to walk in from further out. Acclimate myself to the...mental landscape. The people.
"It felt less like an assault that way."

is considered an advanced technique and is to be used sparingly and only when distraction is paramount.

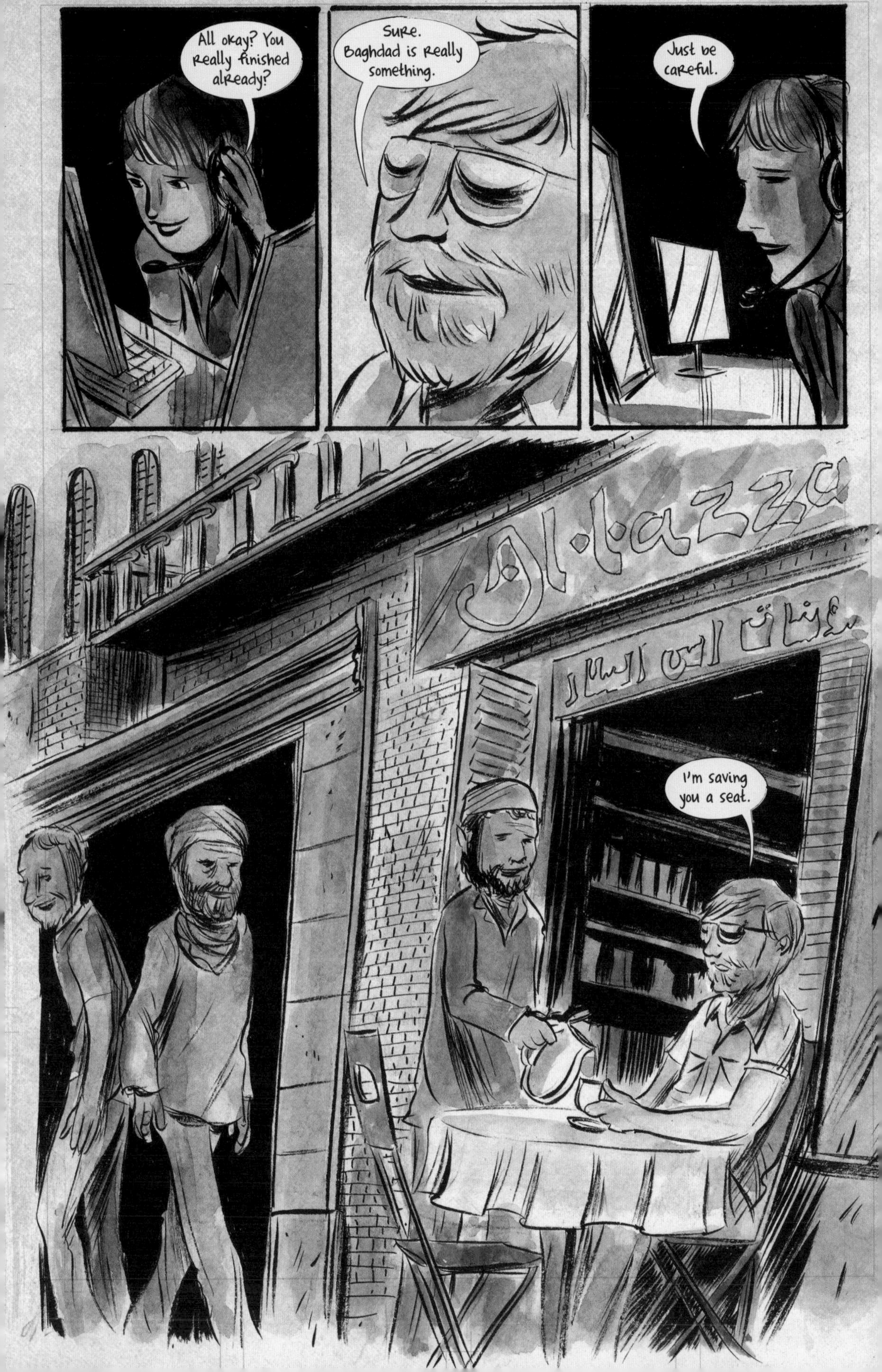
All okay? You really finished already?
Sure. Baghdad is really something.
Just be careful.
Al-Fazza
I'm saving you a seat.

MIND MGMT FIELD GUIDE. 4.13. Hazaras are more likely to be encountered when attempting management of large populations. Currently only two agents have clearance for this activity.

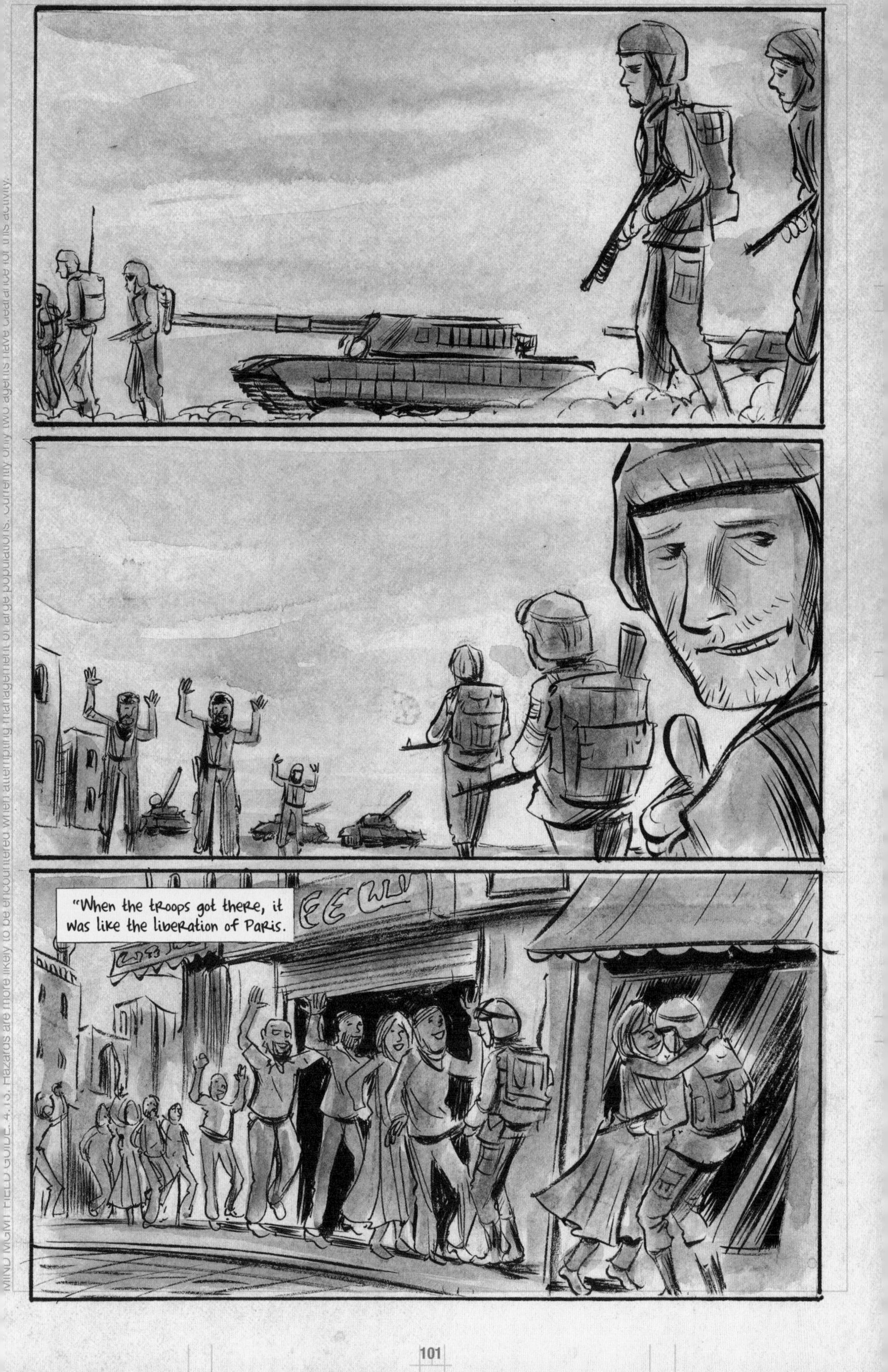
"When the troops got there, it was like the liberation of Paris.

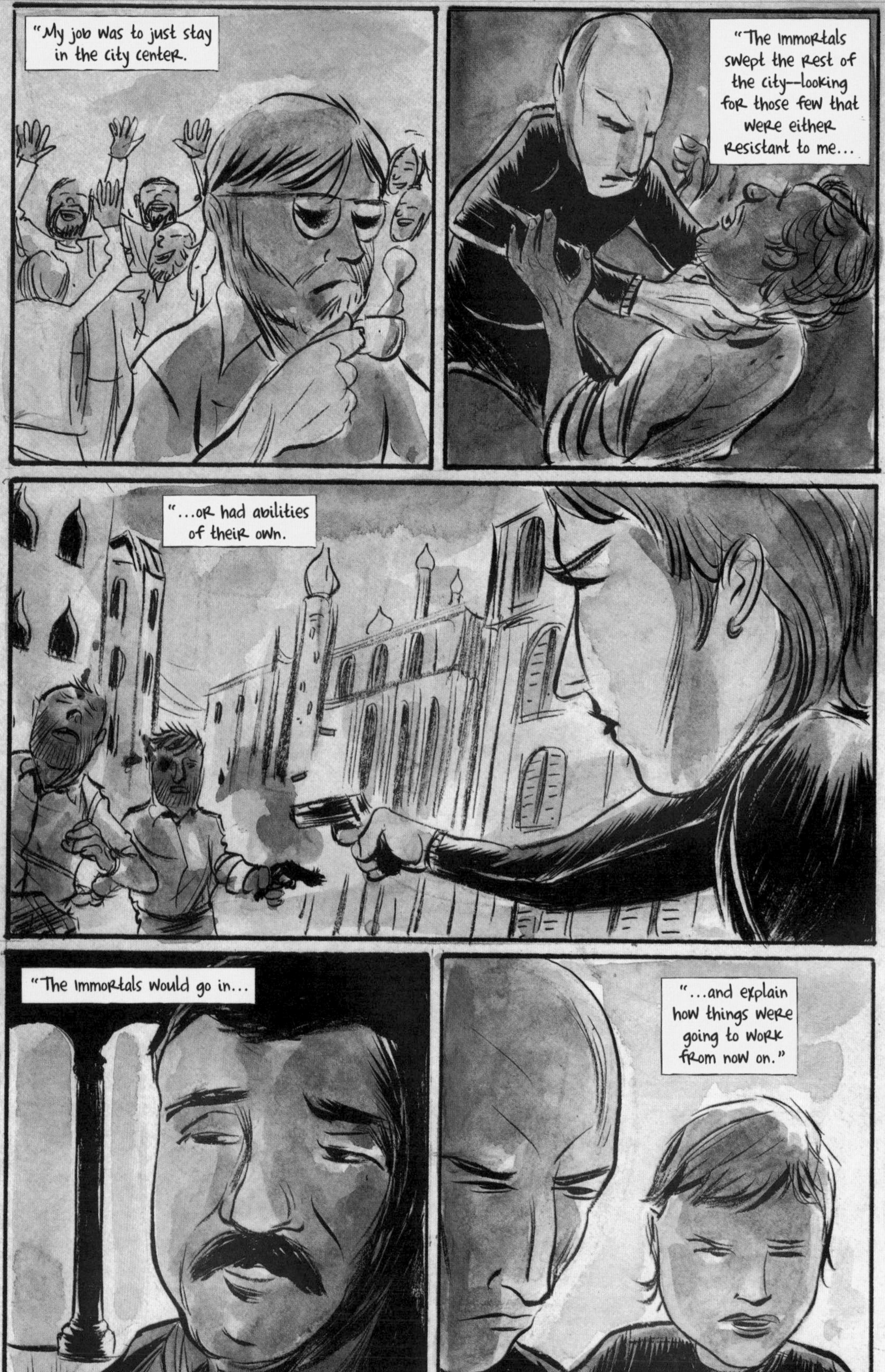
"My job was to just stay in the city center.
"The Immortals swept the rest of the city--looking for those few that were either resistant to me...
"...or had abilities of their own.
"The Immortals would go in...
"...and explain how things were going to work from now on."

MIND MGMT FIELD GUIDE. 4.14. Lethal use of Immortal agents is recommended in large population-control exercises. Stray escapees are often more dangerous than average hostiles.

MIND MGMT FIELD GUIDE: 4.15: After engaging in large population-control exercises, a period of 1-3 days of rest is recommended to maintain peak mind management performance.

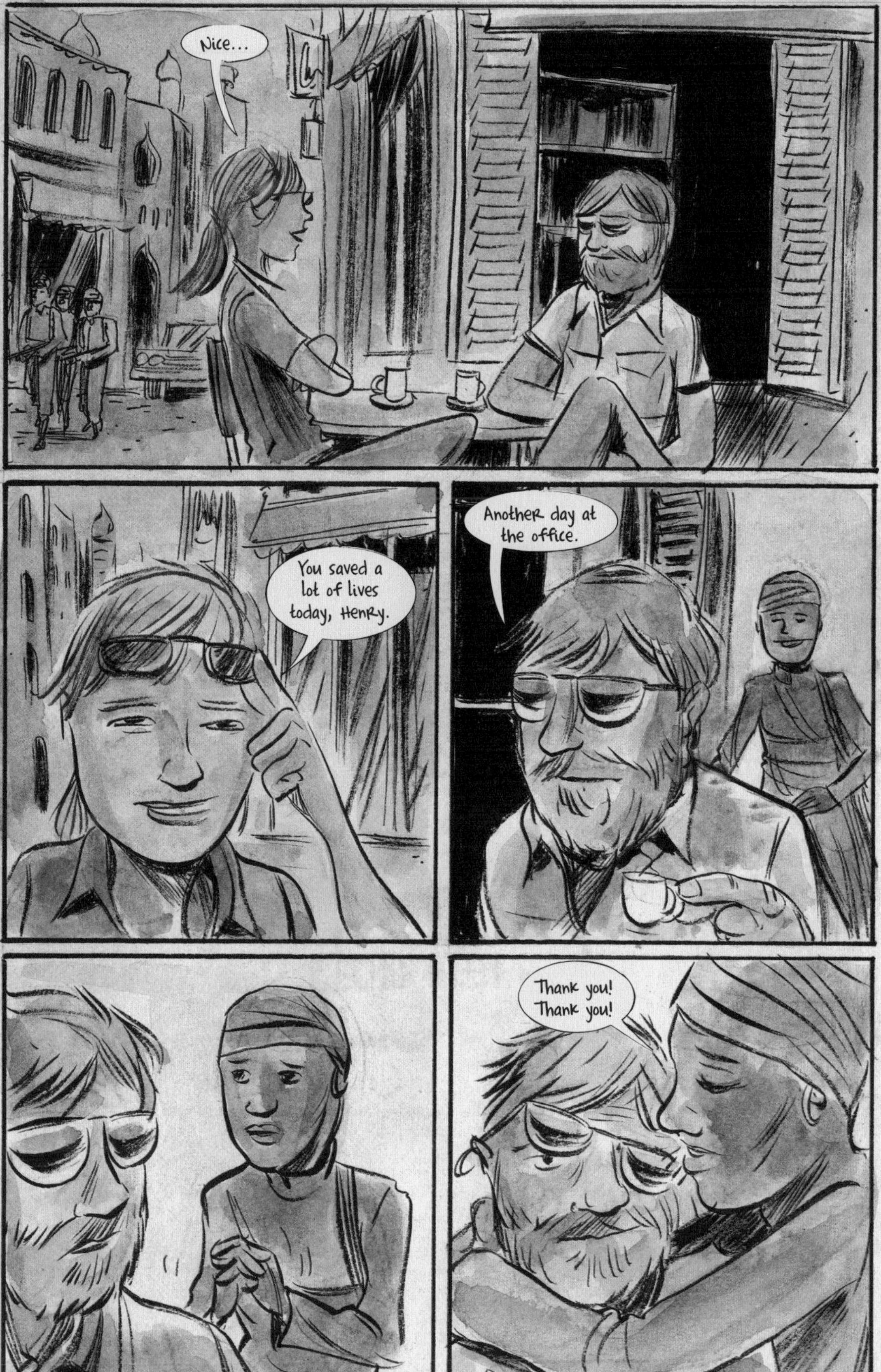
Nice...
You saved a lot of lives today, Henry.
Another day at the office.
Thank you! Thank you!

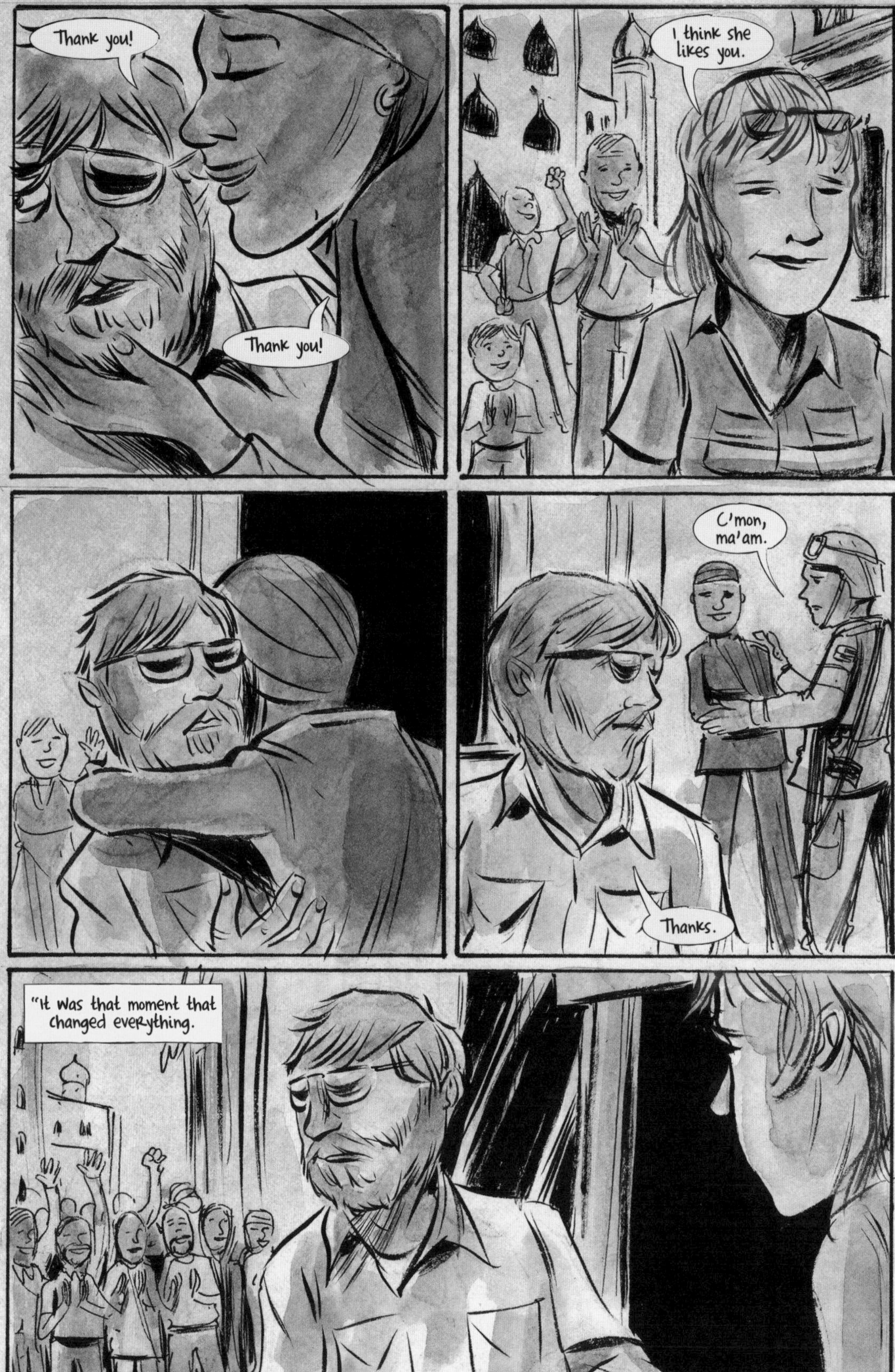
Thank you!
Thank you!
I think she likes you.
C'mon, ma'am.
Thanks.
"It was that moment that changed everything.

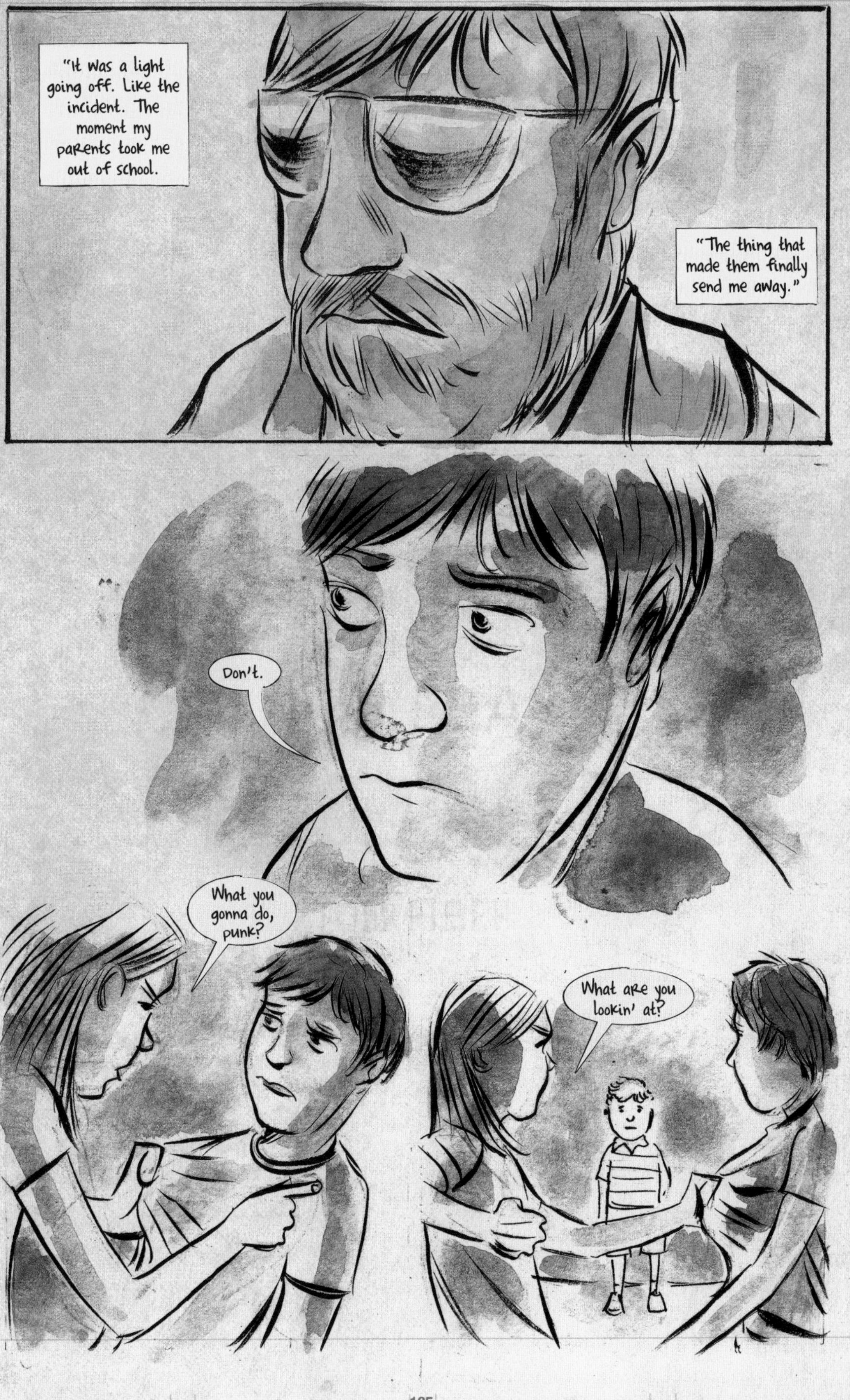
"It was a light going off. Like the incident. The moment my parents took me out of school.
"The thing that made them finally send me away."
Don't.
What you gonna do, punk?
What are you lookin' at?

MIND MGMT FIELD GUIDE: 4.17: During cleansing processARE YOU THERE?

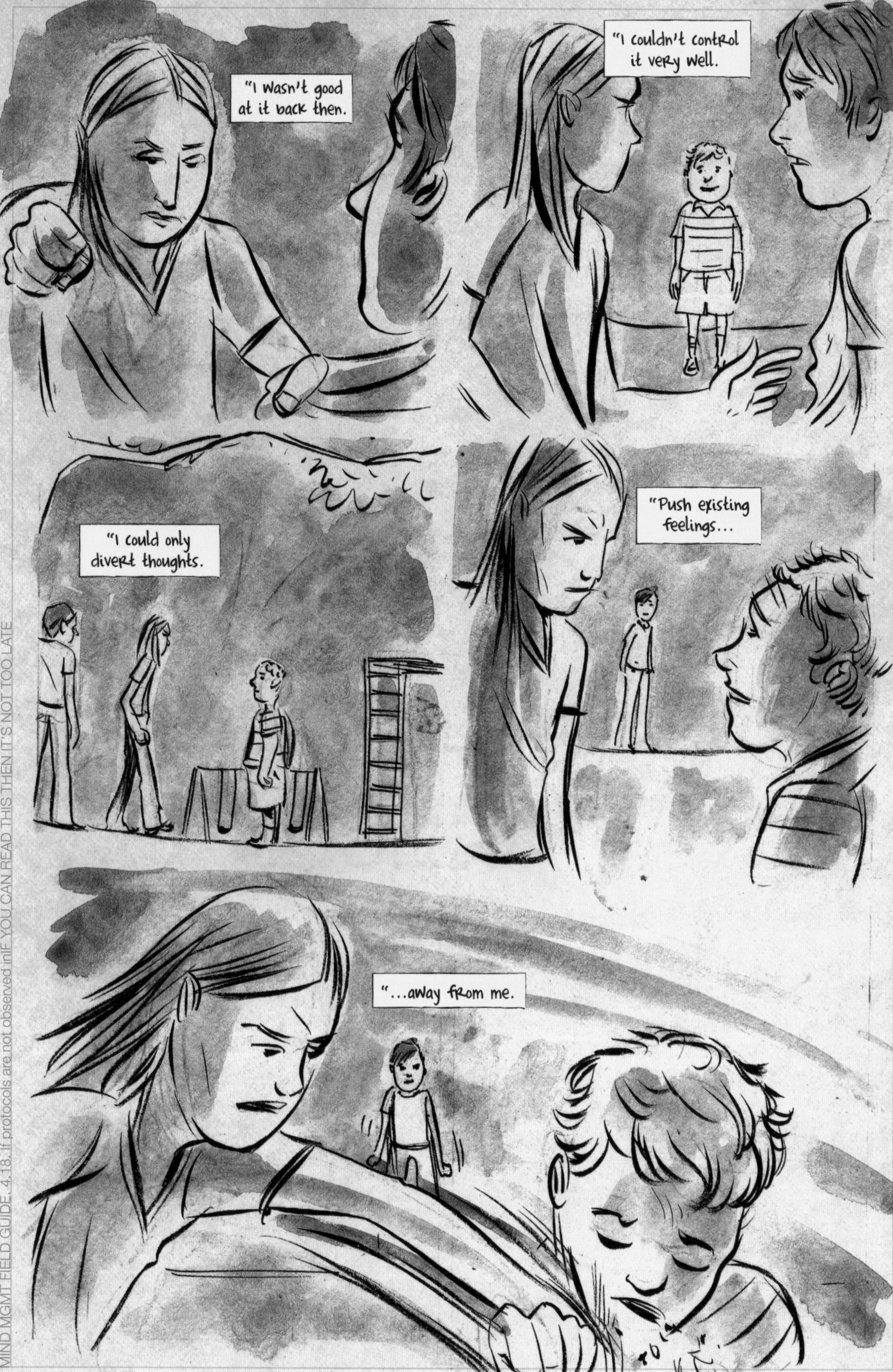
"I wasn't good at it back then.
"I couldn't control it very well.
"I could only divert thoughts.
"Push existing feelings...
"...away from me.

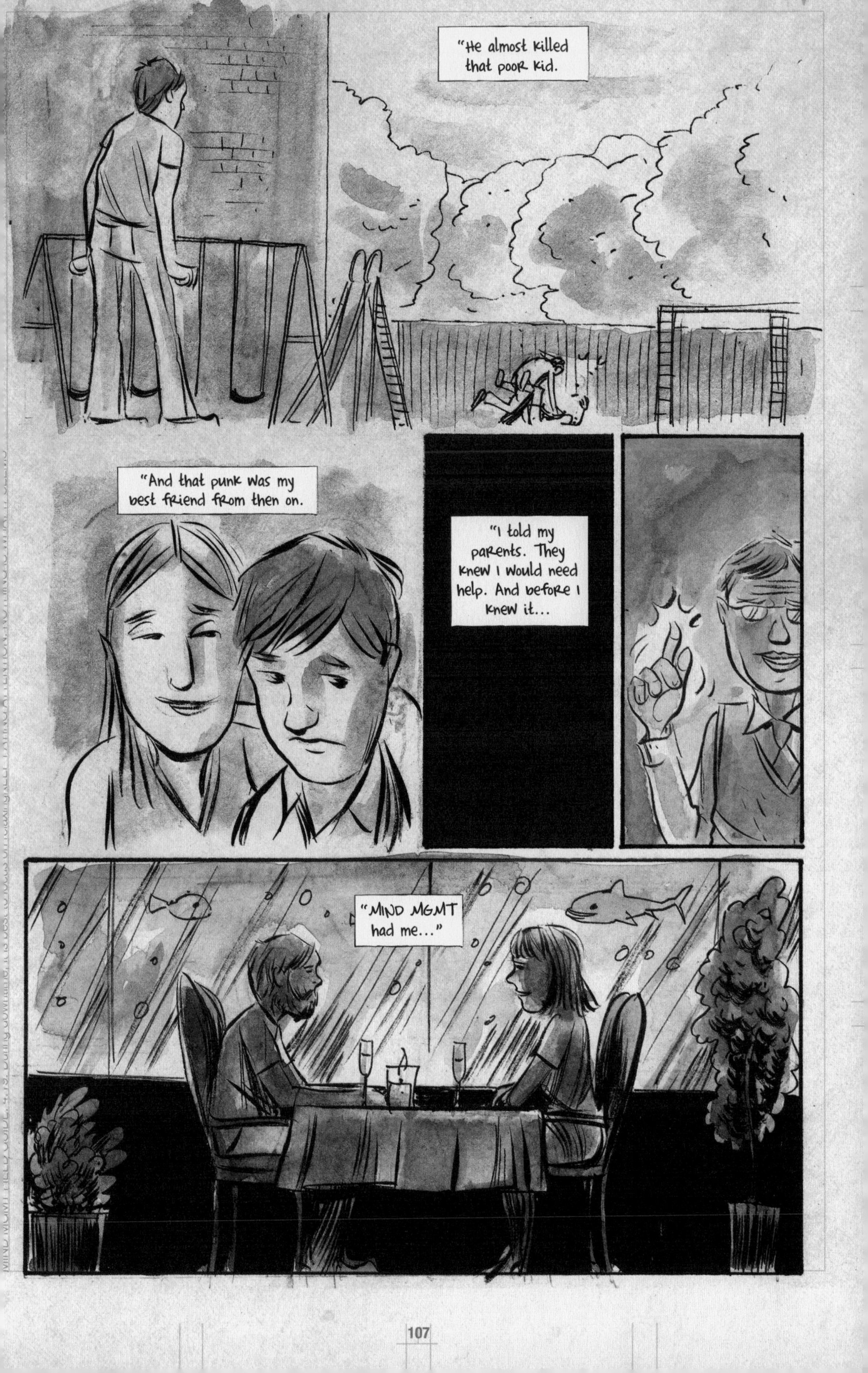
"He almost killed that poor kid.
"And that punk was my best friend from then on.
"I told my parents. They knew I would need help. And before I knew it...
"MIND MGMT had me..."

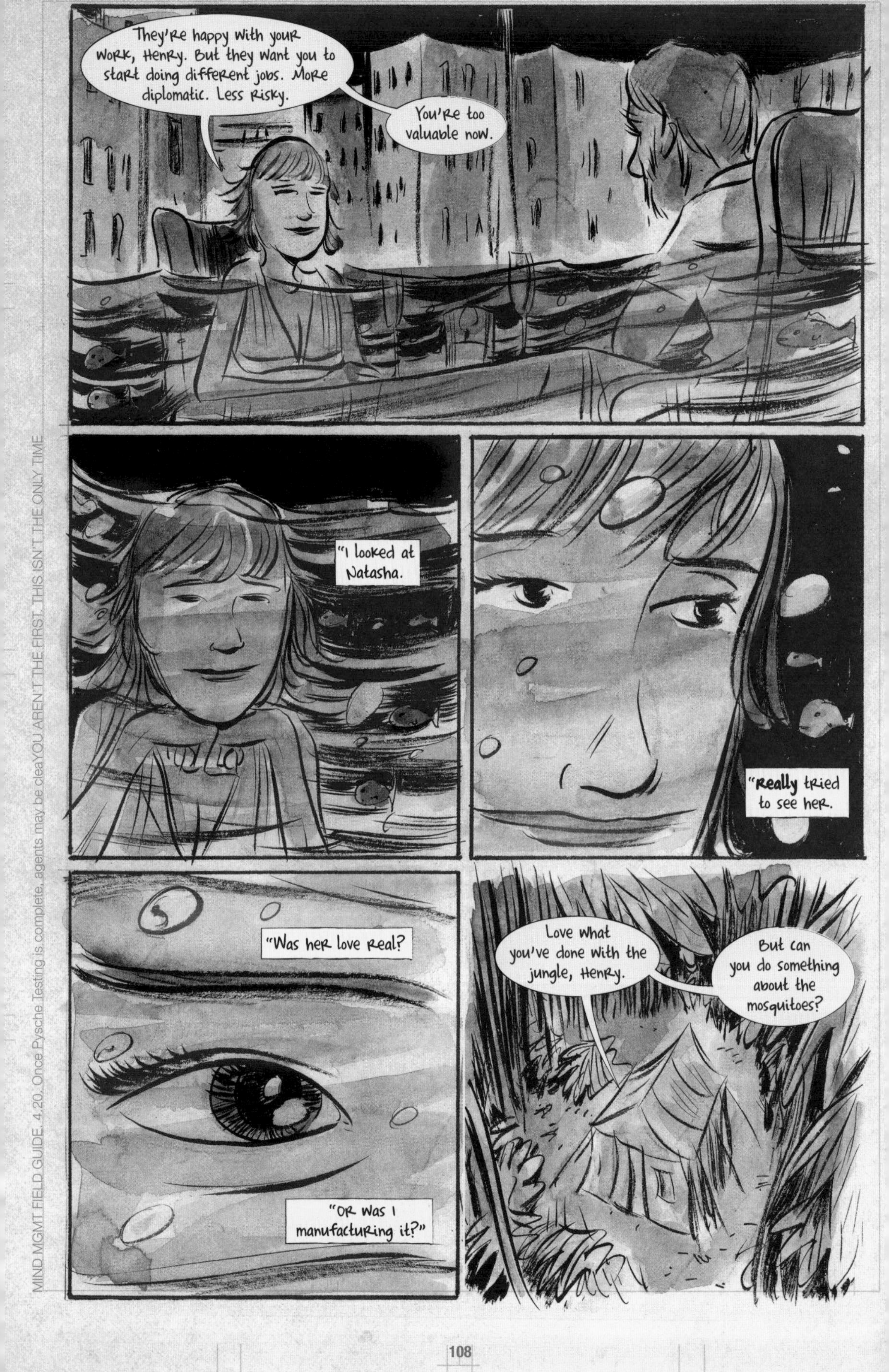
They're happy with your work, Henry. But they want you to start doing different jobs. More diplomatic. Less risky.
You're too valuable now.
"I looked at Natasha.
"**Really** tried to see her.
"Was her love real?
"Or was I manufacturing it?"
Love what you've done with the jungle, Henry.
But can you do something about the mosquitoes?

MIND MGMT FIELD GUIDE. 4.20. Once Pysche Testing is complete, agents may be cleaYOU AREN'T THE FIRST. THIS ISN'T THE ONLY TIME

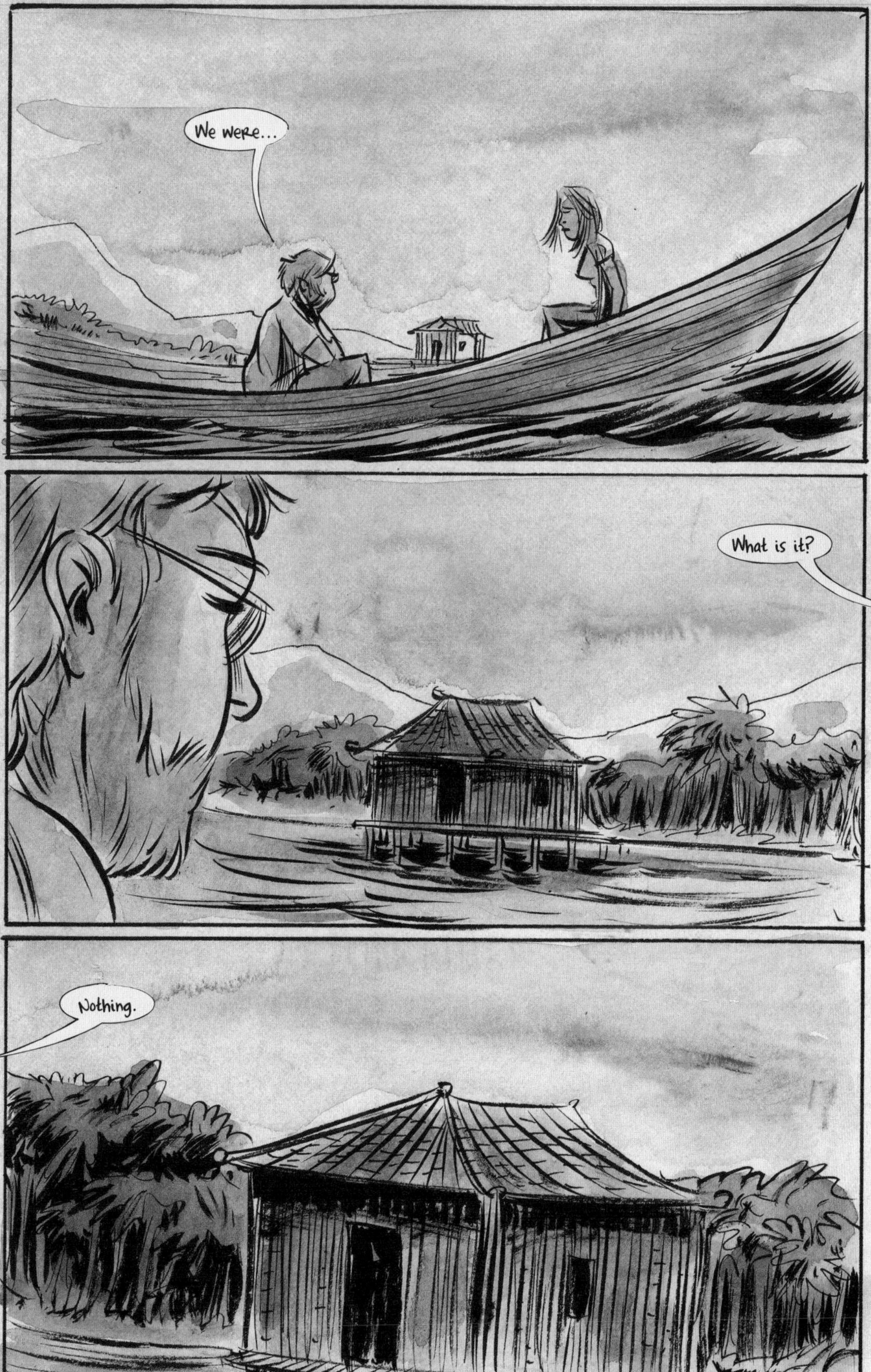
We were...
What is it?
Nothing.

WHEN FILING REPORT ALL ESSENTIAL DETAILS MUST FALL WITHIN THIS SOLID "LIVE AREA" BOX. THIS IS THE BORDER FOR A STANDARD, NON-BLEED FIELD REPORT

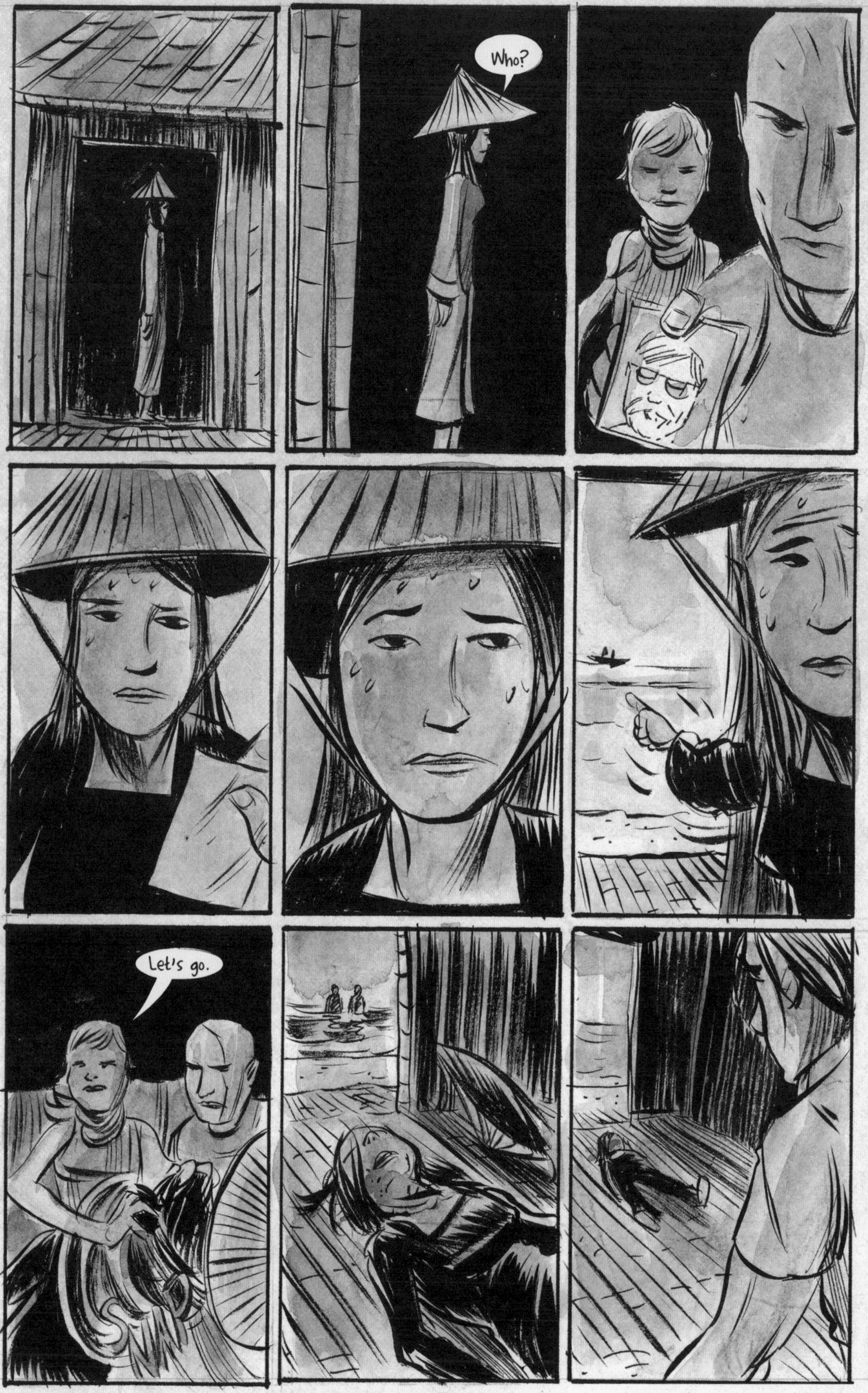

Who?
Let's go.

MIND MGMT FIELD GUIDE. 4:22. Deep breathing and letting go off YOU HAVEN'T DONE IT YET. IT MIGHT ALREADY BE TOO LATE. TAKE BILL AND GET OUT

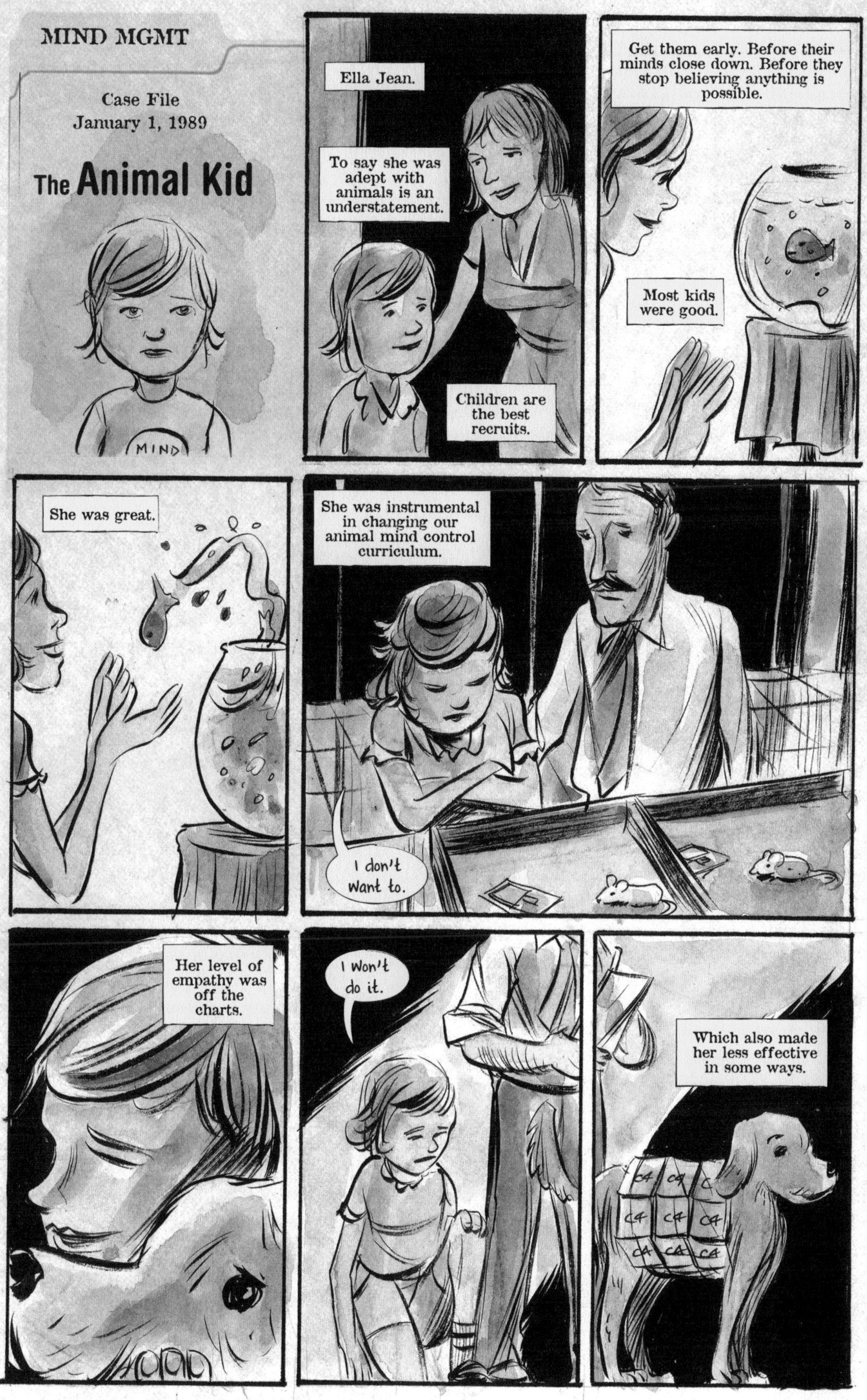
MIND MGMT
Case File
January 1, 1989
The Animal Kid
MIND
Ella Jean.
To say she was adept with animals is an understatement.
Children are the best recruits.
Get them early. Before their minds close down. Before they stop believing anything is possible.
Most kids were good.
She was great.
She was instrumental in changing our animal mind control curriculum.
I don't want to.
Her level of empathy was off the charts.
I won't do it.
Which also made her less effective in some ways.
C4

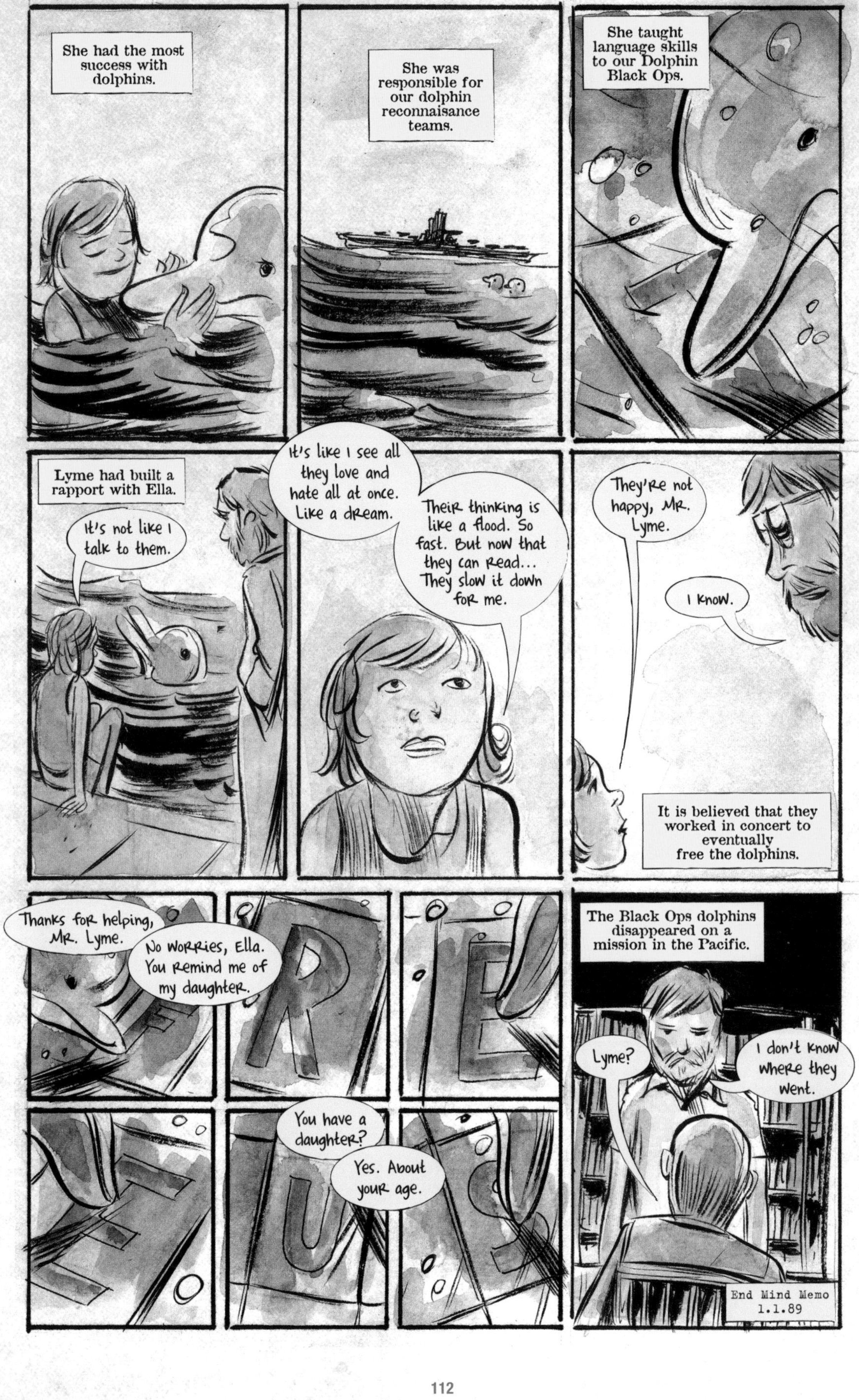

She had the most success with dolphins.
She was responsible for our dolphin reconnaisance teams.
She taught language skills to our Dolphin Black Ops.
Lyme had built a rapport with Ella.
It's not like I talk to them.
It's like I see all they love and hate all at once. Like a dream.
Their thinking is like a flood. So fast. But now that they can read... They slow it down for me.
They're not happy, Mr. Lyme.
I know.
It is believed that they worked in concert to eventually free the dolphins.
Thanks for helping, Mr. Lyme.
No worries, Ella. You remind me of my daughter.
You have a daughter?
Yes. About your age.
The Black Ops dolphins disappeared on a mission in the Pacific.
Lyme?
I don't know where they went.
End Mind Memo 1.1.89

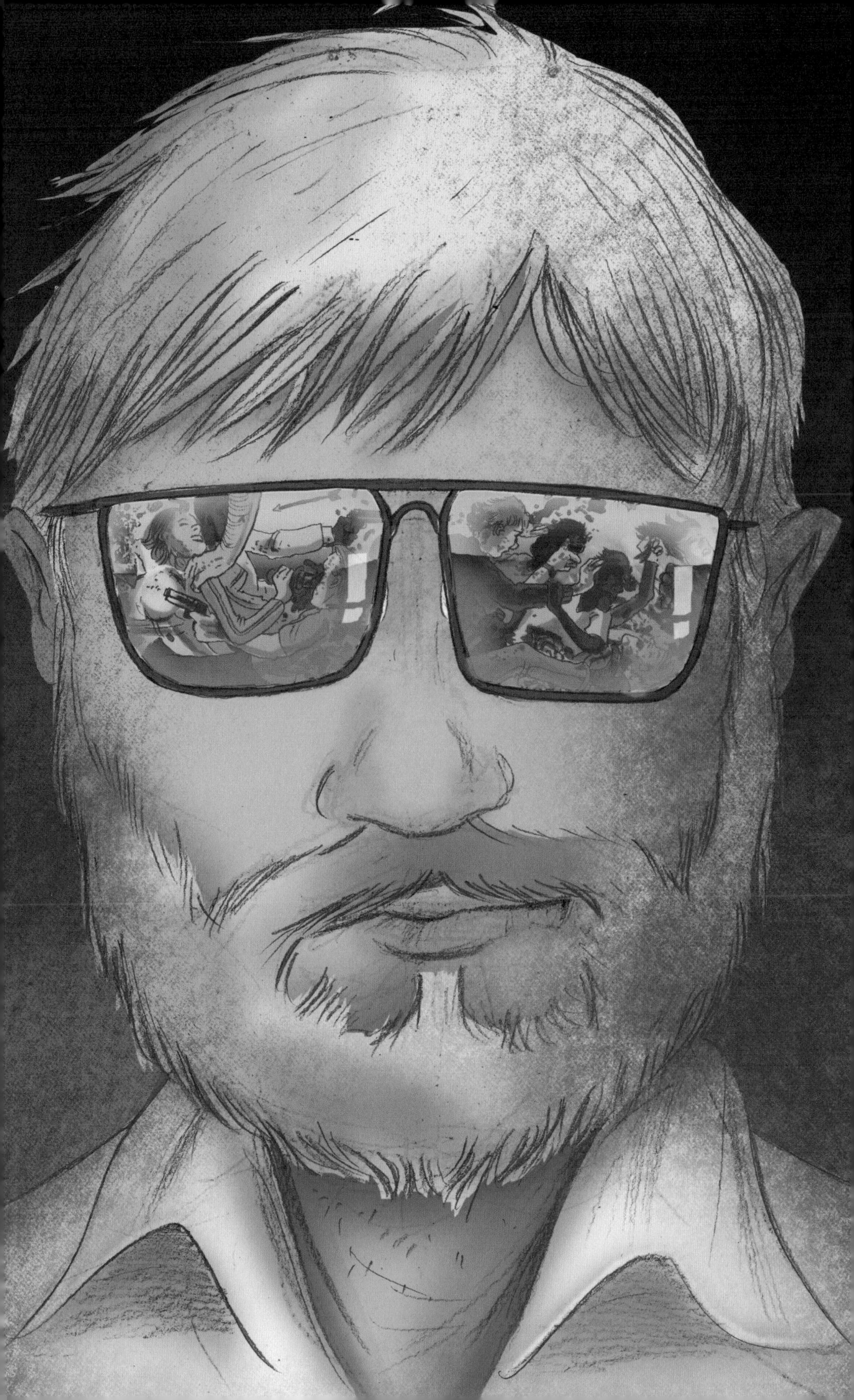

5

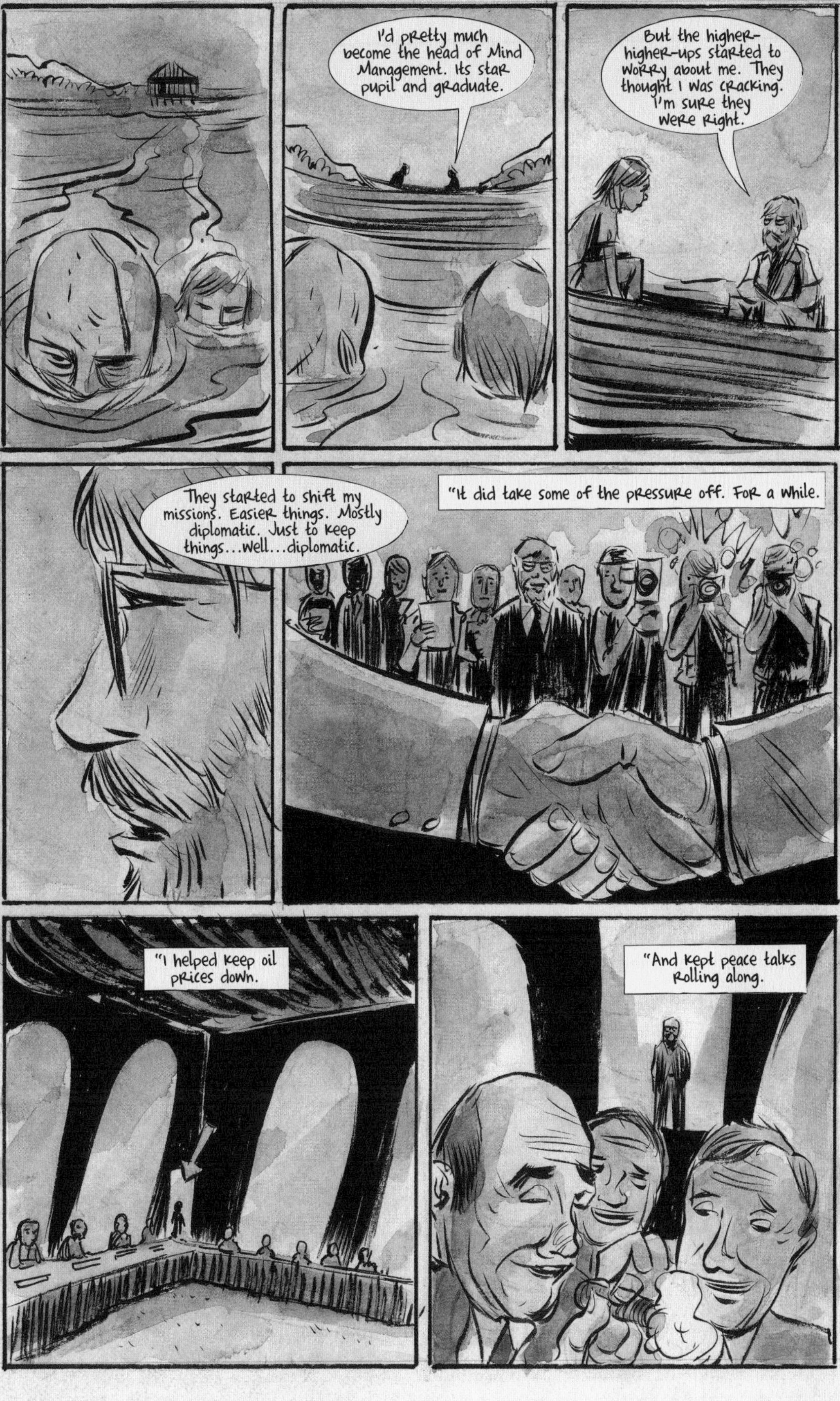
I'd pretty much become the head of Mind Management. Its star pupil and graduate.
But the higher-higher-ups started to worry about me. They thought I was cracking. I'm sure they were right.
They started to shift my missions. Easier things. Mostly diplomatic. Just to keep things...well...diplomatic.
"It did take some of the pressure off. For a while.
"I helped keep oil prices down.
"And kept peace talks rolling along.

MIND MGMT FIELD GUIDE. 5.1. In aquatic scenarios it is best toYOU NEED TO SNAP OUT OF IT

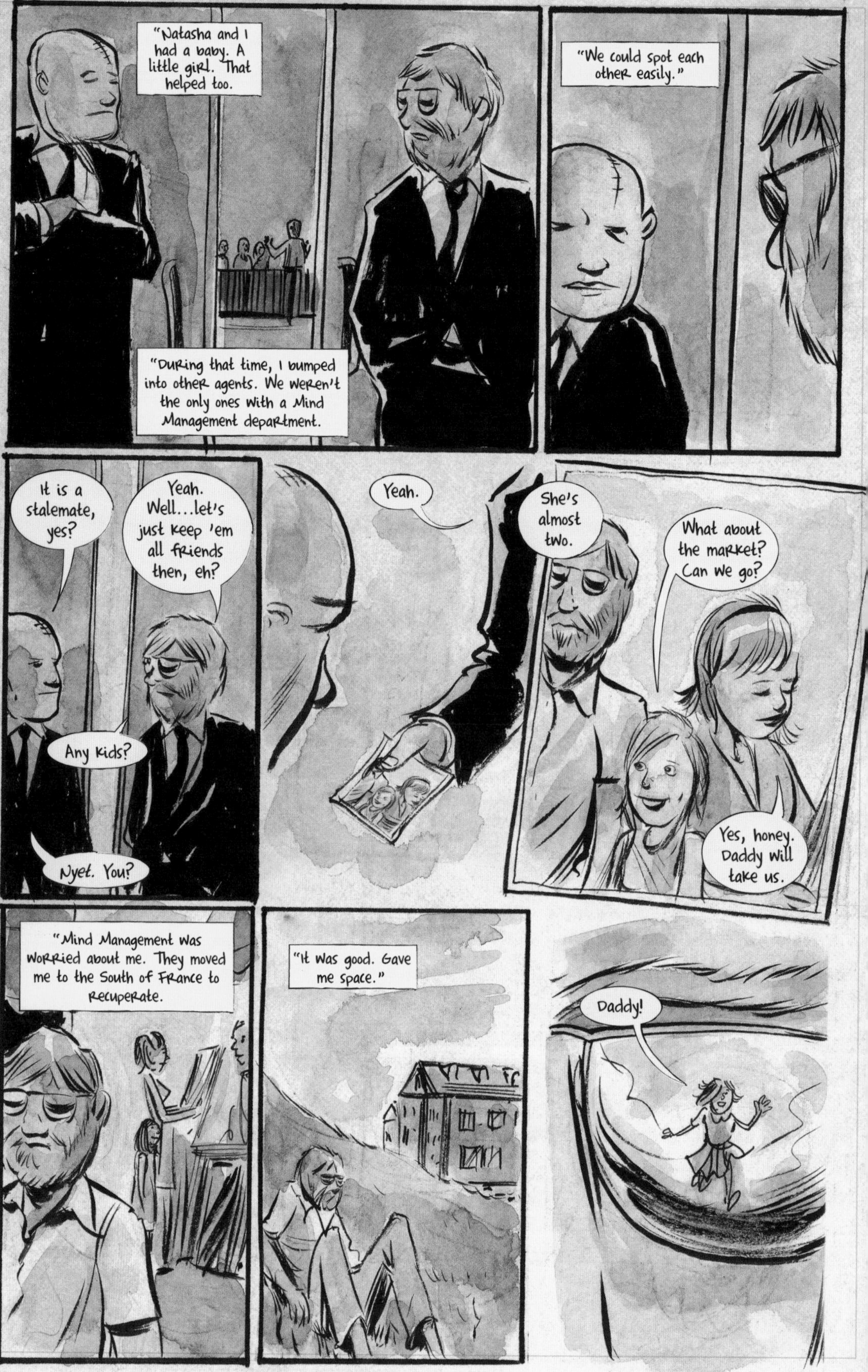
"Natasha and I had a baby. A little girl. That helped too.
"During that time, I bumped into other agents. We weren't the only ones with a Mind Management department.
"We could spot each other easily."
It is a stalemate, yes?
Yeah. Well...let's just keep 'em all friends then, eh?
Any kids?
Nyet. You?
Yeah.
She's almost two.
What about the market? Can we go?
Yes, honey. Daddy will take us.
"Mind Management was worried about me. They moved me to the South of France to recuperate.
"It was good. Gave me space."
Daddy!

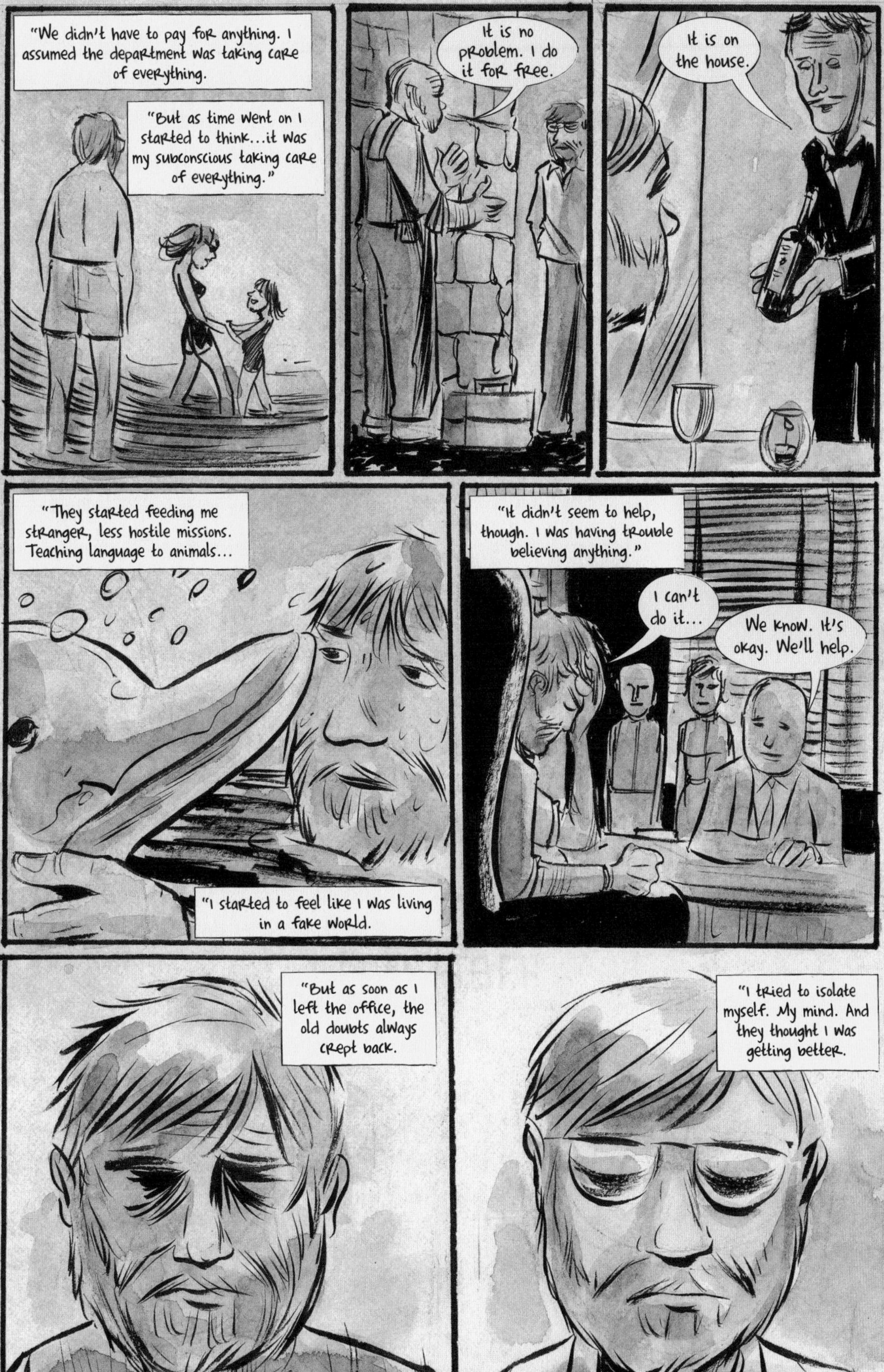
"We didn't have to pay for anything. I assumed the department was taking care of everything.
"But as time went on I started to think...it was my subconscious taking care of everything."
It is no problem. I do it for free.
It is on the house.
"They started feeding me stranger, less hostile missions. Teaching language to animals...
"I started to feel like I was living in a fake world.
"It didn't seem to help, though. I was having trouble believing anything."
I can't do it...
We know. It's okay. We'll help.
"But as soon as I left the office, the old doubts always crept back.
"I tried to isolate myself. My mind. And they thought I was getting better.

WHEN FILING REPORT ALL ESSENTIAL DETAILS MUST FALL WITHIN THIS SOLID "LIVE AREA" BOX. THIS IS THE BORDER FOR A STANDARD, NON-BLEED FIELD REPORT

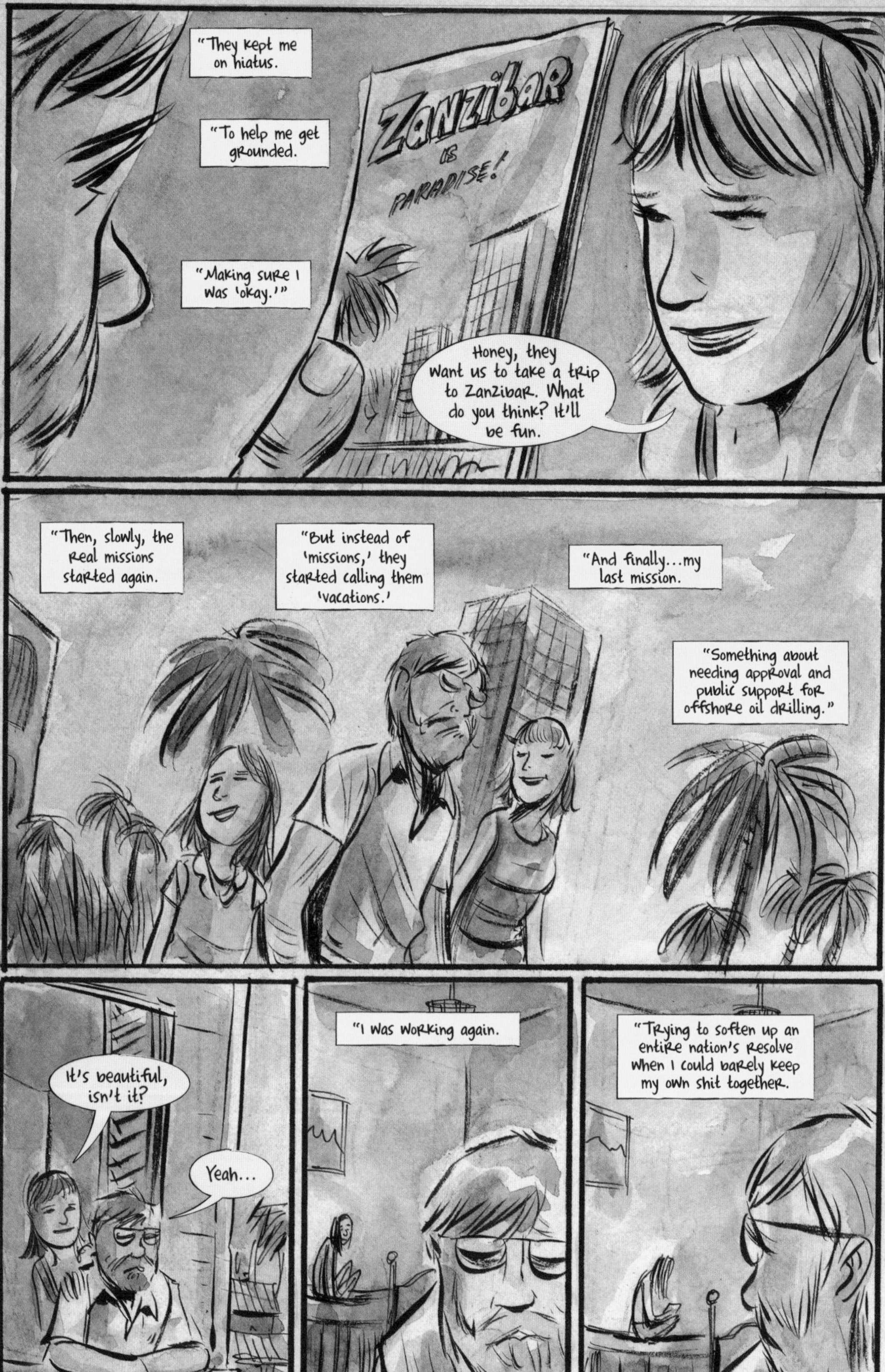
"They kept me on hiatus.
"To help me get grounded.
ZANZIBAR IS PARADISE!
"Making sure I was 'okay.'"
Honey, they want us to take a trip to Zanzibar. What do you think? It'll be fun.
"Then, slowly, the real missions started again.
"But instead of 'missions,' they started calling them 'vacations.'
"And finally...my last mission.
"Something about needing approval and public support for offshore oil drilling."
It's beautiful, isn't it?
Yeah...
"I was working again.
"Trying to soften up an entire nation's resolve when I could barely keep my own shit together.

MIND MGMT FIELD GUIDE. 5.4. Only approved support agents are allowed to accompany primary agents in the field duringBUT I THINK THIS TIME IT WILL WORK

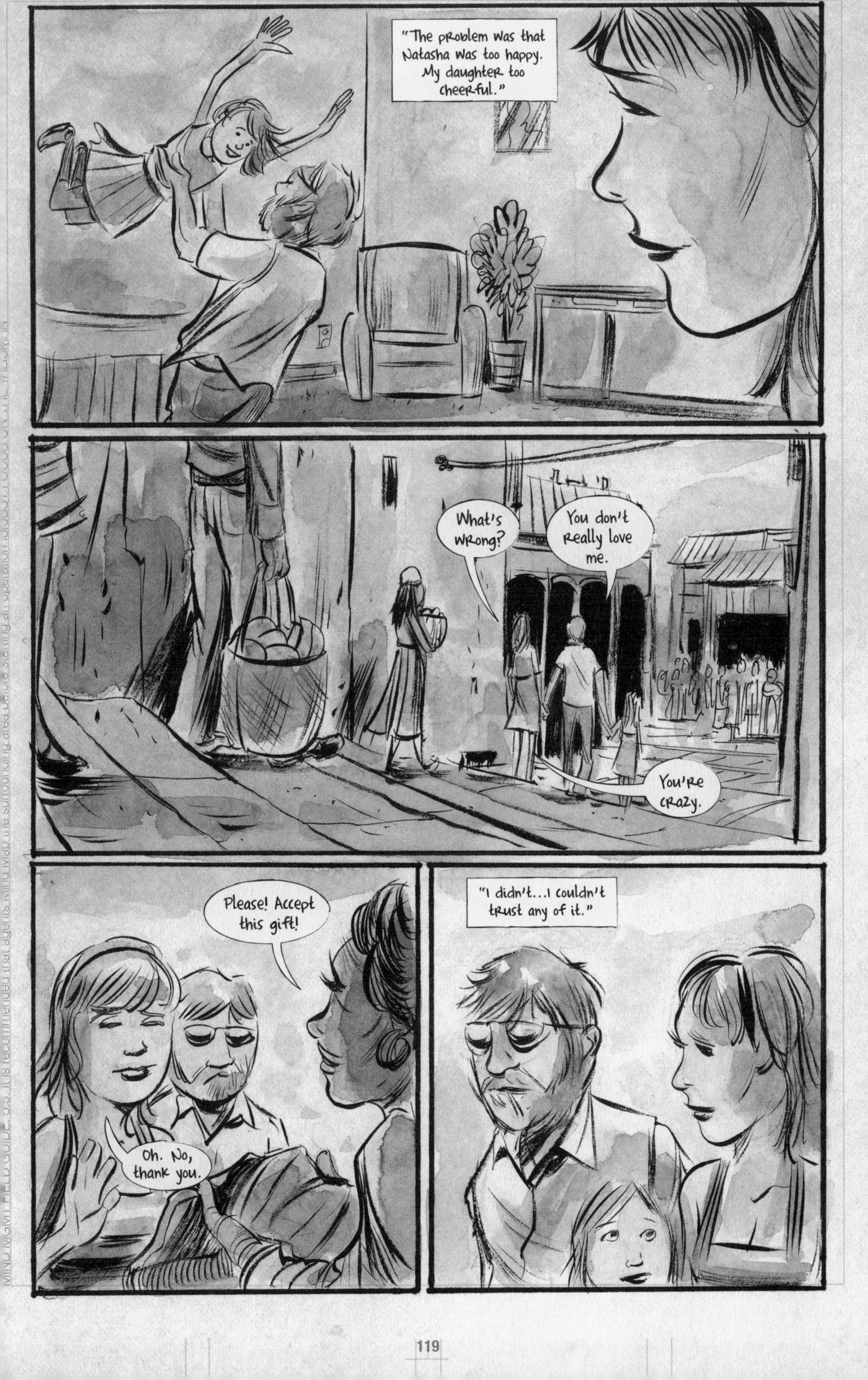
"The problem was that Natasha was too happy. My daughter too cheerful."
What's wrong?
You don't really love me.
You're crazy.
Please! Accept this gift!
Oh. No, thank you.
"I didn't...I couldn't trust any of it."

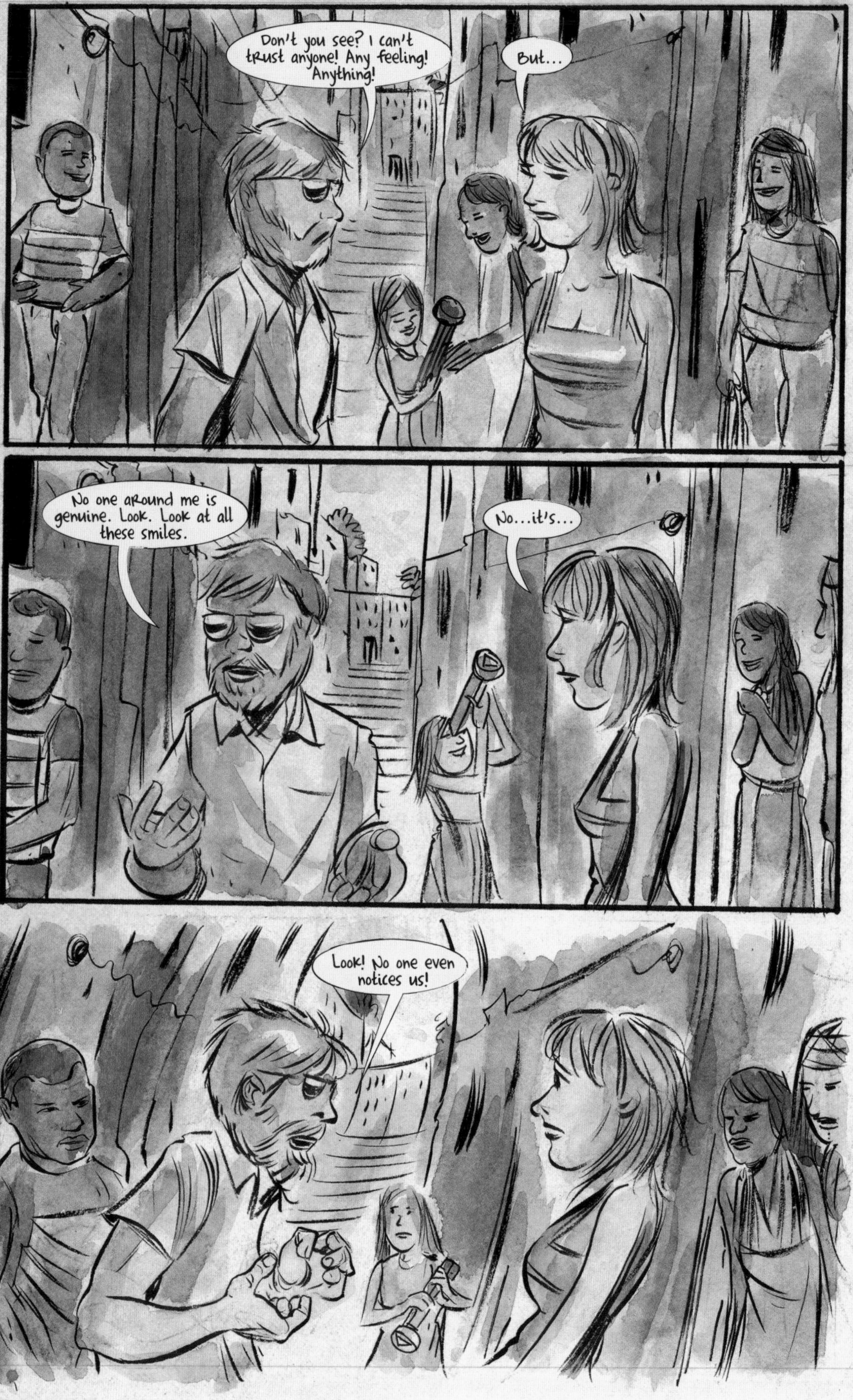
Don't you see? I can't trust anyone! Any feeling! Anything!
But...
No one around me is genuine. Look. Look at all these smiles.
No...it's...
Look! No one even notices us!

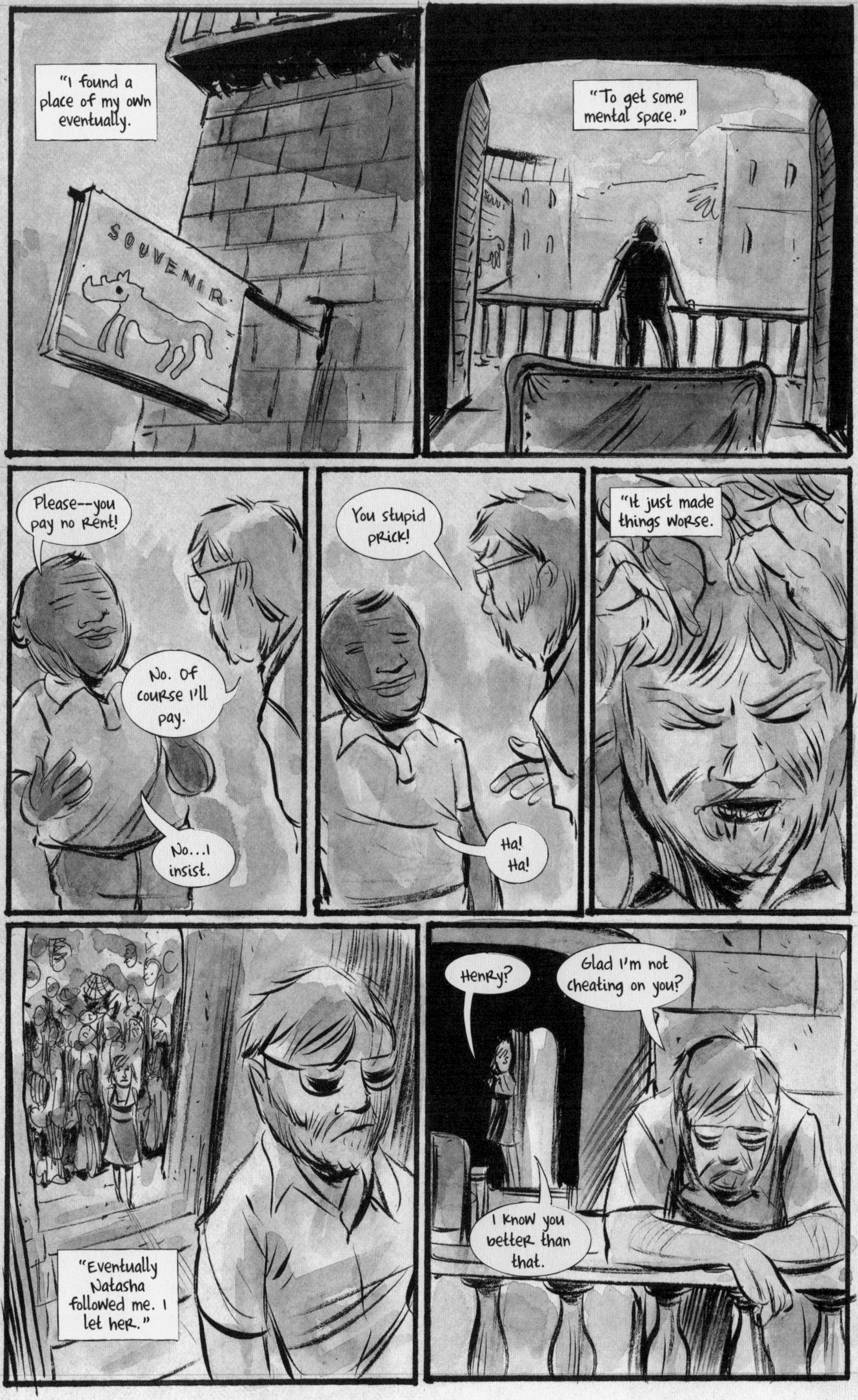
"I found a place of my own eventually.
SOUVENIR
"To get some mental space."
Please--you pay no Rent!
No. Of course I'll pay.
No...I insist.
You stupid prick!
Ha! Ha!
"It just made things worse.
"Eventually Natasha followed me. I let her."
Henry?
Glad I'm not cheating on you?
I know you better than that.

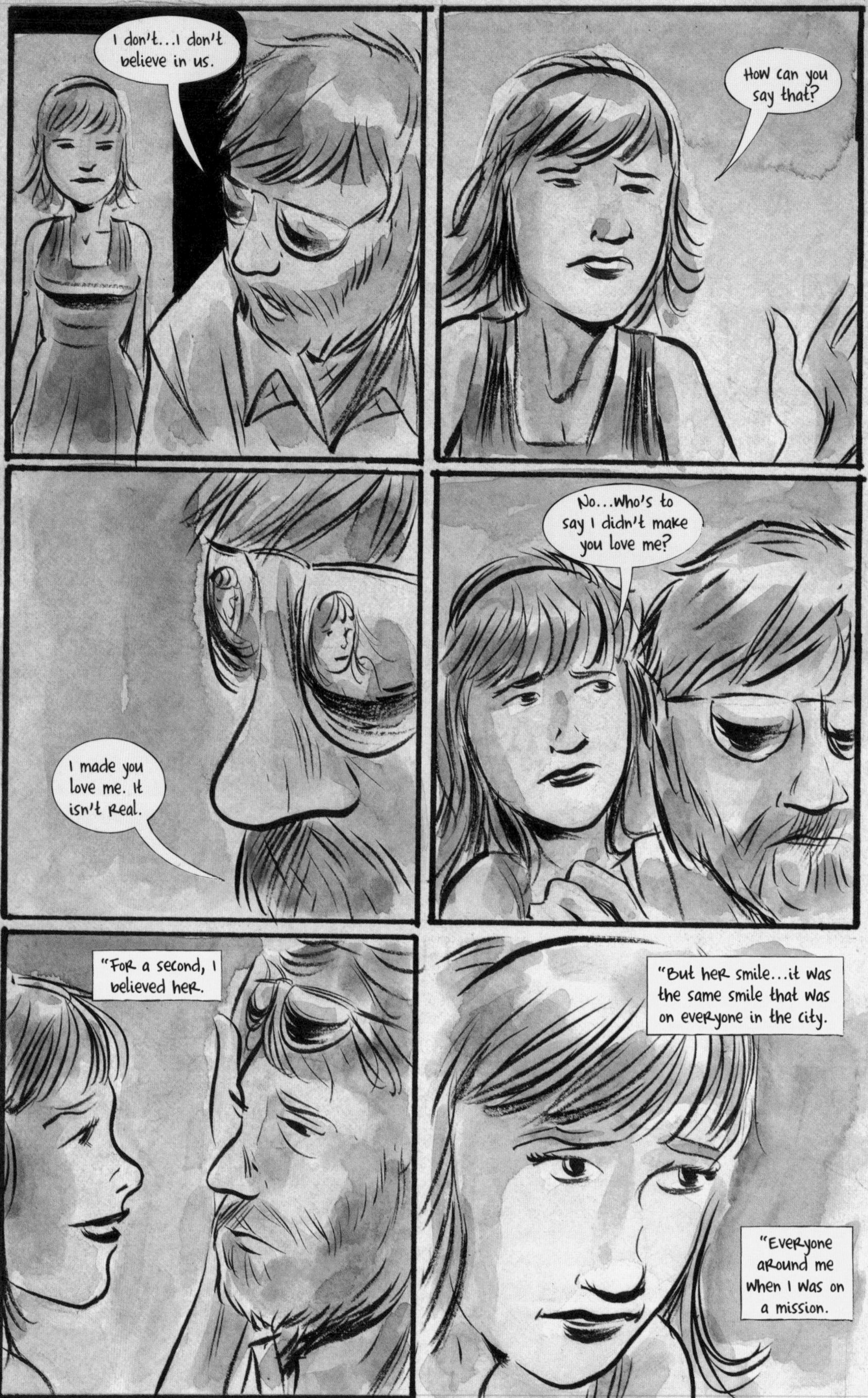
I don't...I don't believe in us.
How can you say that?
I made you love me. It isn't real.
No...Who's to say I didn't make you love me?
"For a second, I believed her.
"But her smile...it was the same smile that was on everyone in the city.
"Everyone around me when I was on a mission.

MIND MGMT FIELD GUIDE. 5.8. Backup agents will be employed to provide cover, support, andKNOW THAT YOU'VE BEEN HERE BEFORE

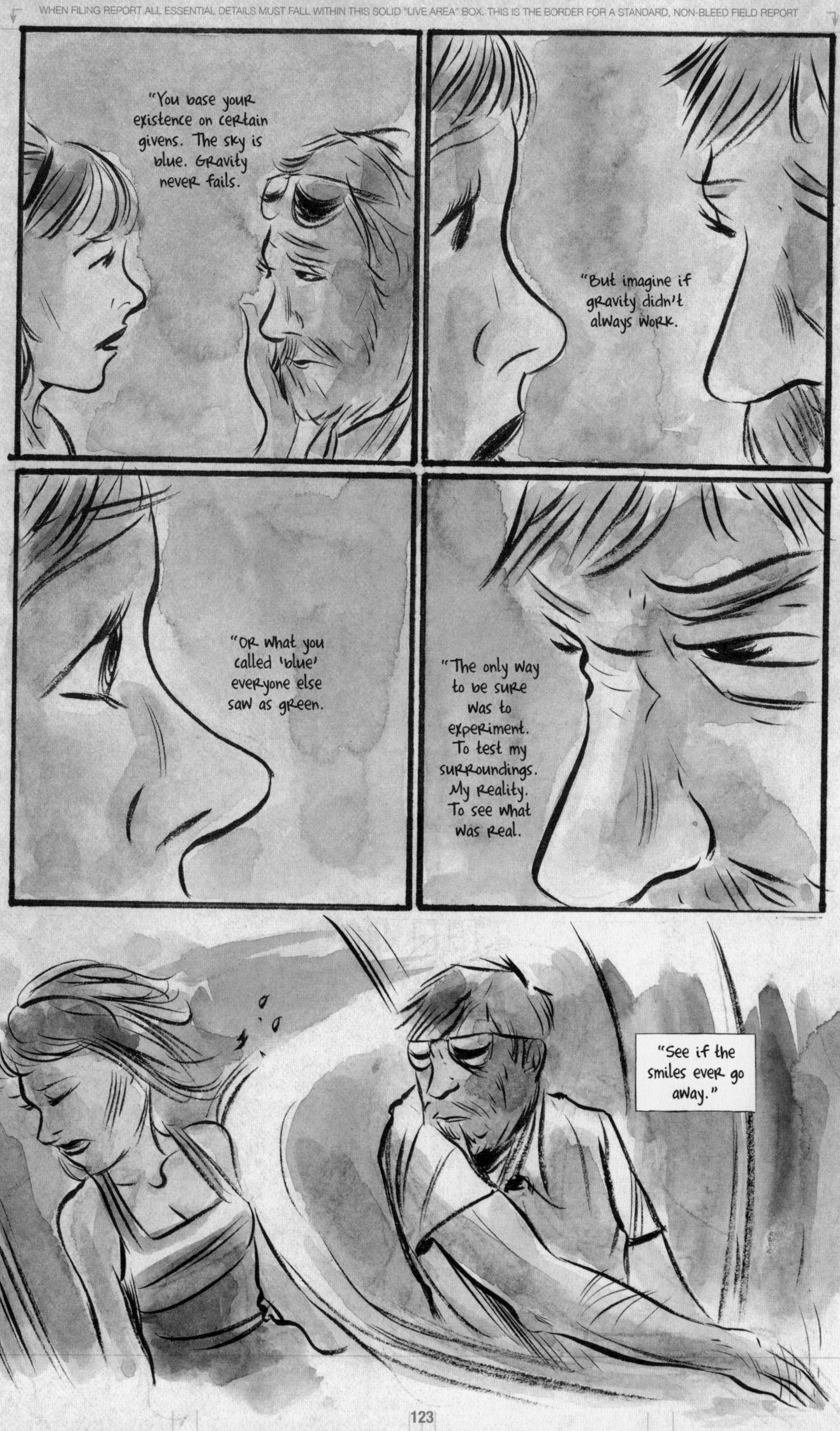
WHEN FILING REPORT ALL ESSENTIAL DETAILS MUST FALL WITHIN THIS SOLID "LIVE AREA" BOX. THIS IS THE BORDER FOR A STANDARD, NON-BLEED FIELD REPORT
"You base your existence on certain givens. The sky is blue. Gravity never fails.
"But imagine if gravity didn't always work.
"Or what you called 'blue' everyone else saw as green.
"The only way to be sure was to experiment. To test my surroundings. My reality. To see what was real.
"See if the smiles ever go away."

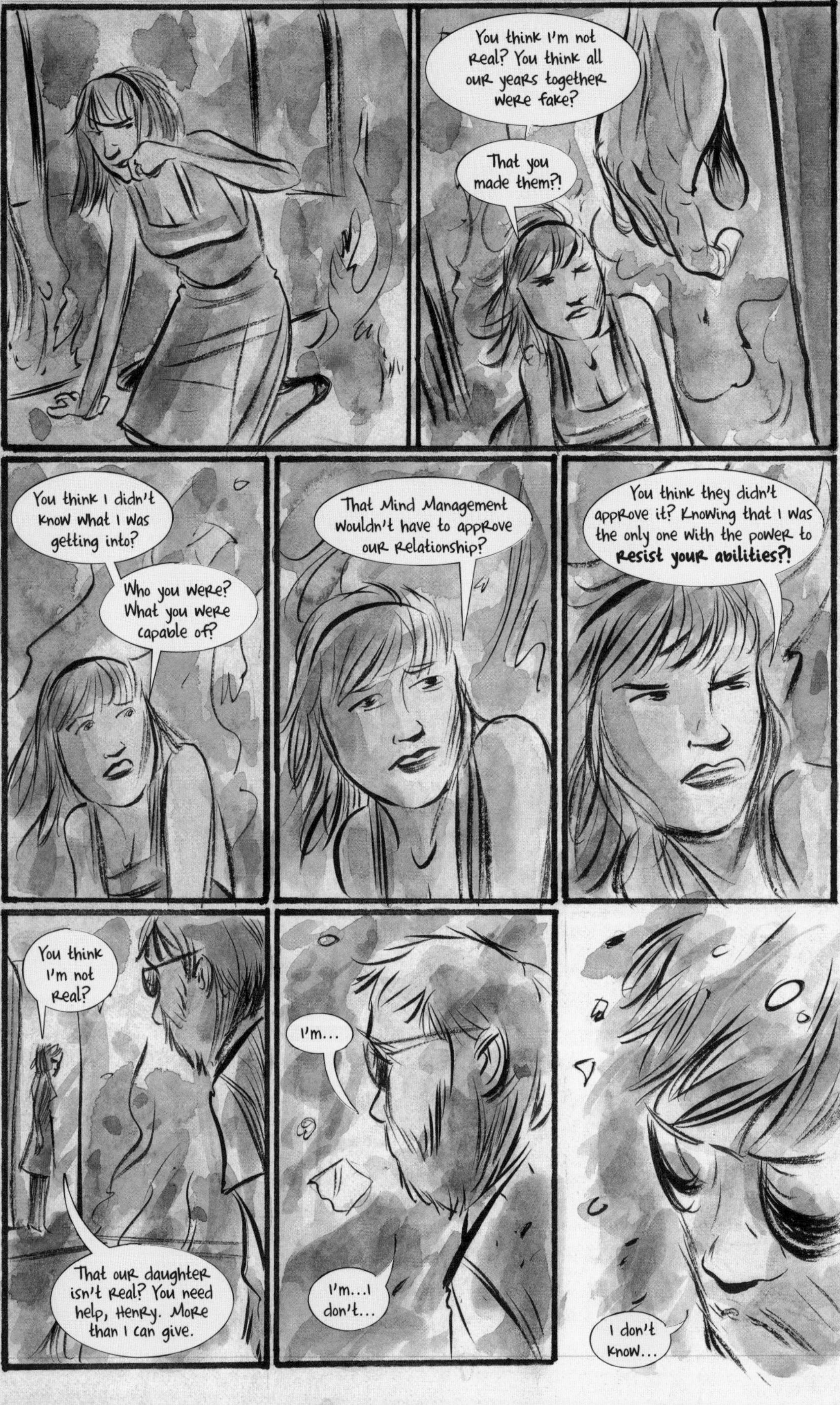
You think I'm not real? You think all our years together were fake?
That you made them?!
You think I didn't know what I was getting into?
Who you were? What you were capable of?
That Mind Management wouldn't have to approve our relationship?
You think they didn't approve it? Knowing that I was the only one with the power to **resist your abilities?!**
You think I'm not real?
That our daughter isn't real? You need help, Henry. More than I can give.
I'm...
I'm...I don't...
I don't know...

MIND MGMT FIELD GUIDE. 5.10. When a physical confrontation is unavoidable, the use of Mental Noise to provide distraction is encouragedIT GETS EASIER EVERY TIME

WHEN FILING REPORT ALL ESSENTIAL DETAILS MUST FALL WITHIN THIS SOLID "LIVE AREA" BOX. THIS IS THE BORDER FOR A STANDARD, NON-BLEED FIELD REPORT

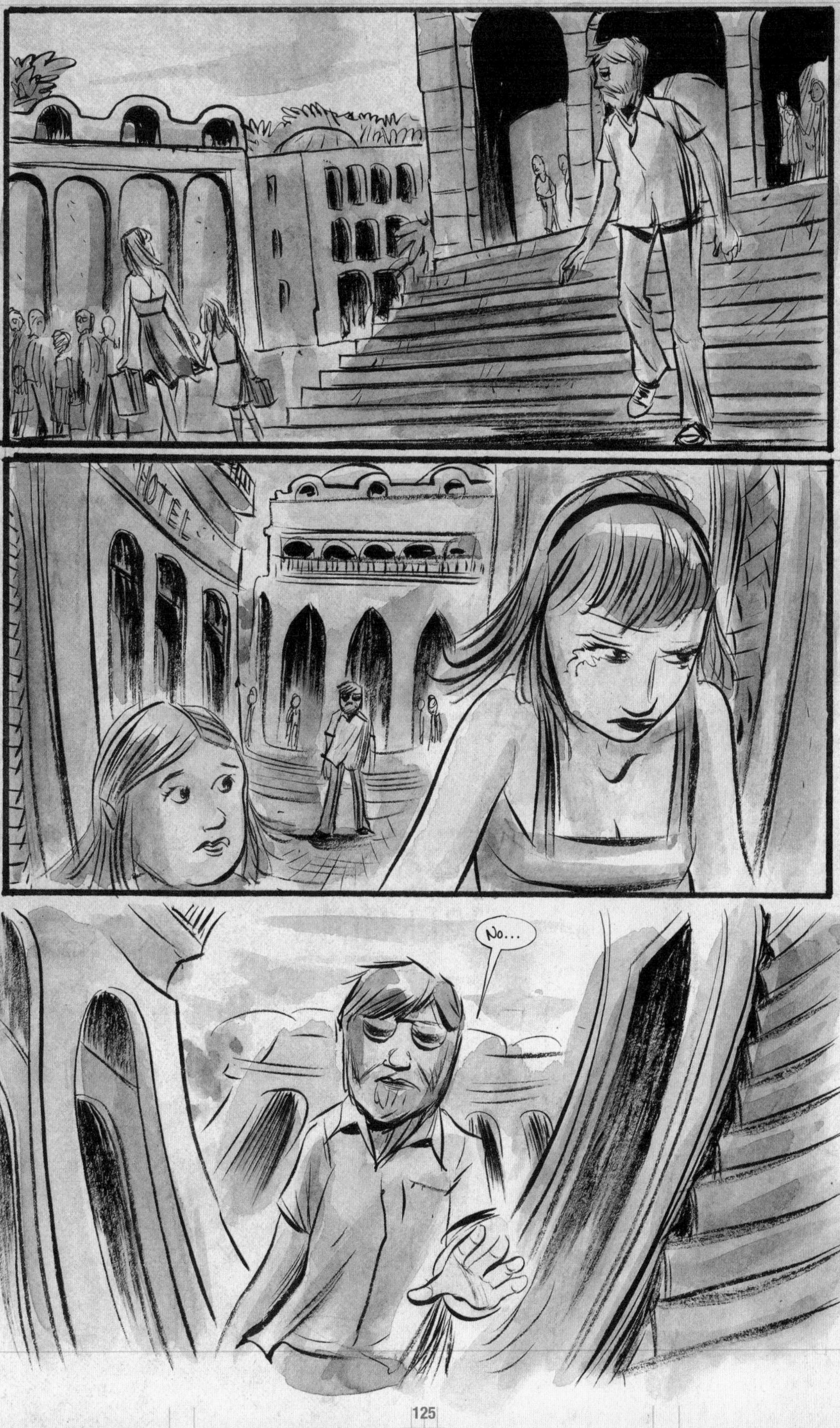

No...

MIND MGMT FIELD GUIDE. 5.11: However, in all cases, retreat and extraction is usually the best option unless YOU'RE WONDERING WHO I AM

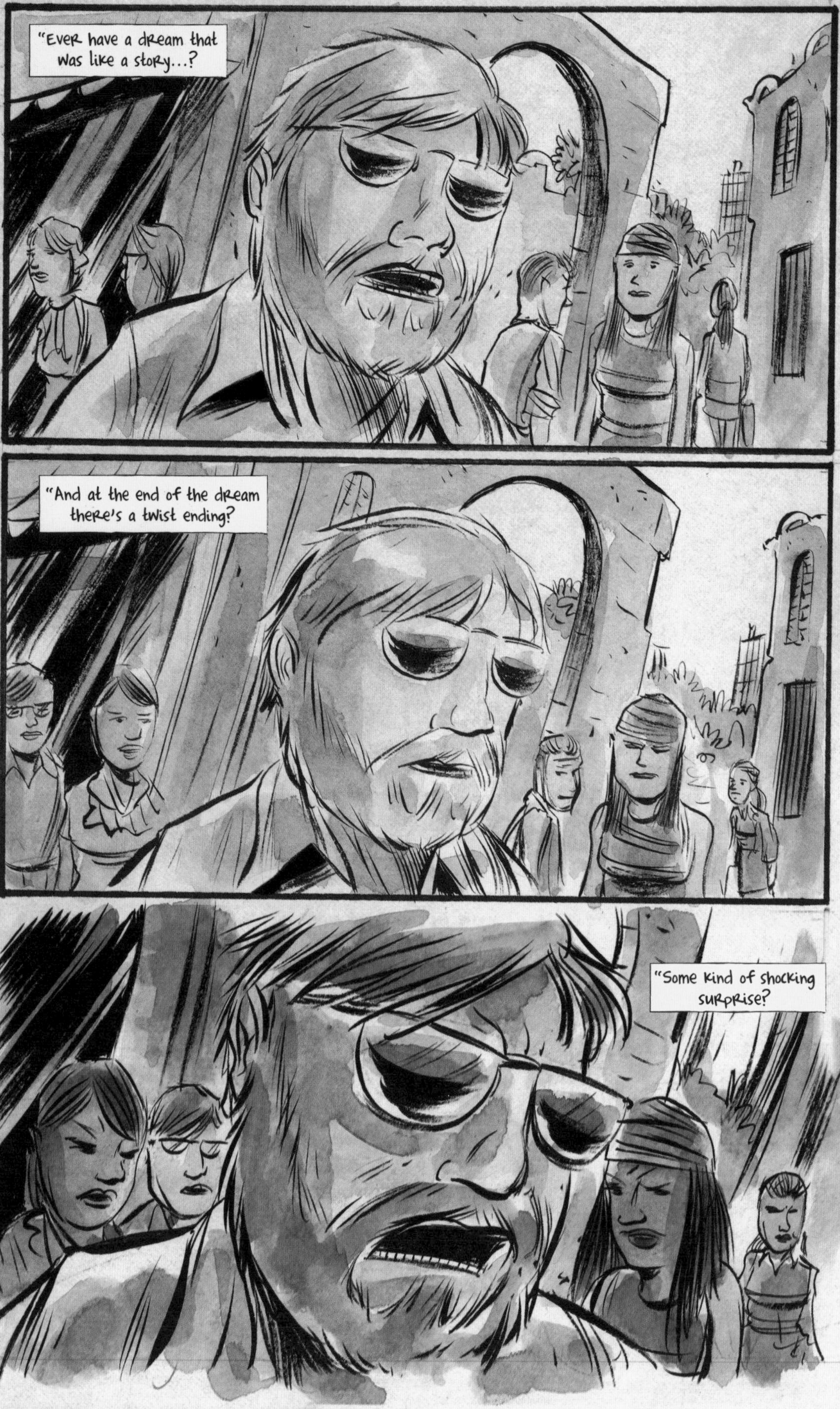
"Ever have a dream that was like a story...?
"And at the end of the dream there's a twist ending?
"Some kind of shocking surprise?

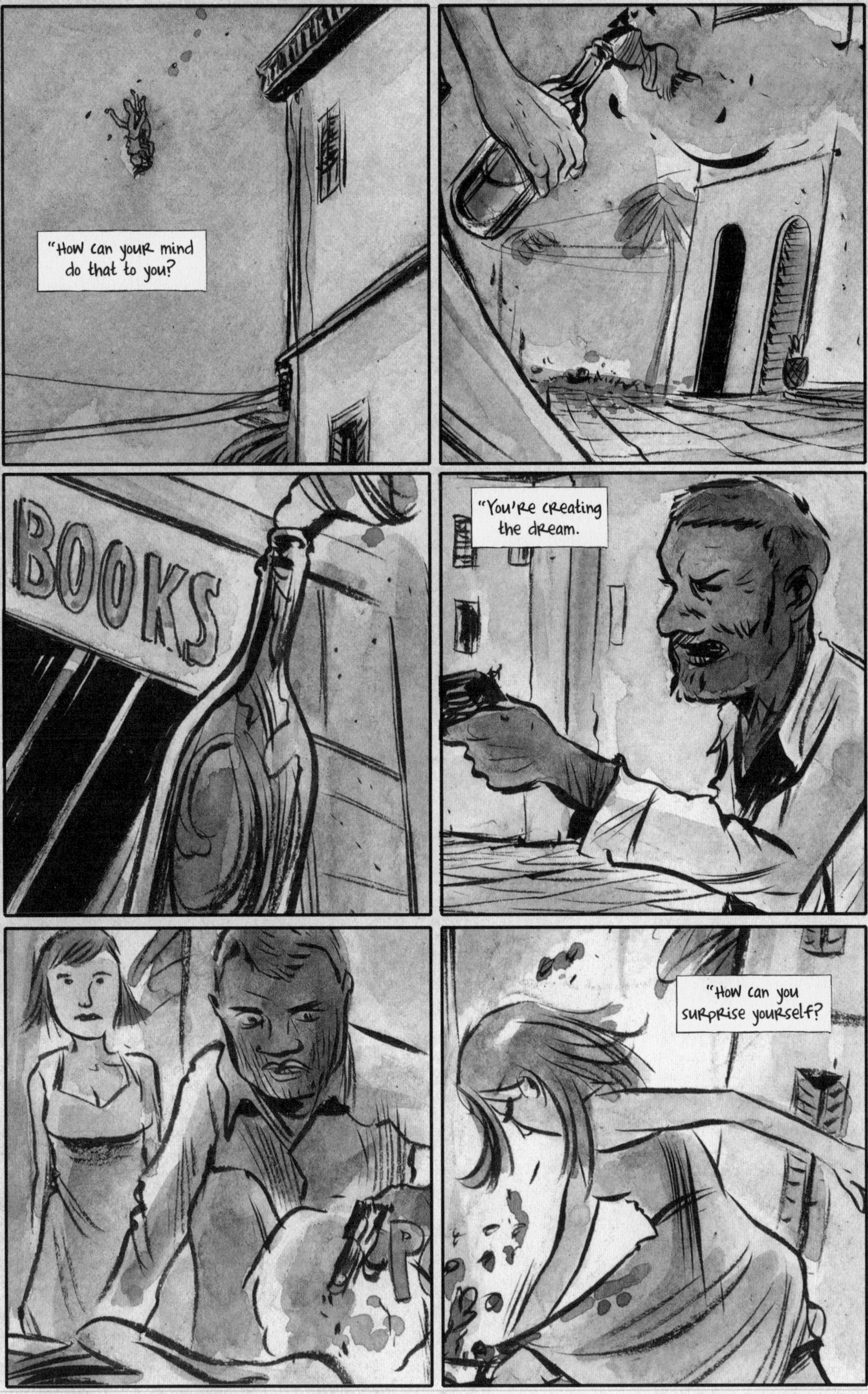
"How can your mind do that to you?
BOOKS
"You're creating the dream.
"How can you surprise yourself?

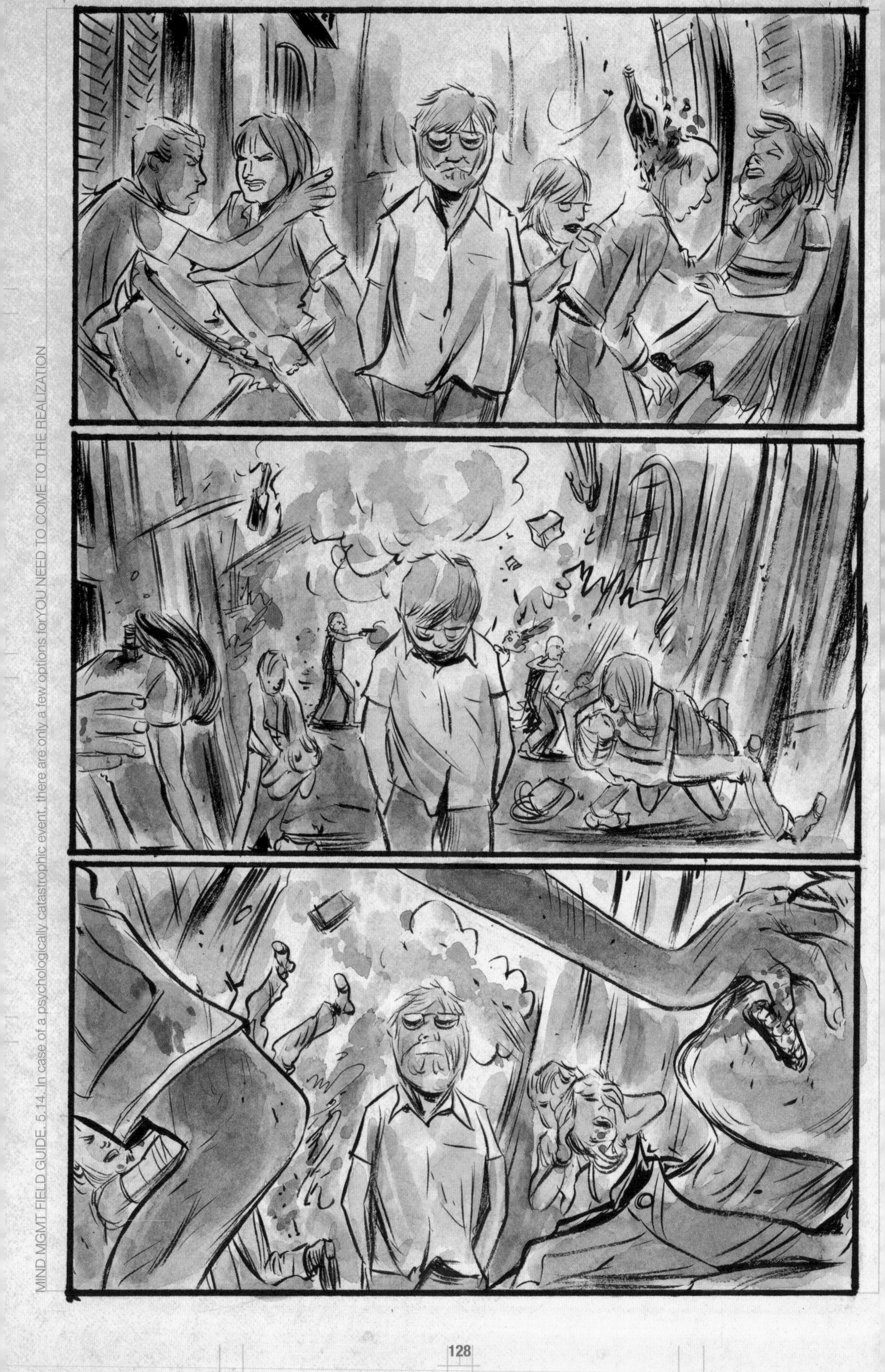

MIND MGMT FIELD GUIDE. 5.14. In case of a psychologically catastrophic event, there are only a few options forYOU NEED TO COME TO THE REALIZATION

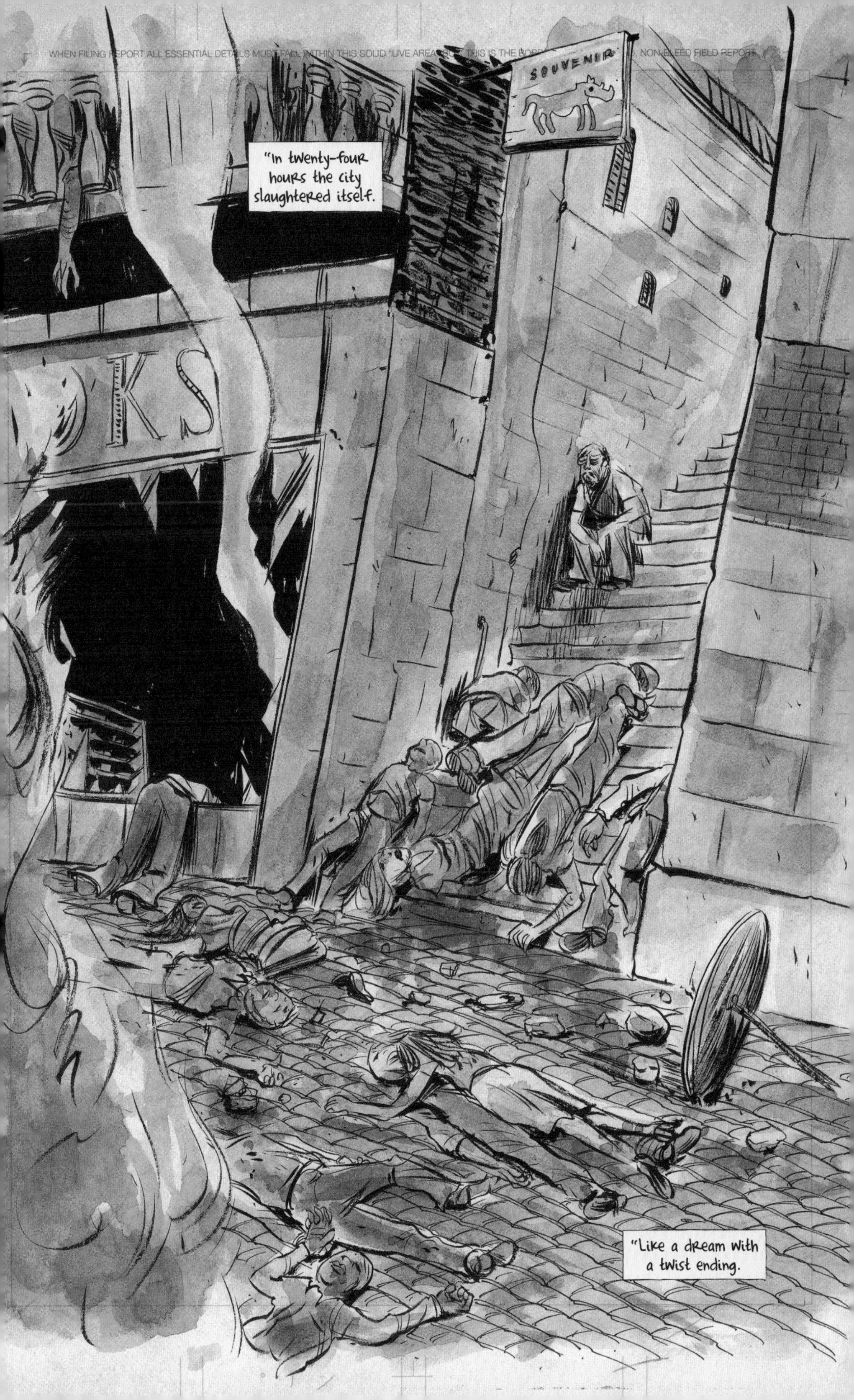
SOUVENIR
"In twenty-four hours the city slaughtered itself.
"Like a dream with a twist ending.

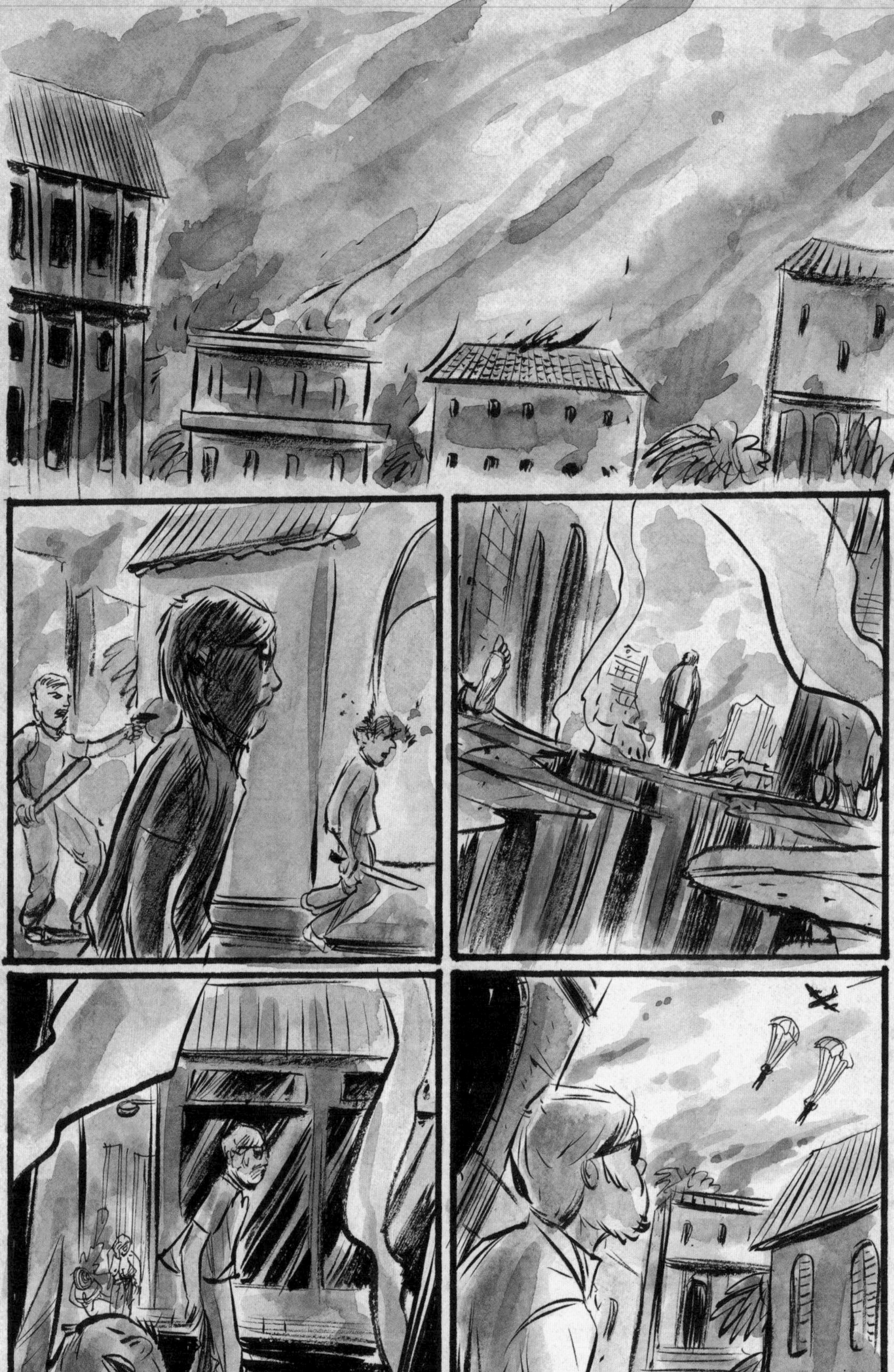

MIND MGMT FIELD GUIDE. 5.16. When escape is not an option, Cerebralflage is recommended to successfully avoid discovery in ON YOUR OWN

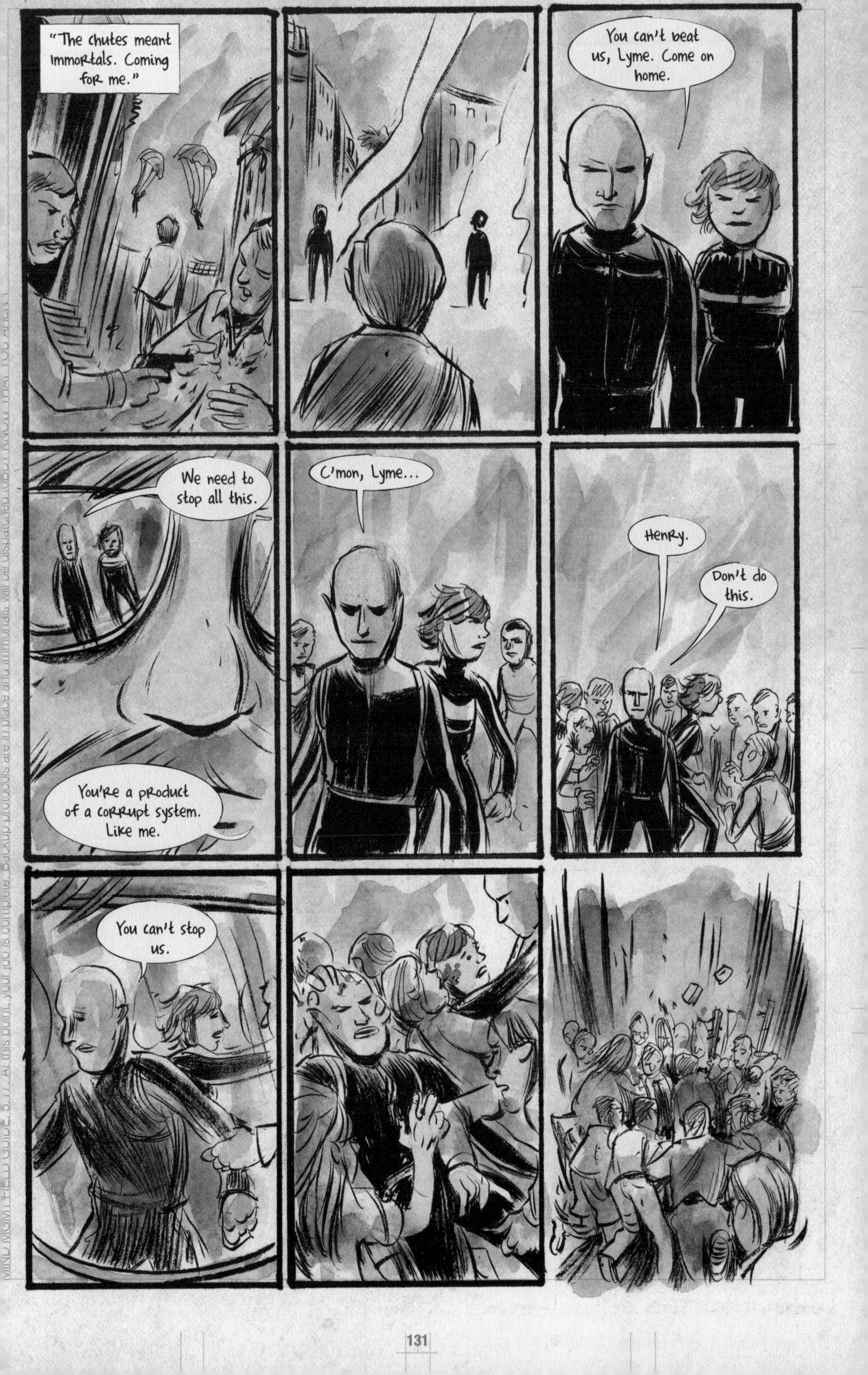
"The chutes meant Immortals. Coming for me."
You can't beat us, Lyme. Come on home.
We need to stop all this.
You're a product of a corrupt system. Like me.
C'mon, Lyme...
Henry.
Don't do this.
You can't stop us.

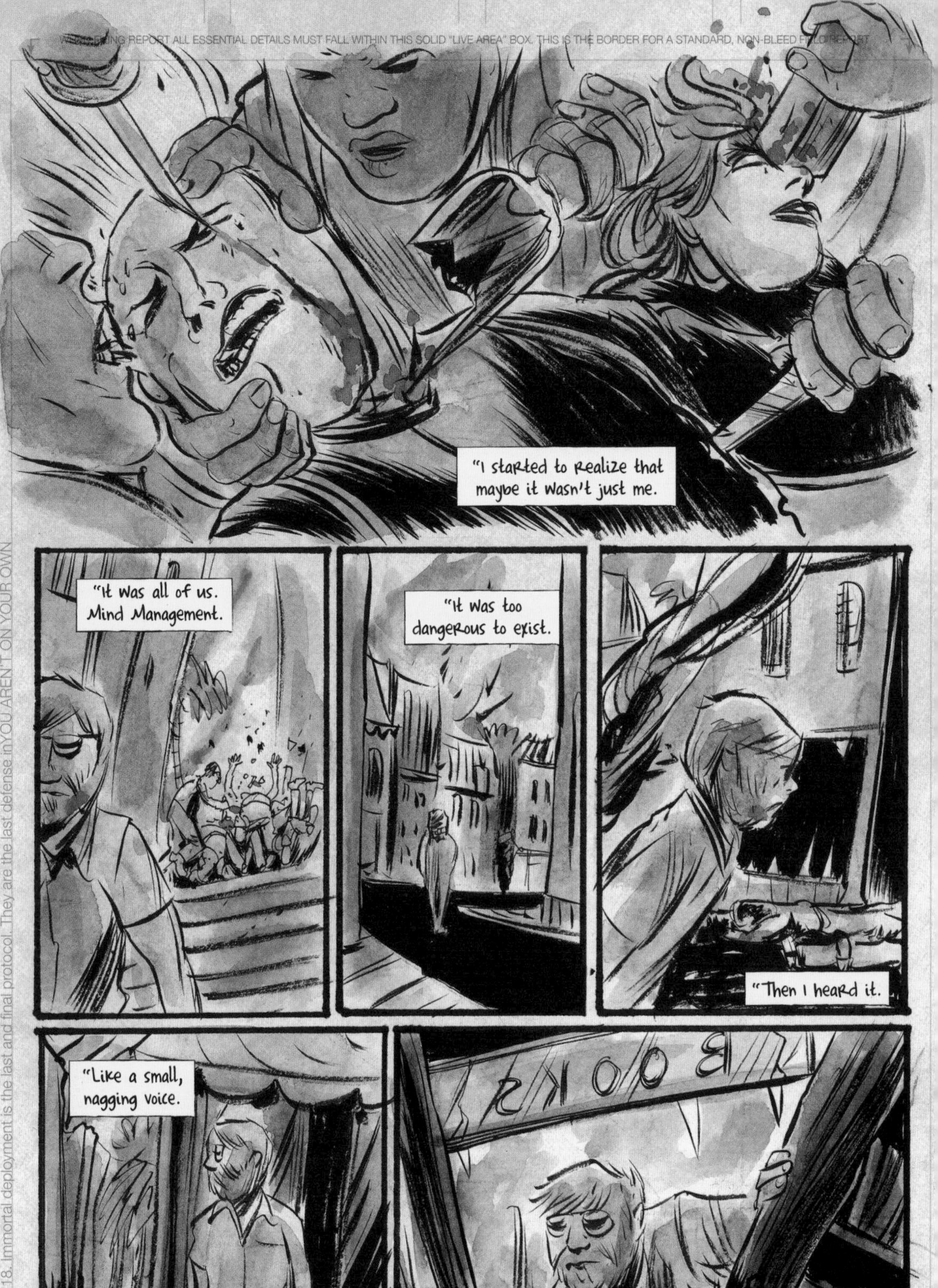
REPORT ALL ESSENTIAL DETAILS MUST FALL WITHIN THIS SOLID "LIVE AREA" BOX. THIS IS THE BORDER FOR A STANDARD, NON-BLEED FIELD REPORT
"I started to realize that maybe it wasn't just me.
"It was all of us. Mind Management.
"It was too dangerous to exist.
"Then I heard it.
"Like a small, nagging voice.
BOOKS
"Telling me what I needed to do."
MIND MGMT FIELD GUIDE. 5.18. Immortal deployment is the last and final protocol. They are the last defense inYOU AREN'T ON YOUR OWN

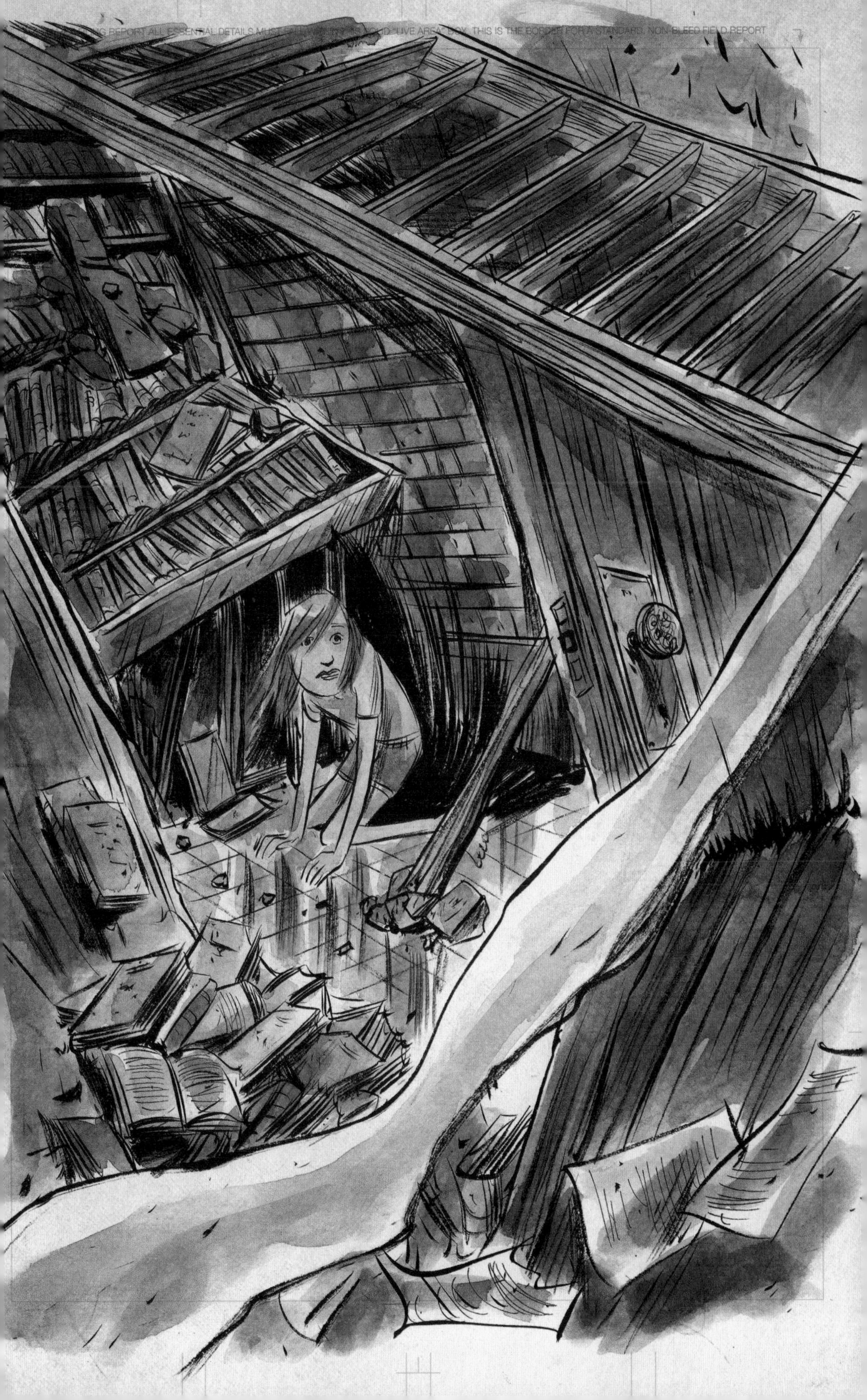

WHEN FILING REPORT ALL ESSENTIAL DETAILS MUST FALL WITHIN THIS SOLID "LIVE AREA" BOX. THIS IS THE BORDER FOR A STANDARD, NON-BLEED FIELD REPORT

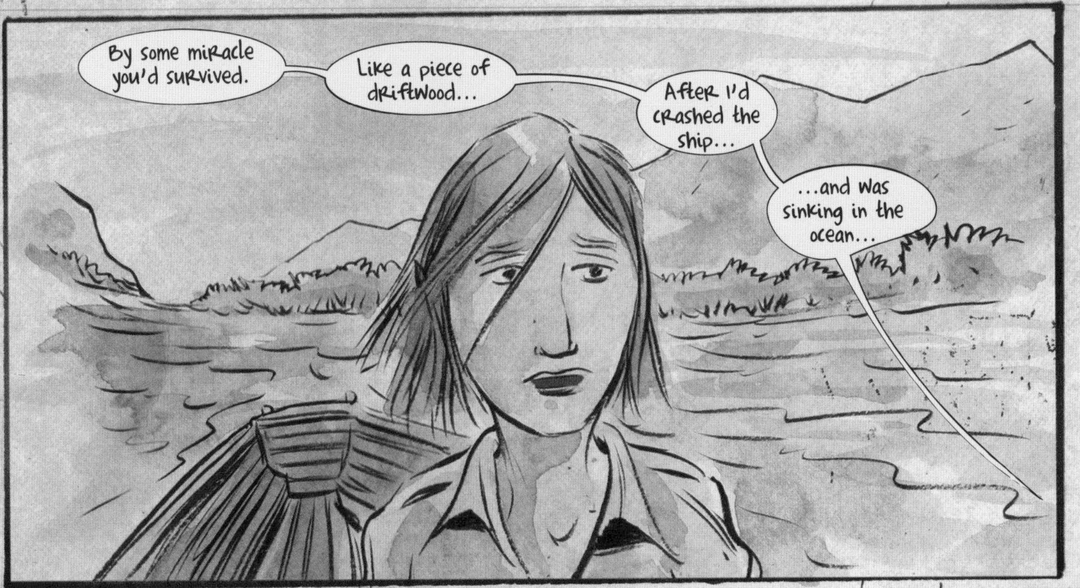

By some miracle you'd survived.
Like a piece of driftwood...
After I'd crashed the ship...
...and was sinking in the ocean...

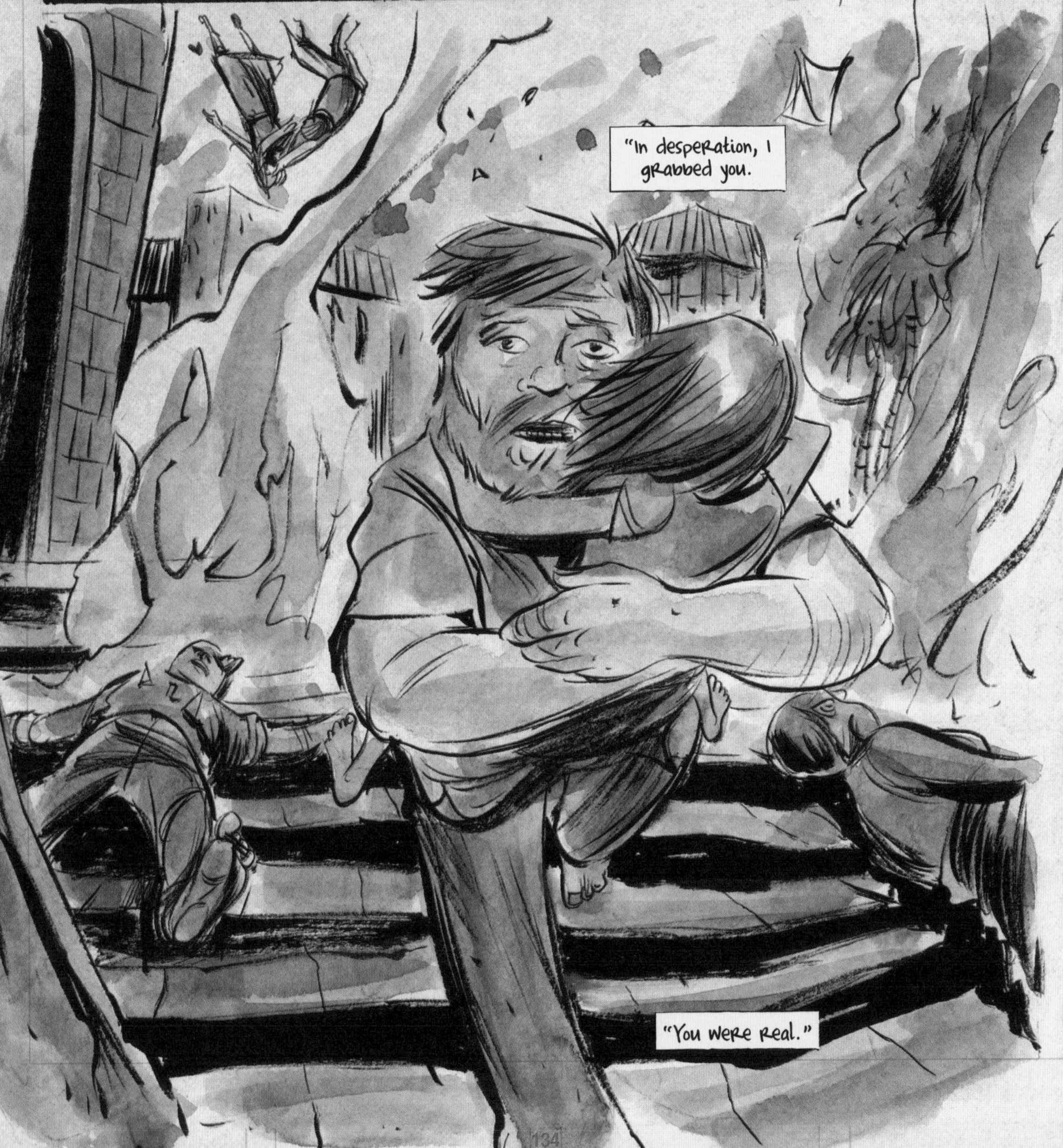

"In desperation, I grabbed you.
"You were real."

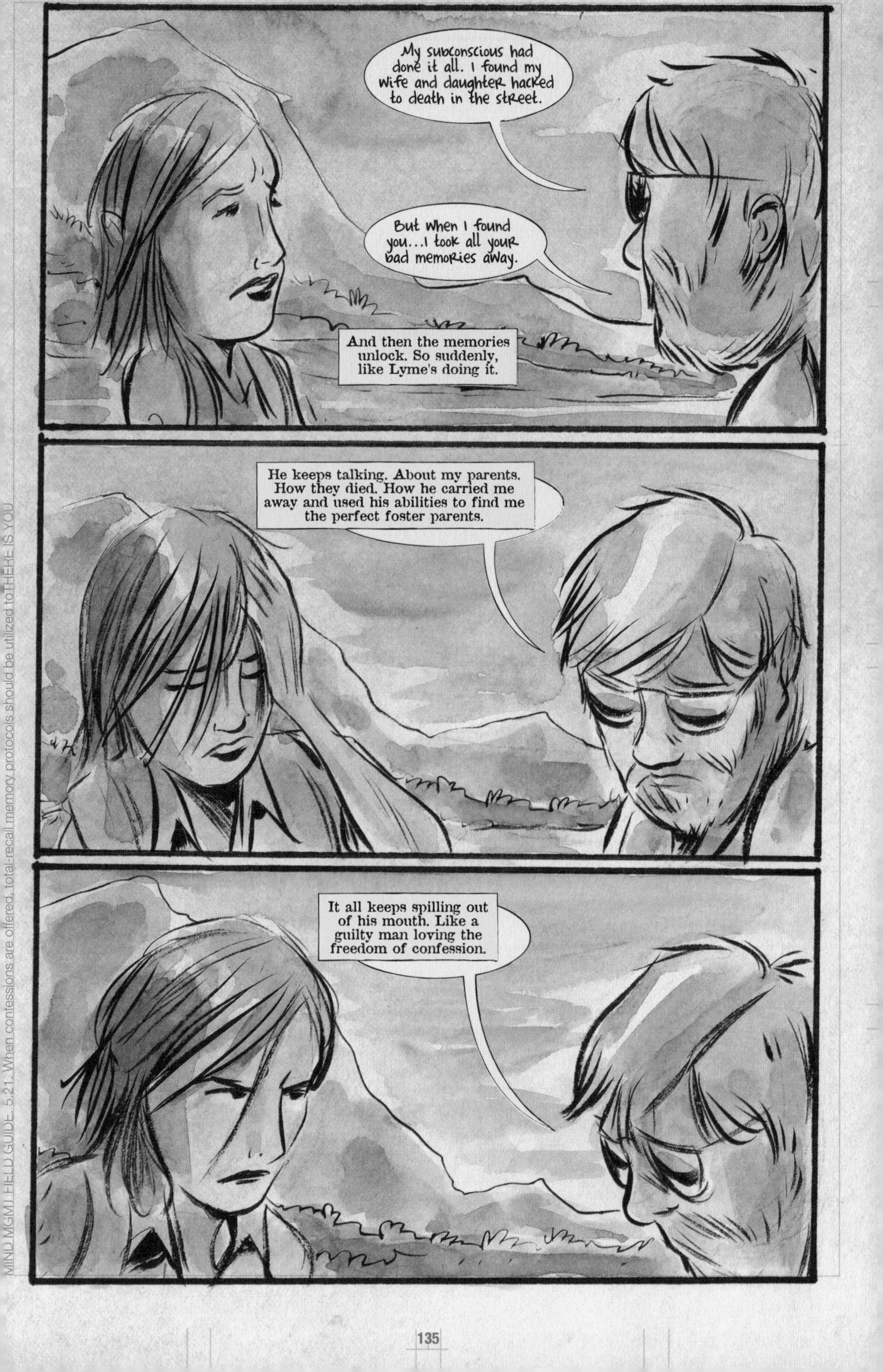
My subconscious had done it all. I found my wife and daughter hacked to death in the street.
But when I found you...I took all your bad memories away.
And then the memories unlock. So suddenly, like Lyme's doing it.
He keeps talking. About my parents. How they died. How he carried me away and used his abilities to find me the perfect foster parents.
It all keeps spilling out of his mouth. Like a guilty man loving the freedom of confession.

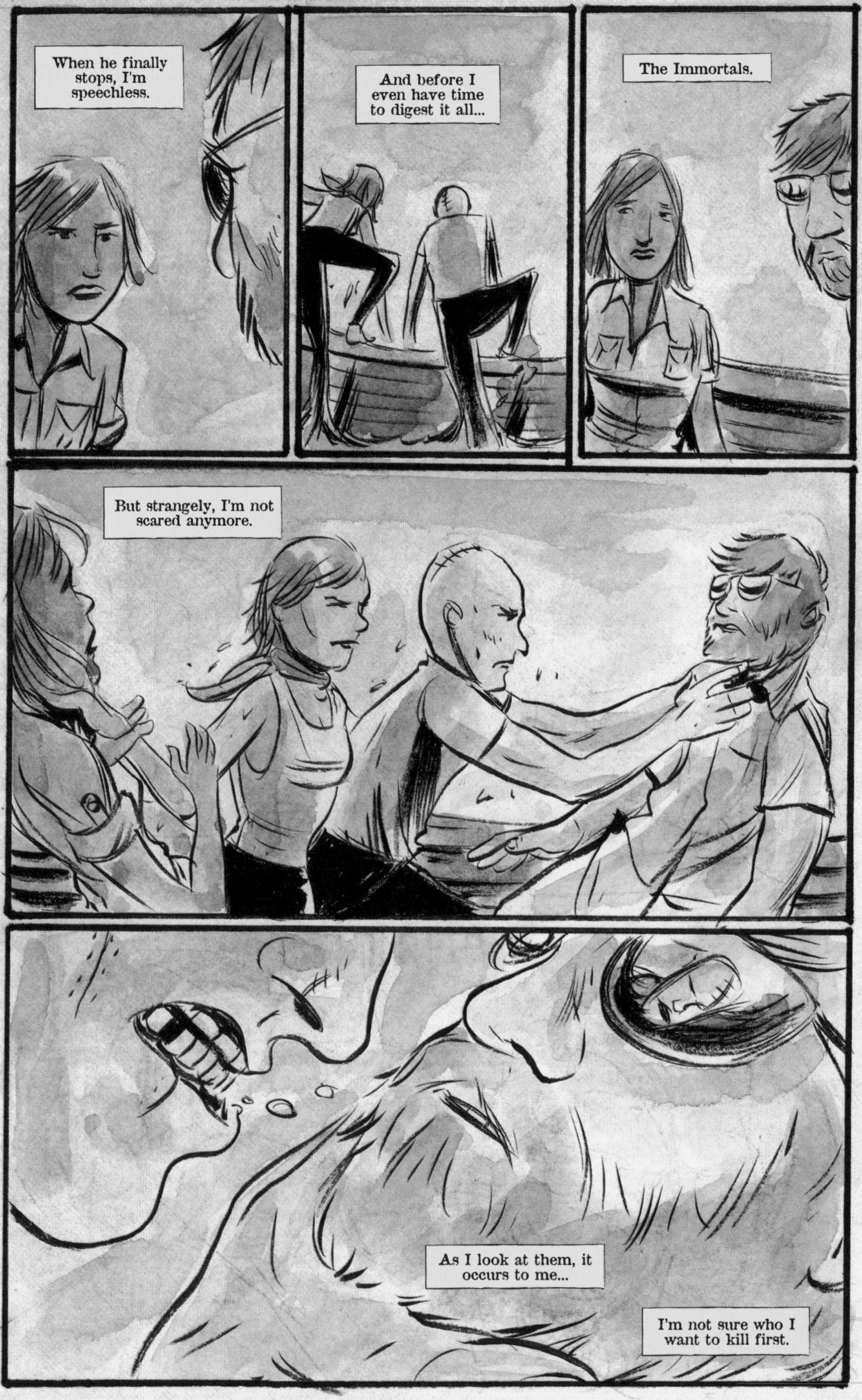
When he finally stops, I'm speechless.
And before I even have time to digest it all...
The Immortals.
But strangely, I'm not scared anymore.
As I look at them, it occurs to me...
I'm not sure who I want to kill first.

MIND MGMT FIELD GUIDE. 5.22. Confessions obtained in the field should never be trusted or acted upon until the veracity ofAND MORE OF YOU.

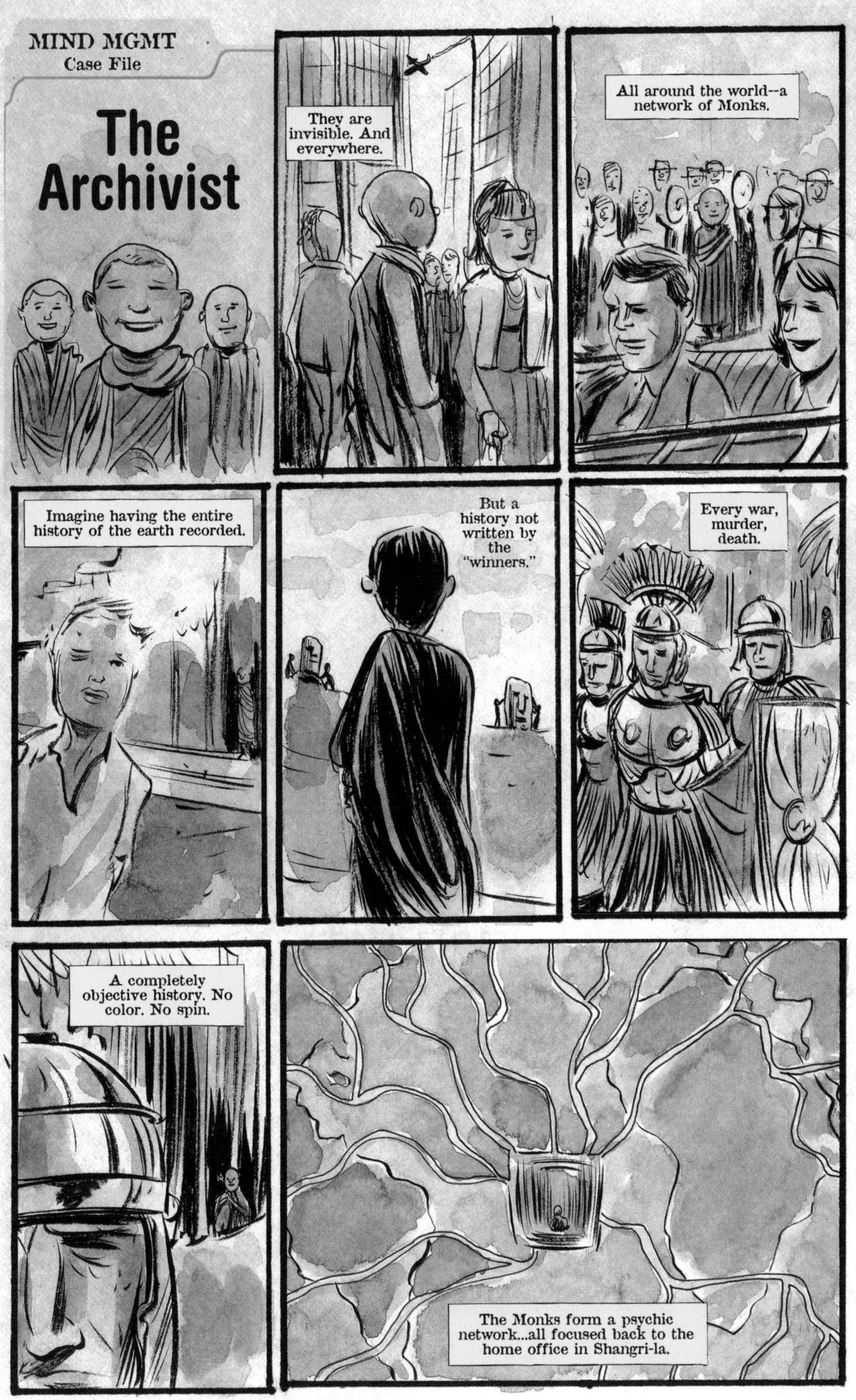
MIND MGMT
Case File
The Archivist
They are invisible. And everywhere.
All around the world--a network of Monks.
Imagine having the entire history of the earth recorded.
But a history not written by the "winners."
Every war, murder, death.
A completely objective history. No color. No spin.
The Monks form a psychic network...all focused back to the home office in Shangri-la.

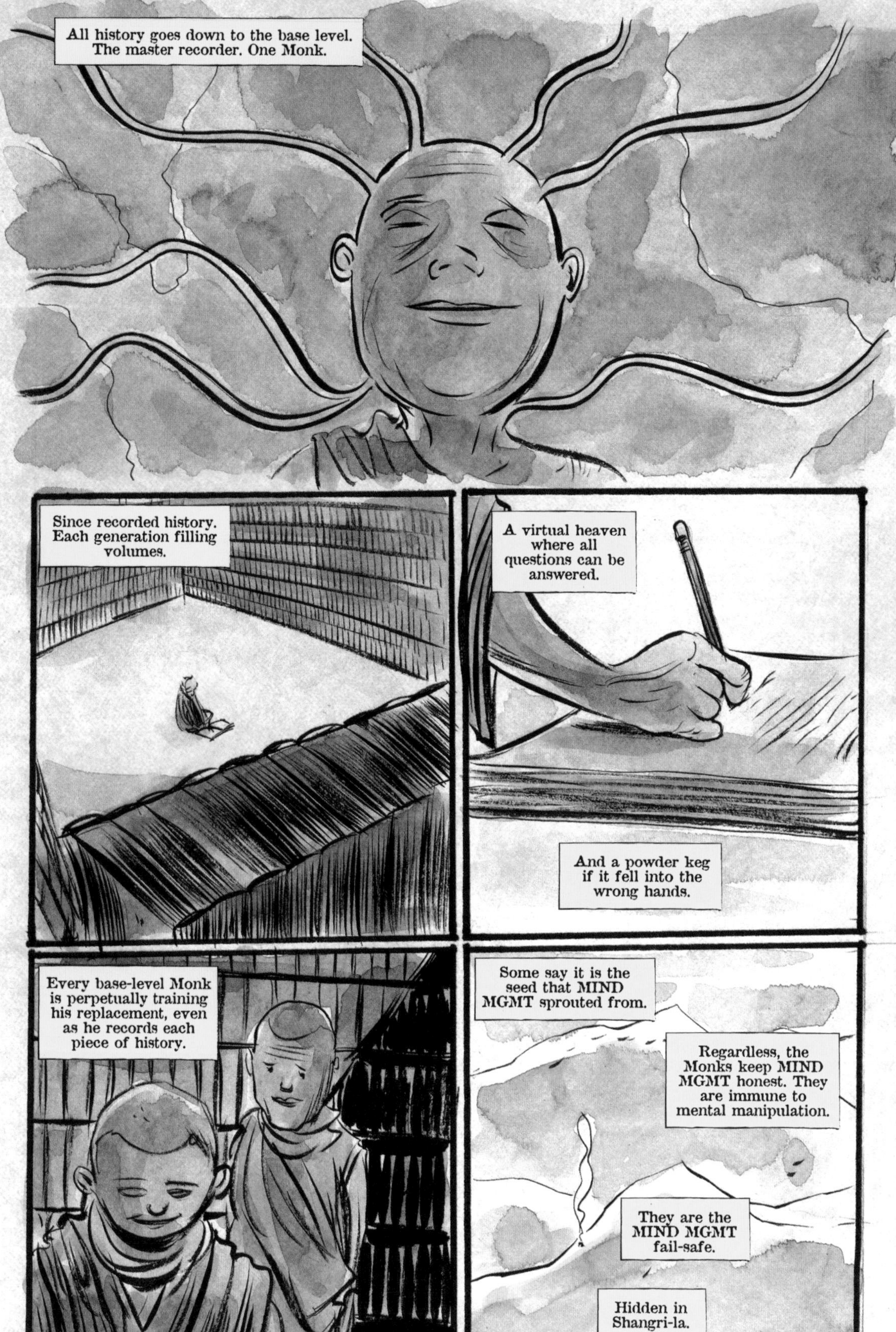
All history goes down to the base level. The master recorder. One Monk.
Since recorded history. Each generation filling volumes.
A virtual heaven where all questions can be answered.
And a powder keg if it fell into the wrong hands.
Every base-level Monk is perpetually training his replacement, even as he records each piece of history.
Some say it is the seed that MIND MGMT sprouted from.
Regardless, the Monks keep MIND MGMT honest. They are immune to mental manipulation.
They are the MIND MGMT fail-safe.
Hidden in Shangri-la.
End Mind Memo
Date Unknown

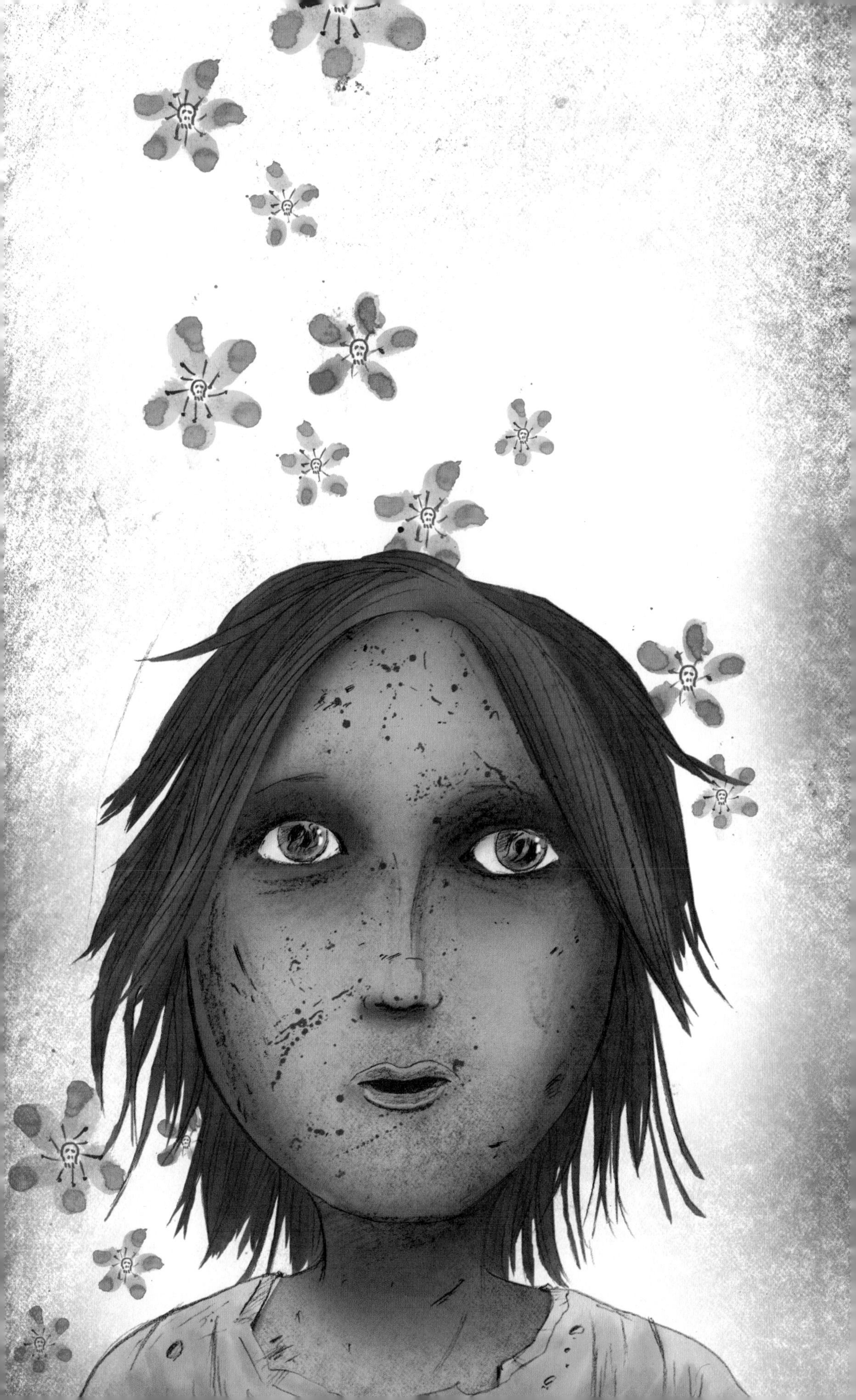

6

WHEN FILING REPORT ALL ESSENTIAL DETAILS MUST FALL WITHIN THIS SOLID "LIVE AREA" BOX. THIS IS THE BORDER FOR A STANDARD, NON-BLEED FIELD REPORT

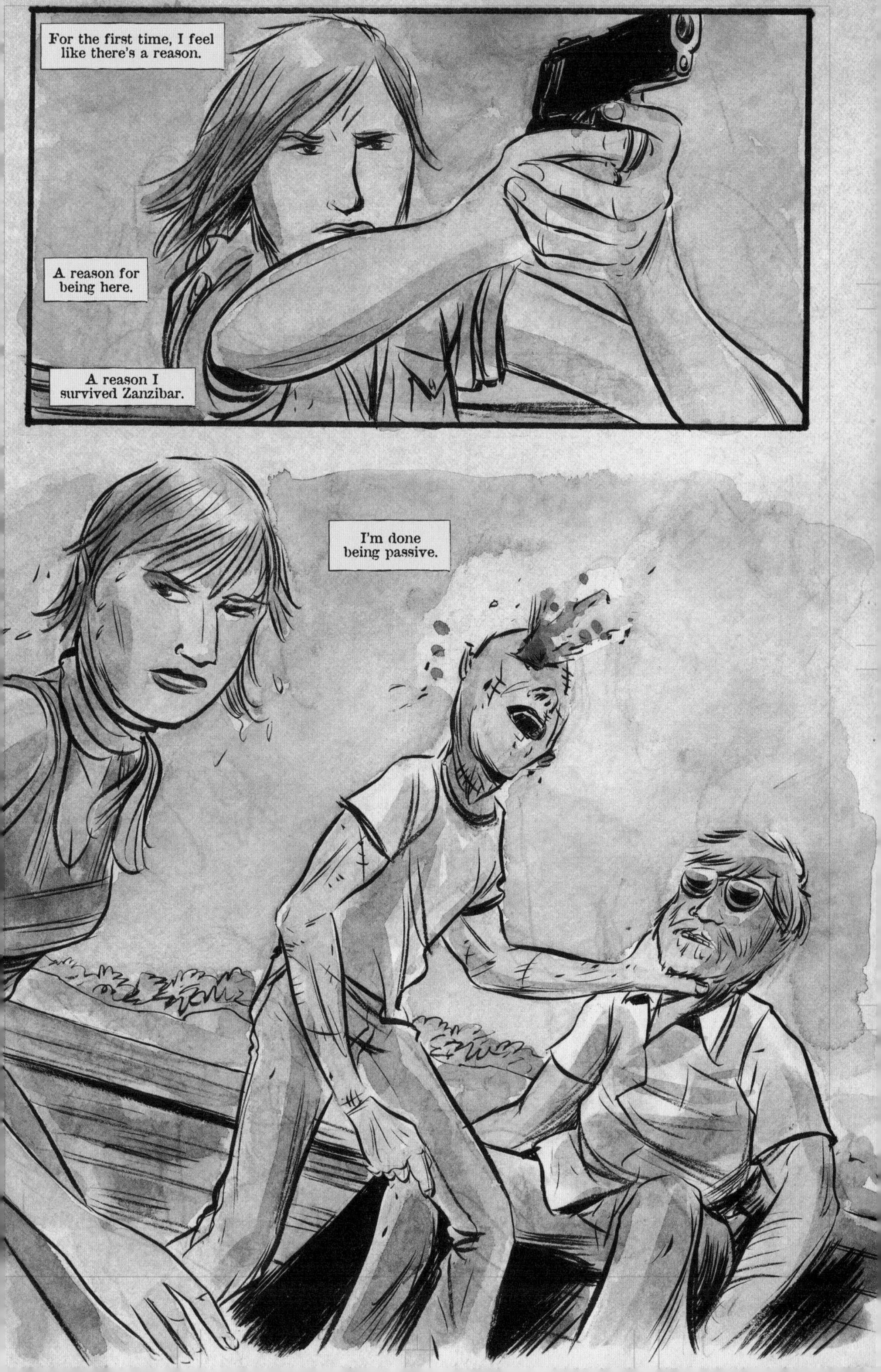
For the first time, I feel like there's a reason.
A reason for being here.
A reason I survived Zanzibar.
I'm done being passive.

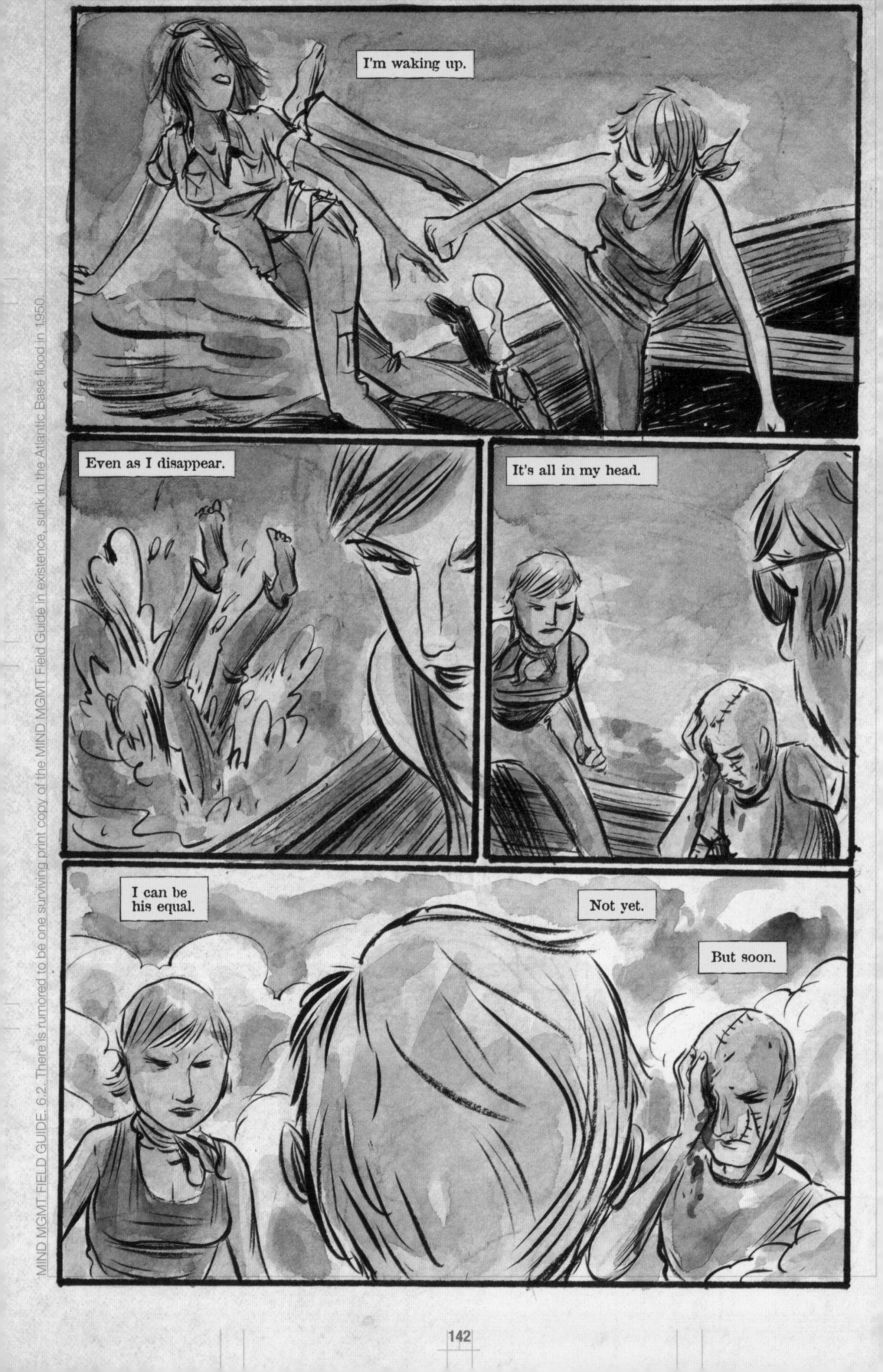
I'm waking up.
Even as I disappear.
It's all in my head.
I can be his equal.
Not yet.
But soon.

MIND MGMT FIELD GUIDE. 6.2. There is rumored to be one surviving print copy of the MIND MGMT Field Guide in existence, sunk in the Atlantic Base flood in 1950.

WHEN FILING REPORT ALL ESSENTIAL DETAILS MUST FALL WITHIN THIS SOLID "LIVE AREA" BOX. THIS IS THE BORDER FOR A STANDARD, NON-BLEED FIELD REPORT

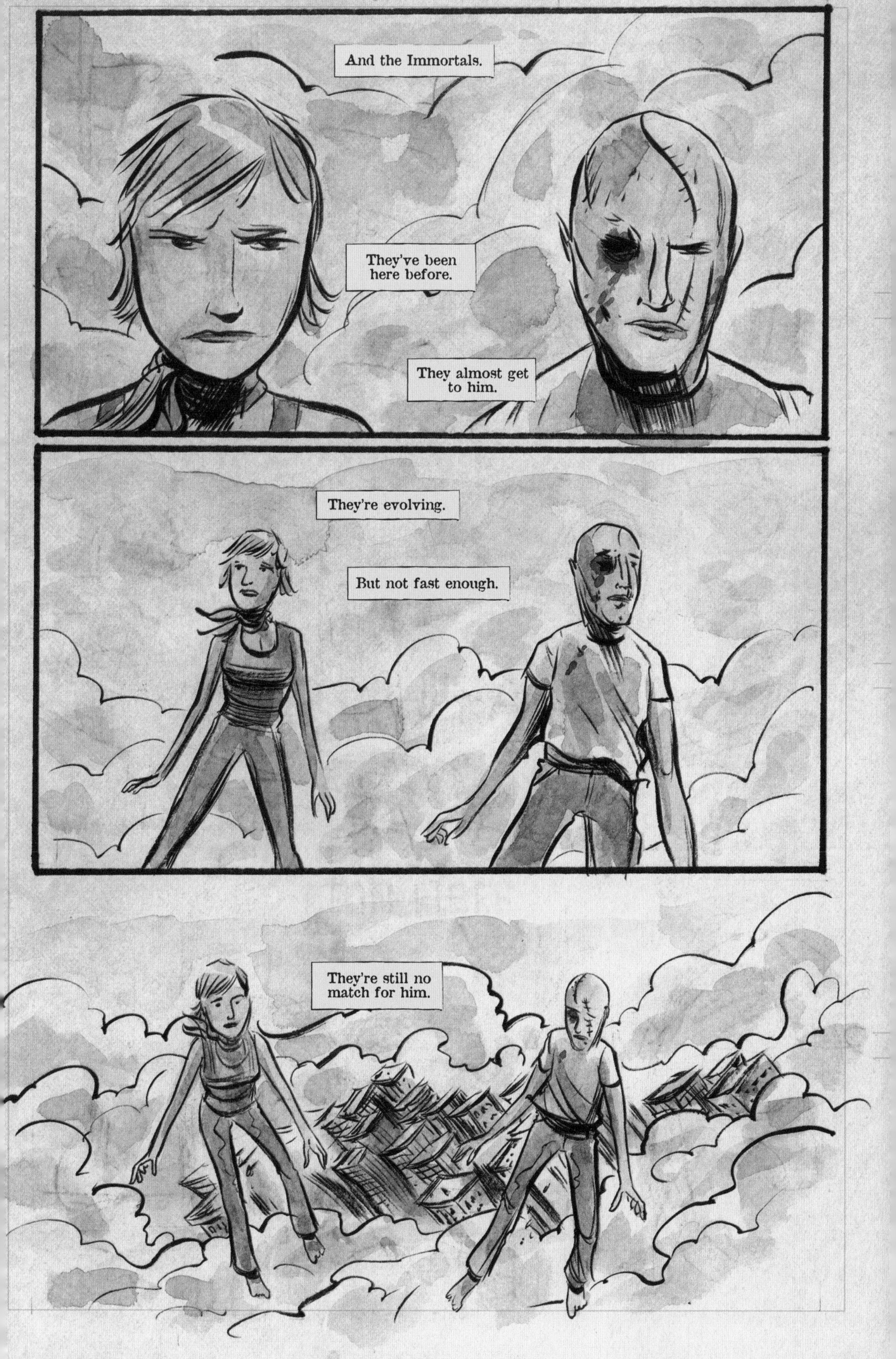

And the Immortals.
They've been here before.
They almost get to him.
They're evolving.
But not fast enough.
They're still no match for him.

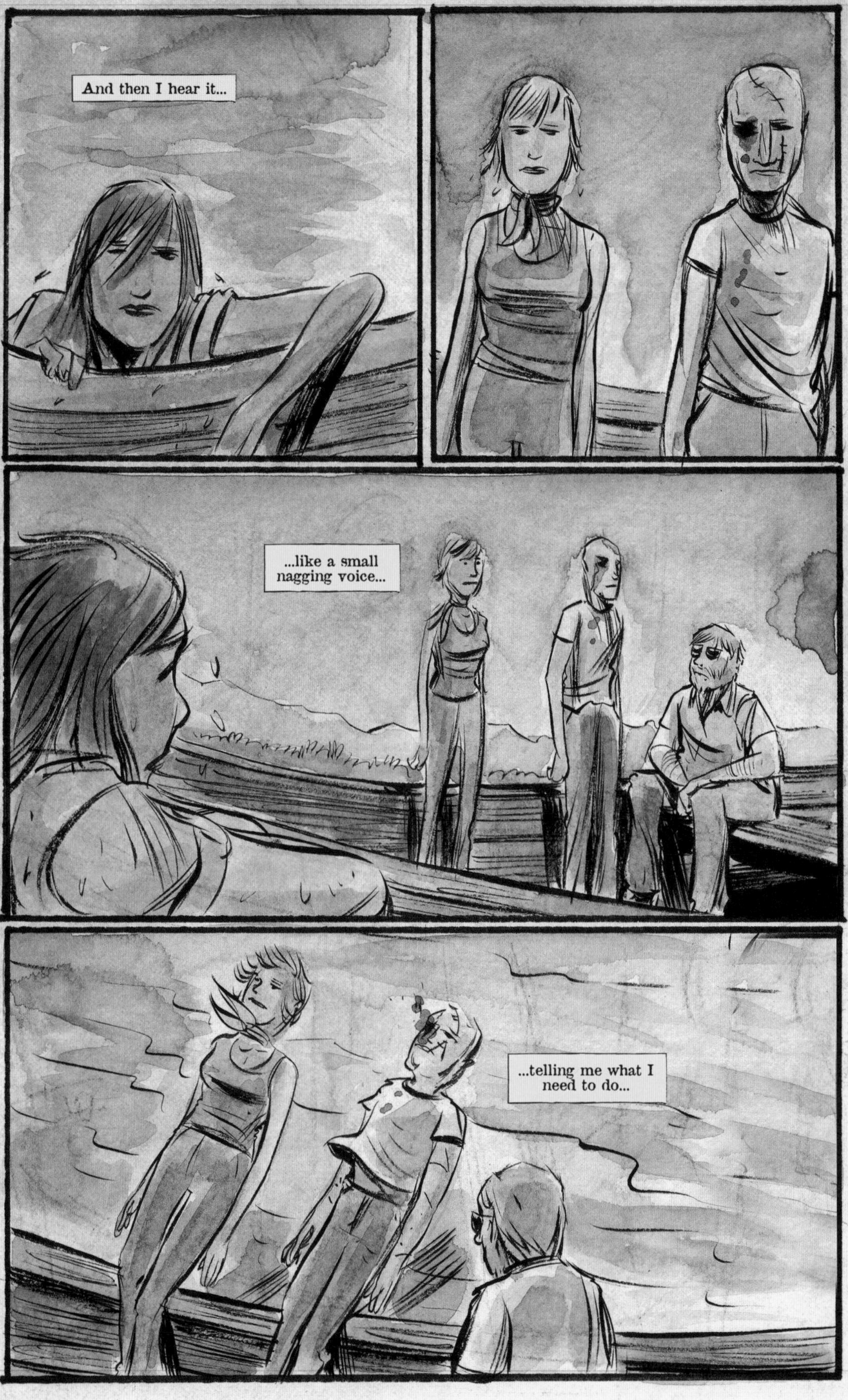
And then I hear it...
...like a small nagging voice...
...telling me what I need to do...

MIND MGMT FIELD GUIDE. 6.4. Over the generations, the Field Guide has not only trained agents, but also rescued them, serving as a mental life preserver.

WHEN FILING REPORT ALL ESSENTIAL DETAILS MUST FALL WITHIN THIS SOLID "LIVE AREA" BOX. THIS IS THE BORDER FOR A STANDARD, NON-BLEED FIELD REPORT

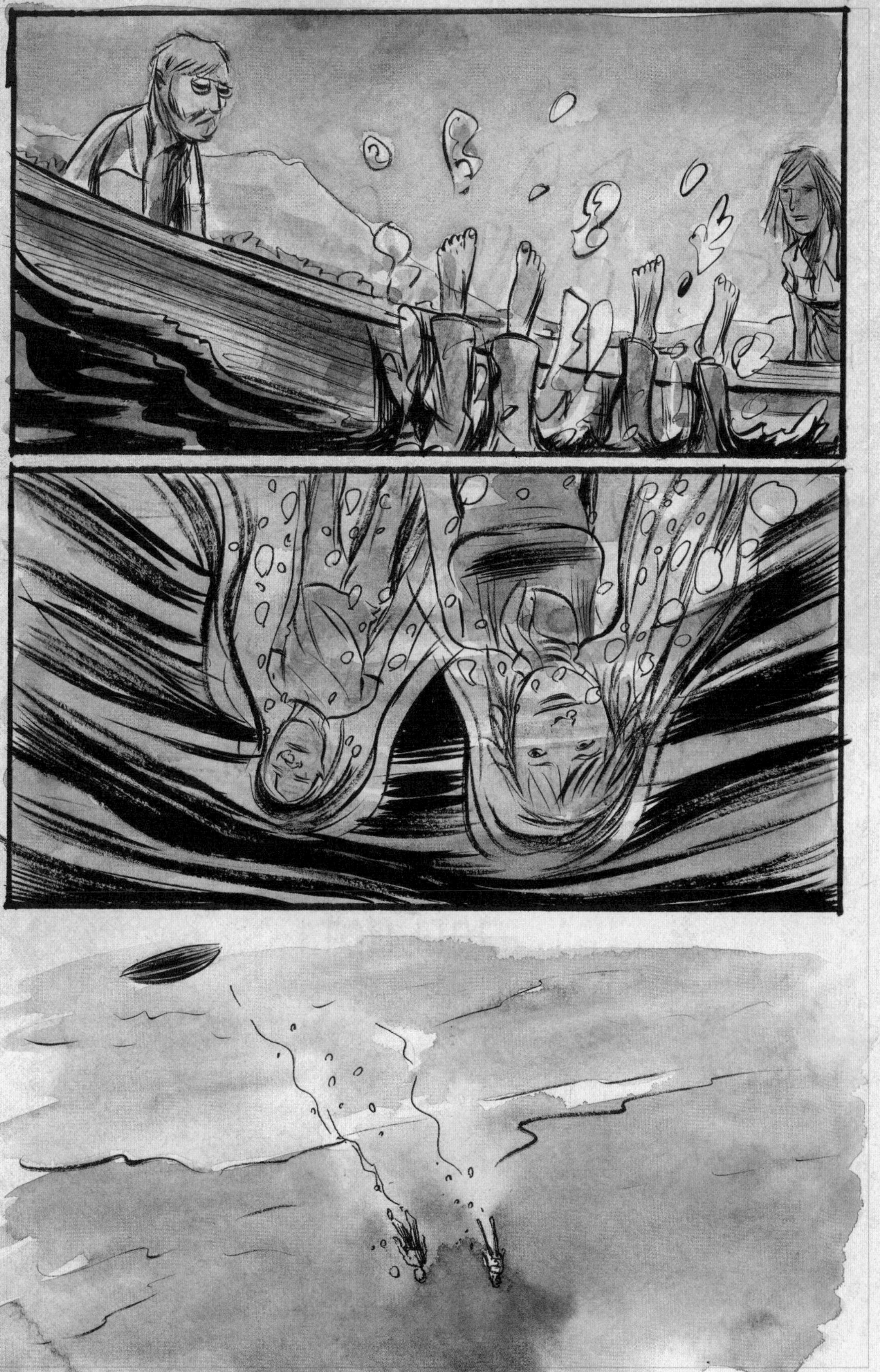

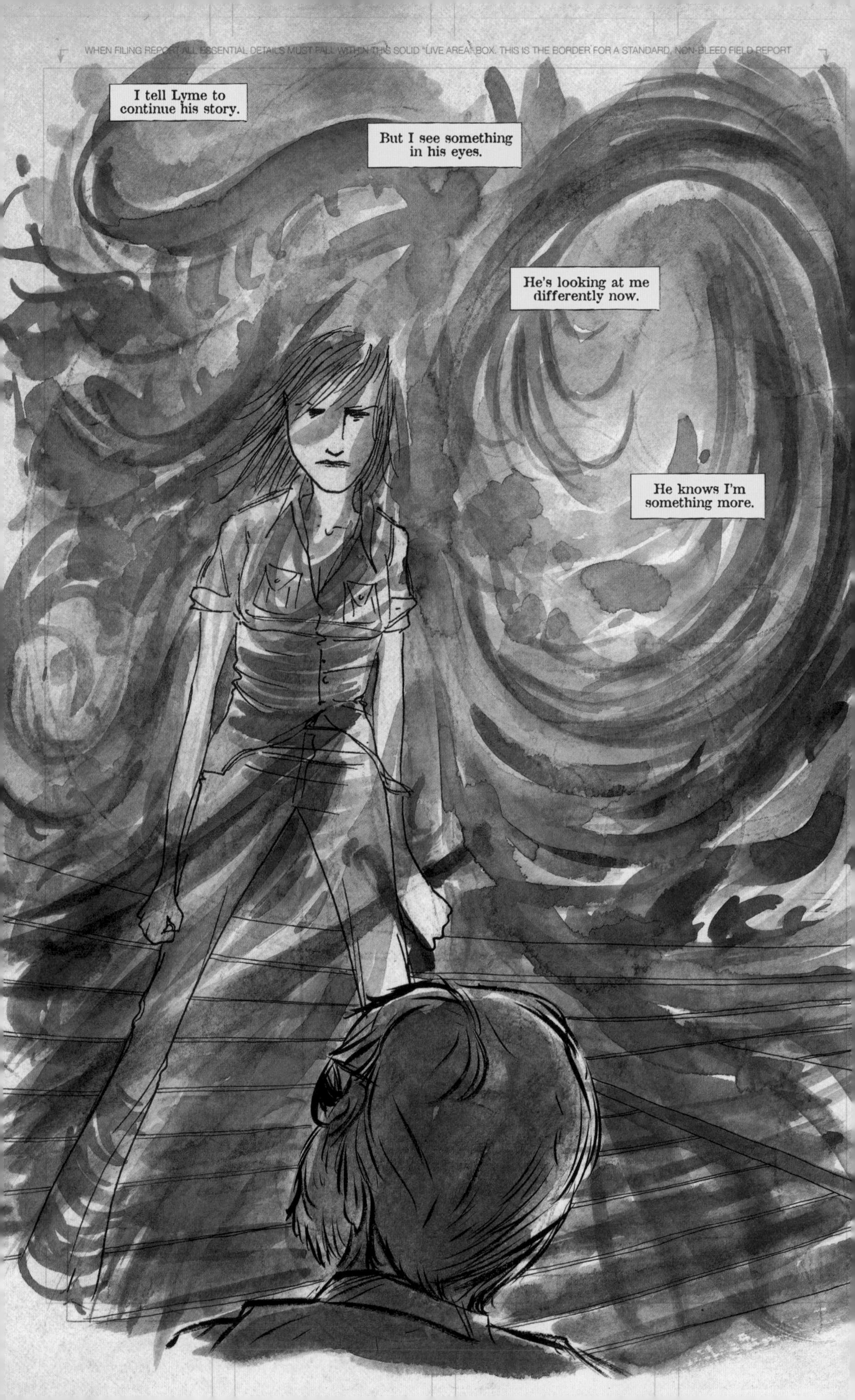
WHEN FILING REPORT ALL ESSENTIAL DETAILS MUST FALL WITHIN THIS SOLID "LIVE AREA" BOX. THIS IS THE BORDER FOR A STANDARD, NON-BLEED FIELD REPORT
I tell Lyme to continue his story.
But I see something in his eyes.
He's looking at me differently now.
He knows I'm something more.

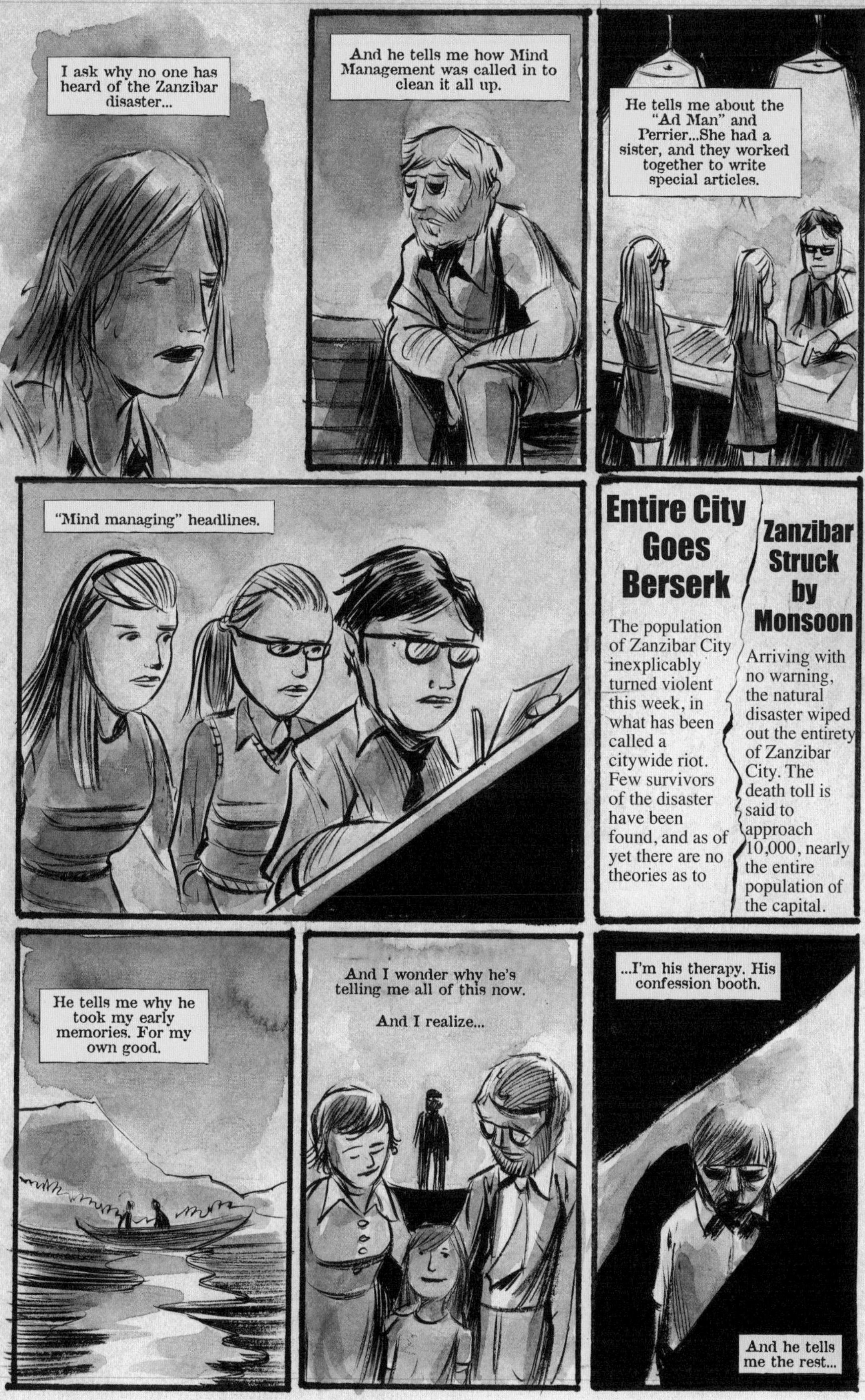
I ask why no one has heard of the Zanzibar disaster...
And he tells me how Mind Management was called in to clean it all up.
He tells me about the "Ad Man" and Perrier...She had a sister, and they worked together to write special articles.
"Mind managing" headlines.
Entire City Goes Berserk
The population of Zanzibar City inexplicably turned violent this week, in what has been called a citywide riot. Few survivors of the disaster have been found, and as of yet there are no theories as to
Zanzibar Struck by Monsoon
Arriving with no warning, the natural disaster wiped out the entirety of Zanzibar City. The death toll is said to approach 10,000, nearly the entire population of the capital.
He tells me why he took my early memories. For my own good.
And I wonder why he's telling me all of this now.
And I realize...
...I'm his therapy. His confession booth.
And he tells me the rest...

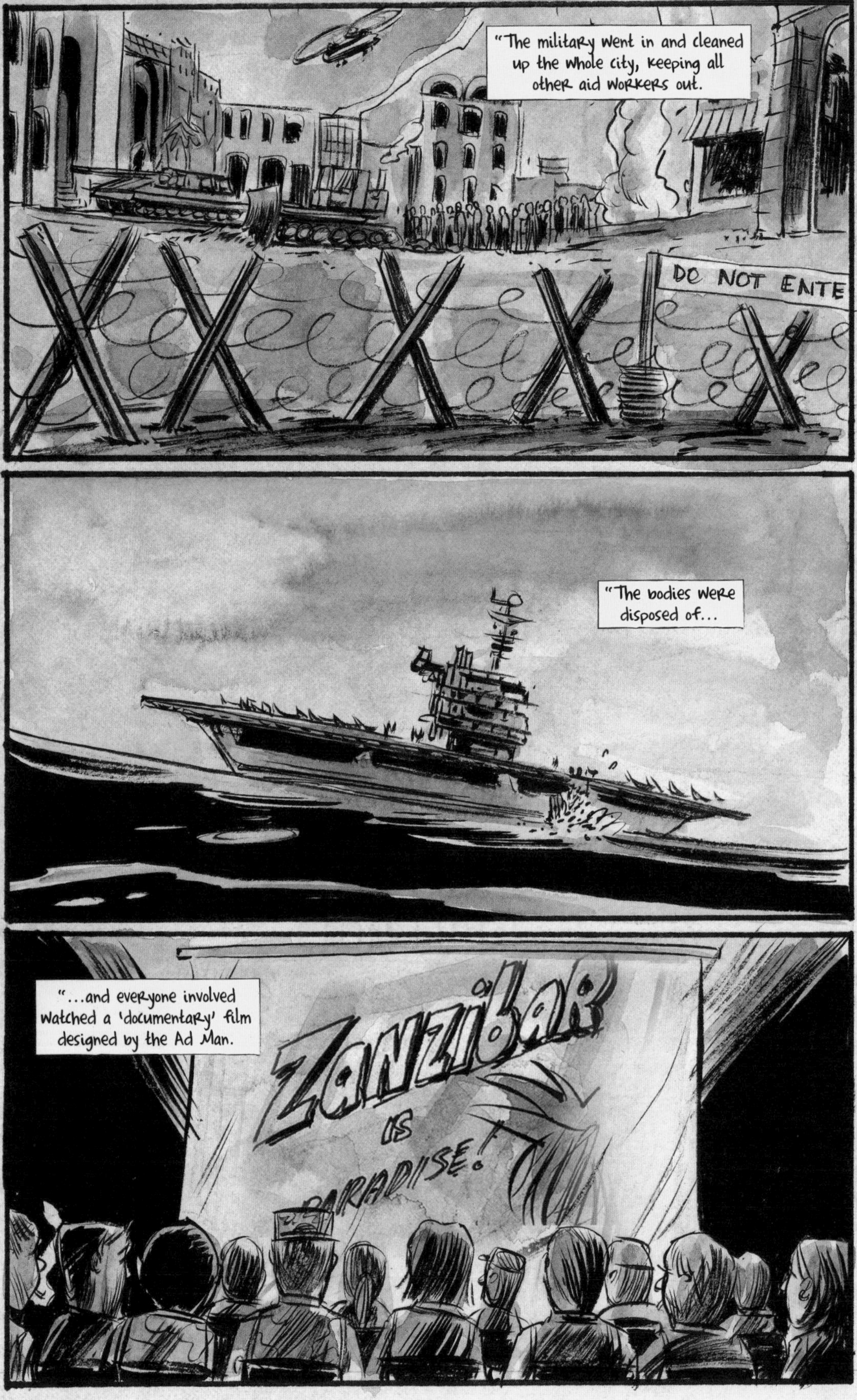
"The military went in and cleaned up the whole city, keeping all other aid workers out.
DO NOT ENTE
"The bodies were disposed of...
"...and everyone involved watched a 'documentary' film designed by the Ad Man.
ZANZIBAR
IS
PARADISE!

MIND MGMT FIELD GUIDE. 6.8. Many ex-agent scholars have poured over transcribed versions of the Field Guide...

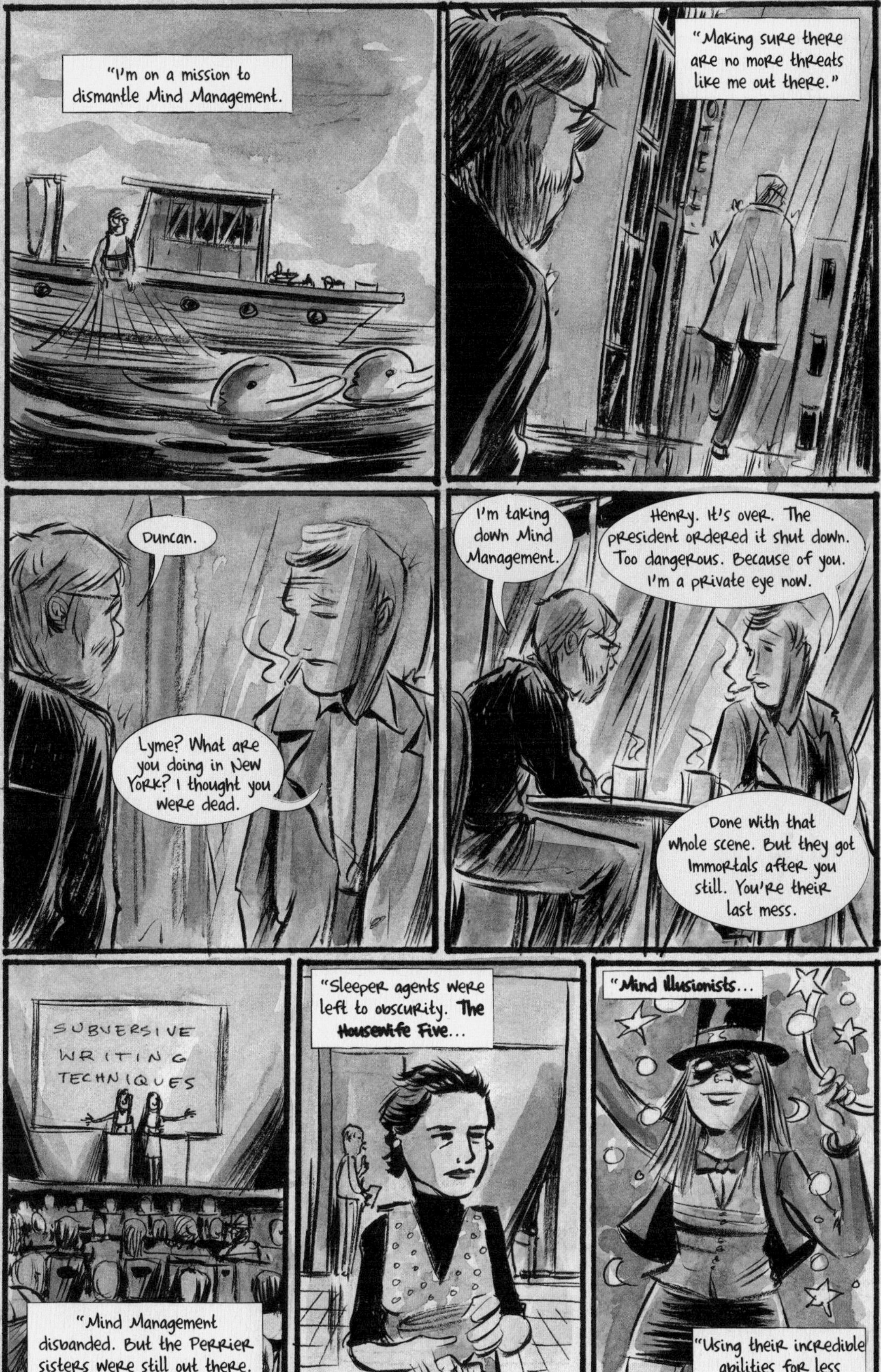
"I'm on a mission to dismantle Mind Management.
"Making sure there are no more threats like me out there."
Duncan.
Lyme? What are you doing in New York? I thought you were dead.
I'm taking down Mind Management.
Henry. It's over. The president ordered it shut down. Too dangerous. Because of you. I'm a private eye now.
Done with that whole scene. But they got Immortals after you still. You're their last mess.
SUBVERSIVE WRITING TECHNIQUES
"Mind Management disbanded. But the Perrier sisters were still out there. Along with countless others...
"Sleeper agents were left to obscurity. The Housewife Five...
"Mind Illusionists...
"Using their incredible abilities for less intrusive goals.

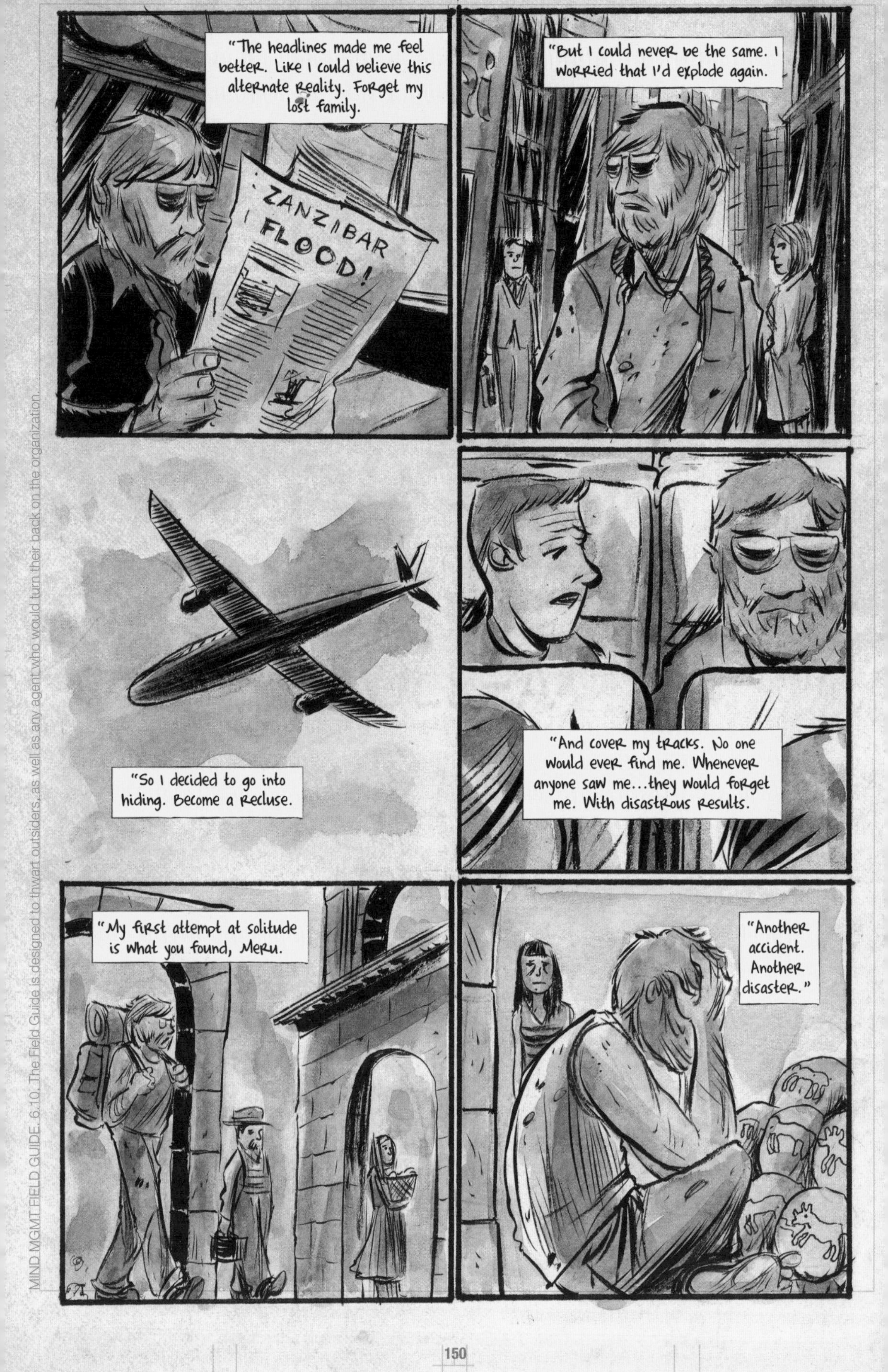
"The headlines made me feel better. Like I could believe this alternate reality. Forget my lost family.
ZANZIBAR FLOOD!
"But I could never be the same. I worried that I'd explode again.
"So I decided to go into hiding. Become a recluse.
"And cover my tracks. No one would ever find me. Whenever anyone saw me...they would forget me. With disastrous results.
"My first attempt at solitude is what you found, Meru.
"Another accident. Another disaster."

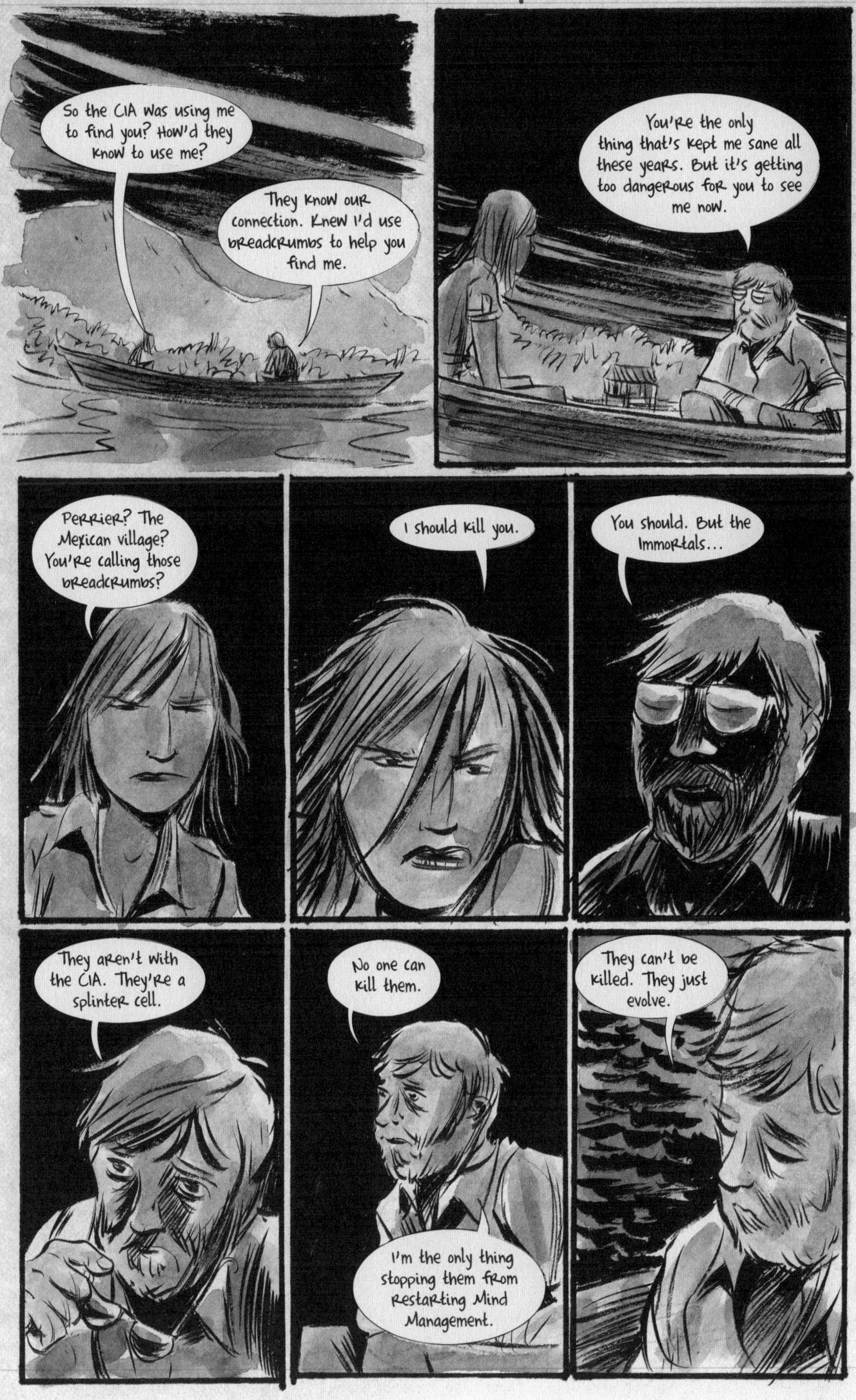
So the CIA was using me to find you? How'd they know to use me?
They know our connection. Knew I'd use breadcrumbs to help you find me.
You're the only thing that's kept me sane all these years. But it's getting too dangerous for you to see me now.
Perrier? The Mexican village? You're calling those breadcrumbs?
I should kill you.
You should. But the Immortals...
They aren't with the CIA. They're a splinter cell.
No one can kill them.
I'm the only thing stopping them from restarting Mind Management.
They can't be killed. They just evolve.

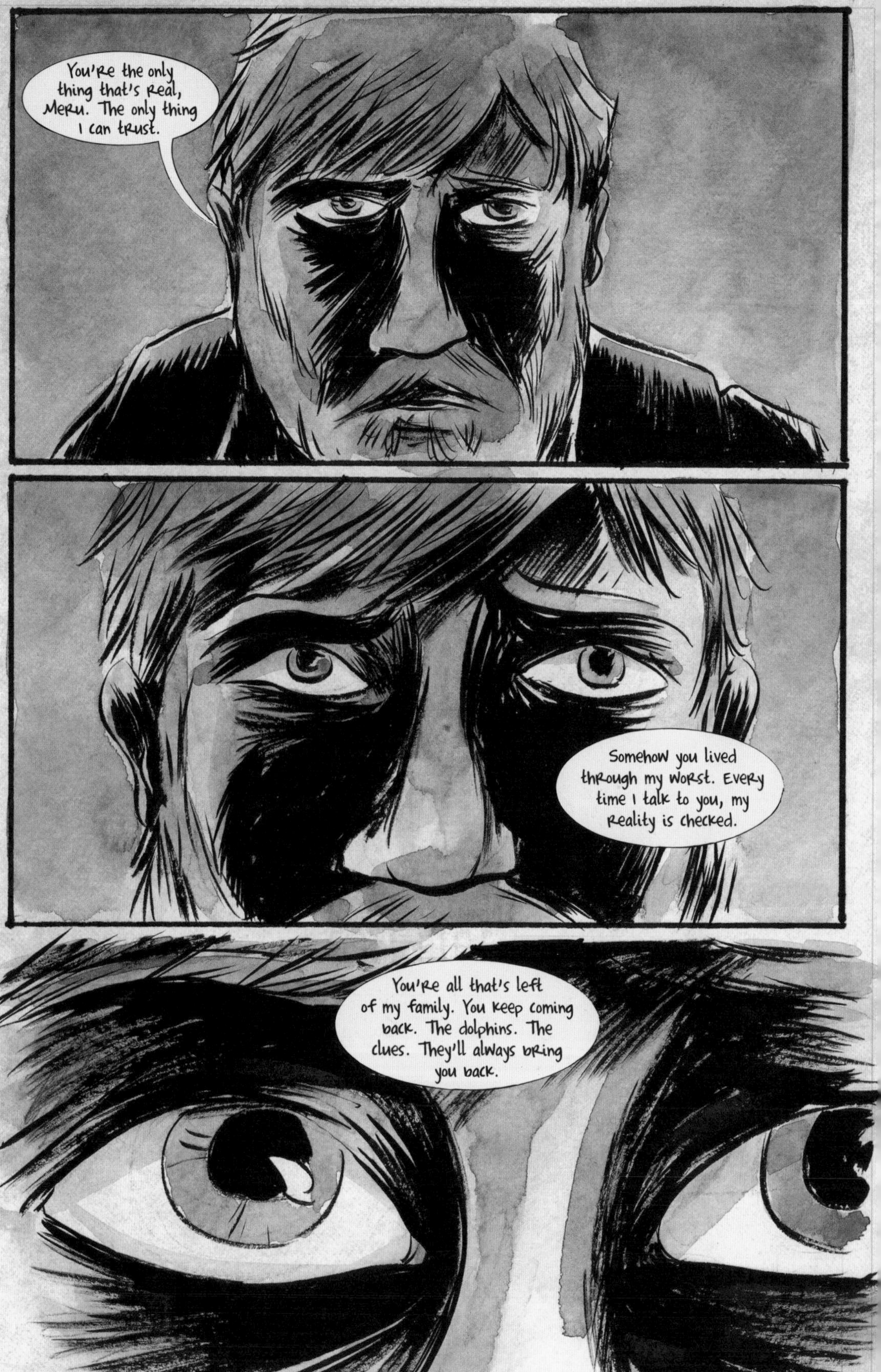
You're the only thing that's real, Meru. The only thing I can trust.
Somehow you lived through my worst. Every time I talk to you, my reality is checked.
You're all that's left of my family. You keep coming back. The dolphins. The clues. They'll always bring you back.

MIND MGMT FIELD GUIDE. 6.12. None of these theories have ever been proven.

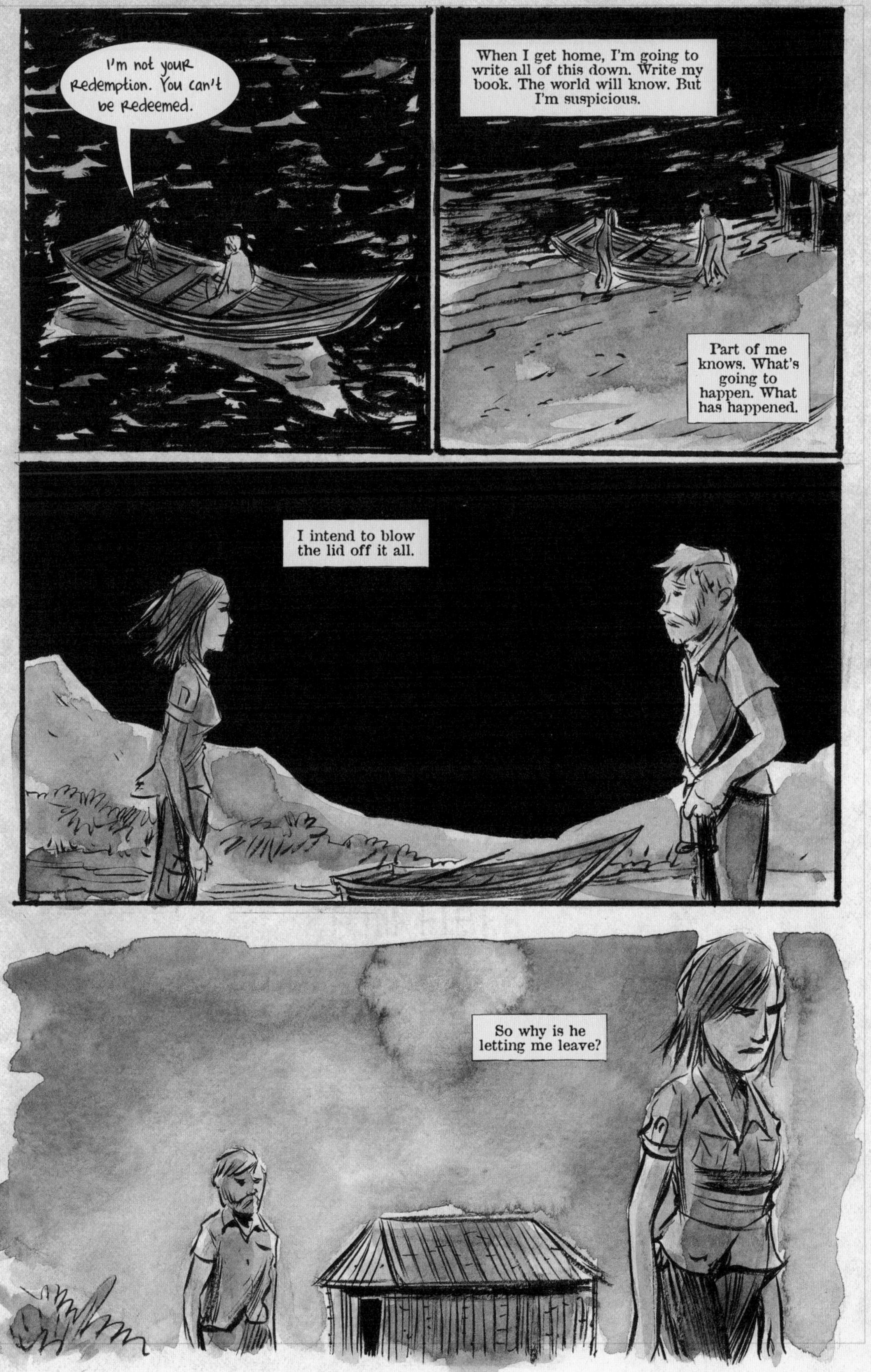
I'm not your redemption. You can't be redeemed.
When I get home, I'm going to write all of this down. Write my book. The world will know. But I'm suspicious.
Part of me knows. What's going to happen. What has happened.
I intend to blow the lid off it all.
So why is he letting me leave?

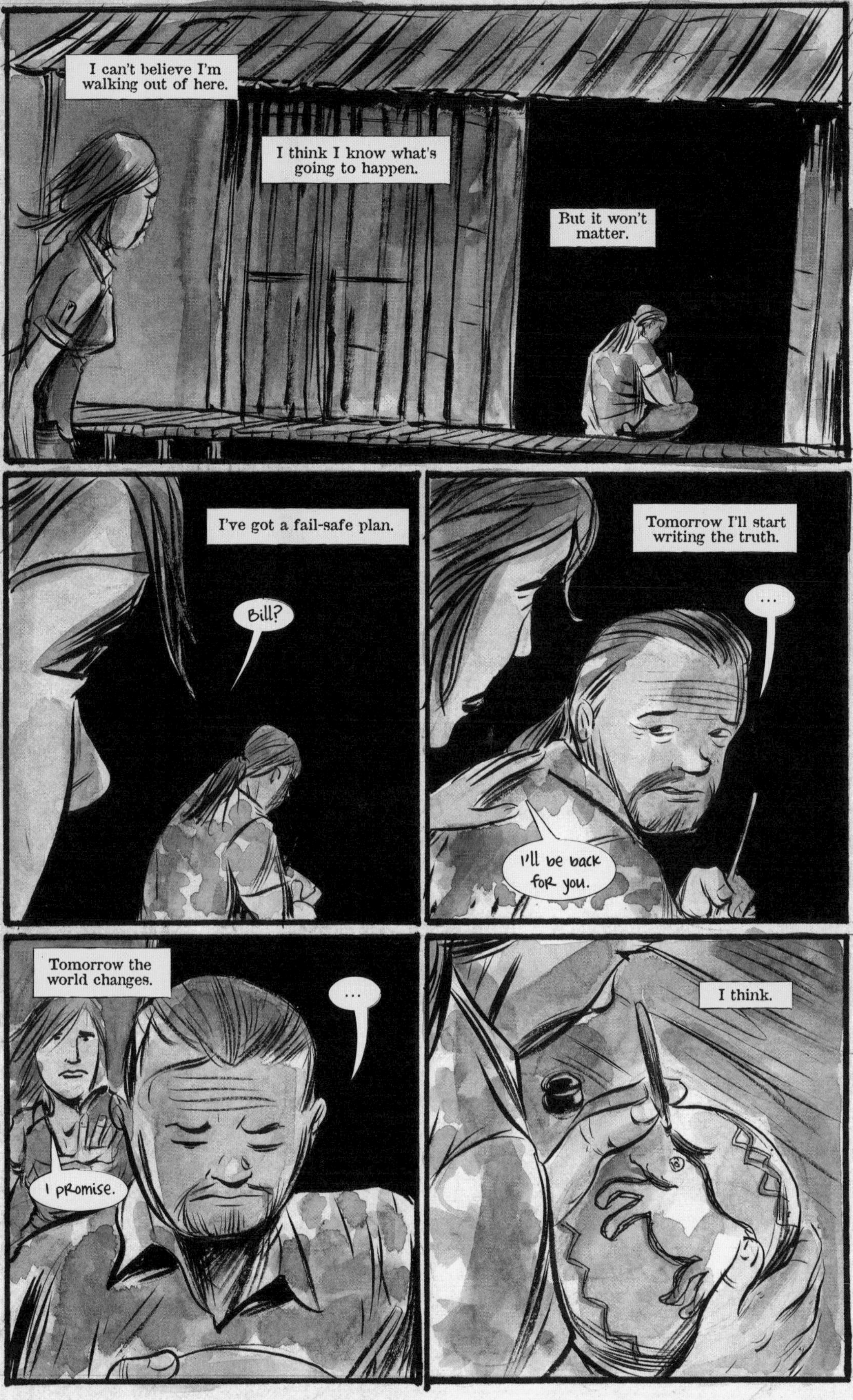
I can't believe I'm walking out of here.
I think I know what's going to happen.
But it won't matter.
I've got a fail-safe plan.
Bill?
Tomorrow I'll start writing the truth.
...
I'll be back for you.
Tomorrow the world changes.
...
I promise.
I think.

MIND MGMT FIELD GUIDE. 6.14. Some suggest that nearly half of the criminally insane are actually ex-agents or failed agents-in-training.

WHEN FILING REPORT ALL ESSENTIAL DETAILS MUST FALL WITHIN THIS SOLID "LIVE AREA" BOX. THIS IS THE BORDER FOR A STANDARD, NON-BLEED FIELD REPORT

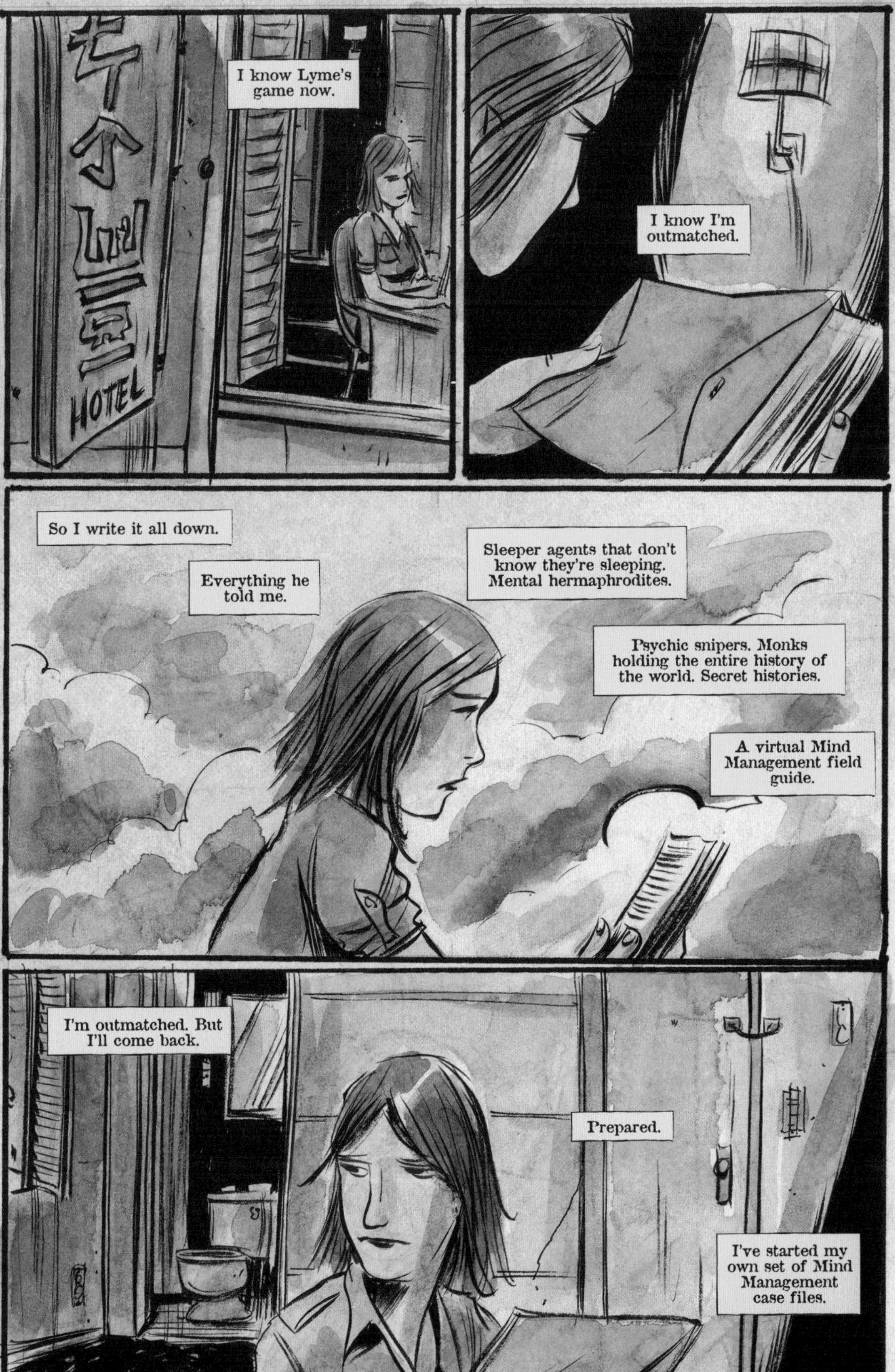
HOTEL
I know Lyme's game now.
I know I'm outmatched.
So I write it all down.
Everything he told me.
Sleeper agents that don't know they're sleeping. Mental hermaphrodites.
Psychic snipers. Monks holding the entire history of the world. Secret histories.
A virtual Mind Management field guide.
I'm outmatched. But I'll come back.
Prepared.
I've started my own set of Mind Management case files.

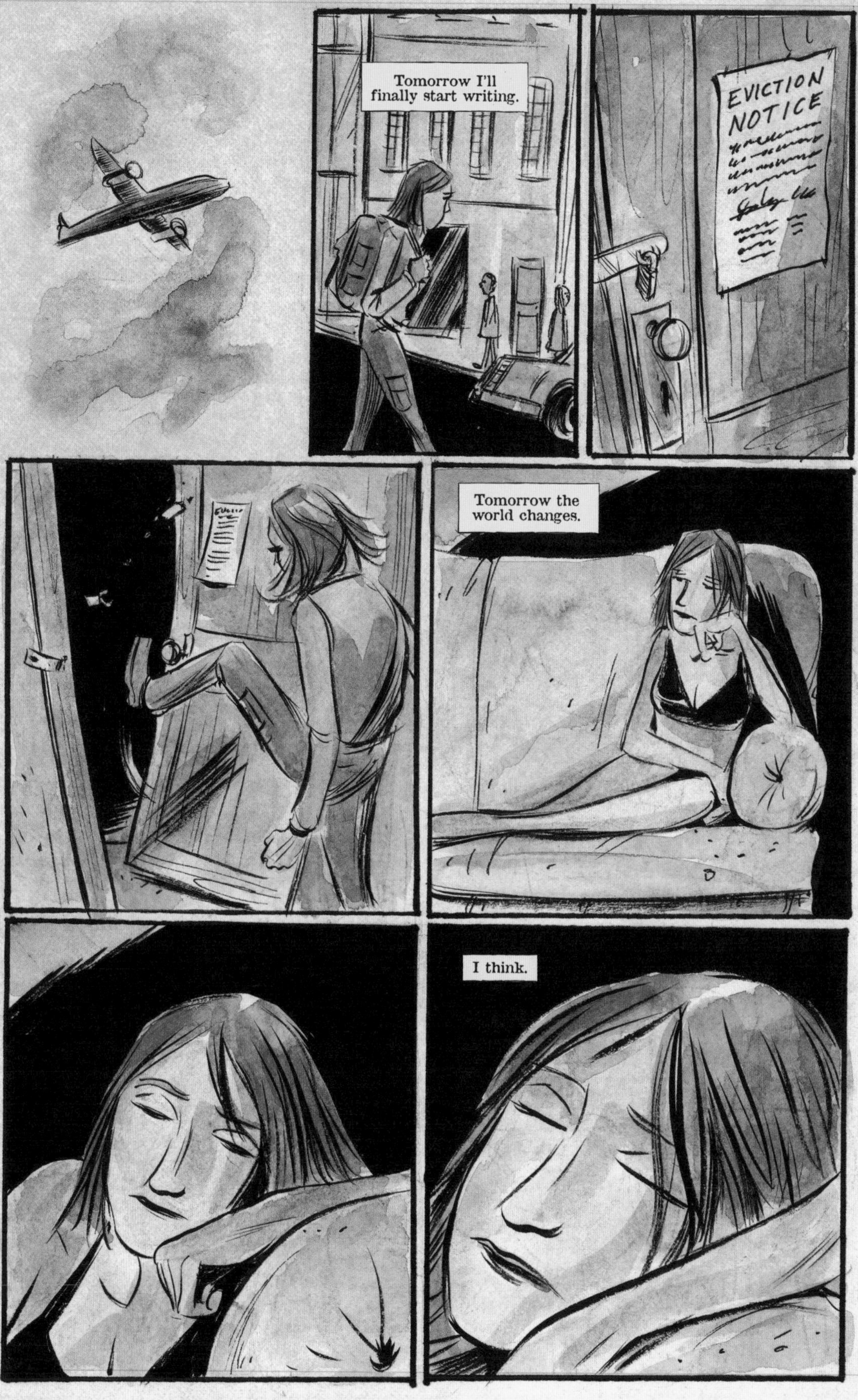
Tomorrow I'll finally start writing.
EVICTION NOTICE
Tomorrow the world changes.
I think.

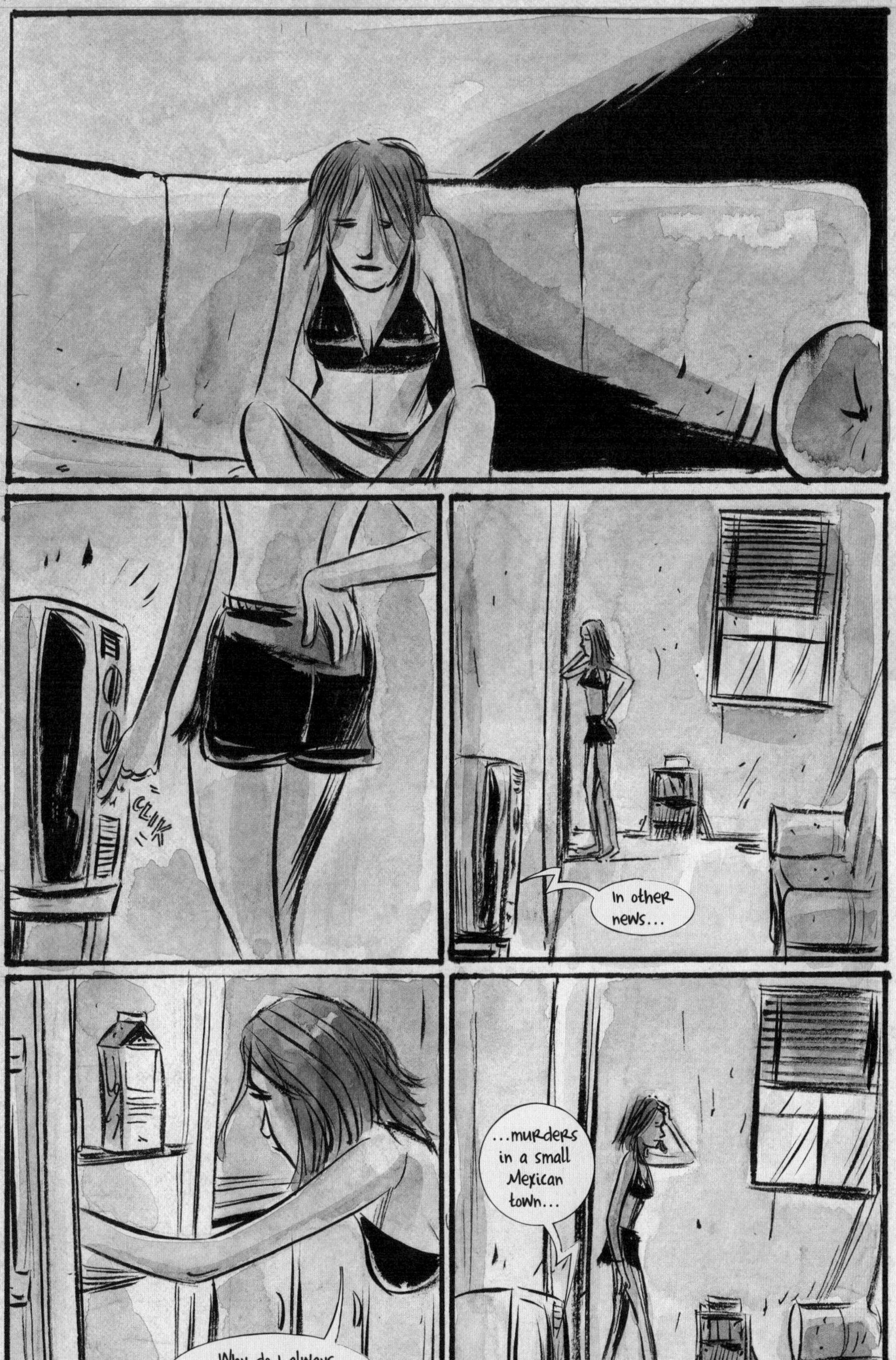
CLIK
In other news...
Why do I always look in here? It's always empty.
...murders in a small Mexican town...

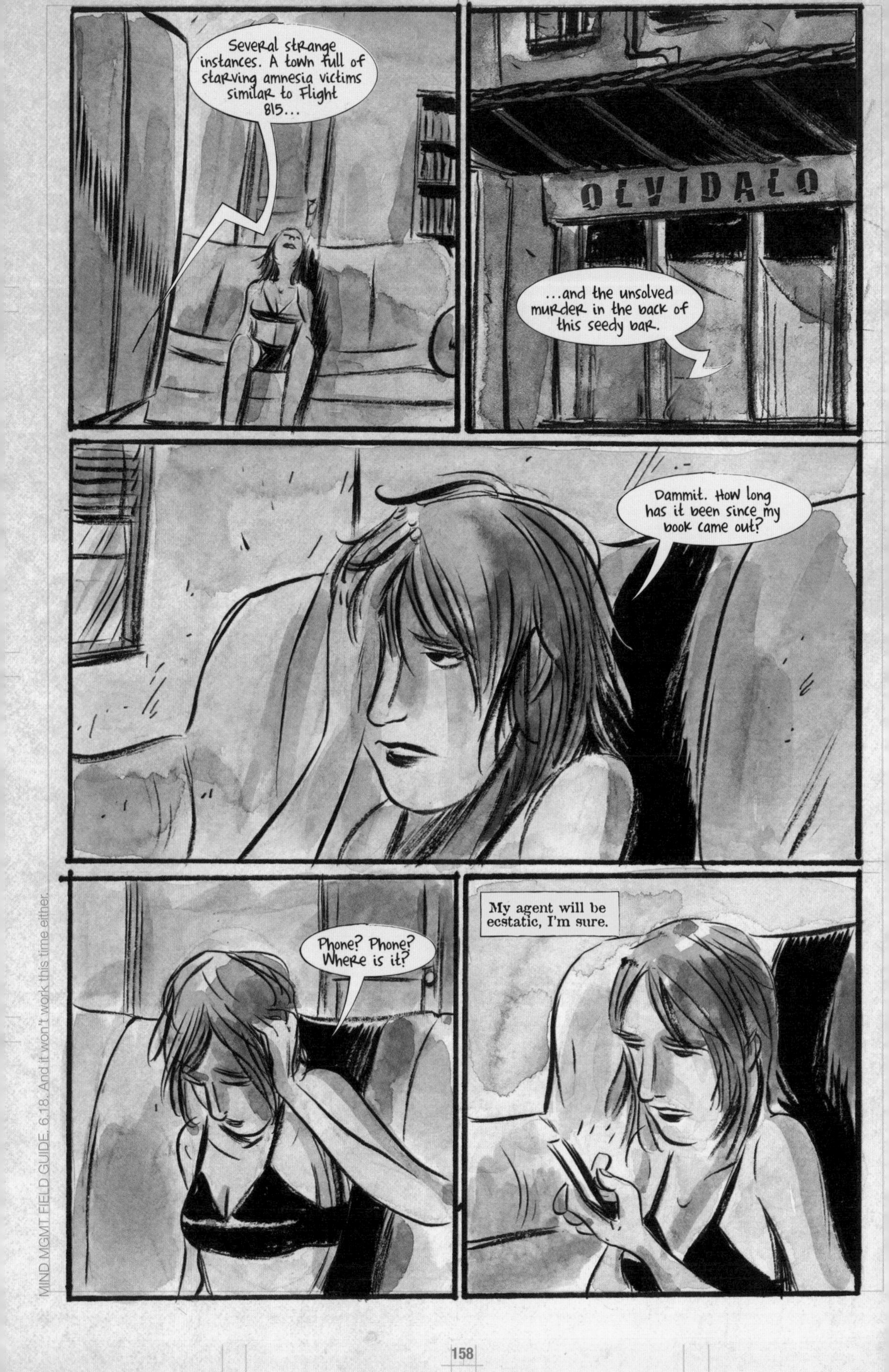
Several strange instances. A town full of starving amnesia victims similar to Flight 815...
OLVIDALO
...and the unsolved murder in the back of this seedy bar.
Dammit. How long has it been since my book came out?
Phone? Phone? Where is it?
My agent will be ecstatic, I'm sure.

MIND MGMT FIELD GUIDE. 6.18. And it won't work this time either.

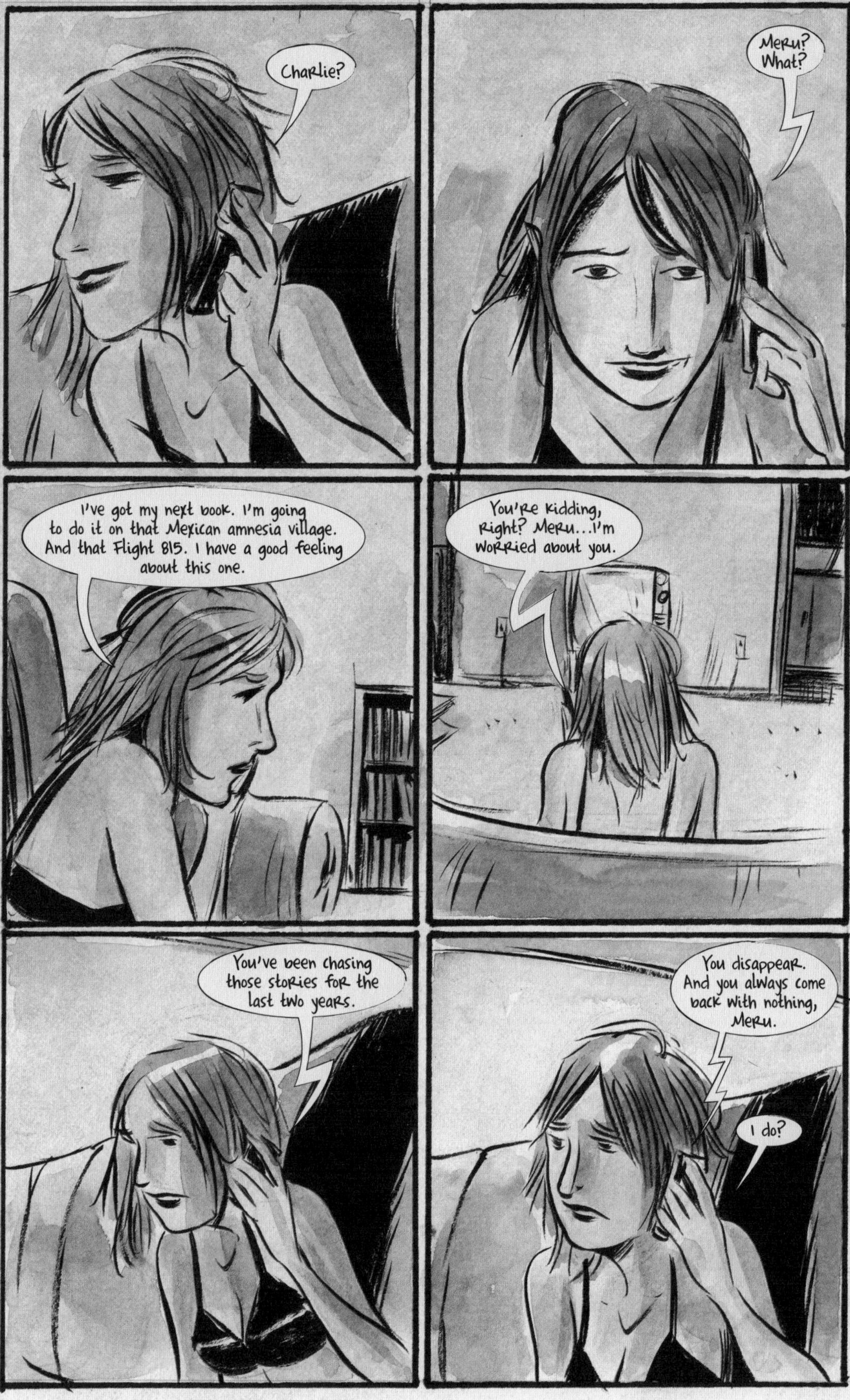
Charlie?
Meru? What?
I've got my next book. I'm going to do it on that Mexican amnesia village. And that Flight 815. I have a good feeling about this one.
You're kidding, right? Meru...I'm worried about you.
You've been chasing those stories for the last two years.
You disappear. And you always come back with nothing, Meru.
I do?

MIND MGMT FIELD GUIDE. 6.20. Having gathered all of this evidence, it is now up to you. To ask yourself the question. The answer that will not be said aloud.

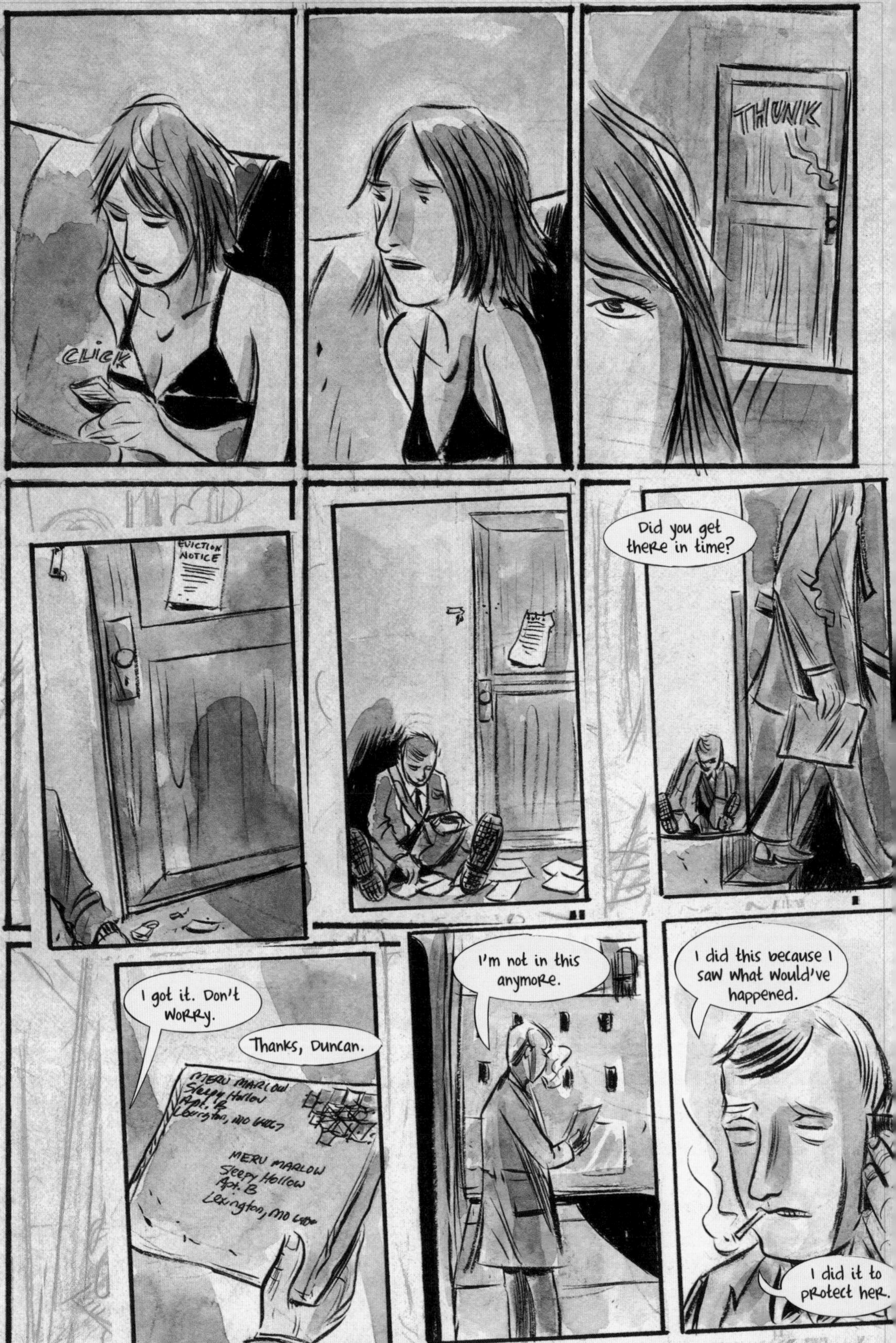
CLICK
THUNK
EVICTION NOTICE
Did you get there in time?
I got it. Don't worry.
Thanks, Duncan.
MERU MARLOW
Sleepy Hollow
Apt. B
Lexington, MO
I'm not in this anymore.
I did this because I saw what would've happened.
I did it to protect her.

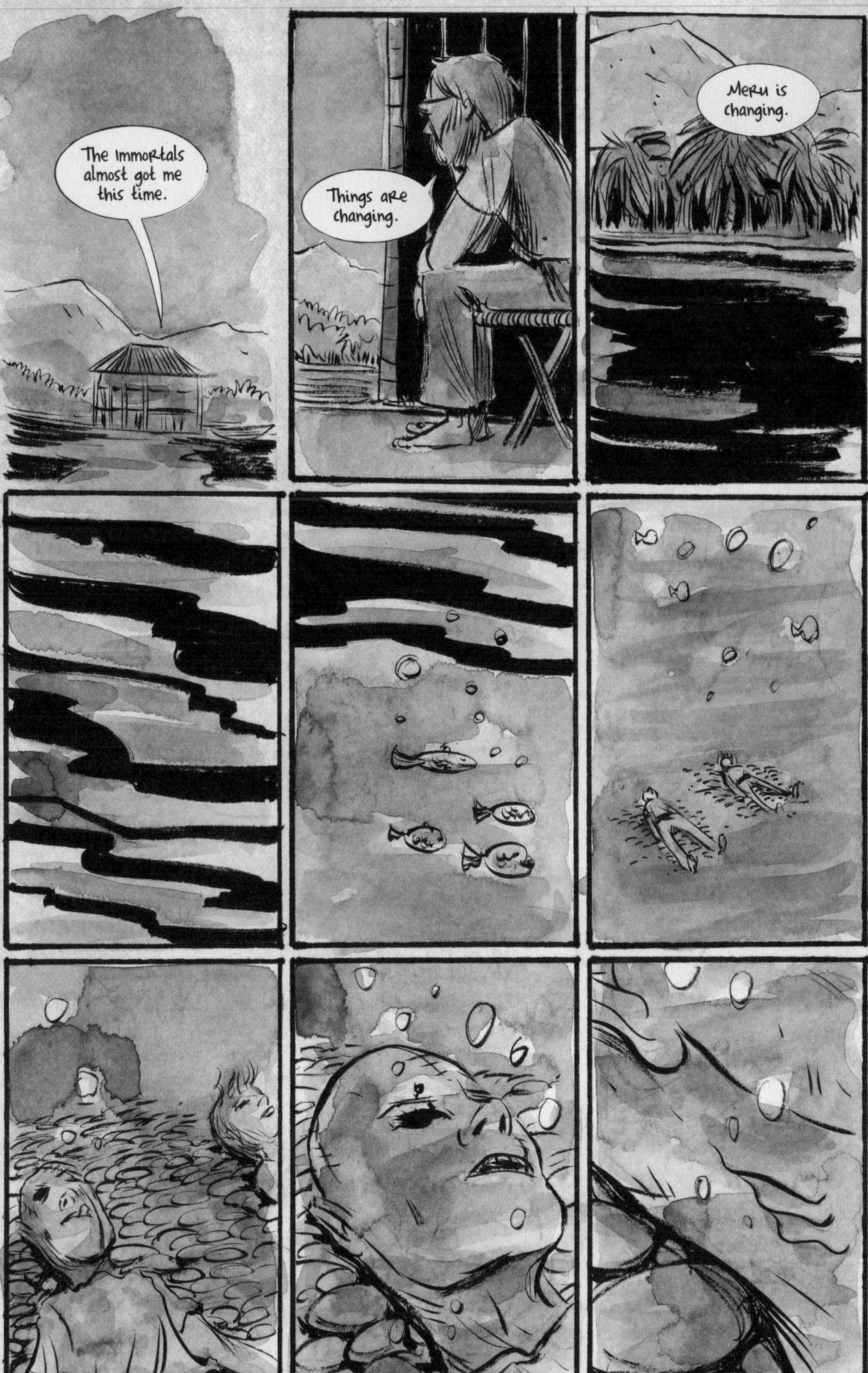
The Immortals almost got me this time.
Things are changing.
Meru is changing.

MIND MGMT FIELD GUIDE. 6.21. You need to ask yourself...

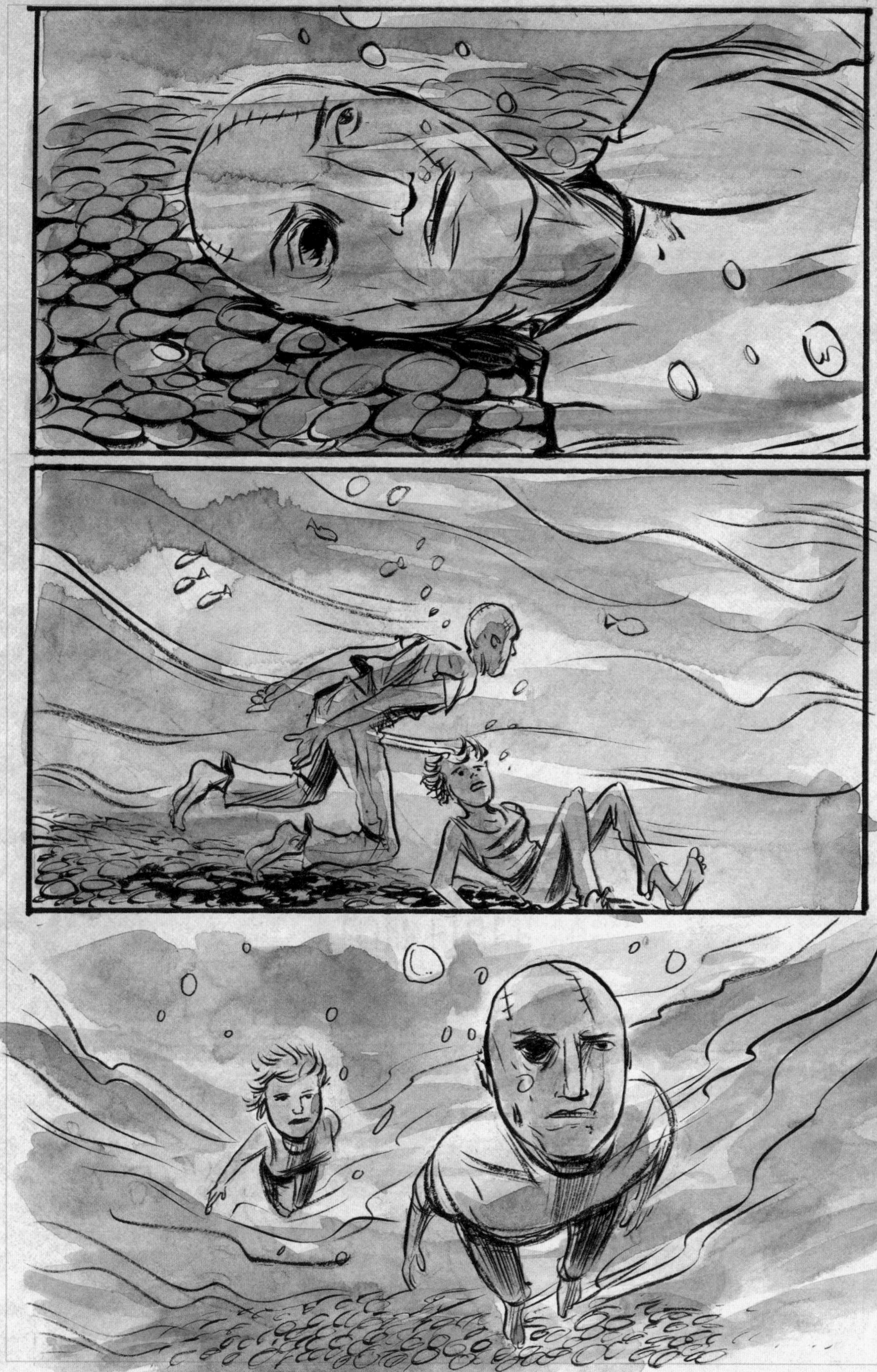

End of Book One

MIND MGMT FIELD GUIDE. 6.22. How do you remember the entire Field Guide?

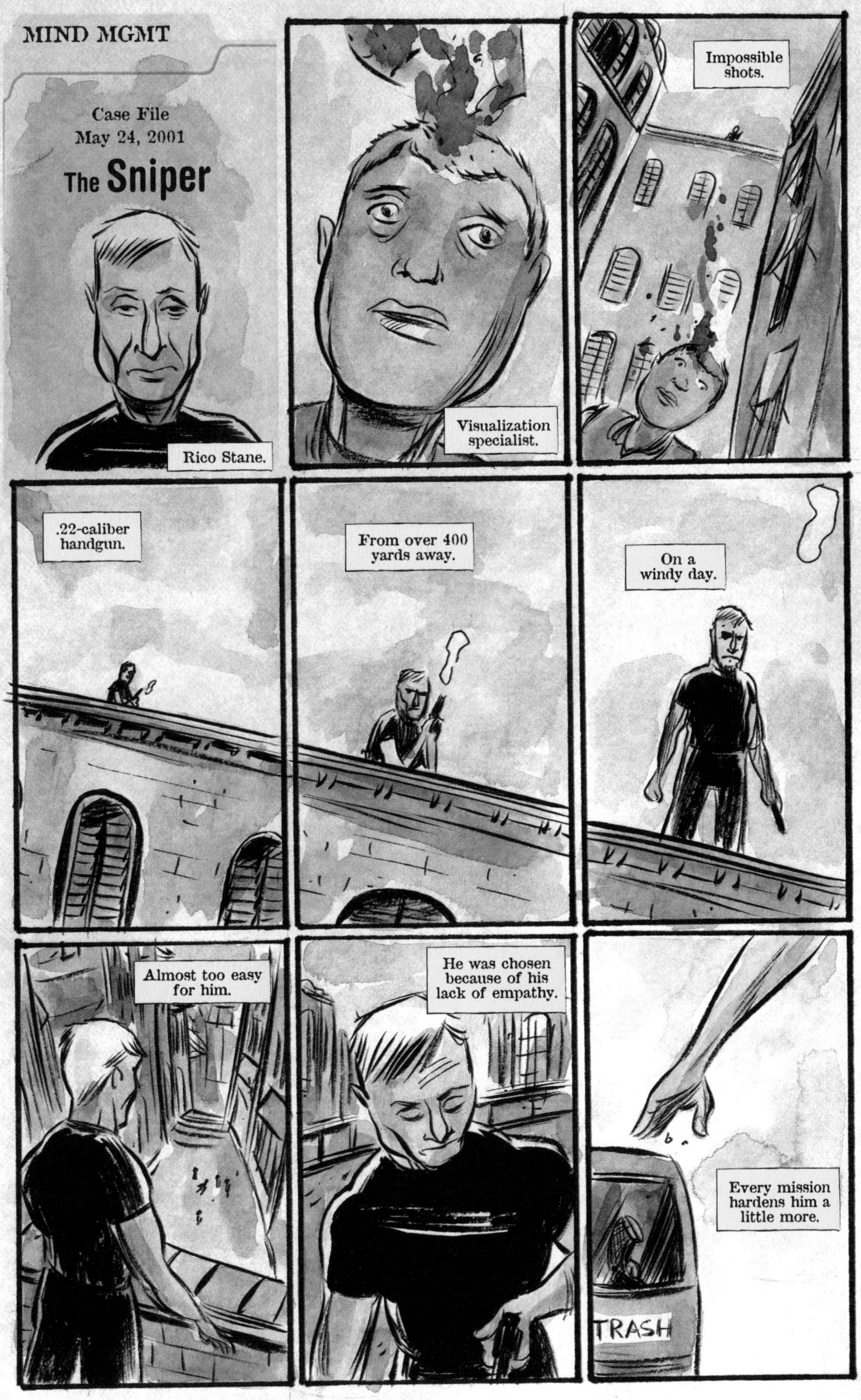
MIND MGMT
Case File
May 24, 2001
The Sniper
Rico Stane.
Visualization specialist.
Impossible shots.
.22-caliber handgun.
From over 400 yards away.
On a windy day.
Almost too easy for him.
He was chosen because of his lack of empathy.
Every mission hardens him a little more.
TRASH

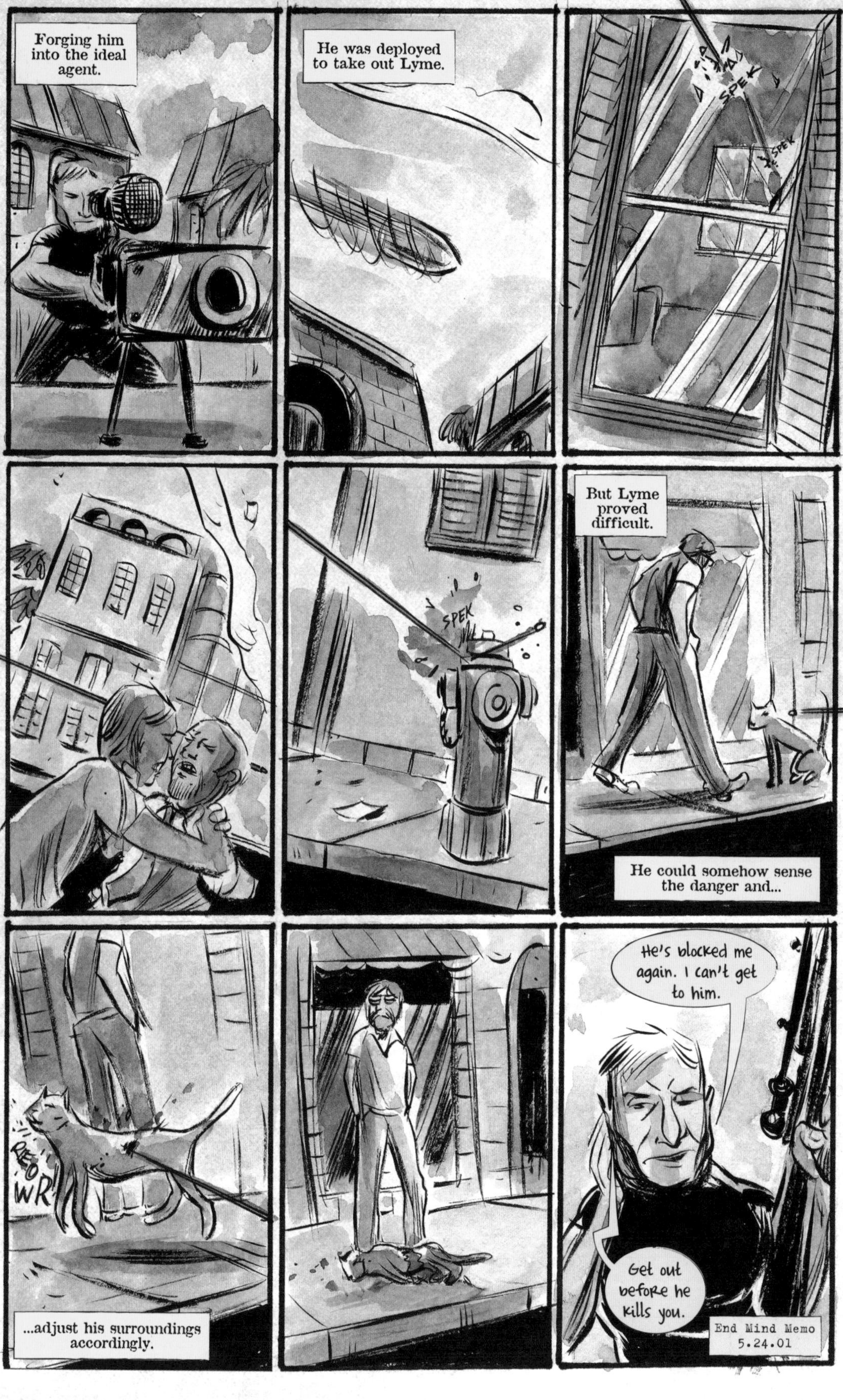
Forging him into the ideal agent.
He was deployed to take out Lyme.
SPEK
SPEK
SPEK
But Lyme proved difficult.
He could somehow sense the danger and...
REOWR
...adjust his surroundings accordingly.
He's blocked me again. I can't get to him.
Get out before he kills you.
End Mind Memo 5.24.01

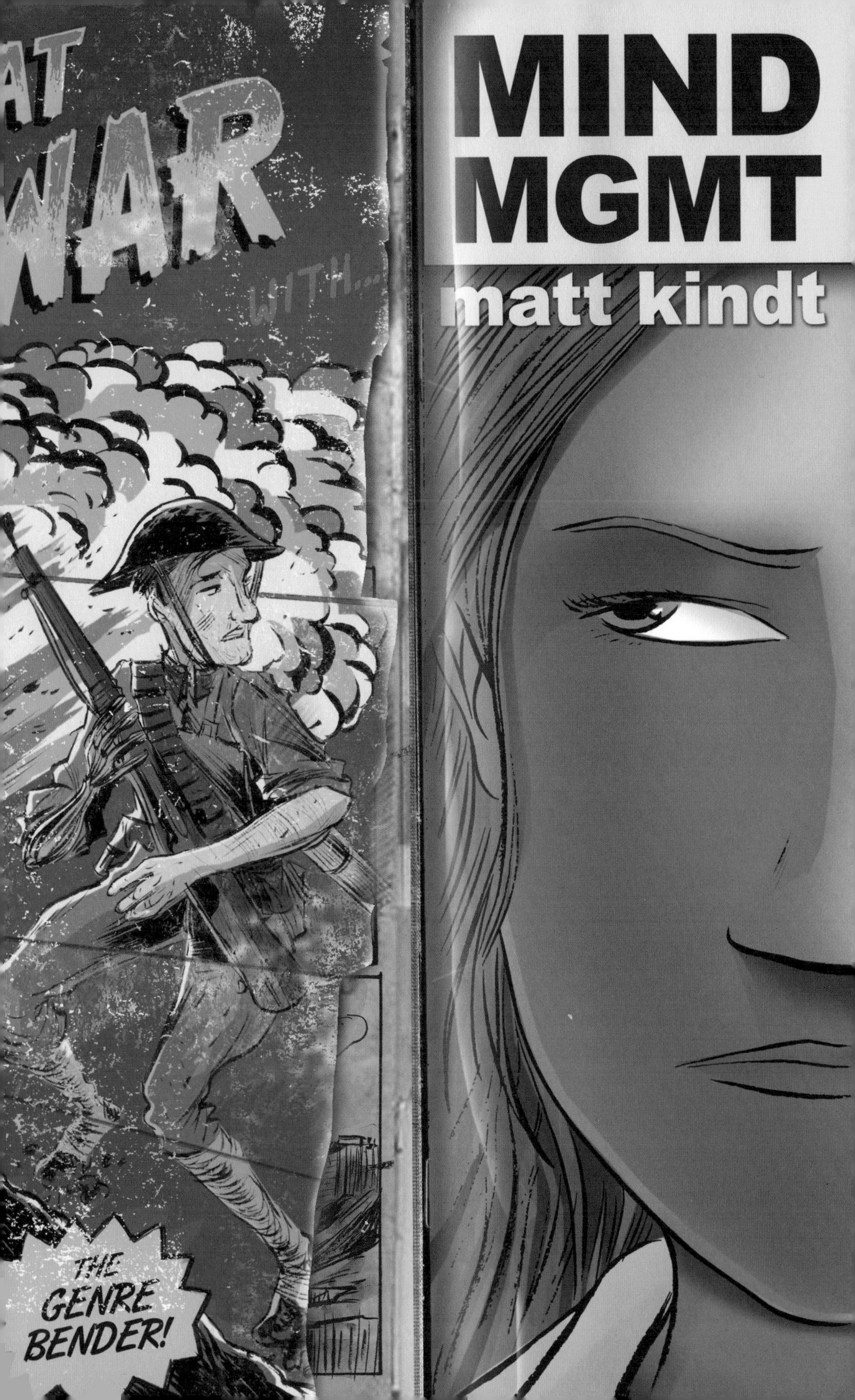

AT WAR
WITH...
THE GENRE BENDER!
MIND MGMT
matt kindt

SECRET FILES

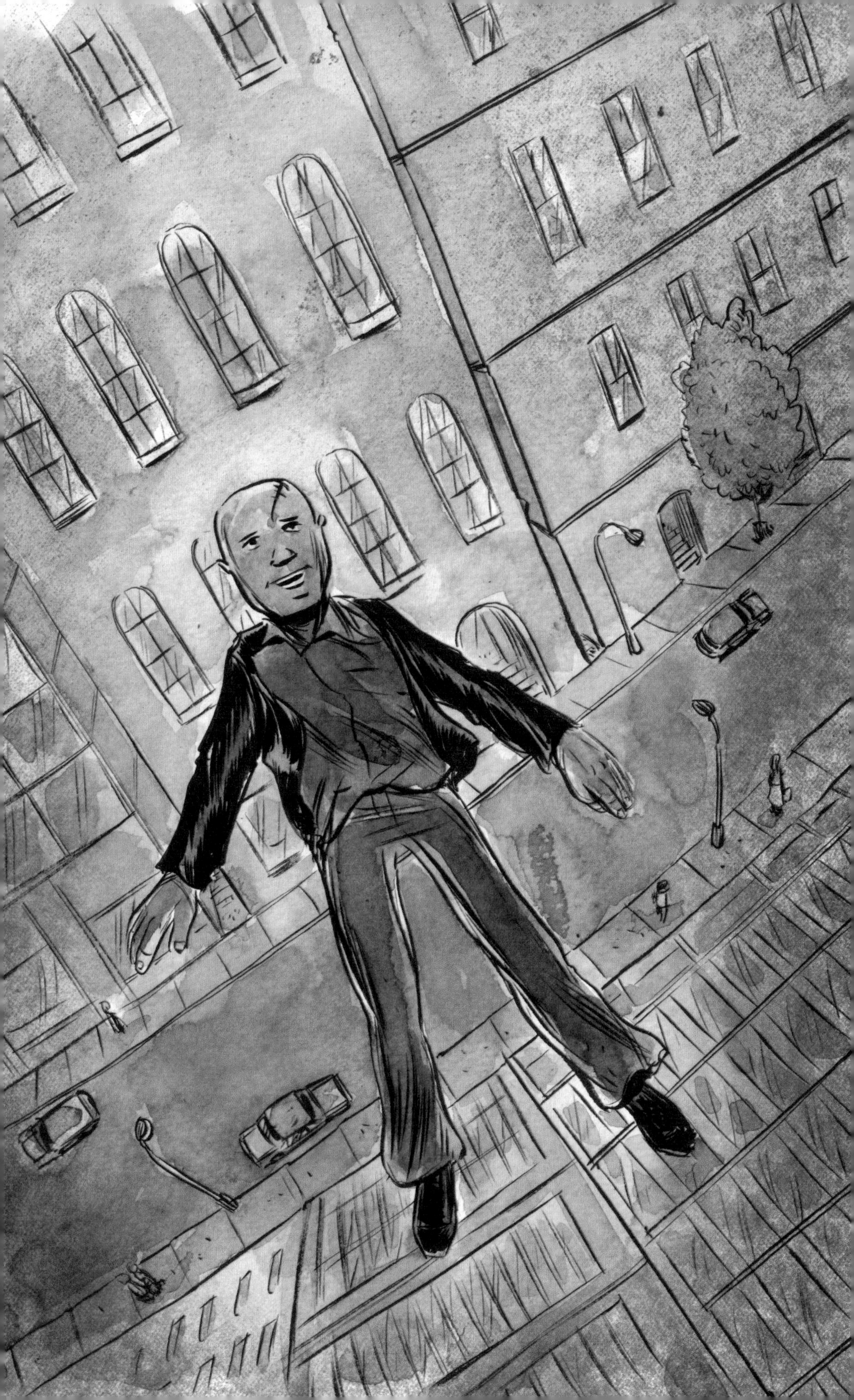

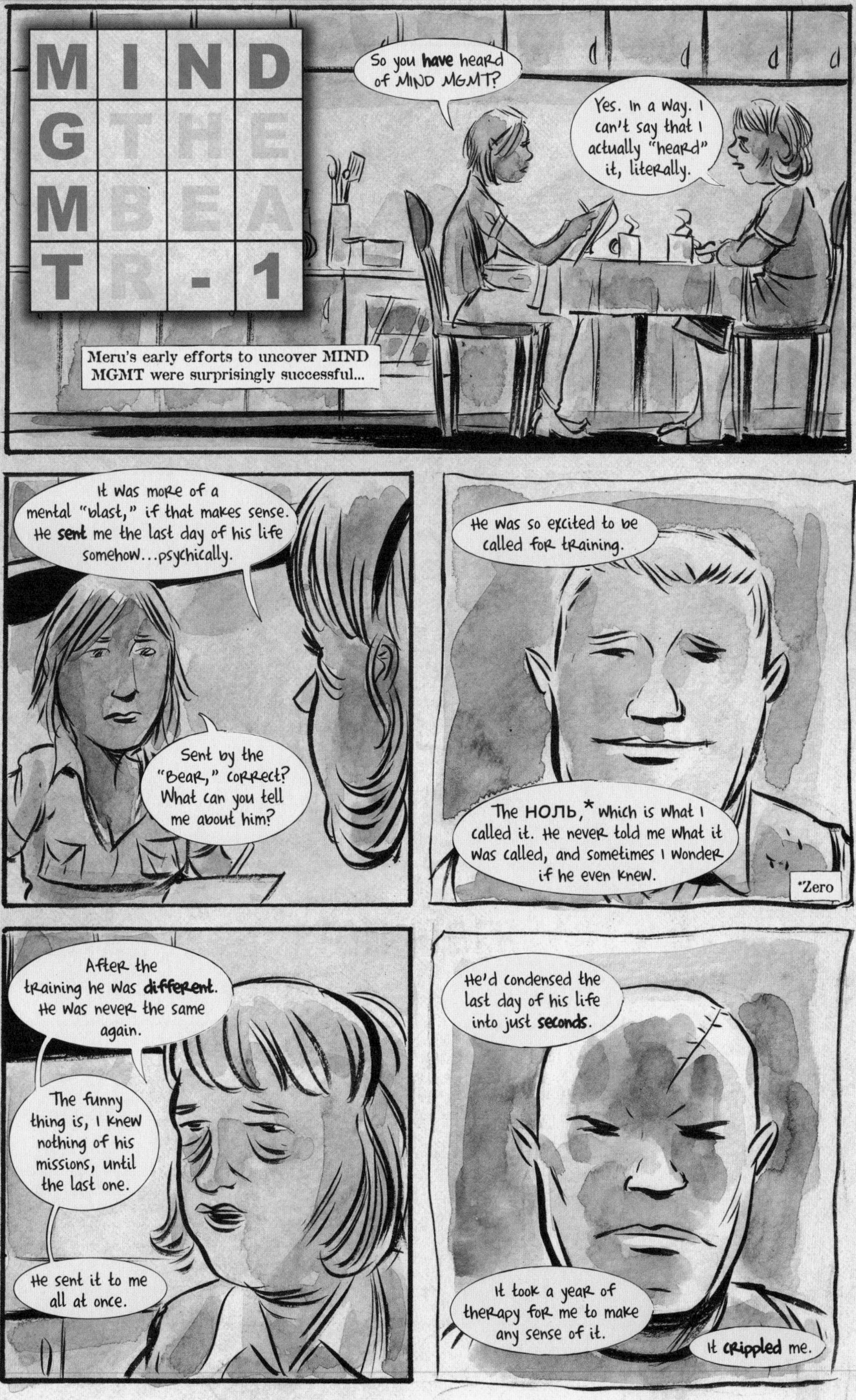
MIND MGMT THE BEAR - 1
Meru's early efforts to uncover MIND MGMT were surprisingly successful...
So you have heard of MIND MGMT?
Yes. In a way. I can't say that I actually "heard" it, literally.
It was more of a mental "blast," if that makes sense. He sent me the last day of his life somehow...psychically.
Sent by the "Bear," correct? What can you tell me about him?
He was so excited to be called for training.
The НОЛЬ,* which is what I called it. He never told me what it was called, and sometimes I wonder if he even knew.
*Zero
After the training he was different. He was never the same again.
The funny thing is, I knew nothing of his missions, until the last one.
He sent it to me all at once.
He'd condensed the last day of his life into just seconds.
It took a year of therapy for me to make any sense of it.
It crippled me.

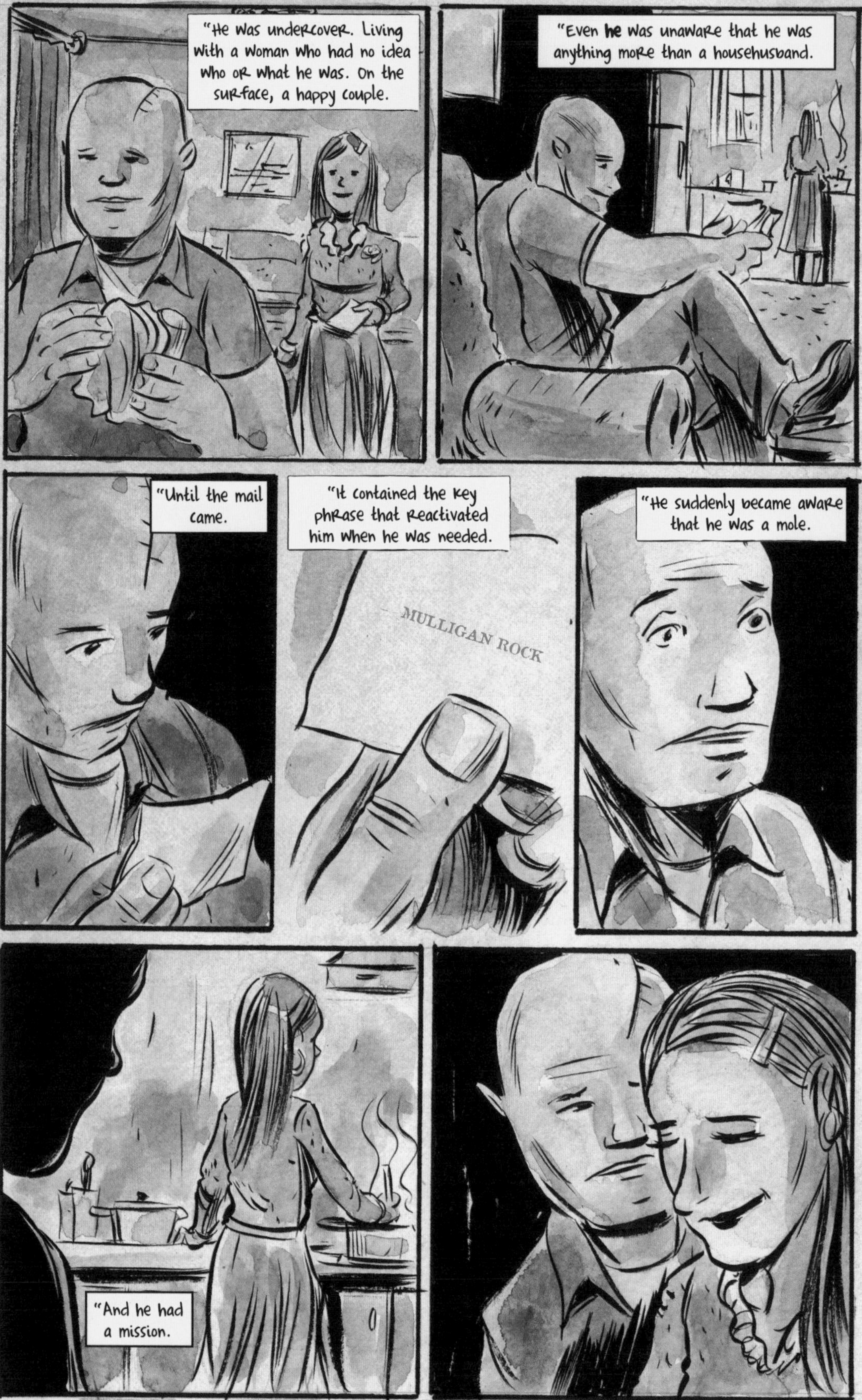
"He was undercover. Living with a woman who had no idea who or what he was. On the surface, a happy couple.
"Even he was unaware that he was anything more than a househusband.
"Until the mail came.
"It contained the key phrase that reactivated him when he was needed.
MULLIGAN ROCK
"He suddenly became aware that he was a mole.
"And he had a mission.

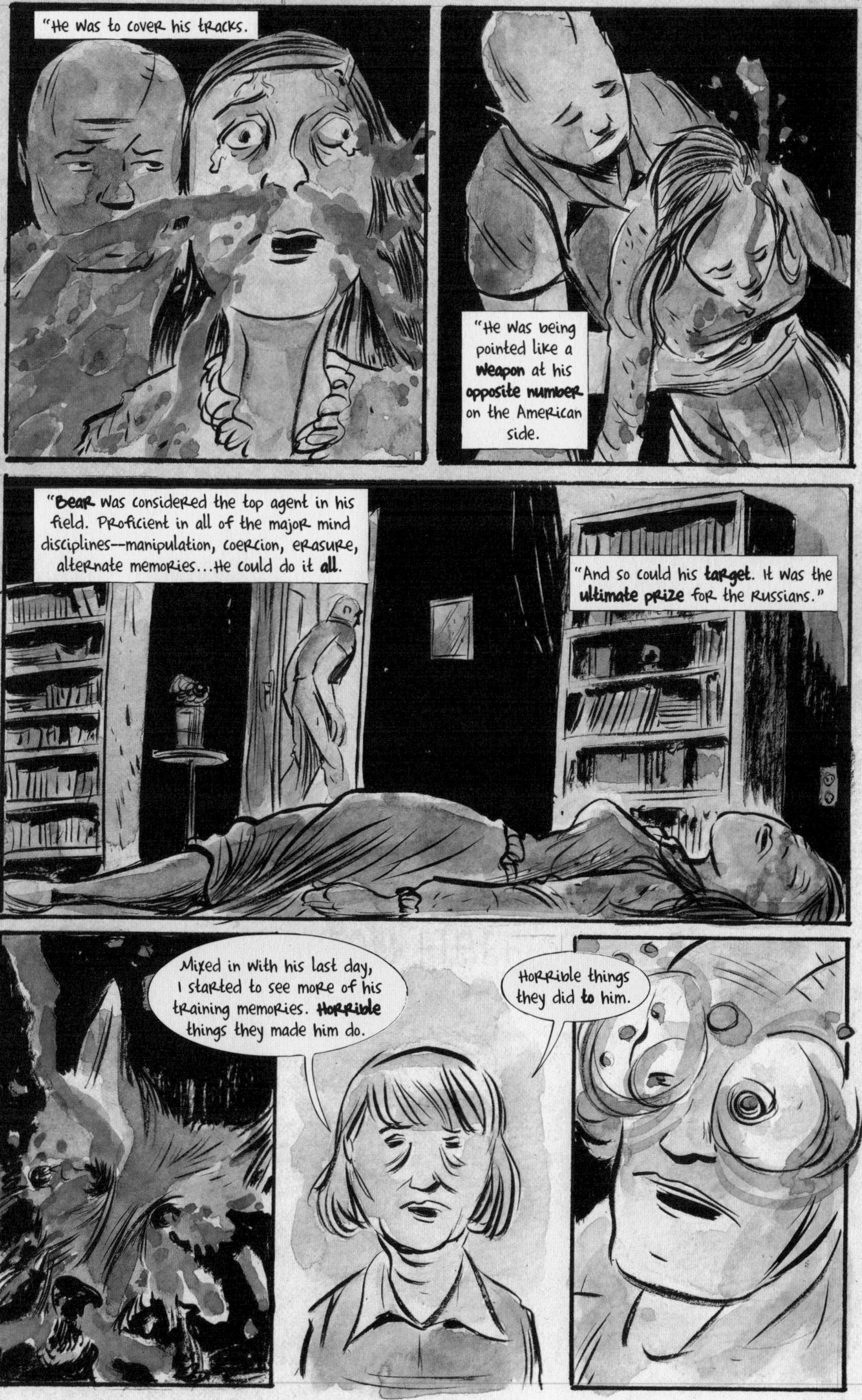
"He was to cover his tracks.
"He was being pointed like a **weapon** at his **opposite number** on the American side.
"**Bear** was considered the top agent in his field. Proficient in all of the major mind disciplines--manipulation, coercion, erasure, alternate memories...He could do it **all**.
"And so could his **target**. It was the **ultimate prize** for the Russians."
Mixed in with his last day, I started to see more of his training memories. **Horrible** things they made him do.
Horrible things they did **to** him.

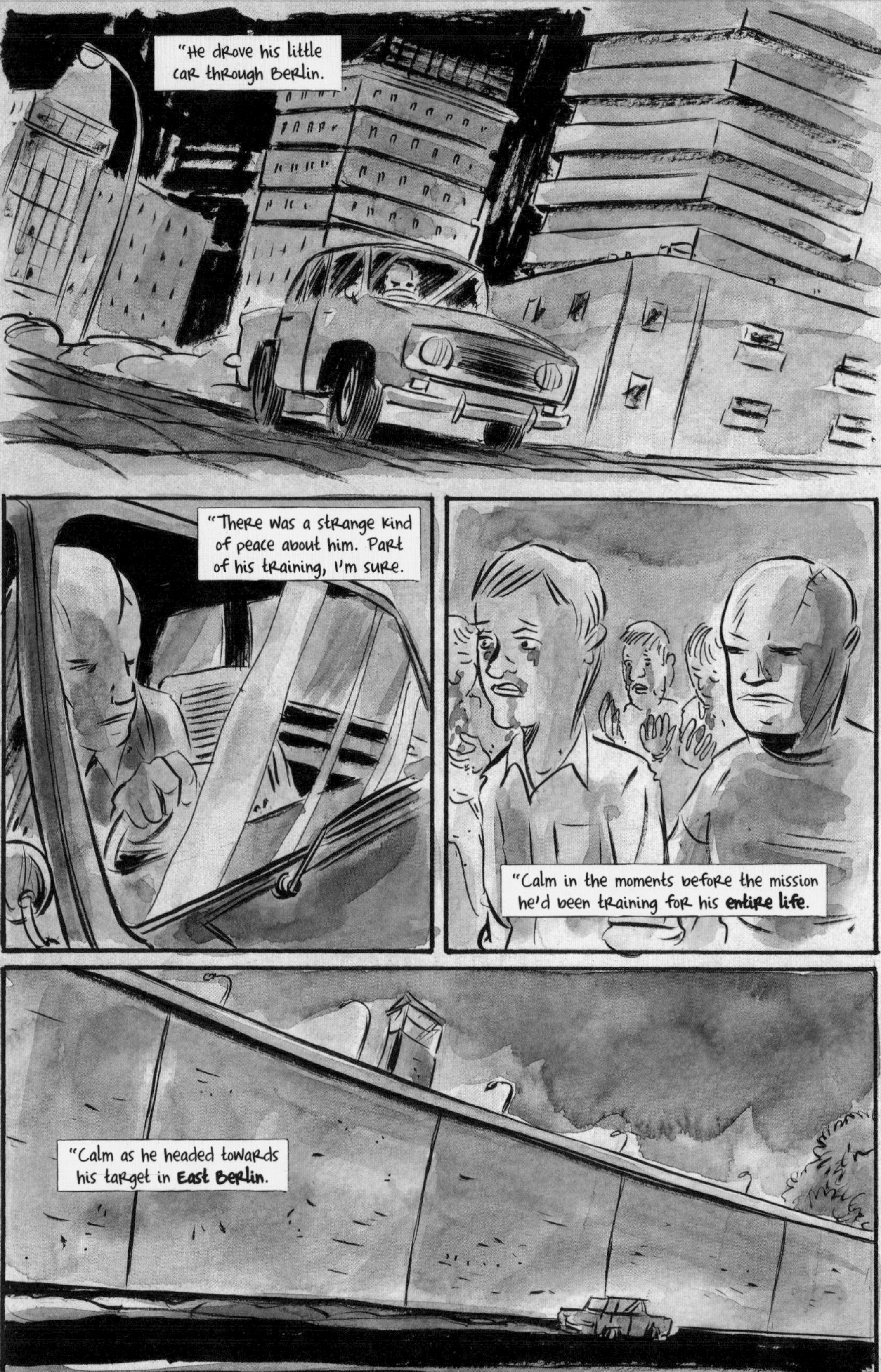
"He drove his little car through Berlin.
"There was a strange kind of peace about him. Part of his training, I'm sure.
"Calm in the moments before the mission he'd been training for his **entire life**.
"Calm as he headed towards his target in **East Berlin**.

WHEN FILING REPORT ALL ESSENTIAL DETAILS MUST FALL WITHIN THIS SOLID "LIVE AREA" BOX. THIS IS THE BORDER FOR A STANDARD, NON-BLEED FIELD REPORT

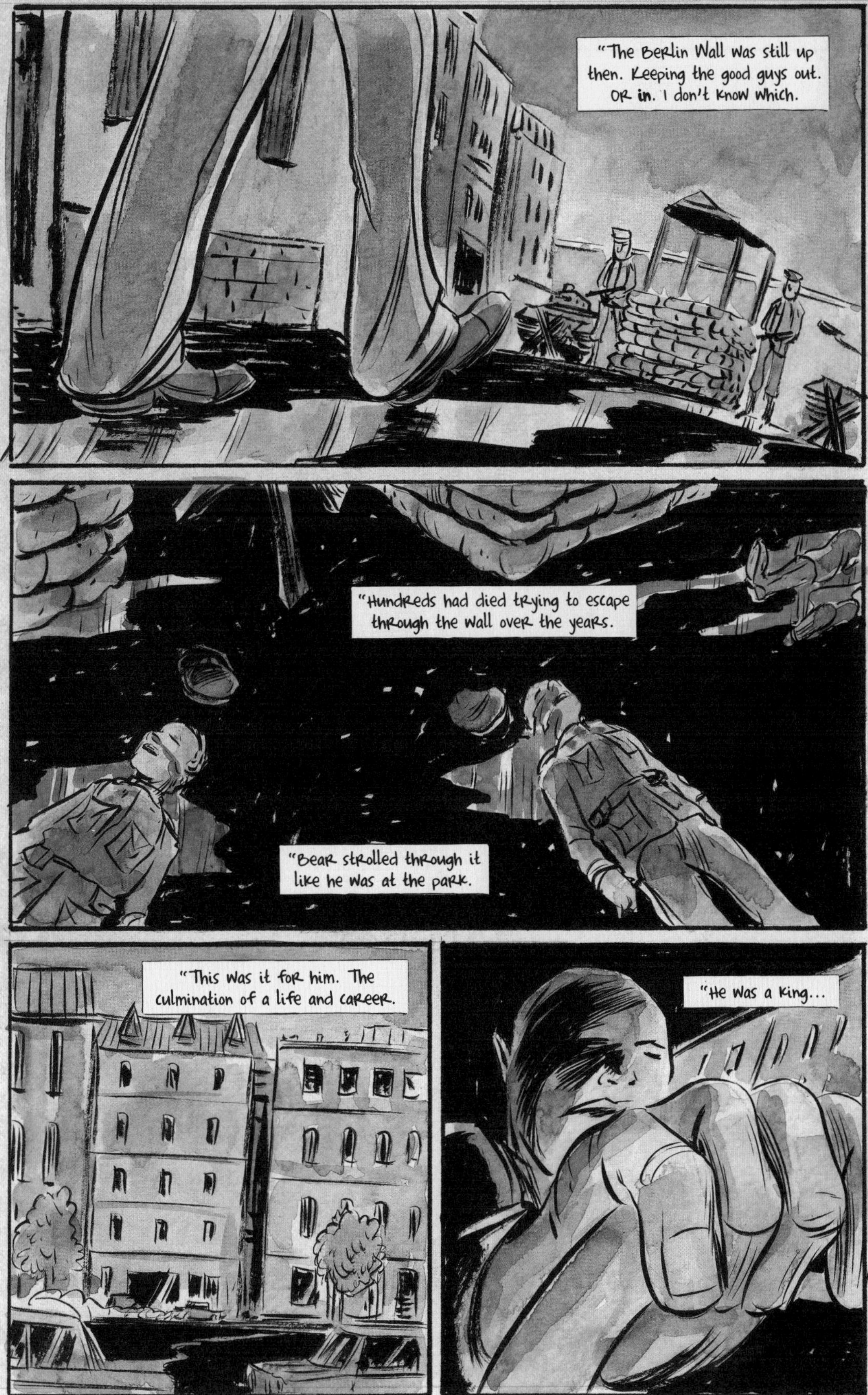
"The Berlin Wall was still up then. Keeping the good guys out. Or in. I don't know which.
"Hundreds had died trying to escape through the wall over the years.
"Bear strolled through it like he was at the park.
"This was it for him. The culmination of a life and career.
"He was a king...

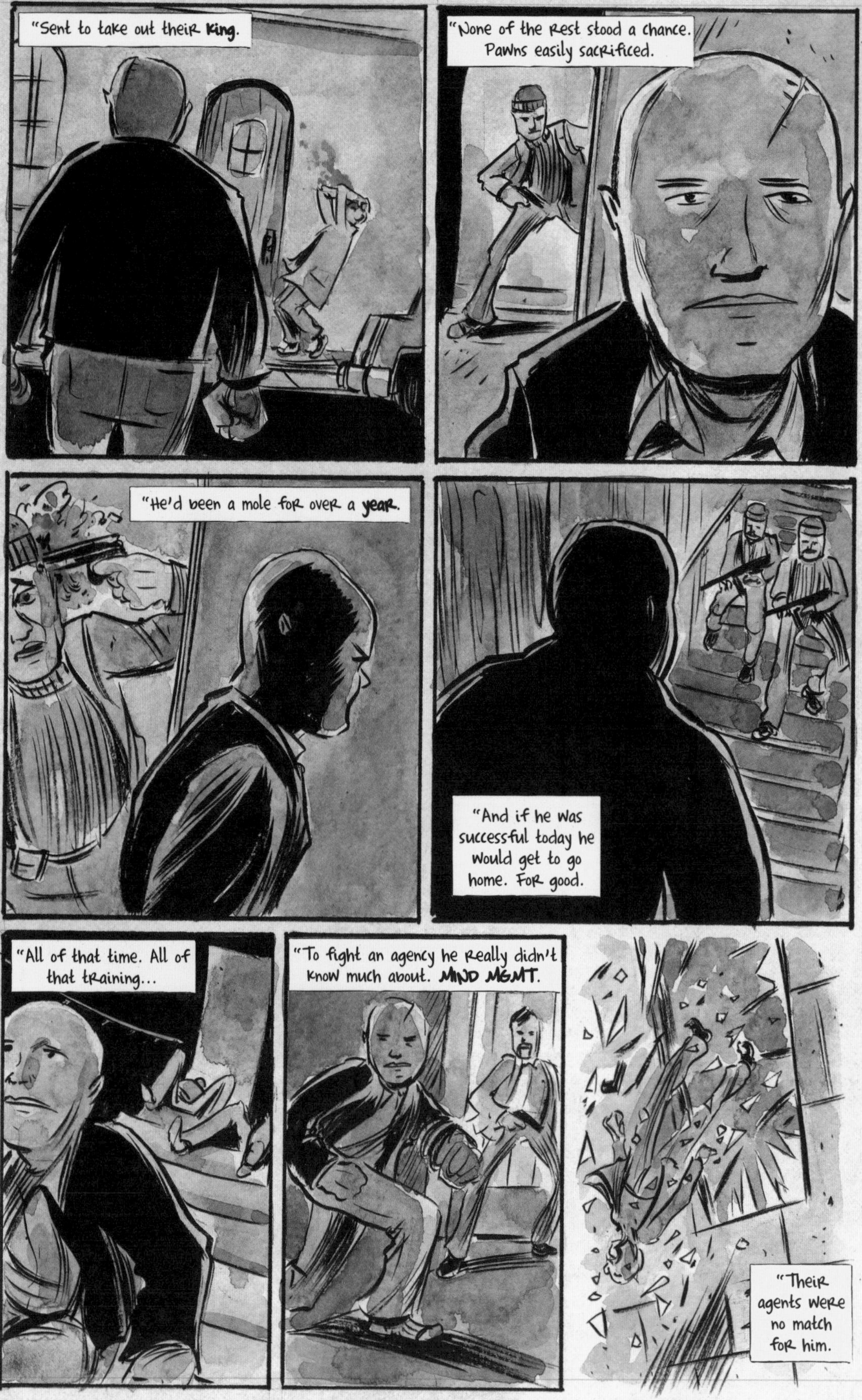
"Sent to take out their King.
"None of the Rest stood a chance. Pawns easily sacrificed.
"He'd been a mole for over a year.
"And if he was successful today he would get to go home. For good.
"All of that time. All of that training...
"To fight an agency he really didn't know much about. MIND MGMT.
"Their agents were no match for him.

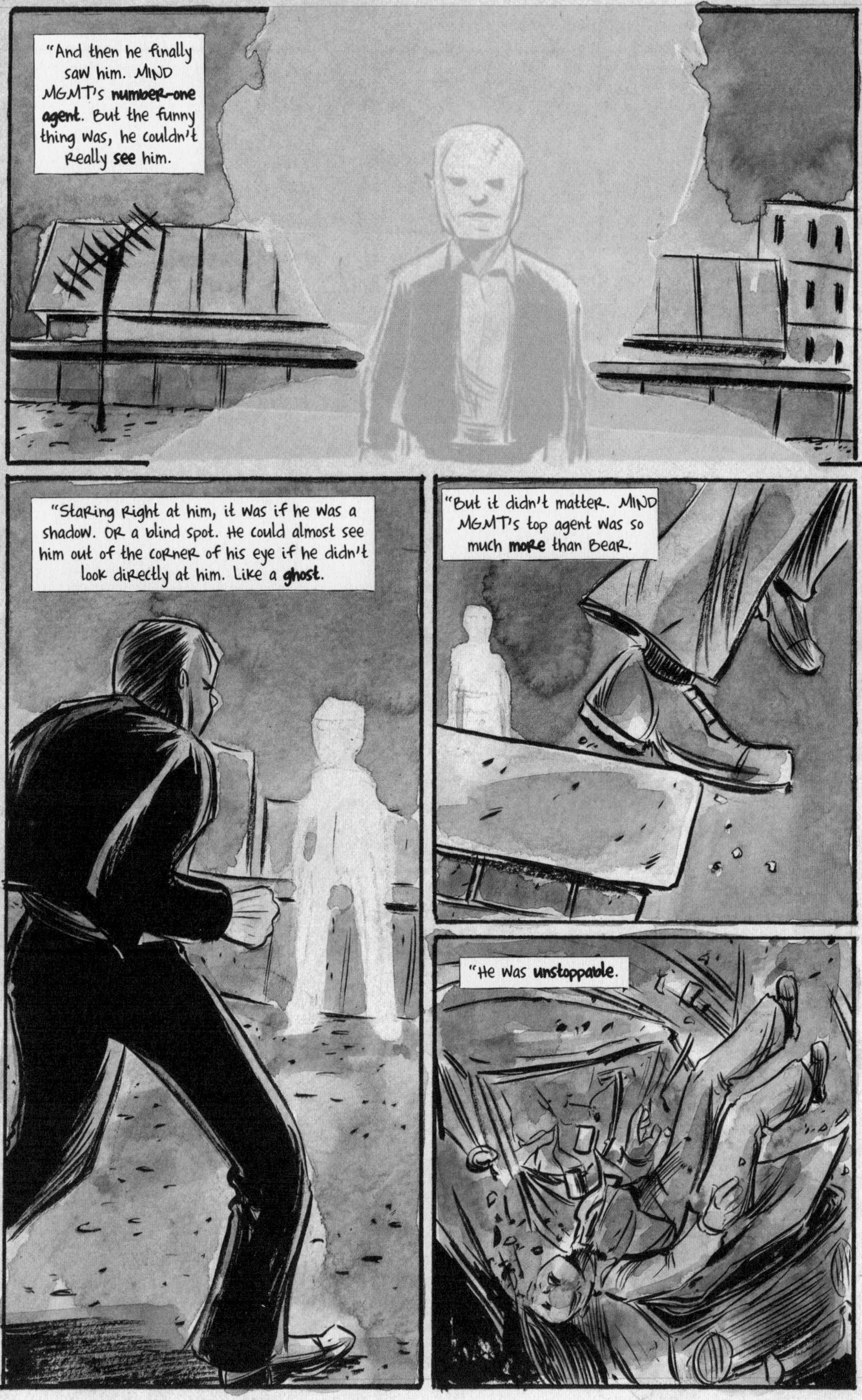
"And then he finally saw him. MIND MGMT's **number-one agent**. But the funny thing was, he couldn't really **see** him.
"Staring right at him, it was if he was a shadow. Or a blind spot. He could almost see him out of the corner of his eye if he didn't look directly at him. Like a **ghost**.
"But it didn't matter. MIND MGMT's top agent was so much **more** than Bear.
"He was **unstoppable**.

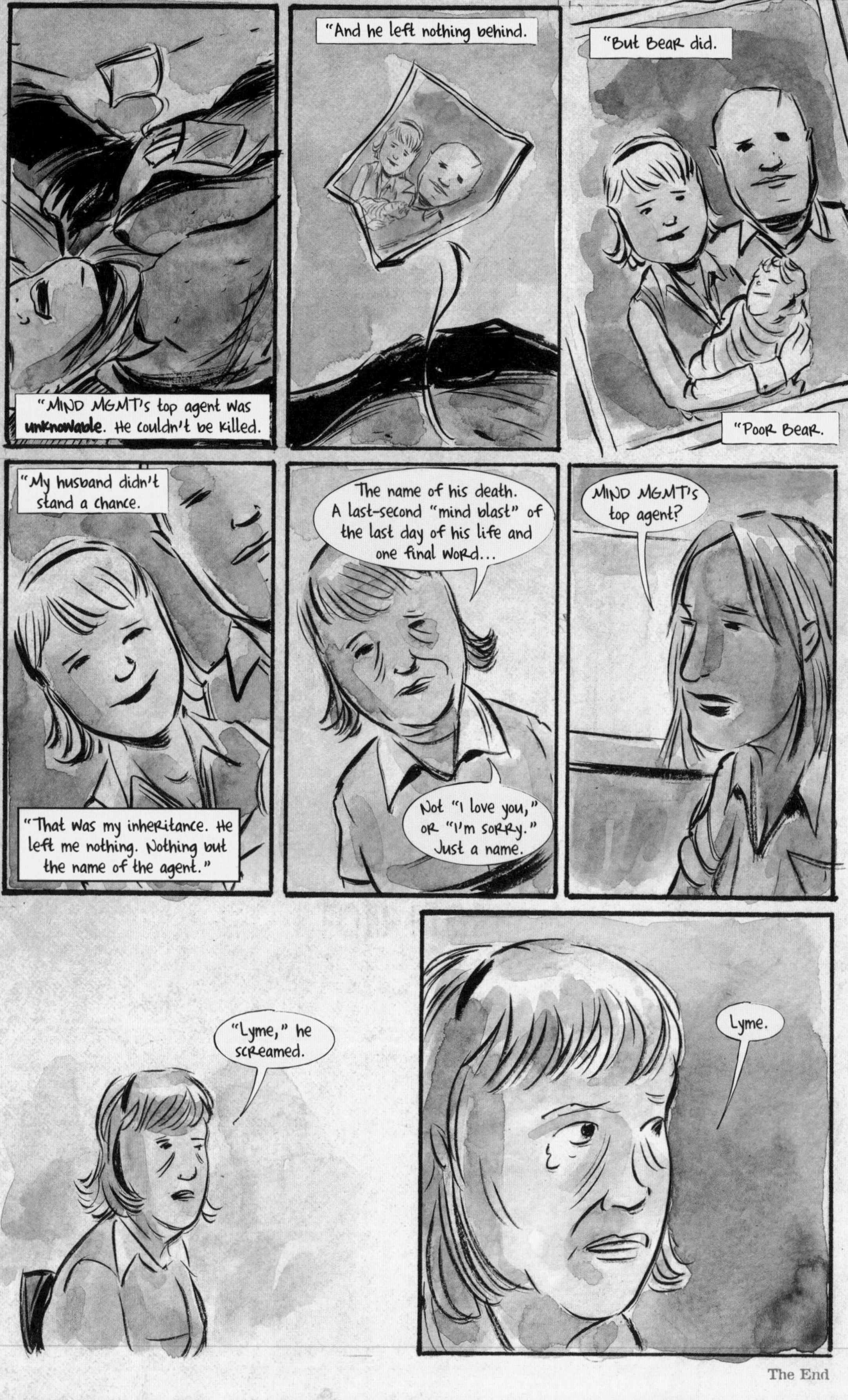
"MIND MGMT's top agent was unknowable. He couldn't be killed.
"And he left nothing behind.
"But Bear did.
"Poor Bear.
"My husband didn't stand a chance.
"That was my inheritance. He left me nothing. Nothing but the name of the agent."
The name of his death. A last-second "mind blast" of the last day of his life and one final word...
Not "I love you," or "I'm sorry." Just a name.
MIND MGMT's top agent?
"Lyme," he screamed.
Lyme.

The End

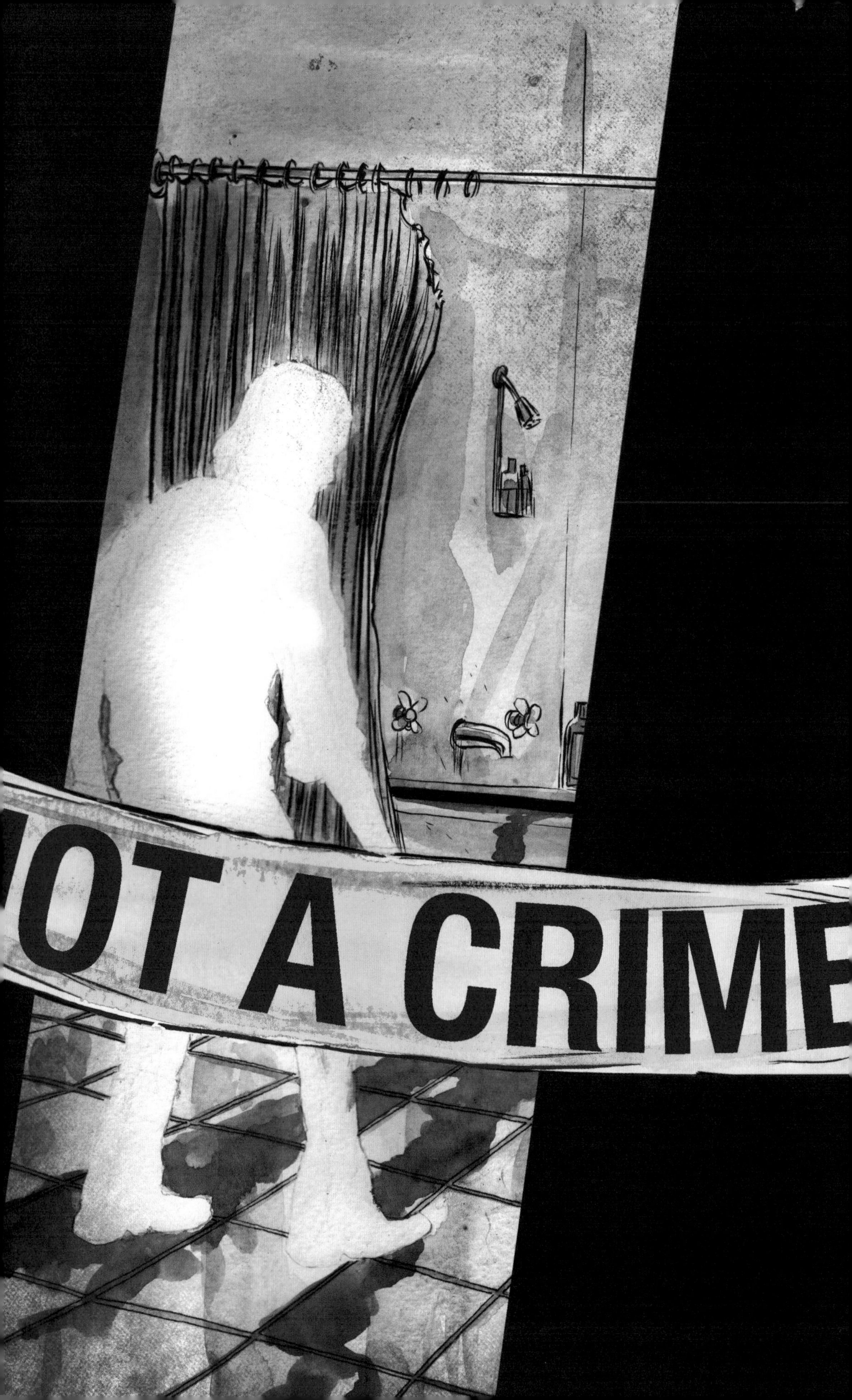
OT A CRIME

WHEN FILING REPORT ALL ESSENTIAL DETAILS MUST FALL WITHIN THIS SOLID "LIVE AREA" BOX. THIS IS THE BORDER FOR A STANDARD, NON-BLEED FIELD REPORT

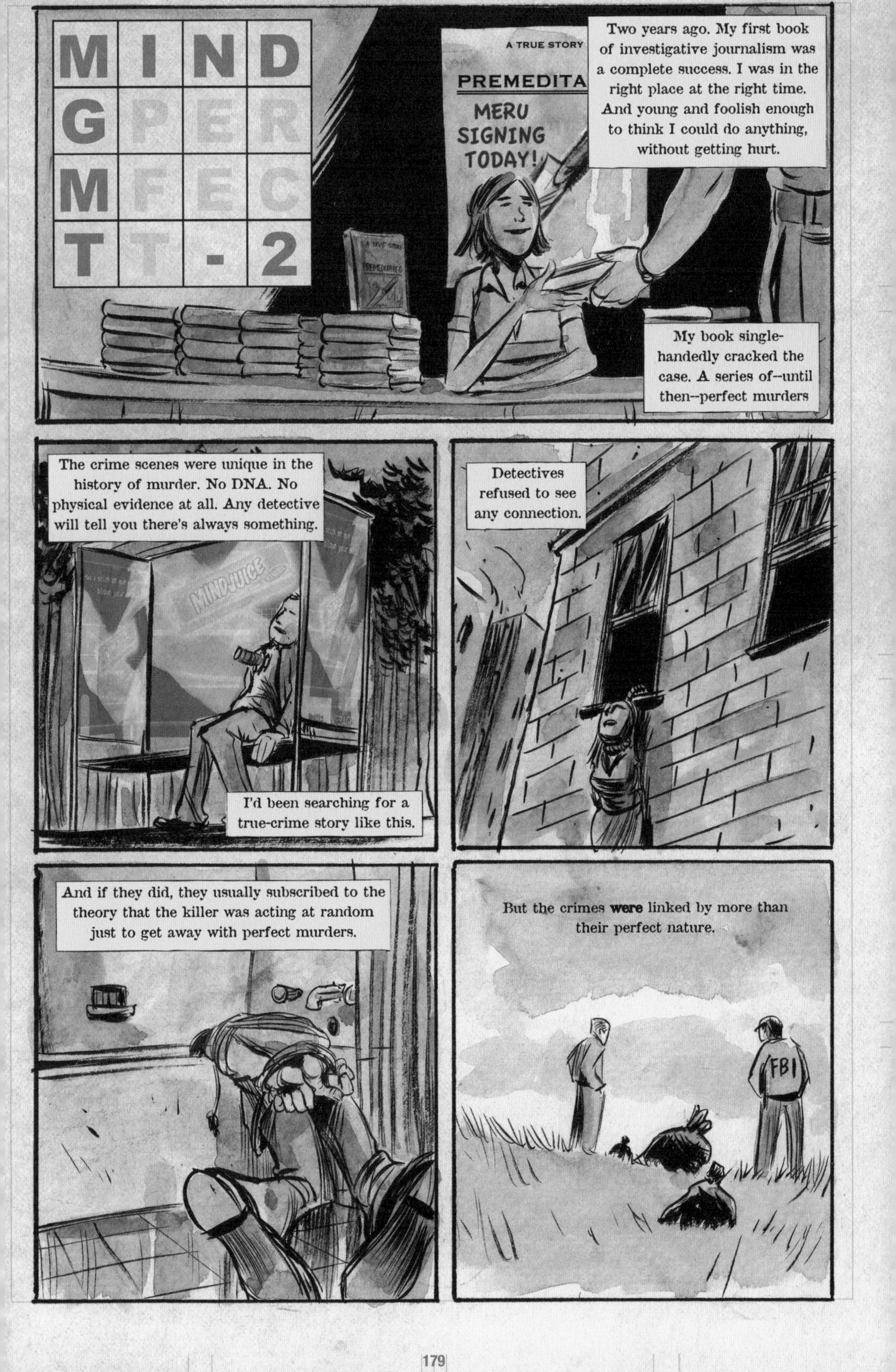

MIND
GPER
MFEC
TT-2
A TRUE STORY
PREMEDITA
MERU SIGNING TODAY!
Two years ago. My first book of investigative journalism was a complete success. I was in the right place at the right time. And young and foolish enough to think I could do anything, without getting hurt.
My book single-handedly cracked the case. A series of--until then--perfect murders
The crime scenes were unique in the history of murder. No DNA. No physical evidence at all. Any detective will tell you there's always something.
MINDJUICE
I'd been searching for a true-crime story like this.
Detectives refused to see any connection.
And if they did, they usually subscribed to the theory that the killer was acting at random just to get away with perfect murders.
But the crimes **were** linked by more than their perfect nature.
FBI

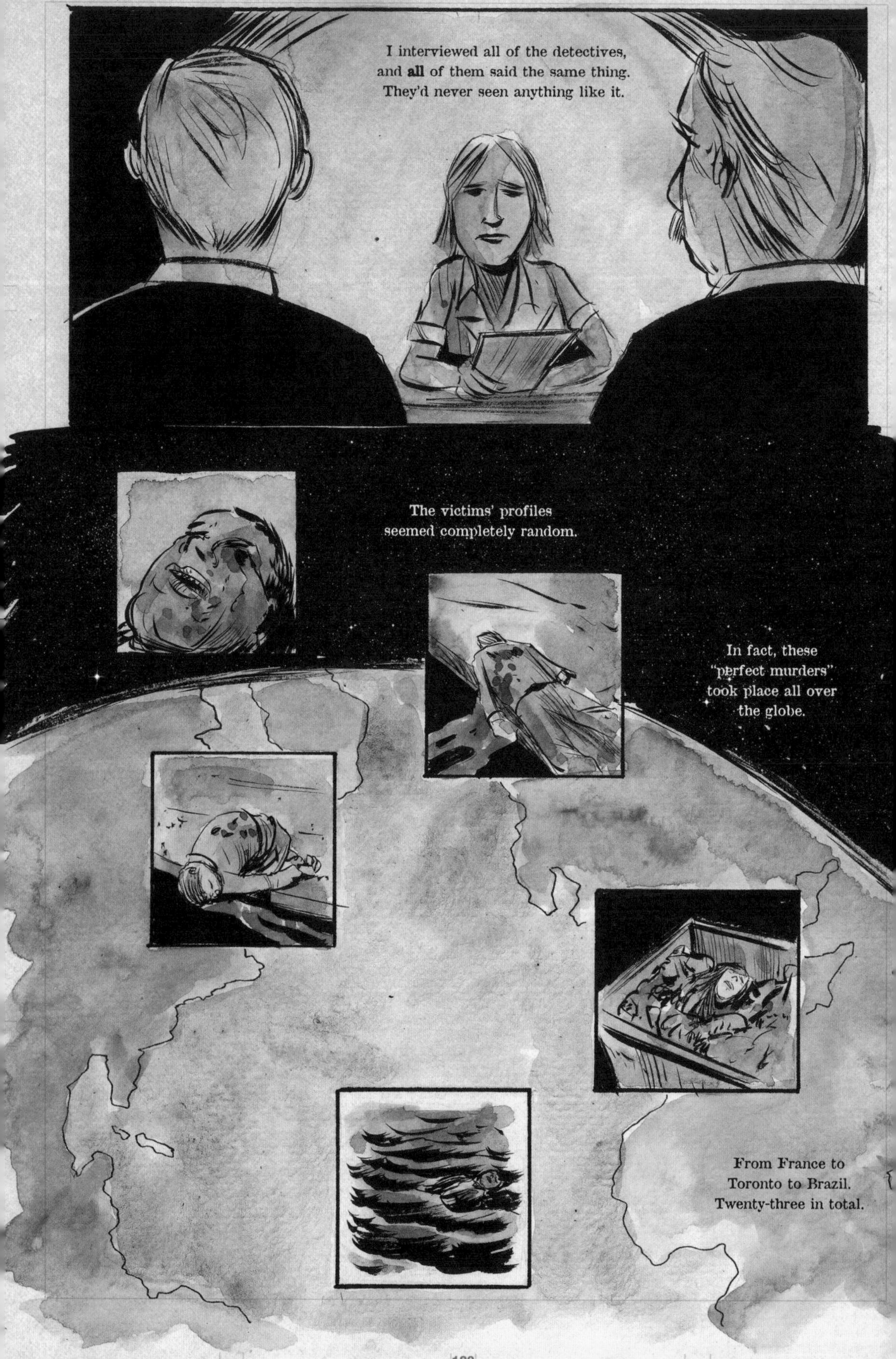
I interviewed all of the detectives, and **all** of them said the same thing. They'd never seen anything like it.
The victims' profiles seemed completely random.
In fact, these "perfect murders" took place all over the globe.
From France to Toronto to Brazil. Twenty-three in total.

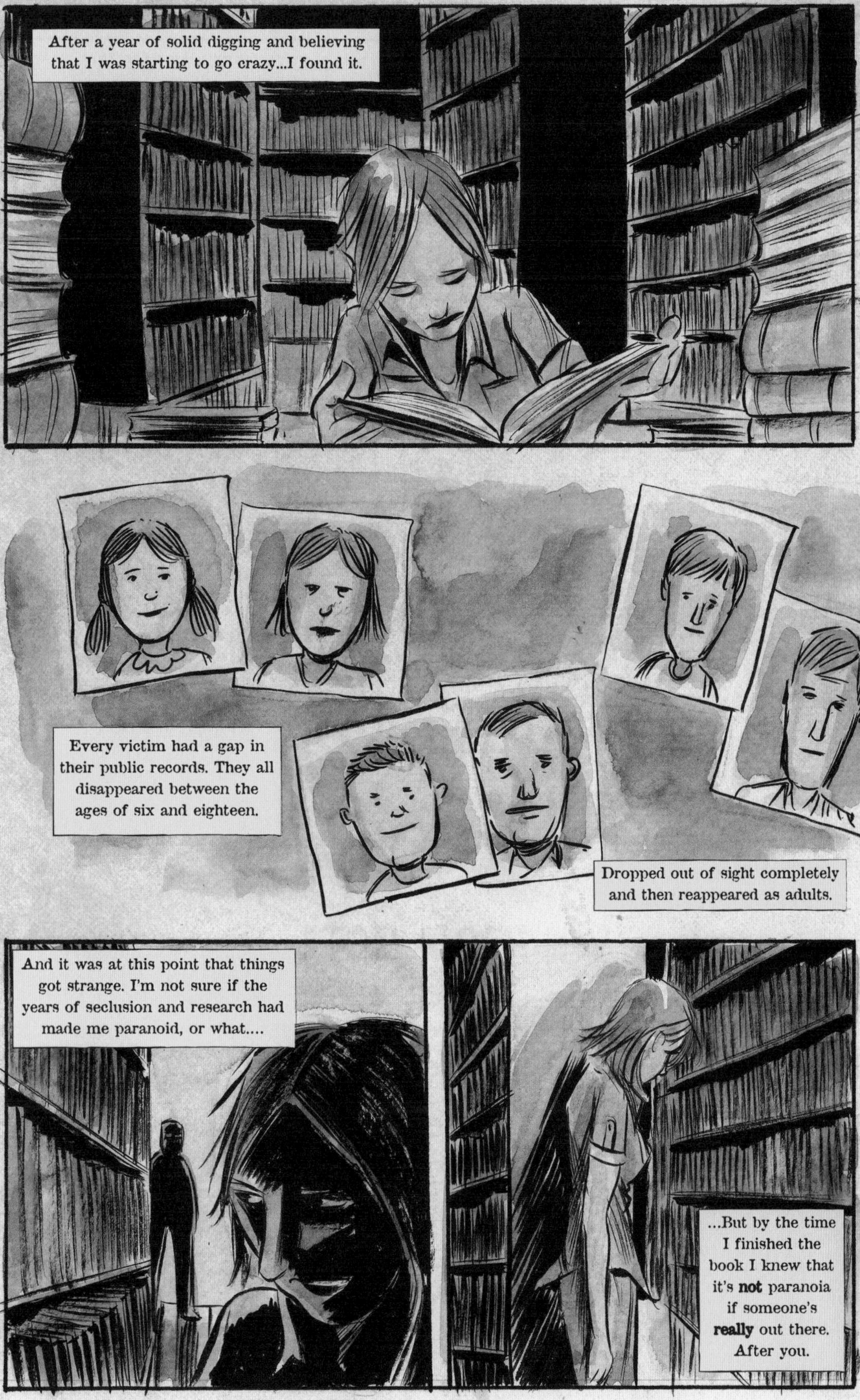
After a year of solid digging and believing that I was starting to go crazy...I found it.
Every victim had a gap in their public records. They all disappeared between the ages of six and eighteen.
Dropped out of sight completely and then reappeared as adults.
And it was at this point that things got strange. I'm not sure if the years of seclusion and research had made me paranoid, or what....
...But by the time I finished the book I knew that it's **not** paranoia if someone's **really** out there. After you.

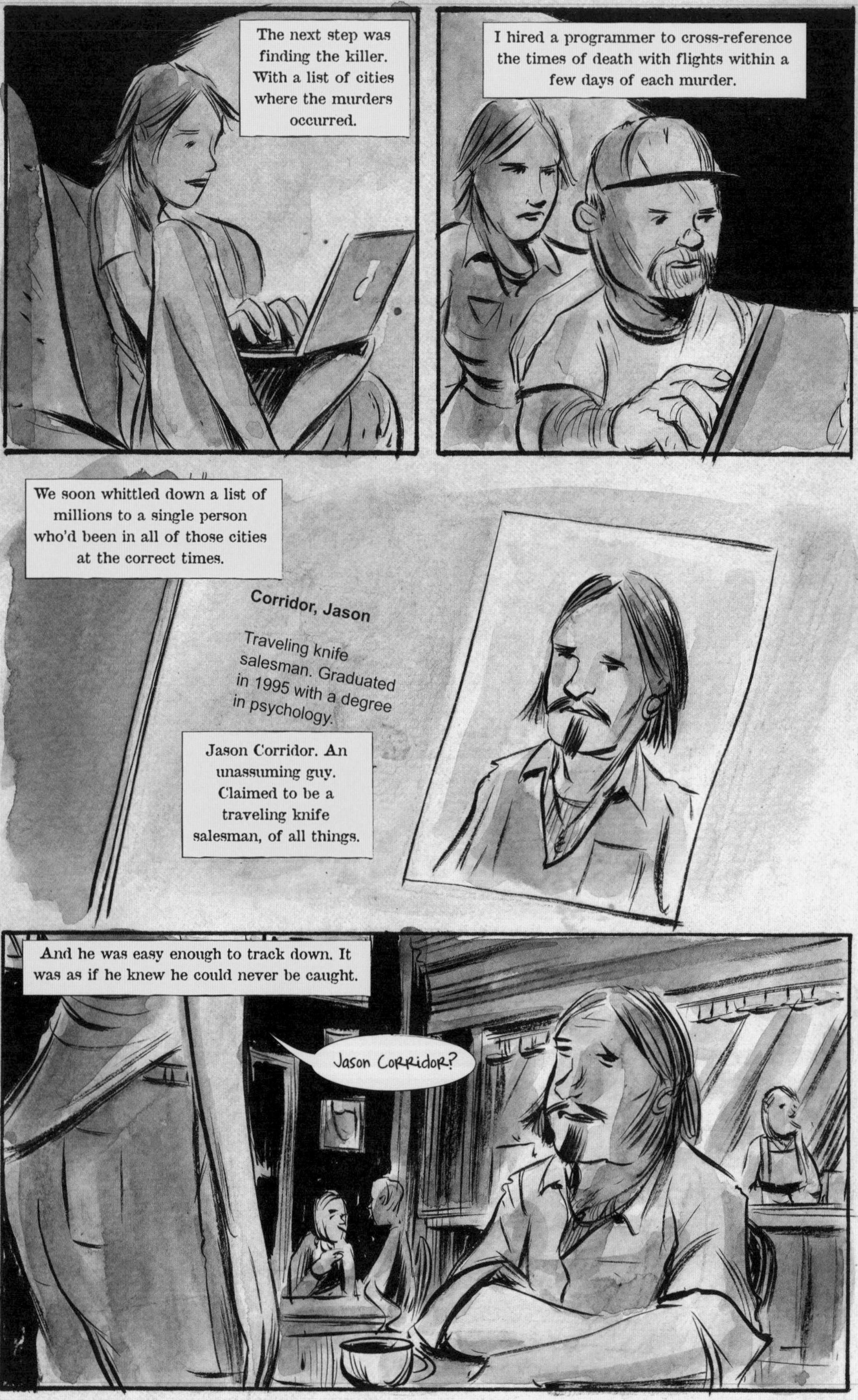
The next step was finding the killer. With a list of cities where the murders occurred.
I hired a programmer to cross-reference the times of death with flights within a few days of each murder.
We soon whittled down a list of millions to a single person who'd been in all of those cities at the correct times.
Corridor, Jason
Traveling knife salesman. Graduated in 1995 with a degree in psychology.
Jason Corridor. An unassuming guy. Claimed to be a traveling knife salesman, of all things.
And he was easy enough to track down. It was as if he knew he could never be caught.
Jason Corridor?

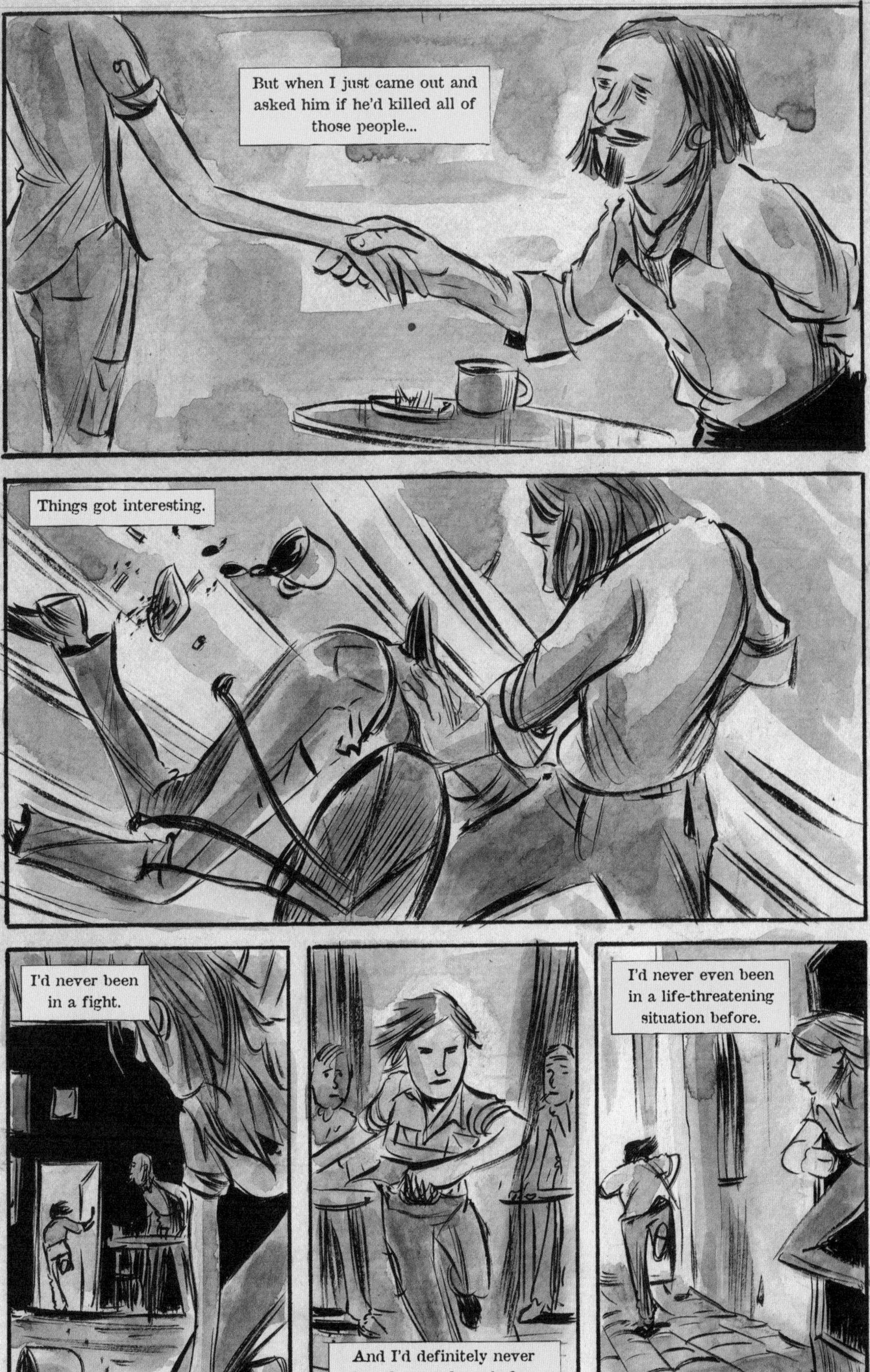
But when I just came out and asked him if he'd killed all of those people...
Things got interesting.
I'd never been in a fight.
And I'd definitely never chased a murderer before.
I'd never even been in a life-threatening situation before.

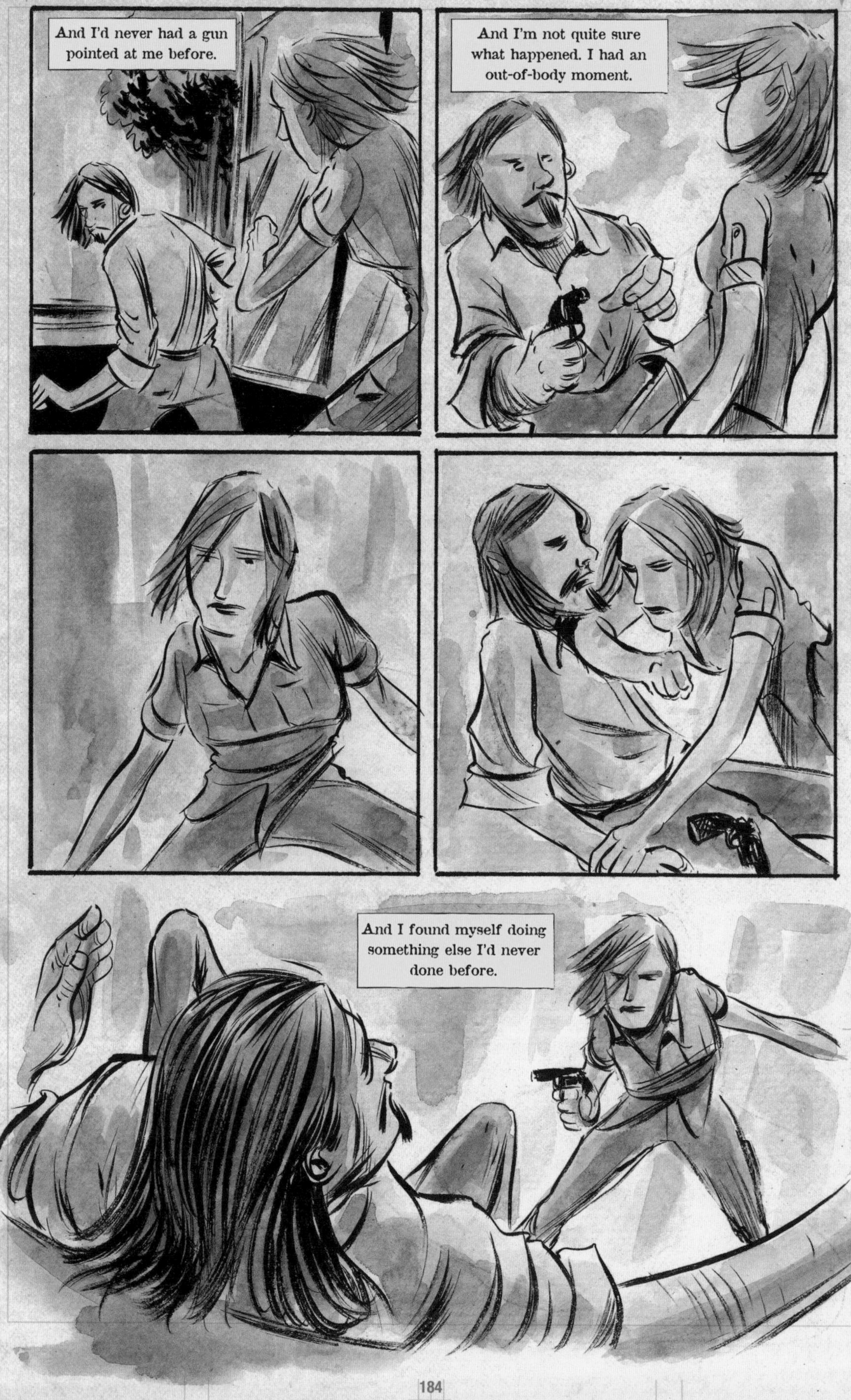
And I'd never had a gun pointed at me before.
And I'm not quite sure what happened. I had an out-of-body moment.
And I found myself doing something else I'd never done before.

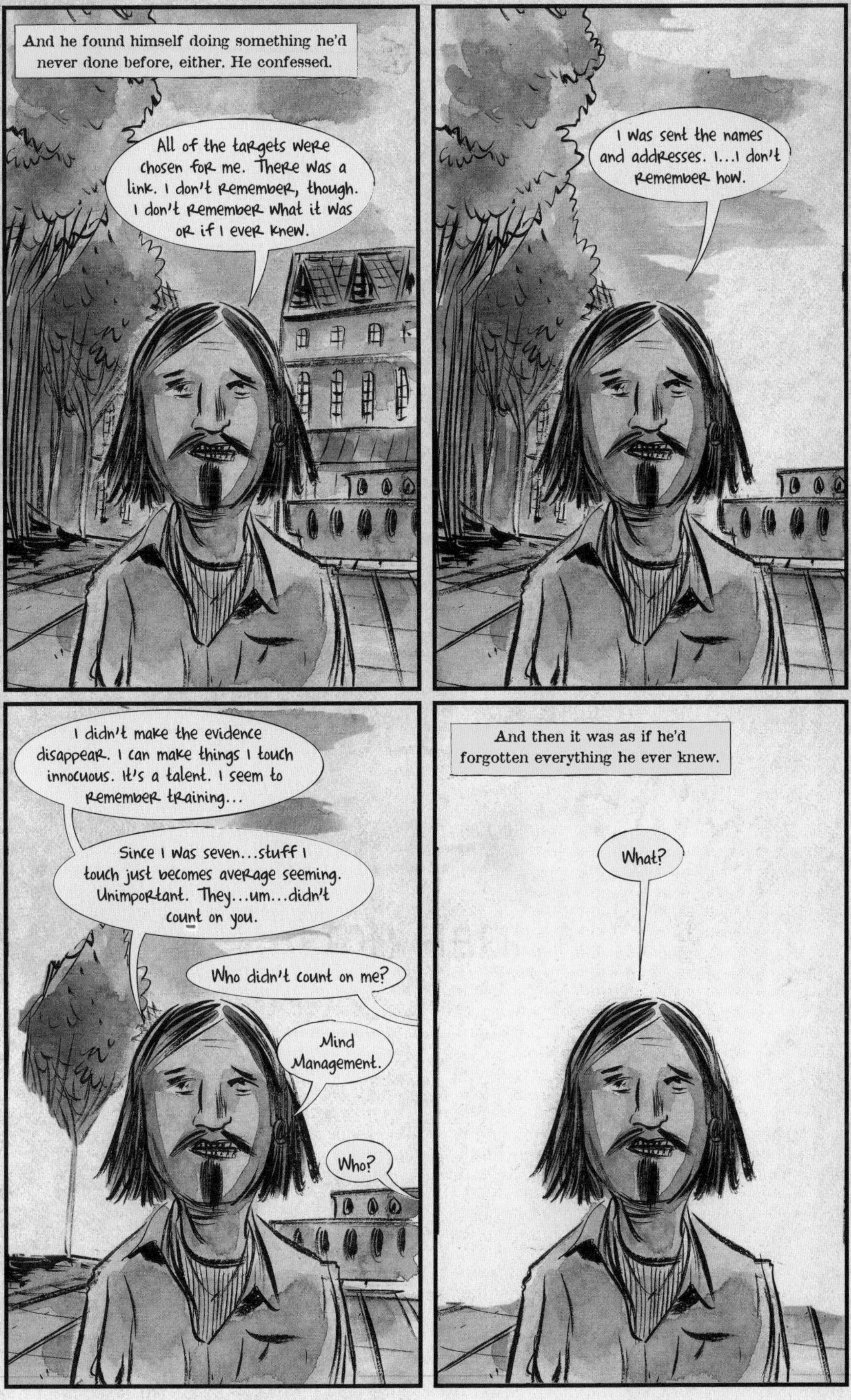
And he found himself doing something he'd never done before, either. He confessed.
All of the targets were chosen for me. There was a link. I don't remember, though. I don't remember what it was or if I ever knew.
I was sent the names and addresses. I...I don't remember how.
I didn't make the evidence disappear. I can make things I touch innocuous. It's a talent. I seem to remember training...
Since I was seven...stuff I touch just becomes average seeming. Unimportant. They...um...didn't count on you.
Who didn't count on me?
Mind Management.
Who?
And then it was as if he'd forgotten everything he ever knew.
What?

Outside investigators came in and found loads of physical evidence linking Jason Corridor to the murders.

Suddenly everything at the crime scenes became relevant somehow.

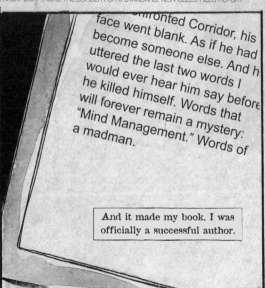

...fronted Corridor, his face went blank. As if he had become someone else. And he uttered the last two words I would ever hear him say before he killed himself. Words that will forever remain a mystery: "Mind Management." Words of a madman.

And it made my book. I was officially a successful author.

I turned the book in to my editor, who didn't have to change a word. And a million copies later, here I am.

Words that will forever remain a mystery: "Mulligan Rock." Words of a madman.

Feeling like I've just hit the tip of an iceberg.

The End

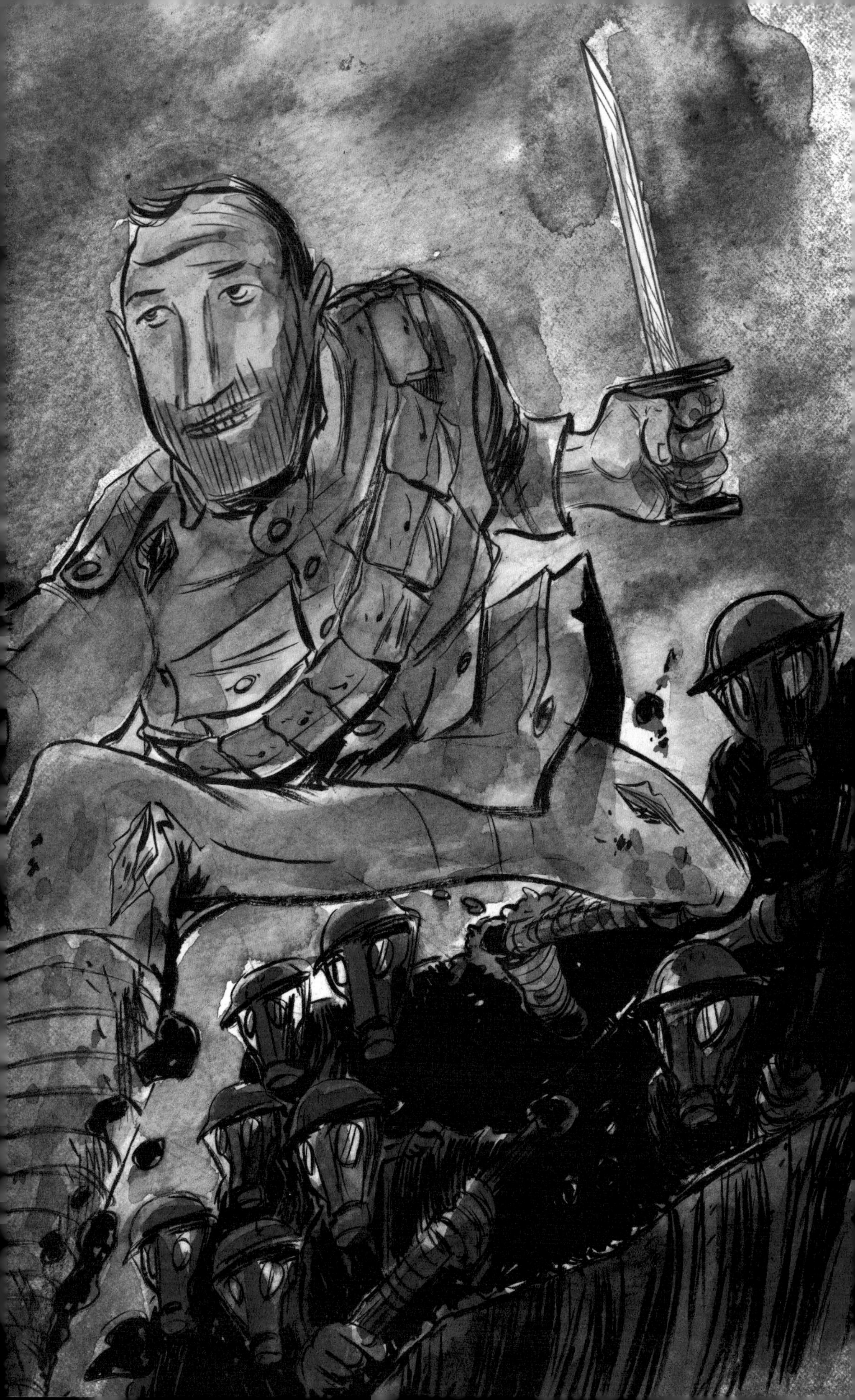

-3

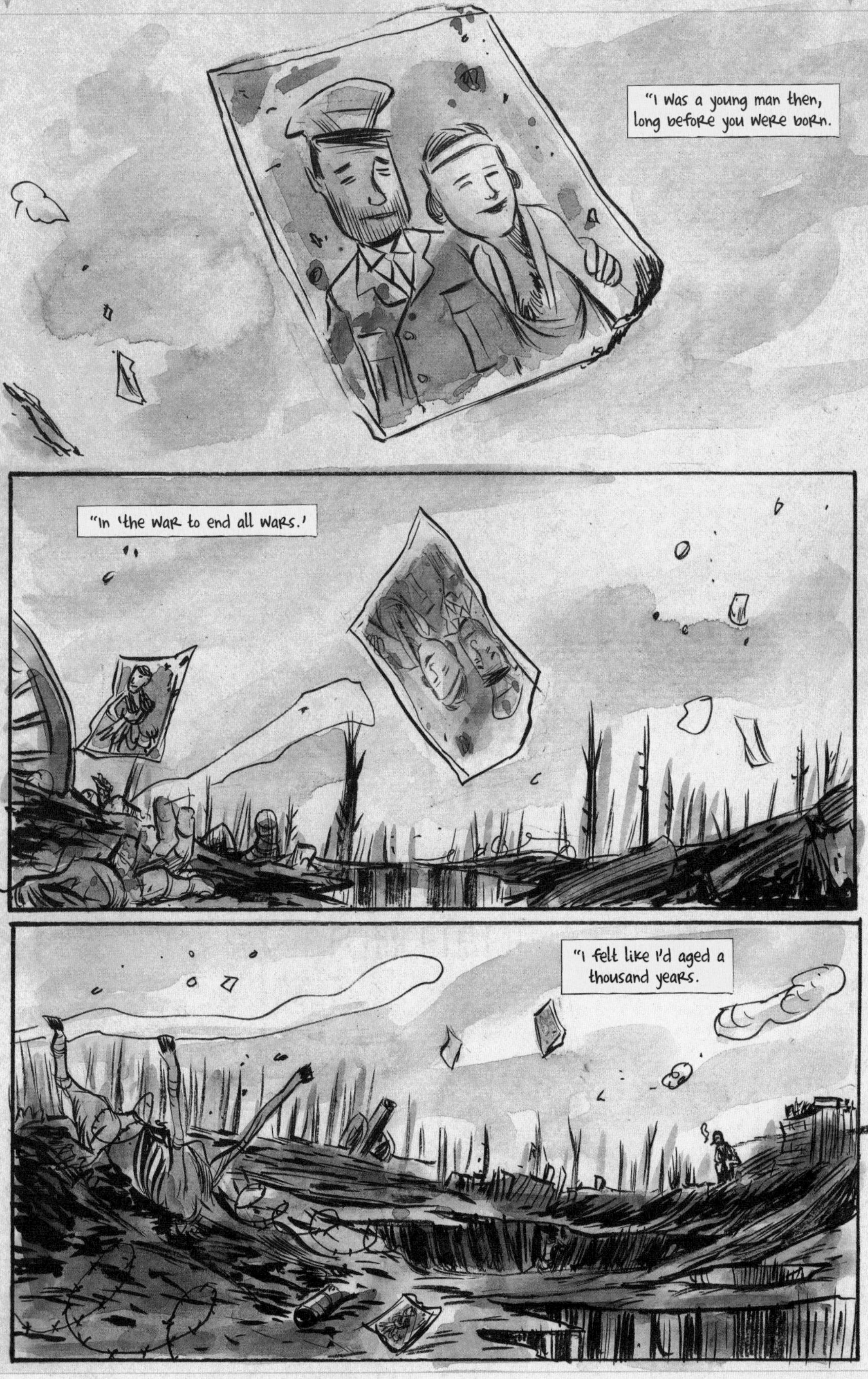
"I was a young man then, long before you were born.
"In 'the war to end all wars.'
"I felt like I'd aged a thousand years.

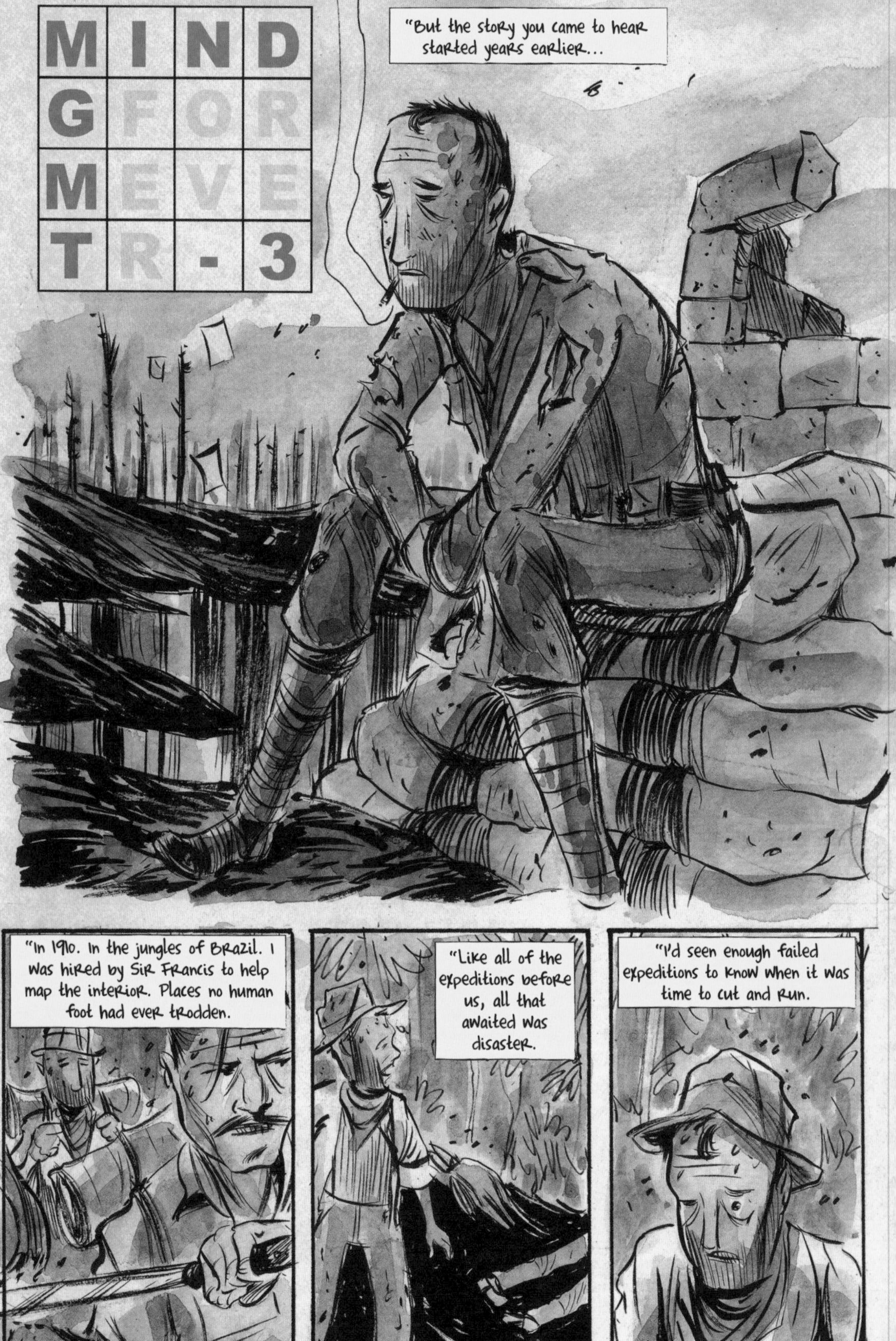
MIND
GFOR
MEVE
TR-3
"But the story you came to hear started years earlier...
"In 1910. In the jungles of Brazil. I was hired by Sir Francis to help map the interior. Places no human foot had ever trodden.
"Like all of the expeditions before us, all that awaited was disaster.
"I'd seen enough failed expeditions to know when it was time to cut and run.

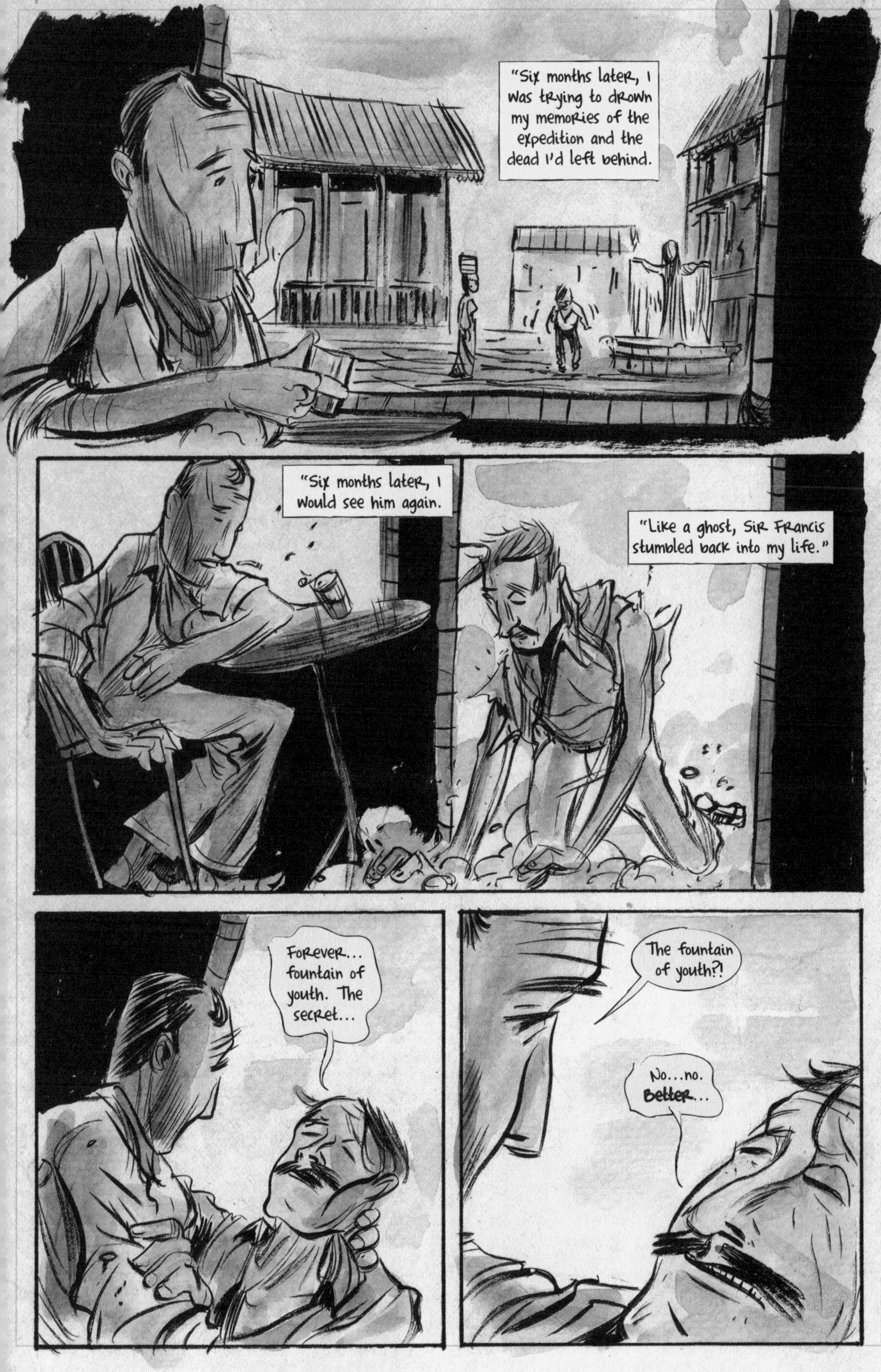
"Six months later, I was trying to drown my memories of the expedition and the dead I'd left behind.
"Six months later, I would see him again.
"Like a ghost, Sir Francis stumbled back into my life."
Forever... fountain of youth. The secret...
The fountain of youth?!
No...no. Better...

"Sir Francis had a vision in the jungle. Of a mind management technique.

"He opened my mind to the concept of mind over matter. Over body.

"Anything was possible.

"This was his revelation. And the knowledge that he slowly trained me with.

"And while initially I was surprised that he wasn't angry at me for abandoning him in the jungle...

"...he was getting a revenge of sorts.

"My body became an extension of my mind. And if my mind was invincible...

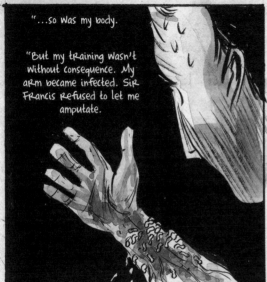

"...so was my body.

"But my training wasn't without consequence. My arm became infected. Sir Francis refused to let me amputate.

"Eventually I fought back the infection, forcing my arm to wither.

"It saved my life.

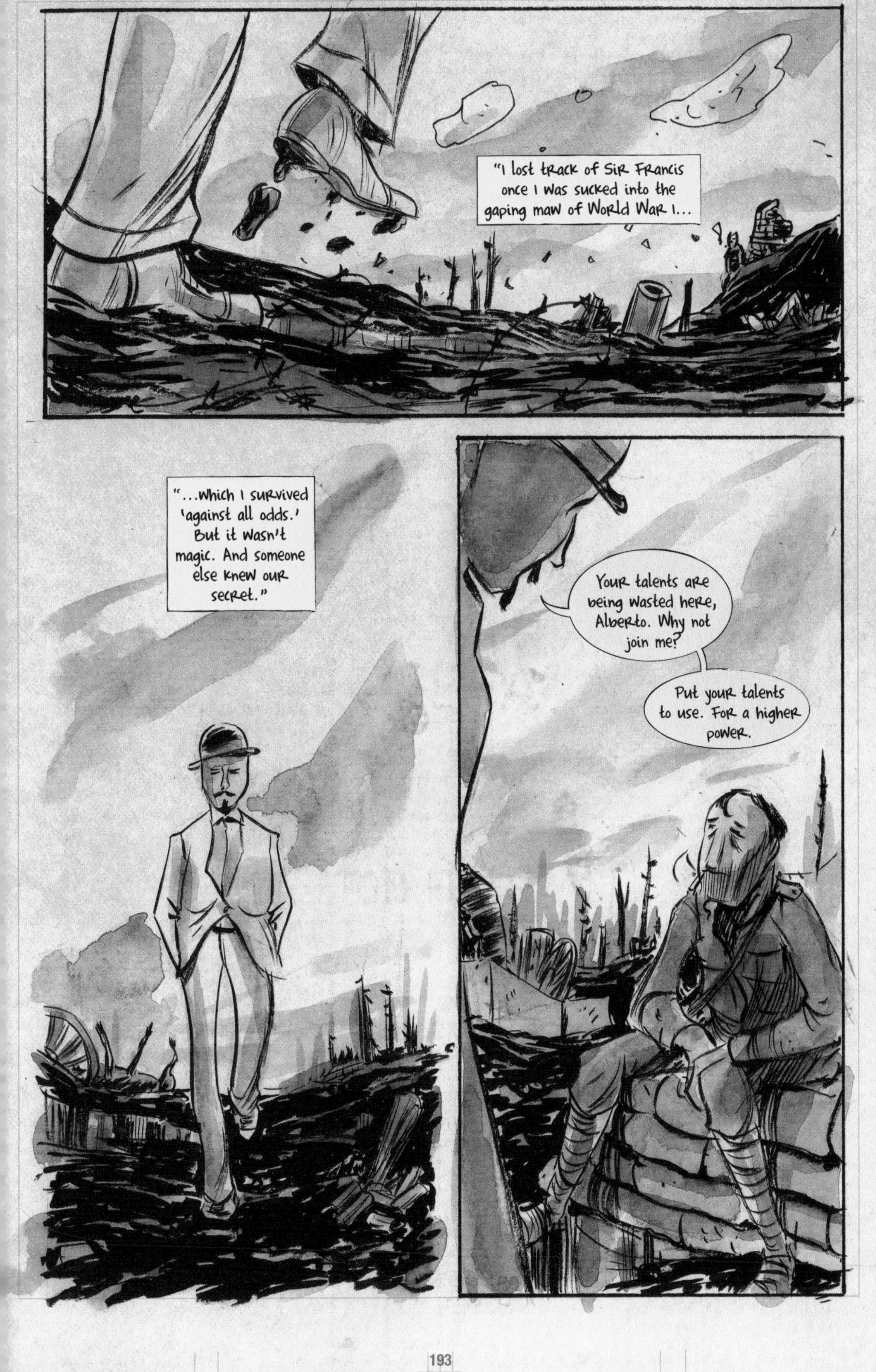
"I lost track of Sir Francis once I was sucked into the gaping maw of World War I…
"…Which I survived 'against all odds.' But it wasn't magic. And someone else knew our secret."
Your talents are being wasted here, Alberto. Why not join me?
Put your talents to use. For a higher power.

"I joined Leopold and his 'Mind Management.' I was reteamed with Sir Francis, whom he had already recruited.

"We acted as scouts, building secret bases that no other humans could reach.

"Miles below the ocean...

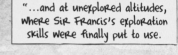

"...and at unexplored altitudes, where Sir Francis's exploration skills were finally put to use.

"Later, our missions became a little more...

"...unorthodox.

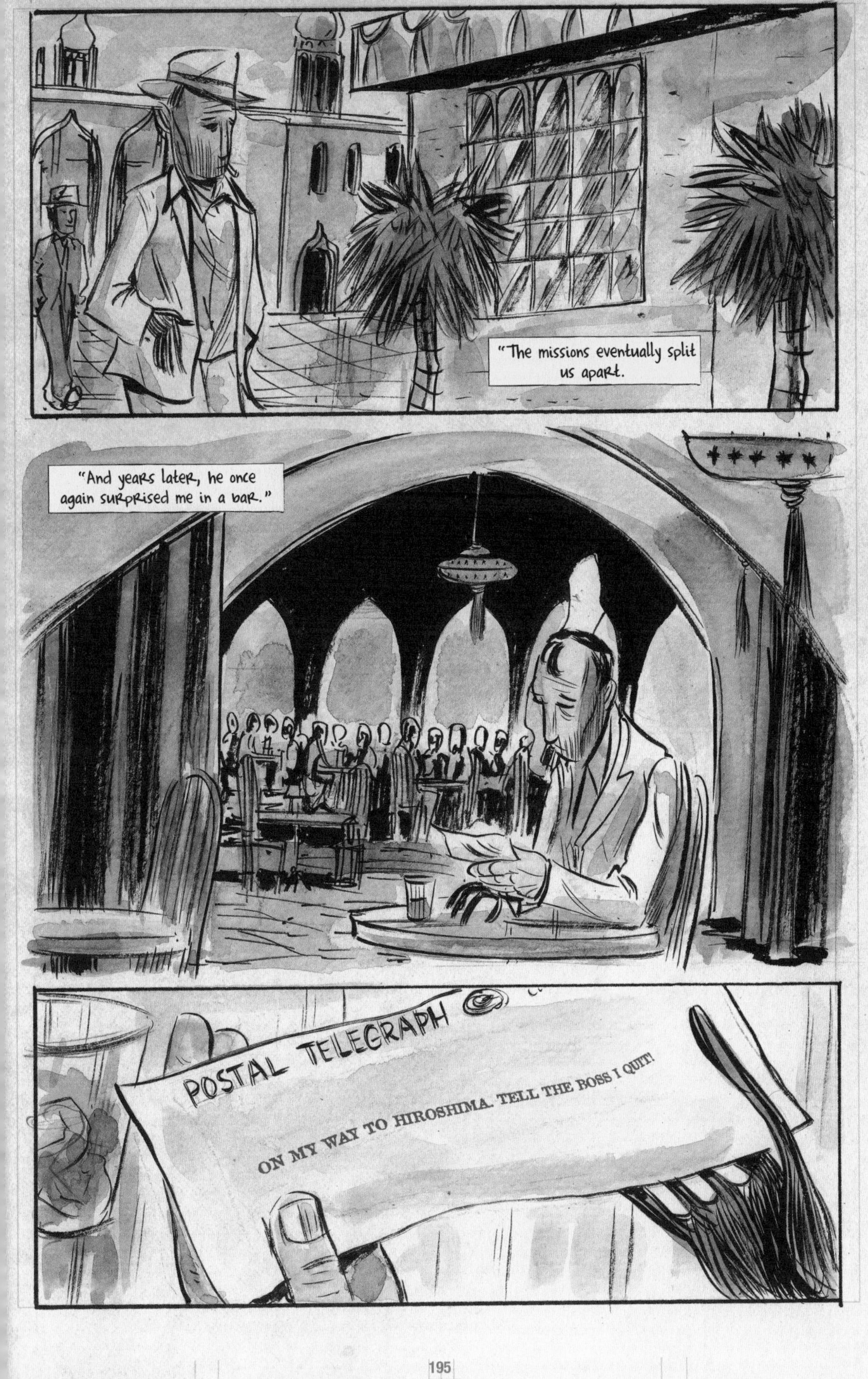
"The missions eventually split us apart.
"And years later, he once again surprised me in a bar."
POSTAL TELEGRAPH
ON MY WAY TO HIROSHIMA. TELL THE BOSS I QUIT!

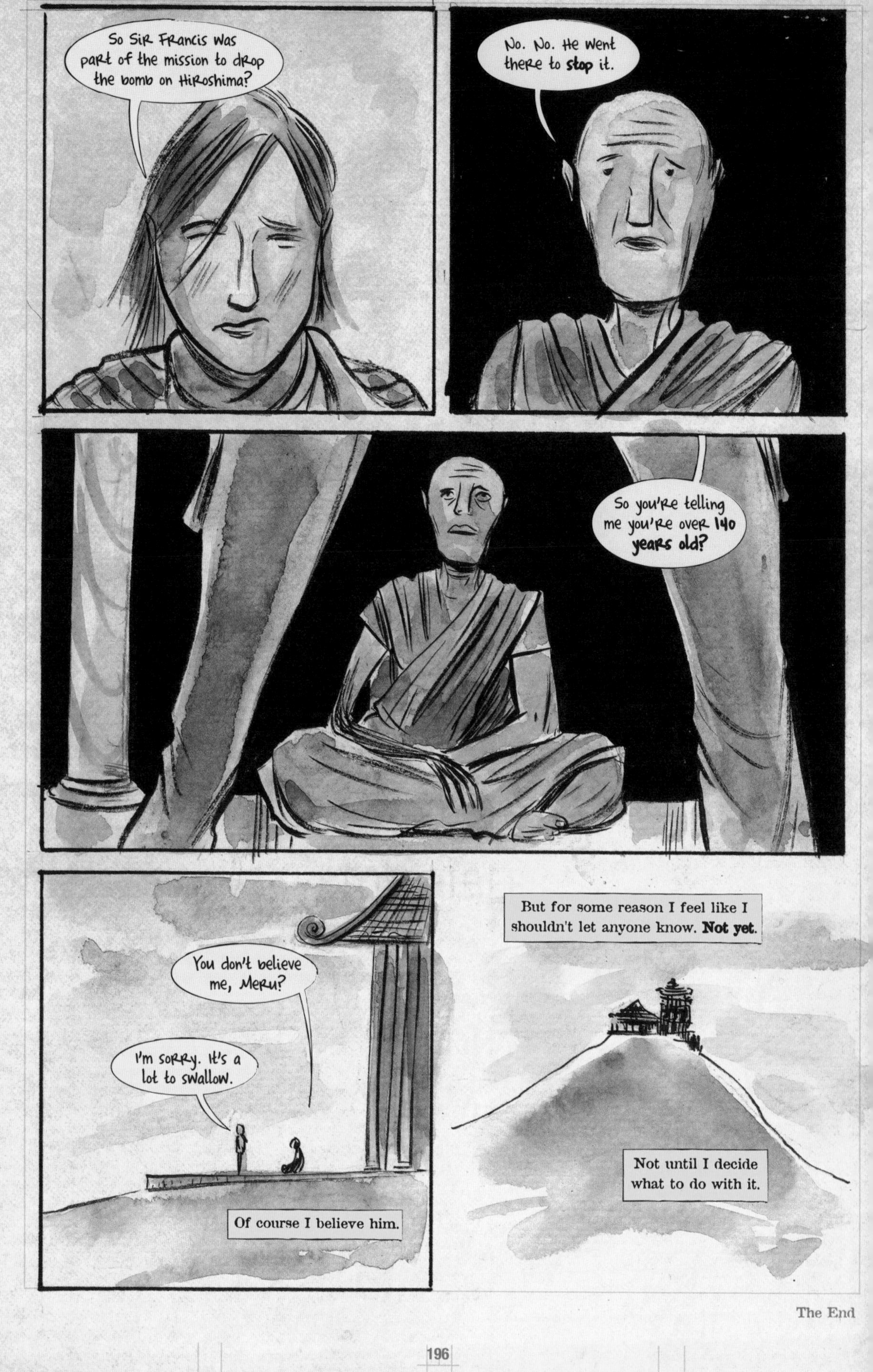
So Sir Francis was part of the mission to drop the bomb on Hiroshima?
No. No. He went there to **stop** it.
So you're telling me you're over **140 years old?**
You don't believe me, Meru?
I'm sorry. It's a lot to swallow.
Of course I believe him.
But for some reason I feel like I shouldn't let anyone know. **Not yet.**
Not until I decide what to do with it.

The End

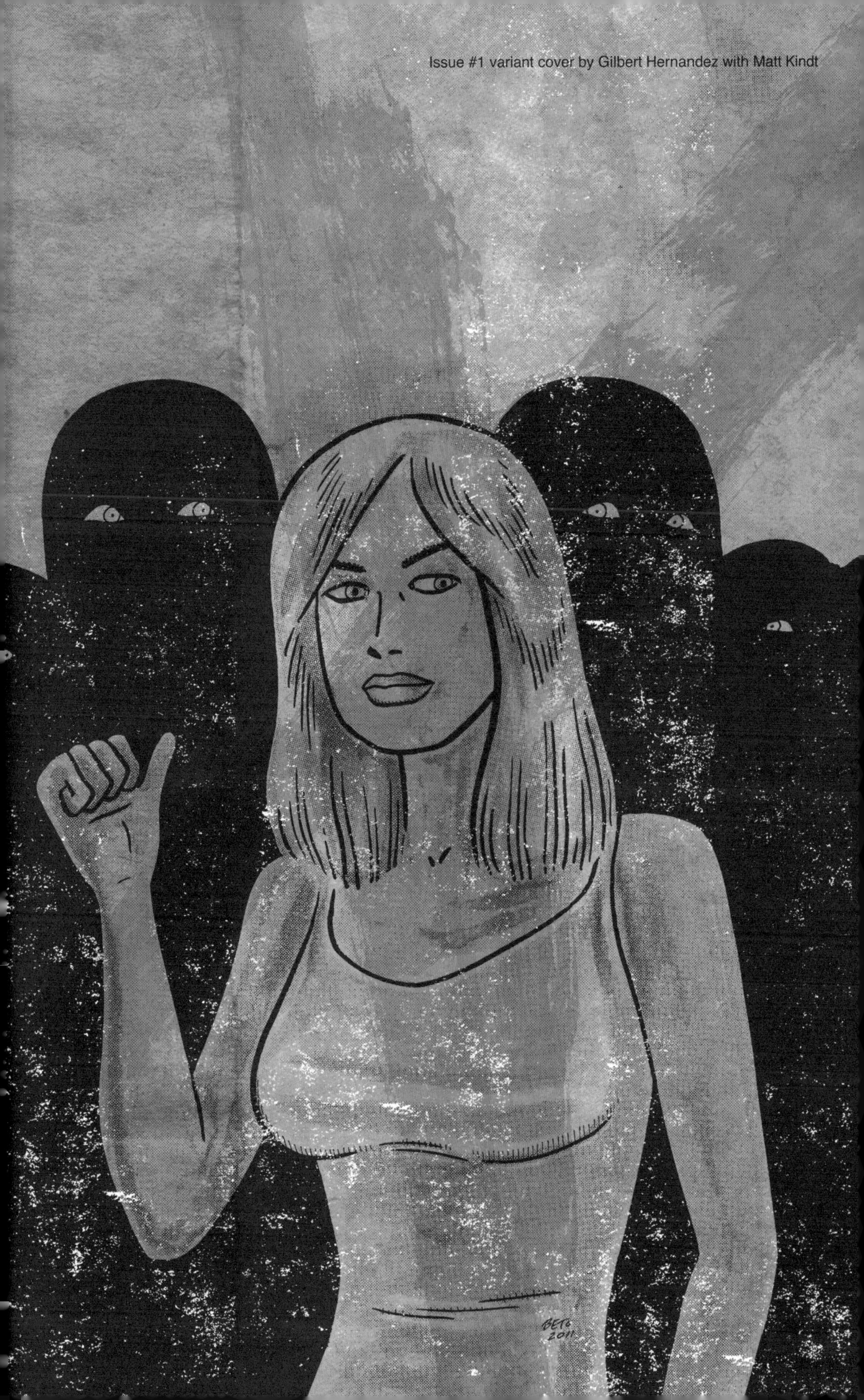
BETO
2011

Issue #1 variant cover by Gilbert Hernandez with Matt Kindt

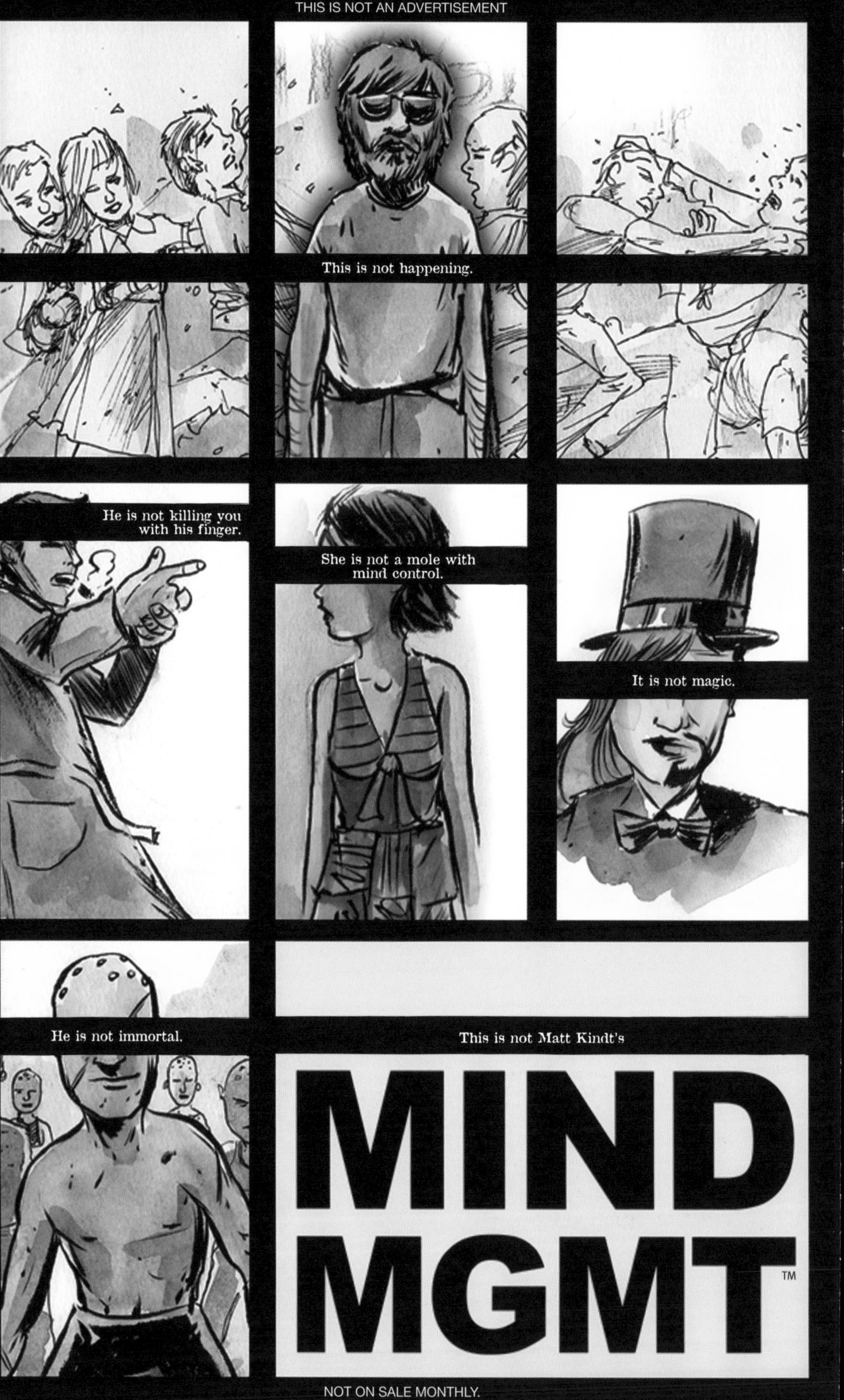
THIS IS NOT AN ADVERTISEMENT
This is not happening.
He is not killing you with his finger.
She is not a mole with mind control.
It is not magic.
He is not immortal.
This is not Matt Kindt's
MIND MGMT™
NOT ON SALE MONTHLY.

ALSO BY MATT KINDT

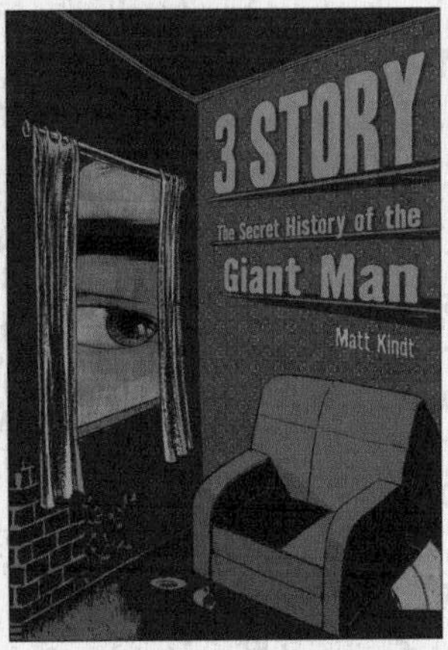

3 STORY
The Secret History of the
Giant Man
Matt Kindt

3 STORY: THE SECRET HISTORY OF THE GIANT MAN
978-1-59582-356-4
$19.99

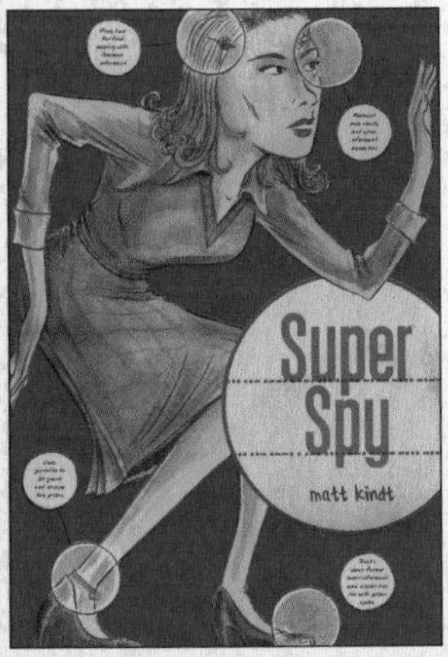

Super Spy
matt kindt

SUPER SPY
978-1-89183-096-9
$19.95

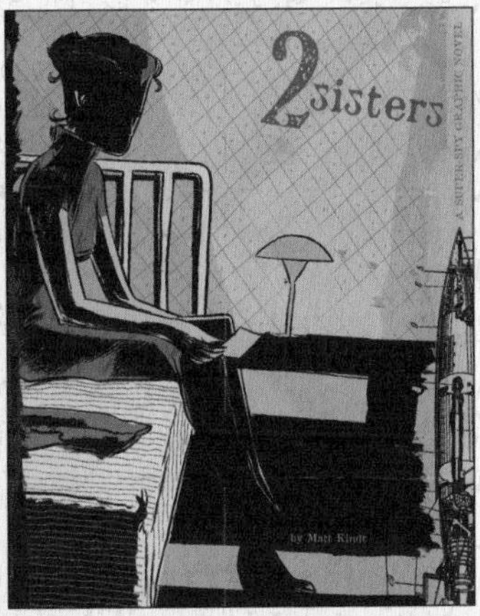

2 sisters
A SUPER SPY GRAPHIC NOVEL
by Matt Kindt

2 SISTERS: A SUPER SPY GRAPHIC NOVEL
978-1-89183-058-7
$19.95

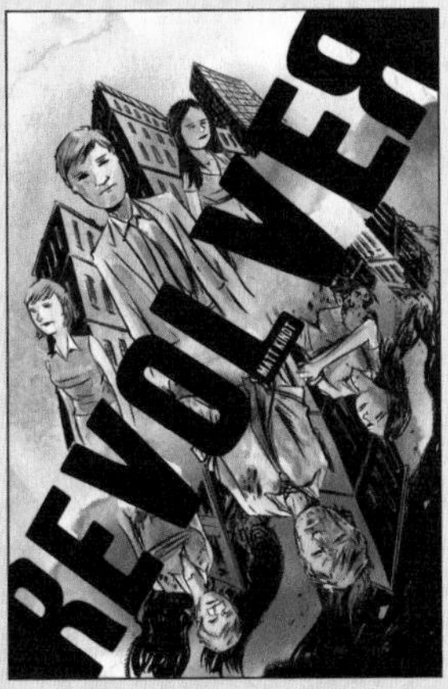

REVOLVER
MATT KINDT

REVOLVER
978-1-40122-242-0
$19.99

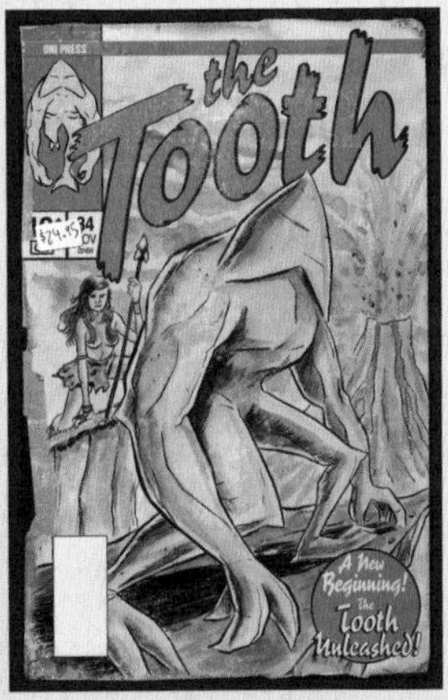

ONI PRESS
the Tooth
A New Beginning!
The Tooth Unleashed!

THE TOOTH
(with Cullen Bunn and Shawn Lee)
978-1-93496-452-1
$24.99

PHOTO BY SHARLENE KINDT

4-09

For Sharlene and Ella.

ABOUT THE AUTHOR

Matt Kindt is the Harvey Award–winning author of the graphic novels *3 Story*, *Revolver*, *Super Spy*, and *2 Sisters*, and the artist and cocreator of the *Pistolwhip* series of graphic novels. He has been nominated for four Eisner Awards and three Harveys. Matt lives and works in St. Louis, Missouri, with his wife and daughter. For more information, visit MattKindt.com.